DONNIE BRASCO

My Undercover Life in the Mafia

A true story by FBI Agent

JOSEPH D. PISTONE

with Richard Woodley

A SIGNET BOOK

SIGNET
Published by New American Library, a division of
Penguin Group (USA) Inc., 375 Hudson Street,
New York, New York 10014, USA
Penguin Group (Canada), 10 Alcorn Avenue, Toronto,
Ontario M4V 3B2, Canada (a division of Pearson Penguin Canada Inc.)
Penguin Books Ltd., 80 Strand, London WC2R 0RL, England
Penguin Ireland, 25 St. Stephen's Green, Dublin 2,
Ireland (a division of Penguin Books Ltd.)
Penguin Group (Australia), 250 Camberwell Road, Camberwell, Victoria 3124,
Australia (a division of Pearson Australia Group Pty. Ltd.)
Penguin Books India Pvt. Ltd., 11 Community Centre, Panchsheel Park,
New Delhi - 110 017, India
Penguin Group (NZ), cnr Airborne and Rosedale Roads, Albany,
Auckland 1310, New Zealand (a division of Pearson New Zealand Ltd.)
Penguin Books (South Africa) (Pty.) Ltd., 24 Sturdee Avenue,
Rosebank, Johannesburg 2196, South Africa

Penguin Books Ltd., Registered Offices:
80 Strand, London WC2R 0RL, England

Published by Signet, an imprint of New American Library, a division of Penguin Group (USA) Inc. Previously published in a Dutton edition.

First Signet Printing, January 1989
30 29 28 27 26 25 24 23 22 21 20 19

To my wife and children, whom I love dearly.
To both sets of parents, brothers and sisters.
To Michael, Sheila, Janie, Bob F., Howard and Gail,
and Don and Patricia—Thank you.

To the FBI undercover agents, who are the best at
what they do.
To the street agents, who make the FBI the best
investigative agency in the world.
To the U.S. Justice Department Strike Force attorneys
in Tampa, Milwaukee, and especially the Southern
District of New York.

—J.D.P.

CONTENTS

1

THE WHIRLWIND

I looked down from the witness stand at five Mafia defendants, five rows of press, and a standing-room-only courtroom filled with more than 300 people. It was an incredible sight to me. This was just the first mob trial, the first group of wiseguy defendants.

Lefty Guns Ruggierro was shaking his head. So were Boobie Cerasani and Nicky Santora and Mr. Fish Rabito and Boots Tomasulo. It was as if these defendants couldn't believe what was taking place either. Lefty had told his lawyer, "He'll never go against us." Up until my appearance on the stand, apparently he refused to believe that I was a special agent of the FBI and not his partner in the Mafia.

But two other defendants had already pleaded guilty before the trial. And later in his jail cell, between court appearances, Lefty had become a believer. He told his cell mate, "I'll get that motherfucker Donnie if it's the last thing I do."

There was a Mafia hit contract out on me. FBI agents were guarding me twenty-four hours a day.

Two days before I took the stand to testify, before my real name was revealed, we got word from an informant in Buffalo, New York, that the mob was going to go after my family.

The chief prosecutor for this case was Assistant U.S. Attorney Barbara Jones. The most powerful Mafia boss, the man who then sat at the head of the Mafia Commission, the boss of bosses, was Big Paul

Castellano of the Gambino family. I told Barbara that I wanted to go to Castellano myself and tell him this: "If anybody touches my wife or kids, I will go after you personally. I will kill you myself." I said I would do that only if it wouldn't jeopardize the cases. "I can't tell you who and who not to talk to," she said.

She was being tolerant and understanding. But I figured it might hurt the cases, so I held off and alerted some people and stayed very watchful.

In the middle of the courtroom, half hidden in the crowd, a Bonanno Mafia family associate I had seen around Little Italy but whose name I didn't know aimed his hand like a pistol and silently pulled the imaginary trigger with his forefinger. At a break in the trial, agents protecting me got the guy in the hallway and talked to him. He never came back.

I had been undercover inside the Mafia for six years. All that time, no more than a handful of people in the world knew who I was in both real life and in the Mafia. Now there was this explosion in the media.

There were huge headlines in the press, some of them covering the front pages: G-MAN CONNED THE MOB FOR SIX YRS; SECRET AGENT BARES MOB DEALS; MAN WHO CONNED THE MOB; FBI UNCOVERS MOB SUPERAGENT; "BRASCO" FACES GRILLING TODAY. *Newsweek* had a full page entitled, "I Was a Mobster for the FBI." They also indicated the threats: MAFIA SEEKS REVENGE ON DARING INFILTRATOR; MOB IS TRACKING FBI-ER WHO FOOLED BONANNO FAMILY.

Before the trial, the media knew that a primary witness would be an FBI undercover agent who had infiltrated the Mafia. They were using every angle to try to find out who it really was. Once the trial began, reporters were always trying to get to me. I had never given an interview, never allowed the press to photograph or film me. We'd finish up in court at five P.M., have to hang around until eight or nine to avoid the press, and even then we'd go out through the marshals' lockup. We couldn't go out of the building to eat lunch, or out of the hotel to eat dinner.

* * *

Before the first trial began, we had definite word of a hit contract out on my life. The Mafia bosses had offered $500,000 to anybody who could find me and kill me. They had circulated pictures of me all over the country. We thought we'd better take some precautions. The federal prosecutors petitioned the court to allow me and another agent I had worked with during the final year to withhold our real names when testifying and use the undercover names the mob knew us by: Donnie Brasco and Tony Rossi.

Presiding Judge Robert W. Sweet, U.S. District Judge for the Southern District of New York, was sympathetic. In his ruling he wrote, ". . . there can be no question but that these agents were, are and will be at risk. Certainly their performance as set forth by the government establishes their courage, heroism and skill as front line fighters in the war against crime and entitles them to every appropriate protection [which includes] the withholding of the location of their homes, family situation, and any additional information which is of tangential relevance and might increase their exposure to risk."

But he denied our motion because of constitutional rights of defendants to confront their accusers. I felt neither betrayed nor surprised. There were never any guarantees.

My real name was not revealed until the first day I testified, when I walked into the courtroom, raised my right hand, and swore to tell the truth. Then I was asked to give my name, and I gave it, for the first time publicly in six years: Joseph D. Pistone.

All those years undercover in the mob, I had been lying every day, living a lie. I was lying for what I believed was a high moral purpose: to help the United States government destroy the Mafia. Nonetheless, I was constantly aware that eventually, on the witness stand, I was going to be confronted with the fact by defense attorneys: You lied all the time then; how can anybody believe you now?

Before, everything, including my life, had been riding on the lie. Now everything was riding on the truth.

When I was undercover, with every step I took I had to think: How will this seem when I testify? I had to be absolutely clean. Money had to be accounted for. I had to document what I could, and remember what I couldn't document. Finally it would come down to my word in front of the juries.

The two prosecutors in the very first trial, Assistant U.S. Attorneys Jones and Louis Freeh, continually drove the point home to me: "No matter how much evidence we put on, the jury has to believe *you*. Without your credibility we have nothing."

From the day I ended my undercover role, July 26, 1981, I was deluged with trial preparations and testimony.

I was in a whirlwind. There was nonstop work with U.S. Attorneys seeking indictments of Mafia members and preparing for trials on racketeering, gambling, extortion, and murder in New York, Milwaukee, Tampa, and Kansas City. I worked with FBI officials at Headquarters in Washington, D.C., to prepare other cases across the nation where my testimony wasn't needed but my information was. As the weeks and months went by, I was working with the prosecutors, testifying before grand juries, and testifying in trials all at once.

In New York City alone, home of the main Mafia families, there were at times five or six Mafia trials going on at once. Trials coming out of our investigations got famous, such as "The Pizza Connection," the biggest heroin-smuggling case, and "The Mafia Commission," the trial of the entire ruling body of the Mafia. Because I had been living within the Mafia for so long, I had information relevant to them all, and I testified at all of them. I would be testifying in more than a dozen trials in a half dozen cities over a span of five years.

Ultimately we would get more than a hundred federal convictions. By 1987, the combination of undercover agents, street agents, cops, U.S. Attorneys, and informants had blasted the heart out of La Cosa Nostra. The Mafia would be changed forever. The boss of every single Mafia family would be indicted and/or in prison and/or dead before the trials were over. We got almost every Mafia soldier we went after.

But the scorecard after all those years wasn't the scorecard right then. In August 1982, we were just launching the courtroom assault that resulted from the years of undercover work and "straight-up" investigation. There wasn't the time or inclination to celebrate. We had stung and humiliated the Mafia, but now, because of that, the Mafia was stirred up like a hornets' nest. The mob was killing its own. Anybody who had trusted me inside the mob was now dead, or targeted for death. A dozen mobsters I knew when I was undercover had been murdered, at least two specifically because of their association with me. One indicted corrupt cop had committed suicide.

For me, there was testifying to do. And I had to avoid the shooters.

In Milwaukee, when I was testifying against Milwaukee Mafia boss Frank Balistrieri, a defense attorney asked me where I and my family actually lived while I was undercover. The prosecution objected. U.S. District Judge Terence T. Evans directed me to answer. Nothing could have forced me to answer that. "Your Honor," I said, "I am not going to answer the question." The judge said he could hold me in contempt. But after consultation with the lawyers he decided that what was relevant was only where the mob thought I lived at the time. Then I answered that question: "California."

My home address and the name my family was living under was a closely guarded secret, and has not been revealed to this day. The FBI installed a special alarm system throughout the house that was wired directly to the FBI office.

Once my real name was splashed around in the media, we got word from a friendly attorney that a New Jersey guy that I grew up with, now in the Genovese family, had gone to Fat Tony Salerno, the boss of the Genovese family, and told him he knew where I was from and where I still had relatives, so maybe they could get at me that way.

When I talked to my daughters by telephone, they were in tears. Grandpa was afraid to go out and start his car in the morning.

The FBI wanted to move my family again. I refused. They didn't want to move again. I wasn't going to run the rest of my life. These bastards weren't going to make me or my family live in fear forever. Could they find me? I take normal precautions. I'm always tail-conscious wherever I am. I travel and have credit cards under various names. But with an all-out effort, sure, they could find me. Nobody's an impossibility. But if they found me, they would have to deal with me. The guy who came after me would have to be better than I was.

I was forty-three years old when the first of the cases came to trial. I had missed six years of normal life with my family. There were huge gaps of experience with my daughters growing up. I hoped that in time this would be balanced by the pride in what I had done, but I never will be able to be a public person. I will always have to use a different name in my private life, and only close friends and associates will know about my FBI past.

My satisfactions are in the knowledge that I did the best job I could, that we made the cases, and that other agents—my peers—congratulate me and respect me for what I did. My family is proud of me.

I am proud of the fact that I was the same Joe Pistone when I came out as I was before I went undercover. Six years inside the Mafia hadn't changed me. My personality hadn't changed. My values hadn't changed. I wasn't messed up mentally or physically. I still didn't drink. I still kept my body in shape. I had the same wife, the same good marriage, the same good kids. I hadn't had difficulty giving up the Donnie Brasco role. I was not confused about who I was. My pride was that whatever my personality was, whatever my strengths and weaknesses, I was Joe Pistone when

I went under, and I was the same Joe Pistone when I came out.

After one trial in New York a defense attorney congratulated me: "You did a hell of a job. You got some set of balls, Agent Pistone."

At another trial years later, in 1986, Rusty Rastelli, boss of the Bonanno family, which I had infiltrated, waited in a hallway outside the courtroom of the U.S. Court for the Eastern District of New York in Brooklyn. He sat in a chair like a throne, with other defendants, Bonanno wiseguys, gathered around him like an entourage. None of them wanted to believe, or admit, even now, what had been done to them. "Even if I wasn't in the can," Rastelli said, "he wouldn'ta met me." "He don't know nobody," one of his members said, "not in six years." A daughter of one of the defendants was brought over to meet Rastelli. She said about me, the agent testifying against them all, "What a dangerous job. I wouldn't want to be in his shoes."

On January 17, 1983, I went with my wife and brother to Washington, D.C., to attend the annual presentation of the Attorney General's Awards. Before the ceremonies we had lunch with FBI Director William Webster and his assistant directors in his private dining room in the J. Edgar Hoover Building, which is FBI headquarters.

The ceremonies were held in the Great Hall of the Department of Justice. The room was jammed with dignitaries and government officials.

Among the awards was one for me. Attorney General William French Smith and FBI Director Webster presented me with the Attorney General's Distinguished Service Award as the outstanding agent in the FBI. They cited my length of service undercover, how no agent had ever penetrated so deep into the Mafia before, and how much personal sacrifice was required. I got a big round of applause.

Next to testifying in my first Mafia trial, this was the best moment in my professional life.

THE BEGINNINGS

I was working out of the Alexandria, Virginia, office in my second year on the job. We had been chasing a bank-robbery fugitive for about a month, just missing him several times. I and my partner, Jack O'Rourke, got a tip that he was going to be at a certain apartment in next-door Washington, D.C., for about a half hour. We alerted the D.C. office so they could send a couple cars, and we took off for the place. When we pulled up, we saw this guy coming down the stairs.

He was a black guy, huge and hard—6'4", 225. He had pulled off a string of bank jobs and hotel robberies, and had shot a clerk.

This is the middle of a black neighborhood. The guy spots us and takes off through an alley. I jump out of the car and take off after him, while my partner wheels the car around the block to cut him off. We go over fences and down alleys, knocking over garbage cans and making a racket. I don't draw my gun because he doesn't show one. Finally, in another alley, I catch up and tackle him. Then we go at each other with fists. Up and down we go, throwing punches. We roll around smacking each other, busting each other up, while a crowd gathers and just watches. I can't subdue him. I manage to get my cuffs out of the small of my back, put a hand through one, and finally I hit him a good shot that dazes him. That buys me a couple of seconds to get him in a hammerlock and slap one cuff on him.

The other cars arrive, and we subdue him.

We're walking him to the car and he says to me, "You gotta be a Eye-talian."

"Yeah?"

"Yeah, 'cause there's only two types that fight like that, a nigger or a Eye-talian. And I know you ain't no nigger."

It was a sad story. The guy was an ex-Marine with medals for heroism in VietNam. He got discharged and came back and couldn't get a job. Nobody wanted him as a VietNam vet. He became a heroin addict and a bank robber. About three years after this bust, he got out of prison and went back to the same stuff, and when they were trying to arrest him, he came out shooting, and a buddy of mine had to blow him away with a shotgun.

I felt bad about that guy. But I wasn't a psychologist or a social worker. I was an FBI agent.

And an Italian. My grandparents came from Italy. I was born in Pennsylvania. I grew up there and then in New Jersey. My father worked in a silk mill and at the same time ran a couple of bars. He retired when he was sixty-two. I have a younger brother and sister.

In high school I played football and basketball, mostly basketball, guard and forward. I was only six feet tall but a leaper, good enough to be second-team All-State. I went to a military school for a year to play more basketball, then went to college on a basketball scholarship. I knew I wasn't good enough to be a pro. Basketball was just a way for me to go to college. I majored in social studies. I wanted to be a high-school basketball coach. After two years of college I left to get married. I was twenty.

I stayed out a year working, as I had during off times from school, in construction, driving bulldozers, in a silk mill, tending bar, driving tractor-trailers. My wife was a nurse. After a year out, I went back to school to get my college diploma. But I didn't resume basketball. My wife was pregnant. I had to work full-time. There wasn't time for basketball. After our first daughter was born, my wife went back to work as a nurse to help put me through college.

Nobody in my family had been a cop. But as a kid I

had thought about being a cop or an FBI agent. In my senior year of college a buddy was going to take the exam for the local police department. He wanted me to go in with him. I said I wanted to finish my last year of school. He urged me to take the exam, anyway. I scored in the top five on the written exam, and number one on the physical exam. I told the police chief that I wanted to take the job with the department, but I was in my last semester of college and I wanted to finish and get my diploma. I asked him if it was possible to get an appointment where I would work only the nighttime shift until I graduated. He said he didn't think there'd be a problem.

But when it came time for the swearing-in, he told me he couldn't guarantee night shifts for me. So I turned down the job with the police department to finish school.

I got my diploma and taught social studies for a while at a middle school. I liked working with kids. By the time I graduated from college, I had two kids of my own.

I had a friend who was in Naval Intelligence. The Office of Naval Intelligence employed civilians to investigate crimes committed on government installations where Navy and Marine personnel were based, or crimes committed by Navy or Marine personnel in the civilian sector. There were investigations of all types: homicides, gambling, burglaries, drugs, plus national security cases such as espionage.

Often Naval Intelligence agents worked closely with FBI agents. In the back of my mind I had always wanted to be an FBI agent. But you had to have three years of prior experience in law enforcement, along with a college degree.

Naval Intelligence interested me. For that you needed only a college degree. I passed the required exams and became an agent in the Office of Naval Intelligence. I had three daughters by then.

I worked mostly out of Philadelphia. It was basically a suit-and-tie job, normal straight-up investigations, some of the work classified. I worked some drug cases, some theft cases, and so on, and did some intelligence work in espionage cases. I made cases, testified in military courts.

My work there satisfied the FBI's requirement for prior law-enforcement experience. I passed the written, oral, and physical exams, and on July 7, 1969, was sworn in as a special agent of the Federal Bureau of Investigation.

For fourteen weeks at the FBI Academy in Quantico, Virginia, I was schooled in the law, the violations that come under the FBI's jurisdiction, and in proper procedures and techniques of interviewing people and conducting all types of investigations. I was trained in self-defense tactics, proper procedures and techniques of car chases and making arrests, and in the use of every type of firearm that the Bureau uses.

In Naval Intelligence I had preferred street work, criminal work, to the intelligence investigations. So when I went into the Bureau, I knew I wanted to do street work. That's where everybody starts, anyway.

I was assigned to the Jacksonville, Florida, office.

I had been on the job less than a month when I had my first serious confrontation as an agent. We had a warrant for a fugitive, an escapee from a Georgia prison. He was a kidnapper and had shot two people. He had fled across the state line into Florida. My partner got a tip from an informant that this fugitive was going to be in the area, driving a van on the way to some kind of crime job.

We stake out the location with a couple of cars, spot the van going by, and tail it, figuring to move in when he gets to where the job is going down. But after a couple of miles he makes the tail and swerves off the highway and onto side roads to try to shake us. We have to make our move. My partner is driving. He draws up alongside the van and forces it off the road to a stop to our right, my side, so that my door is even with the driver's door of the van.

The fugitive and I jump out of our cars at the same time, facing each other maybe five feet apart. He has his gun drawn. I'm new on the job. I haven't pulled my gun. The guy points at me and pulls the trigger. *Click*. He pulls again. *Click*. Two incredible misfires.

This all happens in a few seconds. The guy drops the gun and takes off. I'm right on his heels. My partner is out of the car and running after us. "Shoot him!" he hollers to me.

We have strict guidelines on using our firearms. You're not allowed to fire warning shots. You shoot only to defend yourself; you shoot to kill. But I wasn't going to shoot this guy. I was burning at myself that I had let this guy get the drop on me. It's hard running in a suit and tie, but I catch him and clobber him over the head a few times with my handcuffs before I slap the cuffs on his wrists.

My partner comes running up. "Why the hell didn't you shoot?" he says.

"There wouldn't have been any satisfaction in that," I say. The guy had scared me to death. I was angrier at myself than at him, because I hadn't gotten out of the car with my gun drawn. But by the time the guy panicked and tossed the gun, there wasn't any reason to shoot him, anyway.

In Jacksonville, I worked fugitive cases, gambling, bank robberies. I started developing informants. I feel that one of my better talents was in cultivating reliable sources from the street world.

I grew up as a street guy. I did not look down at guys who survived by their wits and street smarts, tough guys, thieves. You promise informants that you will protect their relationship with you. You never completely trust them, and they never completely trust you—you're on the side of law and they're not.

I didn't try to rehabilitate anybody. If you become too involved in the social-work aspect, it gets in the way of your investigative abilities.

Some of my first informants were women, because I worked a lot of prostitution cases—cases made federal under the Mann Act, for bringing women across state lines for prostitution. The prostitutes were the victims. We went after the pimps who beat them or burned them with coat hangers for not bringing in enough money or whatever.

Sometimes I would try to talk a prostitute into getting away from her pimp. I didn't try to talk anybody out of being a prostitute, because that's just a waste of time. My attitude was: Hey, if that's the profession you're going to choose, I'm just giving you some advice on how to survive, that's all. I got some of them away from their pimps. That made me feel good. And I got some of them to be informants, which made me feel even better.

I had an informant named Brown Sugar. I talked her into at least moving out of the lousy neighborhood into a better, safer area. She didn't have anything for a decent apartment. I asked my wife if we could give her some of our old pots and pans for her apartment. "I'm not giving my pots and pans to any Brown Sugar," my wife said. We didn't have much, either, in those early days of my career, trying to support a family with three kids.

With my partner I did a lot of work in cooperation with the Jacksonville Police Department vice squad. There is a lot of interagency cooperation among guys working the street, because they need each other. Resentment and jealousy between agencies occurs more often at higher levels, where people are looking for publicity.

My partner and I didn't want publicity because we ended up doing some good but unauthorized work to help out the vice-squad cops. I especially didn't want publicity because this was my first year as an agent, and in the first year you are on probation; you can be dismissed without cause.

There was a rash of prostitution at the better hotels in the area. High-class hookers were working the bars and lobbies, picking up businessmen.

Everybody in the hotels knew these vice cops because they had been around awhile, but nobody knew me. So to help them out on local cases I would pose as a businessman, get picked up by a hooker and taken up to a room. The local cops would follow us up and wait outside the door for two or three minutes, long enough for the transaction, then they'd come in and make the bust.

I wasn't a kid—I was thirty—but since I was a new guy on the job, these vice-squad cops liked to have a little fun with me, bust my chops. Like one time I go into the room with this hooker. I give her the money. I wait for them to come through the door. Nothing. She starts undressing. "Come on, honey," she says, "aren't you gonna take your clothes off?" I hem and haw. Nothing is happening at the door. She is naked and starts trying to pull off my clothes. I try to push her hands off my buttons and zippers, and I don't know what to do. My job is on the line here because this is not federal business.

Over the door there is a transom. I hear giggling. They have boosted up one guy, and he is looking through the transom and laughing like hell at my predicament.

Then they come in and make the bust.

We started hearing about armed robberies in the rooms. Pimps would hide in the rooms and stick up the johns when they came in.

One of the girls that was working with her pimp this way picks me up and takes me to the room. This time I know the cops are backing me up because this is serious.

I say I want to hang my jacket up in the closet. The pimp isn't in the closet. Then I have to go to the bathroom. The pimp isn't in there. I go back out in the room with the hooker. I give her the money. She is very edgy. I know the pimp is in there.

It dawns on me he is behind the shower curtain in the bathroom. The curtain was open, gathered at one end of the tub. I hadn't moved it to look in that corner of the tub. I tell her, "Why don't you get undressed. I just want to wash my hands again."

The pimp will have a gun. But if I pull my gun and the girl starts screaming, who knows what the guy will do? So I'll just have to surprise him.

I go into the bathroom, turn on the water in the sink, then spin around and smack the shower curtain away. The pimp is standing there with an automatic in his hand. I slap his arm, put a wristlock on him, make him drop the gun. He starts trying to punch, but it's over. With the commotion the cops come into the room, and I turn the dude over to them and leave.

After eighteen months I was transferred to Alexandria, Virginia. That office had a heavy load of applicant cases—background investigations on people nominated for government jobs. Newcomers to that office were routinely assigned to a squad that got the brunt of those cases. Suddenly I was in a tame area. I asked the Special Agent in Charge—the boss of the office—if I could work criminal cases once I got the applicant cases done. He said he didn't care. So I would get all my applicant cases out of the way by maybe noon. In the afternoon I would hook up with guys who worked criminal cases.

I developed a string of informants who were instrumental in solving a lot of bank robberies and nabbing fugitives. This was the end of the VietNam era, and in Alexandria, like in Jacksonville, I worked a bunch of deserter cases.

I was in Alexandria four years. It was a nice life. We belonged to a country club where my wife was social director.

Along the way I had gone back to school at Quantico for short "in-service" training courses in such things as gambling and undercover work. In those days there was no such thing in the Bureau as long-term undercover assignments. Undercover was a day or two in a "buy-bust" situation. For example, you get information that somebody has some type of stolen property, you negotiate a buy from this thief, and then the thief is arrested.

I also had SWAT training when they first formed the Special Weapons Assault Teams in the early 1970s to deal with hostage situations such as were occurring in skyjackings or with potential terrorist assaults. The teams were formed from specially picked agents who showed superior physical skills. We were trained in the use of various weapons, methods of assault on a building; we rapelled with ropes from buildings, cliffs, helicopters. There was survival training in the wilderness and in the water. We worked on hand-to-hand combat. I loved the camaraderie, the physical challenge.

In 1974, I was transferred to New York City and put on the Truck and Hijack Squad.

We had a good squad, a busy squad. We worked at least six days a week, sometimes two or three days around the clock. But long hours was not unusual in the Bureau. The average agent probably gets to work at six-thirty or seven A.M. and works a twelve-hour day. And we were intercepting six or seven hijacked loads a day.

And then came my break into long-term undercover work—the assignment that led to my work with the Mafia.

The Tampa, Florida, office was working on a ring of thieves that were stealing heavy equipment and luxury cars. They discovered the ring by chance. They had arrested a teenage boy on some unrelated charge. But it turned out that the kid's father was involved in the theft ring.

The father was desperate to keep the kid from going to jail. He came to the agents and said, "You cut my son a deal, I'll work for you busting up a big ring that's stealing heavy equipment and luxury cars all over the southeastern United States."

With cooperation from the Florida Highway Patrol, the Bureau made the guy an informant to see what he could produce. He proved himself. The ring was directed by a guy out of Baltimore and operated all over the southeast. They stole everything to order: trucks, bulldozers, road graders; Cadillacs, Lincolns, and airplanes.

The Bureau thought that maybe they could introduce an agent to work undercover with the guy in busting the ring. It's always better to have an agent's testimony in court. The guy said that the only thing was, the agent would have to know how to drive things like an eighteen-wheeler and a bulldozer. That led the Bureau to me. I was one of the few agents with that kind of experience.

I sat down alone in a room with the guy, whose name was Marshall. We had to get a sense of each other, decide whether we could trust each other enough to risk our lives together. He was massive, maybe 6'1", 250, with reddish hair, a thick red beard, and huge hands. He wore overalls. He was a truck mechanic who could steal anything. I told him I didn't know how to steal cars and trucks. "No problem," he said. "I can teach you that in a minute." We talked about our attitudes, experiences, families. I felt comfortable with him. He felt comfortable with me. He said that prior to meeting me he had the impression that agents were guys with wing-tip shoes and pin-striped suits who didn't know anything about the street. But I was different. "You seem like you could handle yourself okay," he said, "and come off as a thief. I can work you in."

For this operation I needed a name. I didn't give it much thought. For some reason a name had stuck in my head from an old movie or book or something: Donald Brasco. That's who I became. The Bureau furnished me with a driver's license and credit cards under the name. The plan wasn't conceived originally as being long-term undercover. But it ended up extending over about six months.

Marshall gave me a rundown. The head of the ring was a guy named Becker. A lot of the thieves who scouted locations and actually hooked the stuff were young guys, nineteen or twenty years old. Heavy equipment was usually stolen from construction sites. Cars were stolen right off the new-car lots. Customers were construction companies and businessmen. In the case of the luxury cars, customers were just people with enough money.

Marshall had to deliver a stolen Ford XLT pickup to a couple of guys in Lakeland, Florida, who were supplying trucks to outfits working the phosphate mines. That was the first thing I would go along on.

We were about to leave when the agents in charge of the case said they wanted to wire me up. They wanted me to wear a Nagra tape recorder. I wasn't in favor of it because it was so hot and muggy that you couldn't even wear a windbreaker. I had on a Banlon shirt and Levi's. "How the hell am I going to conceal a Nagra?" I asked. "We'll tape it to your back," they said.

This was my first outing, and I didn't want to seem

like a prima donna, so I agreed to it. They taped the recorder, which is four by six inches, three-quarters of an inch thick, to the small of my back. In the mirror I looked like I had a growth under my shirt.

Marshall said he would introduce me to the other thieves as a guy he met through a guy named Bobby, who had been killed in an automobile accident. He told me enough about Bobby to get by. Since Bobby was dead, nobody could question him.

We drove the pickup to the storage garage where we were to meet the customers. We got out and met the guys. They walked around the truck, looking it over. I had to keep moving so that I was always facing them and nobody got behind me, because I had this hump on my back. The customer, Rice, was talking about how many trucks he can sell to the guys in the phosphate mines, and how much other equipment he can use, and he kept moving around, so I kept moving around to keep my back from his view.

The price we put on this truck was $1,500. In 1975, it was worth probably $4,000. Finally Rice decided that this particular truck didn't have enough extras to suit him, so we would have to hook him another one.

When I got back to the Holiday Inn where Marshall and I were staying, I called the agents. "That's the last time I'm wearing a goddamn wire," I said. "I felt like a hunchback."

As it turned out, the machine malfunctioned and the tape didn't come out, anyway.

In a couple of days we were supposed to meet the ringleader, Becker, in Panama City, Florida, out on the panhandle on the Gulf. We stayed at a motel in Lakeland, east of Tampa. Marshall spent the weekend teaching me the business. He taught me how to get into a vehicle using a tool called a "slim jim" that you slide down between the outer door panel and the glass to hook the locking bar. He taught me how to take out a dashboard in five minutes to get at the vehicle identification number. The VIN was stamped in metal and riveted. We would pop the rivets and replace the metal with plastic tape stamped with a new number. He taught me how to "hot-wire" ignitions and how to punch out the ignition barrel on the steering column by using a "slide hammer." Once the ignition is popped out, you've bypassed the ignition lock and can start the engine. You replace the ignition the next day with a part from an auto-parts store. He taught me how to disconnect steering-wheel locks from under the car. It was a real school.

We went to Panama City to meet Becker. He was a rough, ruddy, fast-talking ex-convict and con artist. He bragged about having friends in the mob, in motorcycle gangs, on the docks.

He pumped me on how long I had known the late Bobby and on what I did. I said I hadn't known Bobby all that long, but we did a few jobs together and so on. I didn't try to pass myself off as a longtime car thief because I still didn't know all that much about it. I said I was mainly a burglar and that lately I had spent most of my time in California and Florida.

He bought it because Marshall was there to vouch for me.

I also asserted myself. I told Becker that some of the gang may have more technical knowledge than I do about hooking cars and trucks, but I knew about planning, organization, security. So if I was going to go out with these young punks, I was going to have a say in how the operation proceeded. I said I wasn't going to be just a $100-a-night car thief; I wanted to be in on the business end of it too.

I had to take a leadership attitude, because I had to keep these guys in check when we went out on jobs. While we were getting evidence I had to steer the thing away from violence. So I told Becker that Marshall and I had to call the shots.

He said okay, he would pass that on to the younger guys.

Becker told me about orders he had lined up, specific models, colors, extras. We were selling everything at a price around one quarter to one half of retail value. For Lincolns and Caddies loaded up with extras and worth maybe $12,000, he was getting $2,500. White Freightliner truck-tractors were bringing $10,000 to $15,000. Pickups were bringing $1,500 to $2,000, dump trucks $4,000.

The payoffs we got went to the FBI. Marshall received a monthly fee as an informant. He couldn't keep anything from these jobs.

Becker wanted us to hook a White Freightliner. He had spotted one in a lot just outside Panama City and had a customer in Miami willing to pay $15,000 for it. The next day Marshall and I went to case the lot. We parked across the street at a liquor store. We wanted to see where the truck was, whether it was being moved, and to time the operation.

We're sitting there twenty minutes when a sheriff's car pulls in and the officer comes over to us. He says the liquor-store owner has become suspicious and wants to know why we're sitting there.

"Just making up our minds what to buy, Officer," I say. "Now we know." We go into the liquor store and buy some beer.

That night, before we went back to hook the tractor, Marshall gave me the rundown on it. I was going to hook it myself, to see if I could do it. From memory he described the wiring and what I had to do. The White tractor was a snub-nosed job, complete with a sleeper compartment and air-conditioning, the cab up over the engine. Everything I had to do could be done from inside the cab.

We went to the lot and cased it for a while to check when the sheriff's patrols went by and how much time there was between them. Marshall stayed outside as the spotter. I went into the lot. It took me five minutes to get in, start the engine, and drive the tractor out.

I drove it the first leg, three hundred miles to Lakeland, where we would sleep a few hours during the day before heading on to Miami. We parked it in the parking lot at our motel. While we were sleeping, our agents went over the Freightliner, getting all the numbers and data from it for records.

The next day we drove the tractor to Miami and met with Becker and the customer. The customer was supposed to resell it to a contractor for road building in

Europe. But the customer had changed his mind and didn't want it.

Becker had to go back to Baltimore. He told us: "You guys stash this thing somewhere around here until I can find another buyer."

Where were we going to stash a White Freightliner in Miami? I told our guys about it. The guys from the State Highway Patrol said we could stash it at the Department of Transportation yard, outside of Miami. I wasn't too hot on that, putting our stolen truck in a government yard. But they said it was a big yard with several barns and it would be well hidden.

So that's where we put it, for the time being.

Most of the car and truck lots had no special security, just lights and a chain across the entrances. Usually we had maybe fifteen minutes or a half hour between police patrols. If everything went smoothly, we could hook a car in five minutes.

When we went out on a job, I was on my own. There was no surveillance by the FBI or the Highway Patrol. On an undercover operation like this you don't want either the badguys you're working with or any law-enforcement agency to spot a surveillance. Cops aren't clued in about what's going on. The fewer people who know about it, the better.

I carried no FBI identification. I didn't want to risk getting caught with it. There was no official policy about carrying ID. Some guys carried credentials undercover. My feeling was, carrying ID was just another thing to worry about. You get stopped by cops, you talk your way out of it. Or you take the bust— that's no big deal. If you got into a jam, I felt that one of the most important things was *not* to tell any law-enforcement officer what was going on. You take the bust and let the people running the operation decide what they want to do. Law-enforcement credentials are part of what you have to leave behind you when you're working undercover.

Hooking the stuff was easy, but when I went out to do a job, the adrenaline really flowed. Even though this was a sanctioned operation, I was out there by myself, without surveillance or protection. When you're stealing cars with hardened thieves, ex-cons, guys who may or may not be packing guns, you don't know what's going to happen, and a lot of things are going through your mind.

You want to get the evidence for the case. You're keeping an eye on the subjects to make sure they're not deviating from the plan and heading for something disastrous. You're worrying about getting caught.

If these guys get caught, how are they going to react? Are they going to try to fight their way out of it? If a cop comes across three or four guys stealing cars, what's his reaction? If one of the guys makes a move, will the cop start shooting?

If we're all busted together, what position does that put me in? How do I protect the operation? How do I protect Marshall? How do I protect myself?

All this stuff, all these angles, are going through your mind when you're out pulling or casing a job. And we were stealing five to ten pieces a week.

We had an order for three Cadillacs. We found what we wanted near Leesburg, Florida, in the middle of the state, two on one lot and one on another. That night I went in with two other young guys and got the Caddies. We headed for Lakeland, to our hotel. Marshall drove the tail car. Naturally we were in a hurry. These cars have new-car stickers on the windows, and we wouldn't have the fake registrations until the next day.

We're spread out along the highway, booming along. All of a sudden flashing red lights show in my mirror, and I get pulled over by the Florida Highway Patrol. In these early days I carried a 9-mm automatic, which I had stashed under the seat.

So I get out of the car right away and ask the officer what the problem is.

"You were going over the speed limit, sir," he says.

I have a Donald Brasco driver's license, but no registration for the car, and a gun under the seat, so I figure I better be right up front with him, defuse any interest he may have in looking in the car. While I take out my license and hand it to him, I say, "You know what, Officer, you're probably right. I'm transporting the car from a dealer in Leesburg to a dealer in Lakeland, have to get there so they can clean it up and have it ready on the lot by first thing in the morning." I give him the name of a dealer in Lakeland. Since it's about three A.M., I know there's no risk of him calling the dealer to check. "So I don't even have the papers with me."

He is a real nice guy. "Okay," he says, handing me back my license. "But take it easy, because the next guy may not be so understanding."

I never carried a gun in this operation after that.

Every time we got an order, I called in to the contact agent and told him what we were looking for. Then later I called to tell him we'd found it. After we hooked the vehicle I'd call as soon as I could and give a description of what we hooked, where we took it from, everything about the job, so the Bureau could keep a record, then, later on, after the operation, could work with the insurance companies and dealers in getting the vehicles back.

Becker had finally located a buyer for the White Freightliner that we had stashed near Miami. These guys were dopers. They moved stuff between Florida and California, hiding cocaine and marijuana among boxes of vegetables and fruits in refrigerated trucks.

Marshall and I were staying at our usual place, the Holiday Inn in Lakeland. Becker said his customers would be calling us.

They called and told us to leave the hotel and check into another one. We did that. We waited for two days, and finally these guys came to our room. Two guys, rough and dirty, long hair, in their mid-twenties, both with gun bulges under their belts.

They said they had made the deal with Becker to take the truck for $10,000.

"Bullshit," I say. "The price is fifteen grand."

"We made the deal with him," one guy says, "and you guys were just supposed to deliver the truck."

"We're going to deliver it and make the exchange," I say, "but I'm not just working for this guy; we're partners. He can't make a ten-grand deal on his own when we had all decided on fifteen. That means I would lose more than a grand of my cut on this deal."

"That's your tough luck, pal, because we made the deal and that's all we're paying."

I'm hassling these guys because the original price that I knew of was $15,000, and as a thief you don't just accept somebody's word that the price was changed. Plus, if I accepted their word without checking with Becker, it might make *him* suspicious. If I was such a hotshot, why would I accept a deal different from our original price from guys I didn't know?

If the deal had been changed, Becker should have let me know. But maybe he didn't let me know on purpose; maybe he wanted to see how I'd handle it.

Marshall went into the other room and called him. Becker affirmed the deal. We had had the truck too long, it was too hot, and we needed to get rid of it.

"Okay," I tell these guys. "But anything else you want like this is gonna cost you fifteen grand."

"We'll worry about that when the time comes," the one guy says.

"We won't worry about it at all," I say.

We made arrangements to meet at noon the next day near Miami, at an exit off the Sunshine Parkway.

The next morning Marshall and I drove to Miami and went to the Department of Transportation yard and got the Freightliner.

We meet the guys at the highway exit. "Before I give you the keys," I say, "I want the money."

"Sure," he says. He puts a soggy, grimy, stinking brown paper bag in my hands.

"What the hell is this?" I say.

"That's the money," the guy says. "What we do with our cash money is, we bury it."

Becker got a contract to hook two Caddies down in Miami. He had this dealership staked out, had found two cars fitting the order. Marshall and I went back there with him about an hour before closing time and parked across the street at a Burger King. We hung around waiting for the dealer to close, checking how often the sheriff's patrols went by.

When the place closed, we saw that they had a

guard wandering around the lot. We hadn't known about the guard. Now we had to plan to deal with him.

Becker wanted to go around to the back of this big lot and make noise to draw the guard off back there while the other two of us would hook the cars and go out the front. I didn't like that because of the chance for violence with the guard. I started trying to talk him out of it, saying it was too risky.

A sheriff's car pulled into the Burger King lot and parked near us. Two cops on their coffee break.

We're leaning against our car. Suddenly Becker puts his arm around my shoulders in a chummy way. He nods toward the patrol car. "Don't worry about cops. I been in this business a long time," he says, "and I can smell cops, even plainclothes guys. The easiest to spot, though, are the FBI agents."

"Oh, yeah?" I say. "Why is that? I never met any FBI agents."

"The way they dress, talk, act. I can smell them miles away."

I am thinking: Why is he suddenly talking about FBI agents? Is he testing my reaction? Is he suspicious because I'm trying to talk him out of hooking the two cars across the street? He's never been chummy with me before. I put my arm around *his* shoulders. "How's your nose now?" I say. "You smell anything?"

"No, nothing more than those two cops in the car."

I was able to talk him out of that job because of the guard. He decided we'd go back up north to hook cars. He had to go back to Baltimore. He sent Marshall and me up to the area around Orlando to scout.

We found two satisfactory Caddies again. Marshall brought along two of the younger guys. Marshall was the spotter outside the lot; the other two guys and I cut the chain and went in.

The sheriff's patrol car comes by. Apparently he notices the chain down over the entrance, because he turns into the lot and starts flashing his spotlight around.

I and the other guys dive under cars. I don't know what's going to happen if the cop finds us. Maybe these guys are carrying guns. Maybe this cop will be trigger-happy. I have this vision that I am going to die right here under this car, shot as a damn car thief.

The cop drove around for about five minutes, then went out. We hooked the two Caddies and got the hell out of there.

Becker had stolen a bulldozer in Baltimore and wanted us to deliver it to the customer in Lakeland, so we drove up and put the bulldozer on a flatbed trailer to haul it back. Becker said he was filling contracts for airplanes. He had already had a twin-engine job flown out to Caracas, Venezuela, and now he had another customer for a single-engine Cessna.

When we got the bulldozer back to Lakeland, Marshall and I scouted small airports and found the plane at a strip where nobody was on duty at night. Another guy was going to fly it out, so we took that guy out there that night. Marshall got in and wired the plane up and got it started, and the pilot took off. We didn't want this plane to get out of the country, so I had tipped off our guys ahead of time and they had made arrangements with the FAA to divert the plane to Miami. So when this guy took off, I called in, and they ordered him to land in Miami. So as not to blow our operation, they used as a reason that they suspected it was a drug plane.

A couple of the car thieves lived in Daytona, and one Sunday afternoon we went over there. They lived with their girlfriends in this dumpy little house, and there were two little kids running around in diapers. The place was a mess, and there was nothing in the house to eat except junk food and beer.

Marshall and I went out and bought a load of groceries, including baby food. They served the baby food to the kids while I cooked up pots of spaghetti sauce and pasta and sausage and peppers for the adults. So we had a big meal with the thieves and their girlfriends and kids that Sunday afternoon.

Because we had things going all the time, I got home only twice in five months. In addition to the separation, the operation was putting a financial strain on my family.

At that time all an undercover agent got was a per

diem for expenses. Out of that you had to pay for hotel and meals. It was never enough. Often when I was with badguys, I picked up a check, and often it came out of my own money. I called home a lot, and for security reasons I didn't want any phone numbers on my hotel bill, so I always called collect. I didn't get reimbursed for my home phone bill, so I ended up eating that, which was a big sum over the long haul. Sometimes I had to ask my wife to wire me money because I had run out of cash. Naturally, my wife wasn't happy about seeing our money used this way. In the end I used a total of about $3,000 of my own money in this operation. But I couldn't stop the operation to argue with the office about expenses.

The office had a strict policy about having receipts for everything. I got into a flap over the time when the guys were buying the White Freightliner and they asked us to switch hotels. I had two hotel bills for one day. The auditors at the Bureau rejected my reimbursement claim because the rule was one hotel room per day. I drew the line, flat out refused to eat that expense. I explained about how it was operating undercover, how expenses didn't always fit the normal routine. Eventually that was straightened out. I was given a larger weekly amount, to use how I saw fit.

The problem was, this kind of extended undercover operation was new to everybody.

In February 1976, the FBI and Florida Highway Patrol arrested Becker and the entire ring—thirty people—and recovered a million dollars' worth of stolen vehicles from Florida, Maryland, South Carolina, Pennsylvania, Missouri, Alabama, Georgia, and Virginia. They said it was one of the largest, most lucrative theft rings ever busted.

Trials went on for more than two months. In exchange for his cooperation in busting the ring, and his testimony, Marshall went into the federal Witness Protection Program, on which he and his family were relocated to an undisclosed place and given new identities.

For my work I got a letter of commendation from

Clarence M. Kelley, Director of the FBI, and an award of $250.

What meant more to me than that was a letter that one of the defense attorneys sent to Director Kelley. The letter said, in part, "Mr. Pistone . . . was a most impressive witness and had obviously done an excellent job in his undercover capacity, but the most outstanding elements of his character were his candor, dedication and sincerity."

For a defense attorney who lost the case to take the time to write such a letter—that gave me real satisfaction.

I came back to New York to resume work with the Truck and Hijack Squad. But the success of this operation had changed the course of my career and headed me toward the Mafia.

3

PREPARATIONS

The FBI was finally thinking about getting into long-term undercover operations—long-term being, say, six months. Our success in the heavy-equipment operation helped convince people that using an agent this way, instead of just turning an inside guy into an informant, was effective.

My supervisor in New York, Guy Berada, who has since retired, wanted to get another long-term undercover operation going. He was in charge of the Truck and Hijack Squad, the squad I was assigned to.

Beginning in the spring of 1976, we had meetings and bull sessions and came up with the idea to infiltrate big-time fences—high-echelon dealers in stolen property who were associated with the Mafia. I was a natural link for the hijack squad. You get a report of a hijacking, you investigate it, find out who pulled the job, where the drop was, and who was fencing the load. Our goal was to go strictly after the upper-echelon fences, those who more often than not dealt with the Mafia, the outfit with the money, the know-how, and the connections to distribute the stuff further. Some of these fences owned restaurants or bars or stores; some were actual Mafia members—wiseguys, themselves.

It was decided to make it a one-man undercover job. I was picked because I had just come off the other successful operation, because I knew about hijacking, because I was familiar with the street world.

And not least because I was Italian. That would help me fit in with the types we would be investigating, because if they were not themselves Italians, the people they were dealing with were.

The idea was: You bust the fences, you wound the Mafia. That was the extent of our aims in the beginning, just to get the fences. Having decided on that, though, you don't just walk out the door and begin work undercover. It took months of preparation, both for me and for the bureaucracy.

Eventually we had to sell the idea upstream, to Washington, to the brass at FBI Headquarters. In order to do that we had to have everything calculated—money, time, targets, probabilities for success. Long-term undercover operations were so new to the FBI that there wasn't even a formal set of guidelines issued for undercover agents and their supervisors to go by until 1980, years later. It was pioneer territory, and you had to sell the plan well.

Just launching work on the proposal was exciting for me. I was in on the ground floor with the new long-term techniques. And it was targeted toward the mob, which intrigued me. We had new legal tools to use against organized crime. In 1970, Congress passed the Racketeer Influenced and Corrupt Organizations Act, which everybody refers to as the "RICO" statutes. For the first time we could go after "an enterprise" engaged in a "pattern of racketeering." If we could show people involved in an organization whose purpose it was to commit crimes, we didn't have to show that each member of that organization actually committed each crime.

We had the law we needed against the Mafia.

In this case, with a new type of undercover operation, I and the supervisors would be able to plan and steer the operation the way we wanted it, doing the thing ourselves without a lot of help or intervention from anybody else.

Berada was at that time one of the most imaginative supervisors. We had to get some good targets, and it had to be a feasible plan to sell to headquarters, something that would work, because like most bureaucracies, most people in ours didn't want to put their necks on the line for something new and risky.

There was a lot of research to do before I could go undercover. Even the research was done discreetly. Only four or five people were involved in the entire matter. In the beginning only my supervisor, Berada; the Special Agent in Charge of the Criminal Division of the New York Office, Ted Foley; and the guys who would be my case agent, Joe Connally, and my contact agent, Steve Bursey, were in on it. I went through old, closed files, old reports, and talked to guys who were on the squad, guys I could trust, pumping them for all the information we could get on the fences that we were targeting. For the most part we knew who the fences were. It was just hard to get anything solid on them. So now, for the first time, we would try to plant one of our own men—me—to live and work among them. I gathered names, looked at mug shots. We wanted to know who their mob associates were, who the hijackers were, where they hung out, where they worked out of, what their habits and personalities were, what they looked like—anything that might help me navigate in their world.

In developing the plan and the proposal, there was a handful of people involved, from both New York and Headquarters. Eddie O'Brien was the supervisor at Headquarters who handled undercover work in its infancy. For the proposal we identified some targets that were top fences, and some areas of the city that I would be going into, such as Little Italy in Manhattan and certain parts of Brooklyn, and restaurants and clubs where I might hang out. We left enough leeway so that in case we got other openings, we could take them.

It occurred to us to duplicate the New York plan in Miami, with another agent, the two to work in conjunction with each other. Miami had a lot of wealthy residents and vacationers, and a lot of con men and thieves who were specialists in jewels and stocks and bonds. So there were also a lot of big-time fences who dealt with the Mafia. We could target those fences down there as well, and the agent assigned to that end and I could back each other up.

The Miami office liked the idea. Berada and I went down to help them design the same type of proposal that we had for New York.

Then he and I discussed who I would feel comfortable with as the undercover agent in Miami. Anytime you're working undercover, who you bring into the operation is a crucial choice. It has to be somebody you can trust with the job and your life.

At that time I didn't know anybody from the Miami office who was available. The guy I decided on was a friend whose undercover name was Joe Fitzgerald. He was from Boston, stood about 6'5", was a former defensive end for Boston College. I picked him because he was a good bull-thrower, sharp on his feet, and could really handle himself. He was basically a street guy. He had been in Miami enough to know his way around. So we brought Joe Fitz down to Miami and filled him in on the whole operation, and he accepted the job.

We would launch the two operations together, and the code name for the tandem would be "Sun Apple." Miami Sun, New York Apple.

Next thing we had to plan was me. I had to establish a new identity that would stand up under whatever kind of examination that could arise. On the street everybody is suspicious of everybody else until you prove yourself.

We made a list of things I needed for a credible

background. First was a name. From the heavy-equipment operation I already had the kind of wallet fillers you need for identification—social security card, American Express card, and driver's license (actually I had two driver's licenses, one for Florida, one for New York). So it seemed easiest just to stick with the name Donald Brasco. Under that name I had established some background in California and Florida and made some good contacts. It would be easier just to continue that than to change everything.

But the very background that gave that name an advantage gave it its disadvantage. I wondered whether the publicity I had gotten in the Florida heavy-equipment trials would come back to haunt me. But I hadn't run into any mob guys during that time, so far as I knew. I thought about it for a long time while we were arranging other things. Finally I thought, What the hell, I'll go with it.

As Donald Brasco, I had to have a past. Not too much of a past. Like everything else, I wanted to keep it simple. You have to tell a lot of lies, anyway. The fewer you tell, the fewer you have to remember. In my undercover work I stayed as close to the truth as possible, whenever possible. For this particular aspect—where I came from—the less there was at all, the better.

My background was going to be that I spent time down in the Miami area and out in California, and that I was a jewel thief and burglar—and a bachelor.

We came up with the idea that I would be an orphan. Without a family it's harder for people to check up on you. If you had a family, you would have to involve other agents to speak up for you as family members. If you're an orphan, the only thing they can check on is if you lived in a neighborhood or if you have any knowledge of the particular neighborhood. I had knowledge of areas in Florida and California because I had done some work there.

We knew from our research people about an orphanage in Pittsburgh that had burned down, and there were no records left of the children raised there

That was perfect for me. One of the agents had lived in Pittsburgh, and I had grown up in Pennsylvania.

Being a jewel thief was my idea. There are all kinds of crooks. I needed a specialty that allowed me to work alone and without violence. I couldn't be a stickup man or a bank robber or hijacker or anything like that. We had an okay from the department to get involved in certain marginal activities, but you had to avoid violence. As a jewel thief, I could say I worked alone. I could come and go as I wanted, and come up with scores that everybody didn't have to know about because I committed my "crimes" in private.

For a jewel thief and burglar, it was not unusual for a guy to work alone. And since if you pull off the job correctly you don't confront your victims, there is a minimal chance for violence. That specialty gave me an out whenever anybody would want me to pull a violent job—that's not my thing.

Given the nature of the operation, there was a likelihood that I would wander into gray areas regarding FBI rules and regulations. But we had to take some chances. We would face things as they came up. How far my role could go, what crimes I could participate in and observe and ignore, how far I could go in having a deal instigated and yet avoid the entrapment issue—such things were part of my preparation before I hit the street.

As a jewel thief, I would have appropriate expertise. I knew enough about alarm systems and surveillance equipment to assess prospective "jobs" that I or others might undertake. A prominent New York City jewelry company gave me a two-week gemology course, knowing only that it was for the FBI and not knowing anything about my operation. I spent time with a gemologist at a New York museum and bought books on precious gems and coins. This didn't make me a top-flight expert, but at least I knew what to look for.

I had a name, a background, a criminal career. We had to budget the operation. I would need an apartment, car, money to bounce around with, and so on.

We started modestly. For the New York side of Sun Apple, we figured on a six-month operation with a budget of $10,000. That was low, but with a low figure we felt we had a better chance of getting the operation approved. The main thing was getting it launched. Once you've got something going and can show some results, it's easier to extend it. We were confident. Then if we needed another six months, we could go in with an additional proposal.

Nobody dreamed of going for six *years* and getting where we got to.

We budgeted carefully because the Bureau audits carefully: apartment, phone, leased car, personal expenses, and so on. Our initial figure climbed from $10,000 to $15,000 because we decided to ask to have $5,000 on hand for any special, unexpected expenses, such as if I had to buy into a score.

When all the paperwork was completed, the proposal was sent to headquarters in Washington. They approved it.

Now I had to disappear. Only a handful of people knew about this operation. For their own protection my family knew only that I would be going undercover, not for what. Since the Bureau had no history with deep, long-term undercover operations, we had to make up guidelines as we went along. One of the things we determined was that my true existence as an FBI agent would have to be erased.

In my earlier undercover operation with the heavy-equipment theft ring, everything was treated within the office on a need-to-know basis. Now the security measures would be even more severe. At the New York office of the FBI—then on East Sixty-ninth Street—my desk was cleaned out. My name was erased from office rolls. My personnel file was removed from the office and secretly stashed in the safe of the Special Agent in Charge. Since I was off the office payroll, my paycheck was sent to me outside the normal system. With the exception of those few case agents and contact agents and higher-ups in FBI Headquarters in Washington, nobody in the office or field staffs of the FBI around the country knew what I was doing. If anybody called the office looking for me, they would be told there was nobody employed by the FBI under that name. As far as people inside and outside the Bureau were concerned, nobody by the name of Joseph Pistone had anything to do with the Federal Bureau of Investigation.

We had started thinking about this in April. By the time I was ready to actually hit the street, it was September.

Once I walked out of my FBI office on that September day in 1976, I never returned, never went into any FBI office anywhere, for the next six years that I was undercover.

My coworkers didn't know what had happened to me. My friends didn't know. My informants didn't know. I would utilize no informants in this new Donald Brasco job.

Having disappeared, I proceeded to build my new life. I needed an apartment, a car, a bank account—ordinary things. None of this would be gotten through the Bureau. I would do it on my own, as Donald Brasco, and no strings would be pulled.

I wanted to do everything myself. I didn't want to go through contacts because I didn't want anybody to know it was an FBI operation. You never know if somebody's going to get into somebody else's files, or if somebody will slip and say something. If nobody knows and nobody's involved, nobody can slip. And we knew we might be rubbing up against mob guys through the fences we were targeting, and that any slip could be fatal, so everything I did was done by myself, just as Joe Blow off the street.

We created some references for Donald Brasco. We set up a couple of "hello phones," just numbers people could call to check my references. One was my place of employment. I was a manager of Ace Trucking Company. The other was the building manager at my residence. I was the building manager. The only people who answered those phones were my supervisor or my case agent—or sometimes myself.

I leased a car that fit my role, a yellow 1976 Cadillac Coup de Ville with Florida tags.

Ordinarily I never wear any jewelry, and I don't care about sharp clothes. For this job I had to dress up a little, some rings and chains and sport clothes. In our budget that was a onetime expense of $750.

I went into a branch of Chase Manhattan Bank in midtown to open a checking account. I filled out the forms. There was a space for prior banking, and I left it blank. The officer looked over my application.

"Where did you do your prior banking?" he asked.

"Why you asking me that?" I said.

"Because we have to verify your signature," he said.

"I don't have any prior banking account."

"Well, that's what we require for you to open an account."

It was a quick glimpse into society when you're not playing by ordinary rules. Here I was, looking presentable in new sport clothes, carrying $1,000 in cash for deposit in a new account, and I couldn't open an account because I didn't have any banking history. I wasn't prepared for that. But I didn't want to get into any argument, because I was caught off-guard by this guy.

So I said, "Thank you very much," got up, and left.

There was a branch of Chemical Bank across the street. I decided to try there. But first I thought over what my answer would be if a bank officer there hit me with the same problem.

I walked in and filled out the forms. The guy asked, "Where did you do any prior banking during the last two years?"

"I haven't done any banking during the last two years," I said.

"Then I'm afraid we can't open an account for you," he said.

"You're discriminating against me," I said.

"What do you mean by that?" he said. I wasn't black or female or any of the other things usually associated with discrimination, and he gave me a strange look. "That's our rule," he said, "for everybody."

I said, "I just got out of jail. I did six years in the can. Now I'm out and trying to be a good citizen. I've paid my debt to society, I got a decent job, I want to open up a bank account and be a decent citizen. I've got a thousand dollars with me, and all I want is a checking account. And you're refusing me an account because I haven't done any banking lately. I'd like to have your name and position here, because I'm gonna go downtown to City Hall and put in a complaint to the civil-rights authorities that I'm being discriminated against."

Suddenly he looked intimidated—I think more because he was probably sitting across from an ex-con for the first time in his life than because of potential discrimination problems.

He said, "Well, there are some instances where we can make allowances. I think we can help you out."

So I had a checking account. Now I needed an apartment.

I wasn't fussy about where or how I lived, except for two things: I didn't want to be right in the heart of my target areas, and I wanted the apartment to be in a relatively big building—both of these things for the sake of anonymity. I needed a place where I could come and go without attracting attention.

I scoured the papers and looked for a week. Then I found just what I wanted.

I took a one-bedroom apartment—21-G—in Yorkville Towers at Ninety-first Street and Third Avenue, just a few blocks uptown from the most chic blocks of the city's Upper East Side.

I liked the location and the fact that it had an underground parking garage, and it was not too expensive for what you got—$491.60 per month. It had a big lobby, twenty-four-hour doorman security, and a valet service for deliveries.

I rented furniture for $90.30 per month. I bought sheets, towels, a shower curtain. From my real home I brought in pots and pans and stocked the cupboards.

I told my wife not to call me at the apartment unless it was an emergency. There was a possibility that badguys might be in the apartment when she called, or that my phone might be tapped by badguys. I didn't tell her that. I told her I would be using the same name as before—Donald Brasco—and that I would call her and get home as often as possible. I didn't tell her that I might get involved with the Mafia. Maybe I was being selfish, but to me that was the job.

I was ready to hit the street as Don Brasco, jewel thief and burglar.

4

HITTING THE STREET

We had a list of places where wiseguy-type fences were known to hang out. This was going to be a seven-day-a-week job, going around to these bars and restaurants and clubs. The target places were not necessarily "mob" joints. Sometimes they were—night spots and restaurants owned in whole or in part by the mob. More often they were just places where wiseguys and their associates liked to hang out.

I would cruise these places, mostly in midtown or lower Manhattan, have a drink or dinner, not talking much or making any moves, just showing my face so people would get used to seeing me. Places like the Rainbow Room in the RCA Building in Rockefeller Center, Separate Tables on Third Avenue, Vesuvio Restaurant on Forty-eighth Street in the heart of the theater district, Cecil's Discotheque on Fifty-fourth Street, the Applause Restaurant on Lexington Avenue.

We didn't concentrate on places in Little Italy because I would have been too obvious. You don't just start hanging out in places there without knowing anybody. You're either a tourist or some kind of trouble. I didn't try to introduce myself to anybody or get into any conversations for a while. Mob guys or fences I recognized were mixed in with ordinary customers, what wiseguys call "citizens," people not connected with the mob. After I had been to a place a few times, I might say hello to the bartender if he had begun to recognize me. The important thing was just to be seen and not to push anything; just get noticed, get established that I wasn't just a one-shot visitor.

I didn't flash around a lot of money because that tags you either as a cop or a mark. A mark is somebody that looks ripe for getting conned out of his money. And a cop typically might flash money when he was looking to make a buy of something illegal, like tempting somebody to offer swag—stolen goods—in order to make a bust. No street guy is going to throw money all over the place unless he's trying to attract attention. Then the question is: Why is he trying to attract attention? I didn't want to attract that kind of attention. So to do it right, you don't go in and start spending a lot of money or showing off stuff or trying to make conversation, because you don't know them and they don't know you.

You take a job like this in very small, careful steps—not just to avoid suspicion but also to leave behind you a clean, credible trail. You never know what part of what you do will become part of your history when people want to check on you. You want to establish right away, everywhere you go, that you don't have a big mouth, and that you don't have too big a nose about other people's business. You have to be patient, because you never know where anything will lead. Basically I wanted to keep my own personality, which was low-key. I felt that the time would come in conversation with somebody what my game was.

One of the first places I frequented was Carmello's, a pleasant restaurant at 1638 York Avenue, near Eighty-sixth Street and the East River. It wasn't far from my new apartment, and I wanted a place where I could stop in for a late dinner or drink near where I lived. This wasn't one of the primary places we had targeted, but we knew that some wiseguy types hung out there. Our information was that the restaurant was owned by Joey and Carmine Zito, who were members of the Genovese crime family, headed by Fat Tony Salerno.

For weeks I roamed around and hung out at these

places. Time dragged. I rarely drink alcohol. I don't smoke. Before I came on the job as an FBI agent, I once had a job as a bartender, and it was one of my least favorite things, hanging out in a bar all night watching people drink and listening to drinkers talk. During these weeks, in the evening at a bar, I might start off with a Scotch, then I'd switch to club soda for the rest of the night.

Occasionally I saw somebody we had targeted. I recognized them from the pictures I had been shown in preparation. But I never got an opportunity to get into conversation with them. It isn't wise to say to the bartender, "Who is that over there? Isn't that so-and-so?" I wanted to get to be known as a guy who didn't ask too many questions, didn't appear to be too curious. With the guys we were after, it was tough to break in. A wrong move—even if you're just on the fringes of things—will turn them off. While I was having a couple of drinks or dinner, I was always interested in what was going on in the place. I was always observing, listening, remembering, while still trying to put across the impression that I was oblivious to who was in there.

All through October and November I hung out, watching, listening, not advancing beyond that. It was boring a lot of the time but not discouraging. I knew it would take time. It is a delicate matter, maneuvering your way in. You don't just step into an operation like this and start dealing. Associates of wiseguys don't deal with people they don't know or who somebody else doesn't vouch for. So for the first two or three months I had to lay the initial groundwork that would lead to being known and having somebody vouch for me.

All this time—in fact, for the entire six years of the overall operation—I never made notes of what I was doing. I didn't know if at any time I was going to be braced—somebody might check me out, cops or crooks, so I never had anything incriminating in my apartment or on my person. Every couple of days or so, depending on the significance, I would phone my contact agent to fill him on what was going on, who I had seen where, doing what.

One thing that went on at Carmello's was backgammon. Men played backgammon at the bar. I noticed that a lot of local neighborhood guys would hang out in there, come for dinner, then sit at the bar and play backgammon. And some of the wiseguys that were hanging around would get involved. They played for high stakes—as high as $1,000 a game. That looked like a good way for me to get in, get an introduction, get some conversation going with the regulars. But I didn't know how to play backgammon. I bought a book and studied up. Another agent whose undercover name was Chuck was a good backgammon player. Chuck had an operation going in the music business. He was a friend of mine. He would come over to my apartment, or I'd go over to his, and he'd teach me backgammon. We played and played, in order for me to get comfortable.

Finally, when I thought I was good enough, I decided to challenge for a game at the bar.

It was near Christmastime, so there was a kind of festive mood in the place, and that seemed like a good time for a newcomer to edge in. On this night there were two boards going at the bar. I watched for a while to see which board had the weaker players. The way you got into the game was to challenge the winner, and that's the board I challenged the winner on.

The stakes for the first game were $100. That made me nervous because I didn't have a lot of money to spend. I won that first game, lost the next, and ended up the evening about breaking even.

But the important thing was that it broke the ice. I got introduced around as "Don" for the first time. And now I could sit down and talk to people. We could sit around and talk about the games going on.

After a couple weeks I retreated from the backgammon games. The money was getting a little steep. I played two games for $500 each, lost one then won one. My expense account then was maybe $200 to

$300 a week for everything, and I couldn't go over that without going into an explanation for the accountants at the Bureau. It wasn't worth it, just to play backgammon with some half-ass wiseguys.

Anyway, by then I had accomplished what I had learned backgammon for. I had gotten to know some people, at least enough to be acknowledged when I came in: "Hey, Don, how's it going?"

So I wasn't a strange face any longer. I also got pretty friendly with the bartender, Marty. Marty wasn't a mob guy, but he was a pretty good knock-around guy who knew what was going on. I got to bullshitting with Marty pretty good near the end of December 1976, and early January of 1977. Conversation rolled around gradually, and he asked me if I lived around there, since I was in there so much. I told him, yeah, I lived up at Ninety-first and Third.

"You from around here?" he asked me.

"I spent some years in this area," I told him. "Lately I been spending a lot of time in Miami and out in California. I just came in from Miami a couple months ago."

"What do you do?" he asked me.

That kind of question you don't answer directly. "Oh, you know, not doing anything right now, you know, hanging out, looking around . . ." You bob and weave a little with the guy. I said, "Basically I do anything where I can make a fast buck."

He had a girlfriend that used to come in at closing, then they'd go out bouncing after work, around the city. A couple times he asked me if I wanted to go, and I backed off, said no thanks. I didn't want him to think I was anxious to make friends.

Still, I didn't want him or anybody else in there to think I didn't have anything going for me. So once in a while I'd bring a female in—somebody that I'd met in another bar across the street from my apartment or something—just for a couple drinks or dinner. And sometimes my agent friend, Chuck, would come in with me for a drink. You can't go in all the time by yourself, because they think you're either a fag or a cop. And it's good to vary your company so they don't see you with the same people all the time and wonder what's up. The idea is to blend in, not present yourself in any way at all that makes anybody around you uncomfortable.

Marty's girlfriend had a girlfriend named Patricia, a good-looking blonde who was going out with one of the wiseguys that hung out there, a bookie named Nicky. A couple times she came in when I was in there and Nicky wasn't, and she'd sit down for some small talk with me. At first it was just casual conversation. Then I figured she was coming on to me a little, and I had to be very careful, as an outsider, not to overstep my bounds. The worst thing I could do is appear to be coming on to a wiseguy's girlfriend, because there are real firm rules against that. If I made that kind of mistake I would have shot my whole couple months of work to get in there.

One night this Patricia asked me if I wanted to have dinner with her. "Nicky's not gonna be around," she said. "We could take off and find someplace nice."

"Thanks," I said, "but I don't think so. Not tonight."

Then I grabbed Marty the bartender off to the side. "Hey, Marty," I said, "I want you to know that I'm keeping my distance from Patricia because I know that she's Nicky's girlfriend. But I don't want to insult anybody, either."

Marty said, "I know, I've been watching how you handle yourself."

So I established another small building block in my character: The bartender knew that I knew what the rules were with wiseguys. Most guys who hadn't been around the streets or around wiseguys might have jumped at an invitation from a girl like that—figuring that, after all, if she makes the play, it must be all right. But with wiseguys there's a strict code that you don't mess. I mean, strict.

A week or so later Marty came over to me. "Hey, Don, I just want to tell you that Patricia and Nicky broke up, so if you want to ask her out for a drink or something, feel free."

I said, "Thanks, but I'm not really out hawking it, you know?"

He said, "After work tonight we're going to the Rainbow Room. Come on with us, and bring her."

The four of us went to the Rainbow Room and had a good time. I went out bouncing with him a few times more after that, and that got me in pretty solid in that place.

He started introducing me to the other guys that hung out in Carmello's, including some of the half-ass wiseguys. I never did anything with them, didn't get involved with them, but at least they acknowledged me when I came in, and I began to have a "home base" where people knew me, in case anybody started checking.

It was also a place where I could leave messages and where messages would be taken for me. I would tell Marty, If a guy calls here looking for me, tell him I'll be in here at such-and-such a time. Sometimes I would call and ask for myself, and Marty would take the message and give it to me when I came in. So I established that I had some friends around, people I was involved with.

The important thing here in the beginning was not so much to get hooked up with anybody in particular and get action going right away. The important thing was to have a hangout, a good backup, for credibility. When I went other places, I could say, "I been hanging out at that place for four or five months." And they could check it out. The guys that had been hanging around in this place would say, "Yeah, Don Brasco has been coming in here for quite a while, and he seems all right, never tried to pull anything on us." That's the way you build up who you are, little by little, never moving too fast, never taking too big a bite at one time. There are occasions where you suddenly have to take a big step or a big chance. Those come later.

Finally it was time for me to make my move with Marty the bartender. Typically, what an undercover cop will do, in a buy-bust situation, is try to buy something from you. Cops always buy, never sell. I was going to sell. So I brought in some pieces of jewelry. A couple of diamond rings, a couple of loose stones, and a couple of men's and ladies' wristwatches.

When there was nobody else at the bar, I opened the pouch and showed the stuff to him.

"If you'd like to hold on to these for a couple days," I said, "you can try to get rid of them."

"What's the deal?" he asked.

"I need $2,500 total. Anything over that is yours."

He didn't ask if the stuff was stolen. He didn't need to, because it was understood. During the course of recent conversations I had given him the impression that I wasn't on the legit. So it was obvious. You say as little as possible in a situation like this. Actually, of course, the stuff was from the FBI, things that were confiscated during investigations and used strictly for this type of purpose.

He took the items and held on to them for three or four days. Then one night he said, "Don, some people want it, but I can't get you the price tag that you want."

Now, I don't know if he's testing me or what. You never take it for granted that somebody trusts you. I could have said, "Well, get me what you can for it, and I'll give you a piece." But that's not the way you work. Things have a certain street value, and a street guys knows what that is. I knew what the going rate for swag was from dealing with my informants before I went undercover. So I could talk sense about price for diamonds, gold, jewelry with anybody, whether I was going to buy or sell. So if I have swag worth $2,500, I stick with that. If you say, "Okay, just give me $800," then they might doubt that you know what you're doing.

So I said, "Okay, just give it back, no big deal. I'll be getting more stuff, so maybe we can do business another time."

He said, "Anything you come across, Don, let me see it. If I can get rid of it, I will. I can move a lot of stuff. I come across a lot of swag."

"The only things I'd be interested in," I said, "are jewelry or good clothes for myself." But I never bought anything from him.

I did place some bets through him. He talked about Nicky, the bookie, told me about his business. And I placed some bets on the horses.

All of this served the purpose of solidifying my place.

My agent friend, Chuck, had an undercover operation going in the music business: records and concerts. Sometimes we'd hang out together, back each other up—as when he would come with me to Carmello's. Chuck was putting on a concert at the Beacon Theatre on Broadway, featuring the soul singer James Brown. He asked me if I'd give him a hand. That would help him and would also help me—it would show the mob guys downtown that I was doing something, that I was a mover.

He had sucked into his operation a couple of connected guys with the Colombo crime family. He introduced me to one of them, a guy named Albert. "Connected" means that you associate with Mafia members, do jobs with them, but do not share in all the rewards and responsibilities of an actual Mafia member. A true Mafia member is a "made guy" or "straightened out," or a "wiseguy." Albert's uncle was a made guy in the Colombo family.

Albert was a half-ass wiseguy—just a connected guy, not a made guy. He was a big guy, maybe 6' 2", about thirty years old. He was a con artist dealing in paper—a stocks-and-bonds type guy. I didn't think he ever did anything very heavy. He was a bullshit artist.

But he was not a bad guy to hang around. Chuck introduced me to Albert so that maybe I could get some introductions into the Colombo family. So I started running sometimes with Chuck and Albert, bopping around different night spots. Albert liked to hit all the in spots, discos, and restaurants.

When the James Brown concert was coming up, Albert and a couple of his buddies from Brooklyn came up with the great idea that they were going to stick up the box office. He came to Chuck and me and said, "Look, near the end of the concert, when the box office closes, let's stick it up."

He wanted to stick up our own box office. Chuck

and I couldn't allow guys with guns to come in and do that, but we couldn't just veto it, either, without drawing suspicion. We really didn't know how the hell the thing was going to go.

We told Albert, "Look, if these guys come in and knock off the box office, that's less split for us, because we're gonna cop this box office, anyway. We can split it three ways. If you bring in your two friends to stick it up, that's a five-way split."

He went back to his guys with that explanation, but they wanted to do it, anyway. They wanted it all.

It was the day before the concert. We didn't know what to do. We couldn't tip off the cops, because the tip would have been traced right to Chuck or me.

"What should we do?" Chuck says to me.

"I don't know," I say, "this is your operation. I'll go along with anything you want to do as long as we don't jeopardize *my* operation."

Chuck had an idea. "I think I'll hire a couple of off-duty cops, just have them hang around the front of the lobby, like for crowd control, and maybe it'll deter these guys."

He hired the off-duty cops. They arrived in uniform and stood around. Albert and his friends showed up. "What the fuck's with these cops?" Albert said.

I said, "I don't know. Probably they're on the job and figured they'd stick around and hear James Brown. I don't know."

"What the fuck," Albert said to his friends. "How can we stick up the place with cops around?" They discussed it for a few minutes, standing outside, watching the cops in the lobby. They decided it was a no-go.

So we slipped that one. And it helped me out, because now I could tell guys that I had a piece of this guy, Chuck, who's got this Ace Record Company in his pocket.

I was trying to get home to my wife and daughters at every opportunity, even if it was just for breakfast. I would often just end up the night and head across the George Washington Bridge to New Jersey to spend a few hours at home. My wife and I socialized very little when I was home, and our few social friends were Bureau people. And while of course they knew I, too, was with the Bureau, they didn't know what operation I was on.

I was very friendly with an agent named Al Genkinger in the New York office. All during the time I was undercover, Al and his wife stayed close to my wife, took care of anything that came up. Anything my wife needed, she would get in touch with them. That was a comfort.

We told neighbors and others that I was a salesman, on the road a lot.

My daughters were already developing the habit of evading conversations with others about what I did, or even of asking me questions about my work. They would say, "What do you do when you go to work?" And I would say, "I just do my work like anybody else." After a while they stopped asking.

They were becoming cheerleaders at school. My oldest daughter had boyfriends. My wife and I became friendly with a lot of boys on the athletic teams. We went to high school wrestling matches on Wednesdays when I could make it home. She went without me if I couldn't make it.

I set up a weight lifting program for some of the guys in our basement. I had been a weight lifter for a long time. They ate it up. They didn't ask personal questions. They would come over regularly and follow the program I set up. My wife made pizzas.

It seemed I was home very little. My wife and daughters were not happy with the extended absences, especially when I didn't give much explanation. We didn't know it then, but that period gave me the best home time that I would have over the next five years.

I bopped around with Albert and got to know him pretty well. I took him up to Carmello's a few times, so he could see that guys there knew me. It's the kind of thing that feeds on itself: He sees that people know me and acknowledge me, so he feels he can introduce me to other people who know him. It enhances my credibility to be hanging out with a connected guy whose uncle is a wiseguy in the Colombo family. For his part, Albert sees that I'm accepted where I go, so it's good for him to be seen with me.

Getting established is a subtle business, a matter of small impressions, little tests, quiet understandings.

Albert lived in Brooklyn. But he loved Manhattan. One night there was a big snowstorm and he didn't want to drive home to Brooklyn. So I let him stay over in my apartment. From then on he was always trying to weasel in, to stay over at my apartment so that he didn't have to drive home to Brooklyn. I wanted to keep cultivating him, but I didn't want him parking in my apartment.

Between trying to get myself set up, establish credibility, and hanging around with Albert and others, I hardly got home at all during the month of December—maybe two or three evenings up to Christmas. So I was especially intent on getting home at a reasonable hour Christmas Eve, to spend that and part of Christmas Day with my family. I planned to knock off early Christmas Eve and get home by maybe eight o'clock. I had bought presents for everybody and stashed them in the trunk of my car.

In order to get home to my family, I started celebrating Christmas early in my Don Brasco world. On the afternoon of Christmas Eve, we started bouncing around to the various spots, having drinks and wishing people we knew Merry Christmas. Chuck, who was a bachelor, and Albert, who didn't ever like going home, brought along a couple of girls they had been going out with.

One place led to another. I had to act like I wasn't in a hurry to get anyplace. It was after ten o'clock. We were going down Eighty-sixth Street, heading for Carmello's. The street was pretty empty. On the corner there was a guy still selling Christmas trees. I happened to mention, "It's Christmas, and I don't even have a Christmas tree in my apartment."

Albert yells, "Pull over! Pull over to that guy there—he's got trees! I'm gonna buy a tree!"

I pull over at the corner. Albert jumps out and goes over to where the guy has Christmas trees. The guy has only three or four trees left. They are barely trees, more like sticks tied together. Albert picks one out and brings it over to the car. I never saw anything so scraggly. There was a trail of needles from it on the sidewalk. The top was bent over.

"What are you gonna do with that?" I ask.

"Let's put it up and decorate it in your apartment!"

"Come on, I got no decorations. All the stores are closed."

"We'll find something to decorate it with," he says, "won't we, girls?"

"Yeah, yeah!" they say.

"We can't let you be alone on Christmas Eve," Albert says.

So we go up to my apartment with this scrawny tree. When we stood it up, you could see that it was even missing some branches. "I got no stand to put it up in," I say.

"We'll use this!" he says. I had one of those big water-cooler bottles that I threw pennies in.

They put the tree in that. Then the two women rummaged around in the kitchen and came back with some tinfoil. They started making Christmas balls and decorations out of tinfoil. They hung these things on what few branches there were. Every time they hung a tinfoil bird up, a million needles fell on the floor.

"We couldn't let you go without a Christmas tree," Albert says. "Bad enough you don't have a date on Christmas Eve."

They all proceeded to make sure I enjoyed Christmas Eve and wasn't lonely. They sang Christmas carols until after midnight, sitting around this ugly tree, Albert and the girls all boozed up.

I was thinking about my kids, and all the presents in the trunk of my car, and I was angry for letting myself get into this situation.

I said, "Come on, everybody, that's enough, I've had it with Christmas."

They wanted to keep partying. I took Chuck aside and said, "You gotta get 'em outa here. I want to go home."

So he herded them up and left. I waited about a half

hour, then I went down to the garage, got my car, and headed home.

I managed to have Christmas morning with my family. I was back on the job in the afternoon. Five more Christmases would pass by before I would have a normal one with my family.

Things began to happen, some movement. Shortly after the first of the year, 1977, Albert introduced me to some active Colombo guys. We were out bouncing, and we went to Hippopotamus, the popular disco at Sixty-first Street and York Avenue. A lot of mob guys hung out there.

Albert said he'd like to introduce me to a Colombo guy that did a lot of business with swag.

He brought me over to a table and introduced me to a guy. "Jilly, this is Don, a friend of mine."

Jilly was maybe five years older than me, average build, 5'9", 160, with dark hair, prominent nose.

We sat down and talked for a while, and Albert told Jilly and the guys with him that we had been hanging out for a few months. Jilly headed up a crew that hung out mainly in Brooklyn. He said I should stop by his store over on 15th Avenue and 76th Street in the Bensonhurst section.

"Yeah, maybe I'll do that," I said.

For a couple of months now I had been playing this game of trying to be noticed without being noticed, slide into the badguy world and become accepted without drawing attention. You push a little here and there, but very gently. Brief introductions, short conversations, appearances one place and another, hints about what you're up to, casual mannerisms, demeanor, and lingo that show you know your way around— all these become a trail of credibility you leave behind you. Above all, you cannot hurry. You cannot seem eager to meet certain people, make certain contacts, learn about certain scores. The quickest way to get tagged as a cop is to try to move too fast. You have to show that you have the time to play it by the rules of the street, and that includes letting people check you out and come to you.

You have to have confidence in how you're handling yourself, because while you're playing this game, much of the time you don't know where you stand. Nobody tells you you're getting in solid or getting to know the right people or heading in the right direction. Nobody tells you if you're safe. You have to sense it. Badguys on the street are sensing you. You can be wrong. Obviously, so can they. But the street is no place to doubt yourself.

These initial months were not a time of high excitement in terms of events. But I felt excitement. I had a foothold. Nobody in the outside world knew where I was or what I was doing, hour by hour, day by day. On the street, people didn't know who I was or what I was really doing. I was on the job and on my own. There was excitement in that.

One night I came out of Carmello's and started to drive downtown to make the rounds of the regular spots. I thought a car was following me. To check it out, I didn't try to shake them right away. I just led them on a wild-goose chase for a while. I went across the George Washington Bridge to Fort Lee, New Jersey, turned around, and came back. The other car stayed with me but made no move.

It had to be some sort of law-enforcement unit. Nobody else would have reason to follow me. My assumption was that there was an informant in Carmello's, or one of the other places, who had passed on the information that there was a new guy hanging around, making friends with badguys, a guy who obviously doesn't work and yet has money to spend. Or else they could have been spot-checking the place, surveilling it, and they saw my car there a few times, with out-of-state tags, saw me come and go, and got into it that way.

Law-enforcement units—New York Police, FBI, Drug Enforcement Administration, all the others—have organized crime figures under surveillance all the time. It is standard practice. None of these outfits—including the FBI, for the most part—knew who I was. So if I started coming into their picture, buddying up with badguys, naturally I would become a suspect just like the rest of them.

If it wasn't cops, it could be wiseguys checking me out. I didn't want anybody on either side tailing me. If I was going to meet my contact agent, or going home to see my family, a tail could have blown the whole operation. So every time I left a place, I was tail-conscious. I always "cleaned" myself. I never went directly to my destination. I would ride around, keep checking my rearview mirror to see if I was being followed, lose any suspicious cars with a series of turns and double-backs. When I parked someplace, I would notice whoever parked near me, and anybody who came in a place with me.

The first time I was rousted, I was near Carmello's. I hadn't had time to get rid of the car tailing me. They pulled me over. A couple guys in plainclothes with drawn guns ordered me out, told me to put my hands on my head. They patted me down, checked inside the car. They didn't find anything on me or in the car. When they were finished, they said it was a routine license check because I had Florida plates on the car.

The only thing it was routine for was wiseguys, because they get rousted all the time. That's why you don't usually carry a gun. These guys here who rousted me didn't even identify themselves. I don't know who they were.

I was tailed a few times, stopped and searched a couple of times. It was an inconvenience, but it also made me feel that I was doing the job right.

I drove over to Brooklyn, to Jilly's store at 7612 15th Avenue. The neighborhood was very clean, quiet, working-class, two- and three-story residential buildings with a lot of storefronts on the ground floors. Jilly's store was in the middle of a block of glass fronts. There was a small grocery store, and the Park Ridge Pharmacy on the corner.

A big sign over the door of Jilly's store read ACERG. Jilly's last name was Greca, his store was the name spelled backward. The store part was the front room.

Plain metal racks of expensive clothes, mostly women's stuff: leather jackets, pants, blouses. Everything was marked cheaper than it would be at a regular store. The store was open to the public, but nobody would be coming there from Manhattan. It was a neighborhood store in the kind of neighborhood where outsiders are spotted in a minute.

Everything was cheap because it was all swag. Jilly's crew were hijackers, burglars, all-around thieves. The store sold their loot.

5

BROOKLYN:
THE COLOMBOS

The Acerg store was in the front, and anybody in the crew could act as salesman. There was a back room with a desk and a couple of card tables. That's where the crew hung out during the day. That's where I was introduced to a few guys, ranging in age from maybe late twenties to early forties, who were sitting around playing gin and bullshitting. First names and nicknames only: Guido, Vito, Tommy the Chief, Vinnie, and so on.

I started hanging out there with Jilly's crew. Because I was "known" by other people that this crew knew, and because I was introduced to them by somebody they knew, they were pretty open around me.

Although these were lower-echelon guys in the mob, they always had something going. They always had money. They were always turning things over. They always had swag around. Swag was always going in and out. Everybody dressed well. Ninety percent of what they wore was swag. Latest styles. Sports shirts, slacks, sweaters, and leather jackets. If they had jeans on, they were always designer jeans.

You name it, they stole it. Jilly's crew would hit warehouses, docks, trucks, houses. There was nothing they wouldn't consider stealing. They considered all the time. There wasn't one hour of one day that went by when they weren't thinking and talking about what they were going to steal, who or what or where they were going to rob. There was always a load to go after, or somebody else's load you might get a piece of, always something to hustle.

When they got up in the morning, they didn't think about going to work and punching a time clock. They didn't think about spending time with their wives or girlfriends. The mob was their job. You got up, went to the club or wherever you hung out, and spent your day with those guys.

You've got to be up all day figuring out what you're going to do that night, what scores you're going to go out on. The day basically was: You got to the club at ten-thirty or eleven o'clock in the morning, then sat around all day and discussed scams and scores and hustles, past and future. Somebody would have an idea about a burglary or hijack, and they'd kick it around to see if it was worthwhile. Or somebody else had pulled a score and was looking to get rid of jewelry, furs, or whatever. And they'd discuss the possibility of "middling" it—taking the swag and re-selling it.

All day long, while they schemed, they'd sit in the back room at the Acerg store and play gin and smoke cigarettes and cigars. I don't smoke. They never opened a window. Even with air-conditioning, it got to be pretty dense. There might be two games going, depending on how many guys were in there. I don't even like to play cards. You play gin—never any other game—for maybe ten cents a point. Even while you're sitting around playing gin, you're still talking about making a dollar, what the hustle of the day is. Maybe you go over to somebody else's club, play gin there, or talk up some scheme. Maybe you talk to somebody about a score you're trying to set up or trying to get a piece of. If they had a potential job to case, a couple guys would go out during the daytime and look it over.

If they weren't scheming and dreaming, they were telling war stories, reminiscences about their time in various jails and prisons. Everybody did time in the can. It was part of the price of doing business. They knew all about different jails, cell blocks, guards. I had enough phony background set up to establish my credentials as a serious criminal, to show that I was tough enough to do time if I had to without turning rat. But I never claimed to have done any prison time because I didn't know those places, and that could have just tripped me up. If you do three to five years you get to know the guards—what guard's on what tier. You get to know the inmates, guys who are doing fifteen to twenty, guys who are still there. They knew the lingo and the slang. Everybody remembers those relationships and that time.

My thinking is, if it's not necessary to have done something, don't claim to have done it. When these guys talked about prison time, I just listened like an ordinary citizen.

For lunch somebody would go out to bring in Chinese food or hero sandwiches. Maybe around four-thirty or five o'clock, the guys would split, go home to their wives or whatever, have supper, then go back out on the street, pulling off their scores or bouncing around the night spots or doing whatever they did.

On Tuesdays we went to Sally's club for lunch. Sally was an old-time wiseguy, a capo in the Colombo family. He had a social club on 17th Avenue, not far from Jilly's. Sometimes we'd hang out over at Sally's, divide the time between there and Jilly's. But every Tuesday afternoon Sally cooked a big lunch for our whole crew of about eight, and his own, altogether maybe eighteen or twenty guys. He had a regular kitchen, and he would cook meatballs, macaroni, sausages, peppers, everything. For this lunch we would set up a long folding table. We would sit at the table all afternoon eating lunch, drinking jugs of homemade red wine that Sally produced, and bullshitting.

My day would pretty much follow the same routine as theirs. I'd get to the club between ten and eleven and hang out all day with these guys. By late afternoon or early evening, I'd go back to my apartment, maybe take a nap for an hour, get up and shower, and about nine o'clock or so go back out on the street to wherever it was we were going to meet. Sometimes I would go back to Brooklyn, sometimes bounce around in Manhattan; sometimes with them, sometimes by myself in places where people had gotten to know me through these guys.

But even when we'd cruise around to the different night spots, the talk was always on whatever scams or hustles were going on or coming up. What they did for a living was on their minds more than it was with ordinary people. They never put that aside. Nobody ever had enough money, no matter how much they had, and it was always feast or famine. Half the time their schemes came to nothing. Or worse, they went bad in the execution and cost them either money or jail time. But that didn't cool their dedication. They did not have a sense of humor about their failures, or those schemes they came up with that were harebrained. They stuck to their routine.

A small-time fence named Vinnie, who hung around Jilly's, was overweight and had a bad heart, for which he took some pills—maybe nitroglycerin. One afternoon we were all in a card game. It was a hard game, for quite a few bucks. And at the same time they were kicking around the prospects for a house burglary over in Bayonne, New Jersey.

All of a sudden Vinnie falls down on the floor, gasping for breath and grabbing at his chest.

"Hey, you guys," I say, "Vinnie's got a problem."

Nobody moves. They keep playing cards. Vinnie is gasping and grabbing, and still nobody moves.

"He's having a heart attack!" I scramble over to him. "We gotta get him to the hospital! Come on, somebody help me with him!"

"Aw, he does that all the time," one of the guys says. "He's just having one of his regular attacks. Let him pop a few pills, he'll get over it."

This was one of the situations that often came up where I wanted to fit in with the badguys, but I still had my own sense of morality.

I can't just let the guy croak. I manage to get him up and out to my car. I drive him to the emergency room. A couple of hours later he comes out. "I ran out of my medication," he says.

We drive back to Jilly's. They are still playing cards. "See?" somebody says. "We told you he'd be all right."

It was easy to get lulled by this daily routine with these guys. Most of the time it was boring. They were not Phi Beta Kappas, but they were very streetwise. Just under the surface of their routine there was always something lurking that could trip me up. While I was constantly taking mental notes in order to report relevant information to my contact agent, I had to be alert for traps. Most of these guys were, after all, killers.

The FBI wouldn't let me actually go out on hijackings and burglaries, because the crew went armed. There was too good a chance somebody would get shot. In these pioneering days, thinking upstairs in the bureaucracy was very conservative. Somebody suggested that if I went along on crimes where guys were packing guns, I might be liable for prosecution myself.

The guys would ask me to go out on jobs with them. I would find ways to back off. I would tell them, "Hey, packing a gun and all that stuff, that's too cowboy for me. I'll help you out later on with the unloading." And they had enough guys so that adding me didn't mean anything. It wasn't like I was crucial. Plus the fact that for every man that doesn't go along on a job, that's less split they had to do on the proceeds.

They bought it. But if I had tried to push for myself to go along, get all the information I could about the score, and then back out of it—that would have made them very suspicious. I was always up-front with them.

I stayed low-key, and it was no big deal that I was around.

But once they got a little used to me, they let me sit in on their planning sessions. I'd go out with them when they cased a score. And gradually I started imposing myself. They would come and ask my advice on certain scores. I would sit down with them and go over the plans of the job, pick out flaws in it. That showed them that I knew something about what I was doing. In some cases when I could show them what was wrong with pulling a job, it deterred them from pulling them—part of my job, after all.

It was a delicate situation. I couldn't initiate or encourage crimes. Yet to be permitted to hang around I had to participate in some fashion. The Bureau didn't have any firm guidelines for everything I could and couldn't do. I was pretty much on my own. It required some tap dancing.

I helped unload stuff at the store. They would hijack any kind of truck, from eighteen-wheelers down to little straight jobs. They would seize the truck, unload the stuff into smaller trucks or vans, and take it to the "drop," which might be a vacant warehouse or factory, and bring samples to Acerg to show prospective buyers. The load would be parceled out to fences who could get rid of it.

When they hijacked a truck, they would usually just tie the driver up. But most of the hijacked loads were giveaways—setups. The drivers of the heisted trucks would be in on the heist for a percentage. The crew would go wherever they got the information that a guy had a good load on. Most of the heists were in the city. They'd pull them right on the streets in Brooklyn. Some were in Jersey.

Their burglaries were all over—in the city, out on Long Island, over in New Jersey, in Connecticut, in Florida. Stuff came from the airports all the time. Jilly had a steady supply from JFK International Airport, utilizing somebody inside the cargo operations.

I'd unload cases of coffee, sugar, frozen food, whiskey, bags of cocoa, truckloads of sweaters, blouses, jackets and jeans. They would take anything. The best loads were food loads—shrimp, coffee, tuna—because you can get rid of that stuff anywhere, like restaurants and supermarkets. Frozen shrimp and lobster were favorites. Pharmaceuticals—over-the-counter stuff like razor blades, aspirin, toothpaste—were prime targets because so many stores wanted them and the markup was great, even on the straight market. Clothes were good, especially leather, and women's clothes. Liquor was always a big item, especially around Christmastime. There were women's leather gloves, ski gloves, even a load of hockey gloves.

The commodity didn't make any difference, as long as they could sell it. Now, something like men's hockey gloves—where would you move them? They might have gotten stuck with them. But it was a load they could take, so they took it. It doesn't cost anything to steal hockey gloves.

Managers at places like restaurants and supermarkets had to know the stuff was hot, because the price was below anything on the wholesale market. But they bought it, anyway. Some of the best places. When you see how that works, it changes your view of some of the bargains and discount stores. It makes you more cynical. Sometimes the circle was very neat. They would burglarize an A&P warehouse one night, sell the cases of coffee and tuna to other stores a couple of days later.

TVs and VCRs were big. Robbing boxcarloads of them from the railroad freight yards was nothing unusual. They had a railroad employee who would give them a bill of lading and point out the right boxcar. Just back up a truck and load it.

When they hit houses, they were usually looking for jewelry, stocks and bonds, cash, or guns.

Anything that wasn't tied down, they would steal. Those were the days when Mopeds—motorized bikes or motor scooters—were popular. They would steal Mopeds off the street and rent them by the day out of the store.

I maintained a low profile, the way I'm comfortable. I didn't volunteer more about myself than was necessary; I didn't ask questions that didn't need to be asked—even though information I wanted was often just out of reach. But I knew that certain things I did would catch the eye of people or have people talking. I had to be patient, just let things develop.

Guido was Jilly's right-hand man, and he was a tough guy. He was tougher than the other guys in this crew. He looked different too. An Italian with blond hair and blue eyes. He had a mustache. Because he wasn't a made guy, he, like me, could have a mustache. He was about 6'1", 200 pounds. Late thirties. His arms were tattooed with snakes. He wore tinted glasses. He told me he had been in and out of jail most of his life, for various offenses. He was a shooter, but he had never been convicted of murder. Guido's crew under Jilly was sophisticated enough to operate with walkie-talkies. Jilly told me he thought Guido was too much of a cowboy, took too many risks, but that he had done a lot of "work" for the Colombos, meaning he had participated in hits.

If Guido was your friend, he would be with you till the end. If he was your enemy, forget about it—he would get you. Everybody showed respect for Guido.

One day soon after I started hanging out with the Jilly crew, Guido and I were riding around in my car.

He said, "Hey, Don, what's that squeak?"

"I don't know," I said. "Doesn't bother me."

"Yeah, it's a squeak," he said, leaning forward and cocking his head, "in the dashboard."

We got back to Jilly's, and I pulled up at the curb across the street.

He said, "I'll take that dashboard off and find that squeak and fix it."

"Hey, Guido, don't waste your time. It don't bother me."

"It bothers me. It won't take long."

Guido always carried a set of burglar tools in a toolbox in his car. He went and got them and crawled in under the dashboard and started taking it apart.

I said, "Why go through all this trouble just to find a squeak? It's no big deal."

In five minutes he had the whole dashboard off. He

looked all over behind it. "It's okay," he said. He started putting it back in place.

"Well, what the hell did you take it apart for?" I said.

"To tell you the truth, you're new around here. I just wanted to see if your car was wired up or anything. It's clean."

"Well, fuck you," I said. "You think I'm a fucking cop with a fucking recorder in my car? Why don't you just ask me, face-to-face?"

"Take it easy, Don. We gotta be careful, that's all. There's lots of operations they got going on around here. You're just new to us, that's all. Forget about it."

Actually I wasn't all that surprised to have somebody snooping around to check me out. If they did it once, they could do it again. So for all the years I was on this undercover job, while I would eventually have reason to wear hidden transmitters and tape recorders and would ride around in other agents' cars which were equipped with recorders, I would never have my own car wired.

I couldn't play it entirely safe. Any chance I would get, I myself would snoop around. If the guys were out front in the store or outside, and I was alone for a couple of minutes in the back room, I would always be looking in the desk drawers. There would usually be guns, both automatics and revolvers. There would also be other burglary paraphernalia stashed in there, like wigs and ski masks. If anybody had come in, my snooping would have been fatal. But my job was to find out what was going on, after all. I wasn't just curious.

If I was who I said I was, I couldn't just be sitting around listening to their schemes. I had to have some things of my own going.

Early in 1977, I made a few small deals with Vinnie the fence. Vinnie wasn't a heavy-duty guy. He was a family-type guy, from Staten Island, who used to hang around Jilly's during the day and then go home to his family at night. He didn't go out on actual jobs; he wasn't a tough guy. He just got rid of swag for people.

I wanted to make it look like I was moving stuff here and there to make a few bucks and trying to work my way up the line to bigger fences. Vinnie started me out with perfume.

We arranged a meeting for downstairs from my apartment, outdoors at the corner of Ninety-first Street and Third Avenue. Around noon he arrived driving a rented white Ford Econoline van. It was filled with cartons of perfume—by Lanvin. "I pick this up every week right at the factory where they make it," he said. "I pay a couple of guys who work there."

Perfume wasn't really my line, but it's not too far removed from jewelry. And mob thieves don't turn up their noses at anything where they can make a profit. You want to be a good customer, but not so good that you become a mark. I bought one carton of the perfume—Eau My Sin and Yves St. Laurent Rive Gauche—for $220.

The perfume, like everything else I bought in my role, I turned over to the FBI.

A few days later I met him at the Woodbridge Auction on Route 9 in Woodbridge, New Jersey. The auction was like a flea market and drew big crowds. Vinnie had a booth there where he sold swag that he hadn't sold to other fences. There, with the public and families all milling around, Vinnie would be in his booth selling stuff from hijacks or burglaries. I used to swing over there to see what new stuff he had, or if I had something that he might want to sell out of the auction. He got rid of a lot of swag from that booth.

I even took my wife there once. I got to spend so little time with her in those days that I figured the risk was tolerable. She got a kick out of it. The only problem was that once, right in front of Vinnie, who called me "Don," she called me "Joe." But he didn't seem to pick up on it. And, anyway, supposedly she was just some broad I knew—I could have been using any name with her.

He had some Enigma perfume for me, $250 a case, which contained fifteen boxes. "This stuff retails for forty dollars a box," he said. I bought a case.

I told him I had made a score, and had fifty to sixty watches and a good haul of fine turquoise jewelry. I showed Vinnie two sample wristwatches—gold Pateau Mitsu Boshi Boeki digitals, which were fairly new at the time, with red faces, worth maybe $80 apiece—and he bought them for $20 each. "I'll show these to Jilly in Brooklyn," he said, "and see how many more he wants."

Most of the "swag" I sold was stuff confiscated by the Bureau, loot recovered from previous thefts but which could not be traced back to the owners. These watches and jewelry were not from the Bureau. I had wanted the stuff in a hurry to make this deal, so I had bought them at a wholesale place on Canal Street. I worked it this way a few times. It meant there was no paperwork, nobody would know where the stuff was going. Like some other things I did, it might have left me open to internal criticism, but I had to make the decisions about my own security and pace. And nothing I did was a shortcut that would damage a case.

Vinnie said that he and his partner were about to make a score on a load of Faded Glory jeans, for which a buyer had already agreed to pay $125,000. "The load is a hundred and twenty-five thousand pairs," he said, "so it comes out to a buck a pair."

Three weeks later he called and said he wanted fifteen more watches, which I sold him for $300, and some of the turquoise jewelry. I sold him necklaces and bracelets for $150.

I said, "Did you get that load of jeans?"

"Part of it. The guy who took it, he made a couple other deals. So we only got part. You know how it is."

These small deals helped me get accepted by the crew at Jilly's store and by the people they associated with. One of the first things Jilly himself offered me was a white sable coat, part of the haul they had taken in a burglary the night before. "It's worth eleven grand," Jilly told me. "You can have it for twenty-five hundred bucks if you want it."

I passed on that, told Jilly I didn't think I could move it.

There wasn't any sense in buying anything expensive that I couldn't identify, couldn't eventually trace back to the owner. If you can't trace an item back to the owner, you can't prove anything in court. Jilly didn't tell me where he got the coat, and you don't ask somebody where they got something like that. Unless he had, say, seven or eight of them—a really big score. Then you might say, "Hey, where'd you make a score like that?"

At that point the only reason I had for buying the stuff was to establish credibility, as I'd done with the perfume. But I didn't need to spend $2,500 for credibility.

The crew was either talking about, or bringing in, loads every day. Price isn't always negotiable. Even if a potential buyer feels that the price is too high, that doesn't mean the sellers will drop the price. The high price probably means that they have to give somebody else an end of it: Whoever they got it from wants x amount of money, so for these sellers to make anything they have to put a few bucks on top of that, and they can't really drop the price. No deal is ever really dead, it just keeps being shopped around.

Tommy the Chief was a fat hood, probably in his fifties. He brought in a case of crushed salted almonds, the kind used in making ice cream. He told Jilly he had fifty-eight more cases in his cellar, stolen from Breyer's Ice Cream in Long Island City. He had a list of other stuff he said he could get—cocoa, dried milk, and so on, from Breyers. "We got it set up with one of their guys that works as a roaster inside," Tommy said. "And we also got the security guard who will be on duty when we go in next week. The haul will be worth a hundred G's."

Jilly decided to go for it, to rent three twenty-two-foot trucks to haul the stuff away, and a garage to store the swag in over the weekend, until it was moved to the buyer. They brought one truckload of cocoa to the club. They just parked the truck right on the street, and I helped unload it. In that neighborhood, who's going to say anything about what goes on at the

Acerg store? Two days later the load was sold to some guy in Yonkers.

One night Guido took a crew to burglarize a warehouse. They were going to heist four thousand three-piece men's suits. They had some kid with them to be the outside man, the lookout. While they were inside, somebody tripped a silent alarm. The owner arrived at the warehouse. The outside man panicked and took off without notifying anybody inside. The crew heard the owner coming in and managed to sneak out the back.

When Guido was telling Jilly this the following day, I wondered what the punishment might be on the kid. The crew boss had a wide range of options. Punishment depended on who the boss was and what kind of mood he was in. If Jilly was really ticked off, they might do a bad number on the guy.

Jilly decided they would go back in the next night. As for the lookout, all he said was, "I don't want that cocksucker with you when you go back in. He can't come around no more."

They went back into the warehouse. They didn't get all four thousand suits. They got about half of them.

I was always on the lookout for an opening to get to the bigger fences, the guys Jilly's crew was selling to. But whenever I'd suggest that I might be able to use a couple of contacts, they'd say something like, "Give it to us, we'll bring it to the guy. Don't worry about it." And if I said I might have some big score coming, their reaction would be, "Hey, you got a big load, we can get rid of it for you." They weren't about to give up their fences.

There was no acceptable reason for me to push to meet the bigger fences, except by coming up with bigger swag to sell.

I wasn't spending all my time in Brooklyn. I kept poking around in other directions. While bouncing around the Manhattan night spots with the Colombo guys, I met Anthony Mirra. I was introduced to him in a disco then named Igor's, which later became Cecil's, on Fifty-fourth Street.

I knew who Tony Mirra was. He was a member of the Bonanno crime family. He had done about eighteen years in the can for narcotics and other convictions, and he had only gotten out a year or so earlier. I knew that he was involved in anything and everything illegal to make money—gambling, drugs, extortion, and muscle of the type that leads to "business partnerships." I knew that he was a contract man, with maybe twenty-five hits under his belt. He was mean, feared, and well connected, a good guy for me to know.

I started hanging out with Mirra while I was still running with the Brooklyn guys. Through Mirra I met a good thief. I needed some more potent swag to bring to Jilly's crew. This thief had a haul of industrial diamonds. I decided to take a shot with these diamonds. I asked the thief if I could take a few samples on consignment to see if I could "middle" them—be the middle man for selling them off. He agreed and gave me ten diamonds.

Selling stolen property like this would not have been sanctioned by the Bureau. I didn't want to argue with anybody about it. I decided it was worth the chance.

The diamonds I had were worth about $75,000 on the street. I didn't really want to sell them to Jilly's crew, I just wanted to show them what I could do. I decided on a price that would be higher than a good street price—to discourage the sale—but not so high that it would look like something was wrong or I didn't know what I was doing.

I brought the pouch of diamonds into the store and showed them to Jilly and the guys.

"I hit a cargo cage out at the airport," I said. "I got a guy inside. I give him a cut. I got a buyer already, down on Canal Street. But if you could sell them, I'll give you the shot. All I want is a hundred grand out of the deal—seventy-five thousand for me and twenty-five thousand for my inside man."

"That's kind of high," Jilly said, "a hundred grand."

That price would force them to ask for $150,000 to $200,000 in reselling them.

"Hey, what can I tell you?" I said. "My inside guy that set it up wants twenty-five grand. The guy on

Canal Street is willing to give me a hundred grand. I'm giving you a shot because I'm with you guys. I need seventy-five grand. So if you could sell them for more than a hundred, anything over that is yours."

Jilly said to give him a couple days to check with a guy who was out of town. I did. He checked with the guy and said to me, "He's willing to go for seventy-five."

"I can't do it, Jill. I would only get fifty thousand out of the deal, and it's not worth it. I'll just off 'em to the guy down on Canal Street."

"Yeah," he said.

Jilly understood, which was just what I wanted. I had made some moves, got some stones—no cop is going to come up with $200,000 of diamonds to sell—showed them that I knew what I was talking about. If Jilly had come back with an offer of, say, $125,000, I couldn't have backed out of the deal. I would have had to keep my word and sell them to him. That was the chance I took.

It gave me a jump up in credibility, up from the ground floor.

When I first met Jilly, he wasn't made. Nobody in that crew was. He told me he had grown up in Brooklyn, had been stealing all his life. His dream was to get made, become a true member of the Colombo family.

One morning in early May, I arrived at the club to see Jilly all dressed up—pin-striped suit, dark tie, the works. You don't usually hang out in a suit and tie. He looked excited, strutting around. He also looked nervous.

He was just leaving when I came in. "Jill," I said, "where you going dressed like that?"

"I gotta go somewhere," he said. "I'll tell you about it later, when I get back."

He left, and I turned to Vinnie. "What the fuck's going on?"

"He's getting his badge today," Vinnie said. "He gets made."

We waited all day for Jilly. When he came back, he was ecstatic, as proud as a peacock. "Getting made is the greatest thing that could ever happen to me," he said. "I been looking forward to this day ever since I was a kid. Maybe someday you'll know how it feels. This is the fucking ultimate!"

"Hey, congratulations!" I said. "Who you gonna be with?"

"Charlie Moose."

Charlie Moose was going to be his captain. "Charlie Moose" Panarella was well-known to law-enforcement people. He was a mean guy, an enforcer. He was a high-ranking captain, and Jilly would now be a soldier in Charlie Moose's crew, and Jilly couldn't have been prouder.

That night we all partied together for his celebration. But now everybody treated him with more respect. He was a made guy now.

To become a made guy, to a street crook who is Italian, is a satisfaction beyond measure. A made guy has protection and respect. You have to be Italian, and be proposed for membership in the Mafia family, voted on unanimously by bosses and captains, and inducted in a secret ceremony. Then you are a made guy, "straightened out," a wiseguy. No one, no organization, no other Mafia family can encroach on the turf of a made guy without permission. He can't be touched. A Mafia family protects its members and its businesses. Your primary loyalty is to your Mafia family. You are elevated to a status above the outside world of "citizens." You are like royalty. In ethnic neighborhoods like Jilly's, nobody has more respect than a made guy. A made guy may not be liked, may even be hated, but he is always respected. He has the full authority and power of his Mafia family behind him.

One Friday, Jilly was keyed up over a big score he was setting up for the weekend. He had a man inside a trucking company who was going to give him the keys to three trailers loaded with furs and leather jackets. That same inside guy was going to deactivate the Babco alarm systems in the trucks.

Monday morning, Jilly was pissed off with everybody. On Sunday night they had gone into the truck yard. They had opened two of the trailers. When they opened the third, the alarm went off. The whole crew panicked and took off from the scene without grabbing a single item.

It drives the guys crazy to miss a score like that when they were so close, just because somebody fucked up. It also makes them look bad. Jilly had had to get permission to take those loads. On a big score like that, when you're a low-echelon made guy, a soldier, you have to get permission to make sure you're not stepping on anybody else's toes—and also to put the higher-ups on notice that some money will be coming in.

For permission Jilly had gone to his captain, Charlie Moose.

Your captain gets a piece of the action on whatever you do. So you go to him and tell him you're going to pull a big job. If you don't tell him ahead of time and he finds out about it, or you tell him after the fact, the captain might start thinking, They got more out of this job than they're telling me, and that's why they didn't ask me up front.

Because that's what happens all the time. It's all a big bullshit game. You go to your captain and tell him you're going to pull off a job worth a hundred grand. Usually the split is half with your captain. So right off the bat you have to give him fifty percent. The captain in turn has to kick in, say, ten percent upstairs, to the boss.

Captains are greedy, just like everybody else. And each captain sets the rules for his crews. He can set any rules he wants. So maybe a captain says, "I want sixty percent, instead of fifty." Because what he will do is keep fifty and give the other ten percent to the boss. Instead of taking it out of his end, he's taking it out of yours. Some captains demand that each one of their guys give them a certain amount of money per week, say $200, like a rent payment. That insures they get some money. Plus a percentage of the action.

And that's because everybody's playing this same bullshit game, trying to keep as much as they can, pass along as little as they can get away with, regardless of what the rules say. They always fudge. They figure they're out doing the job, who wants to give up half of what they get to somebody that's not even there?

So you never told anybody the whole story with money. If you made $100,000 on a score, you might tell your captain you came out with $80,000. That was the standard. It goes that way right up the line. That's why nobody totally trusts anybody.

Later on, when my position became a connected guy, I had to split whatever I supposedly made on scores with the soldier I was under. He kicked in to his captain. That shows the captain two things: that the soldier is out earning; and that he's loyal in kicking into the treasury. Same thing with the captains; they keep in good favor by throwing a piece of the action to the boss and the underboss.

Simply put: When you're operating within the mob, for every score you do, you know that you're going to split it with somebody at one point or another; you're going to give some of your earnings up. Everybody plays the game of holding something back. Just so you don't get caught.

Now, the thing is, it's a dangerous game, because if you get caught, you're liable to get whacked—killed. Holding out money from partners, captains, and bosses is, in a business strictly based on greed, a serious offense. If you did get caught, the questions are: How much did you skim and who did you keep it from? Some captains or bosses would have you whacked for withholding $5,000. The thing to remember is, no amount of money is insignificant to these guys. You might get whacked for $200—if it wasn't your first time skimming, or if other guys needed to be shown a lesson, or if your captain or boss just felt like having you whacked.

So the practice of skimming, from your own family, was common, and so was the result of getting whacked. It would be nothing to have these guys whacked, the guys in Jilly's crew. They weren't even heavyweights, just underlings.

So in this case, Jilly and the failed score on the loads of leathers and furs, he had gotten permission from

Charlie Moose to take the load, and then he had to go back to Charlie Moose and tell him that the score fell through. Nobody likes to be in a position of having to give his captain such news because, first of all, Charlie Moose would be very disappointed to hear that the money he counted on will not be forthcoming; and second, it would be obvious to Charlie Moose that this crew of Jilly's fucked up like nitwits.

That was why Jilly was pissed off that particular morning.

Charlie Moose squeezed his crews. That was a subject of common complaint among Jilly's crew. They'd bitch and moan about Charlie Moose. They'd complain that they couldn't do anything without his say-so and that he was taking too big a cut of every score. They were all agreed that they'd short him every chance they got.

"What that lousy son of a bitch does," Guido told me one day at the store, "is whenever anybody in the crew makes a score, you have to take all the money into him, and then he divides it up. He don't trust us, then we don't trust him. Fuck him. We pull in a hundred grand, we tell him we got seventy-five. How the fuck's he gonna know the difference?"

Jilly said, "You better shut up with that stuff. You'll get us all killed talking like that."

One way Charlie might know the difference was if somebody there was a snitch, a rat. But that was unlikely. The mentality of these guys is: Once a snitch, always a snitch. So if a snitch rats out these guys to Charlie Moose, even though it might be to the captain's benefit, Charlie is thinking, "These are the guys he's with all the time, his own crew, and if he's willing to rat them out, how do I know that if he gets caught in a box sometime, he's not gonna snitch to the cops?"

So a snitch would be running at least as much risk as the guy he was ratting on. Nothing is hated more in the mob than a snitch.

While I was not getting to the big fences, I was getting a lot of information. Every few days, or when there was anything significant to report, I passed on the information to my contact agent. Occasionally, when they had pulled a particularly big job, we were tempted to have them busted from the outside. The contact agent and I talked it over. But we couldn't do that. Since I was the new guy on the block with this Colombo crew, if any busts did go down, the finger would point at me. I'd be the guy that was the snitch. I was caught in the middle. Like everything else I was involved in at this stage, we couldn't make any busts that might compromise me as a snitch. So a lot of my information just went into the files for later. And later—years later in some cases, because of my continued involvement—the Bureau busted people for some of these scores, or we turned the information over to local police departments for action.

Two guys from Jilly's crew got out of prison, Frankie and Patsy. And naturally they came back and picked up right where they left off with the gang. They were a couple of tough guys, hard-nosed general-purpose thieves who were used to calling their own shots. And right away they were not too pleased with my presence, because I was new and had worked my way in while they were away in the can.

Frankie was about 5'10", slim and stylish, in his late thirties. If you were casting for the movies, he would be perfect for the classic, shifty-eyed thief. Patsy was maybe ten years older, three inches taller, and ten pounds heavier.

They were big on daytime house burglaries. They would get information on a house where there was cash or jewels or guns. Their gimmick was to pose as detectives to gain entry, then handcuff anyone who was home and ransack the place. They had regular detective shields they could show, and they always had a guy in a getaway car outside.

They decided that a couple of houses in Hicksville, Long Island, were great prospects for burglaries. They went out there and posed as morning joggers to trot by and case the places. They would park their car down the road a ways and jog by the houses in their sweat suits.

The morning they were to hit this one house, they drove up and discovered there were a whole bunch of cars parked in the driveway. They canceled the job.

They jogged past the second house to case it. When they jogged back to their car, they saw a woman writing down their license-plate number. They canceled that job.

Jilly and Frankie and I went out in Jilly's car to case a job in Hicksville. They had information that the owner of the house, supposedly the head of some retail dry-cleaners' association, had a bed built over a safe in which there was a lot of cash. Apparently our car was noticed as being strange to the neighborhood and suspicious, because somebody called the cops. The cops came by, stopped, and talked to us. They asked us what we were doing. We said we were just looking for potential properties to buy. On the car seat was a black attaché case in which were two revolvers, one a .38 and one a .32; some loose bullets; and several sets of handcuffs. The cops were satisfied with our explanation. But that blew that job.

By now I was used to putting my two cents' worth in on plans for scores, while still trying to avoid participating. It was part of my function to discourage them from pulling jobs, especially those where somebody might be in the house or somebody might get hurt. So when I had a chance, that's what I did. Anyway, at the same time I was gathering a lot of information on criminal activity, which was also my job.

They had cased a job in Mountainside, New Jersey, and they wanted me to take a run over there and check out the alarm system, see if they could get by it. Since I was a burglar and a jewel thief, I had to know about alarm systems.

So I went over to this house. It was a mansion surrounded by a big fence. It looked like it would be a good house to hit. Of course, I didn't check out the alarm system. I didn't go anywhere near it.

But I went back to Jilly's and told them it looked like the place had a very complicated alarm system that I didn't know how to bypass, plus probably a secondary backup system that I couldn't observe. Plus, it looked to me like there wasn't a good escape route for getting out of the place in case the alarm was tripped. My recommendation was that they forget about that job.

Patsy really wanted to pull that job. He was pissed because I was trying to squelch it.

"It's not worth a shot at getting caught," I said.

"You just don't want to come with us on this," he said. "You're fucking afraid."

"You're right, I don't," he said. "If I can't get by that alarm, what am I gonna do? Break a window and go in like some fucking two-bit junkie? But you guys can go ahead and do it, just count me out."

Then the other guys decided they didn't want to do it, either.

Their next house job they pulled off without telling me about it—some wealthy woman's house over in Jersey someplace. When I came into the club the next morning, Patsy was parading around showing off this huge diamond he was so proud of. Everybody was oohing and aahing because of how much money it would bring. It was three carats, Patsy said.

He got around to me. I took the diamond and looked it over. "I wouldn't get too excited about it," I said, "because this is fake, a fugazy."

"What the hell are you talking about?" Patsy said, grabbing the stone.

"It's a zircon, is what I'm saying."

Patsy snapped his head back like I had shoved a stick up his nose. "You're full of shit," he said. "That broad wouldn't have no fugazy diamonds in her house. We had information the broad didn't have no fake jewelry. It's three fucking carats!"

"It's a fugazy," I said. "Take it home for your kid to play with."

"You're such a smartass, like you know everything."

"Hey, Patsy," I said, "you just got out of the can, and I never been in jail, so I must be just a little smarter than you. You want to embarrass yourself, pal, take that stone to your fence, the jeweler you talk about."

"That's exactly what I'm gonna do," he said. He

stomped out with the gem. I could have been wrong, of course, and at least my credibility would have been hurt. But I had taken that gemology course, and I wanted to demonstrate that I knew something about gems. The stone was just too big—nobody would have this big a stone lying around in their house. And the color was a little off. I just had a gut feeling about it.

Half an hour later Patsy was back, his tail between his legs. He wouldn't look at me. "How'd you know?" he said.

"I'm a jewel thief all my life, so I shouldn't know about diamonds? You oughta stick to hijacking coffee and sugar, because that's what you know."

"Gettin' on my nerves," he muttered.

"Hey, I was trying to do you a favor. You're supposed to know this shit. You take it to the guy and he tells you it's a fugazy, what's he gonna think of you next time you come in with a stone?"

"Your fucking time will come when you won't be such a smartass," he said.

A couple days later I came in and they were planning a burglary of a clothing factory nearby in Brooklyn. The job was to involve me and six other guys, including Frankie and Patsy.

This was a small place that made sport clothes, jeans, blouses. They had been discussing this idea for days, and I had stayed out of it. Now they had it finalized.

I sat down at the table and said, "How we going about doing it?"

It was a beaut. Supposedly there were about twenty or twenty-five people working at this place, most of them women, most of them Italian. Quitting time was five P.M., so at around four-thirty, when most of the salesmen would be gone and just employees left in the place, they'd back a forty-foot trailer truck up to the loading dock. The crew would go in, announce a stickup, handcuff everybody, and load up the trailer.

I had to try to talk them out of it. First, with all this handcuffing and so on, somebody was going to get hurt. Second, because of that first reason, there was no way I could go along on the job, and when the shit

hit the fan and the operation got busted up—which in all likelihood would happen—I didn't want the fingers pointing at me as the snitch.

"Well, it sounds good," I said. "But how long is it going to take to load up the trailer and get out of there?"

Two hours, was the answer.

"Wait a minute," I said. "Quitting time is five o'clock. What happens when the husbands and boyfriends of the women who work there come to pick them up? They just gonna sit and wait in the car for a couple hours without checking inside, while their wives are inside handcuffed and you load your truck? Or if a husband is home at five-fifteen and his dinner isn't on the table by five-thirty—his wife isn't even home— what's the first thing he's gonna think? That she's out screwing somebody. What's the first thing he's gonna do? He's coming to this factory and backtrack to find his wife. They're all gonna come right down to the factory. It's gonna be like a zoo. You're gonna have a hundred fucking people coming down there while you're loading the trailer. What are you gonna do, barricade the fucking doors while you load the trailer and every-body's handcuffed inside? I think it's a pretty stupid idea."

Patsy started fuming. "Every time we plan to pull a fucking score, you got something to say, throw a mon-key wrench in. We think this is a pretty good fucking idea."

"You'll be back in the can," I said, "thinking up such good ideas. But you do whatever you want. I don't have to be in on it. I'm just trying to save your ass. But I ain't the boss."

Jilly said, "I don't think it's good. That joint is only half a mile from here. Too close. Not good."

Jilly was the boss. So that blew off that plan. But there was a lot of heat in that room.

6

THE BONANNOS

One morning not long afterward, I walked into the store. Everybody was there, but nobody was saying much. Jilly took my elbow and said, "Don, let's take a walk."

We went outside. He said, "Look, Don, nothing for nothing, but Patsy and Frankie, they don't feel comfortable around you. They got a beef."

"What's the problem?"

"They feel like they don't know you well enough. They don't want you involved in any more jobs until they know more about you. They want the name of somebody that can vouch for you down in Miami where you said you did a lot of work, so they can feel more comfortable with you."

"Well, how do you feel, Jilly?" I said. "We've done stuff together, right? You know who I am. You got any problems with me?"

"No, I got no problems with you." Jilly was uncomfortable. "But I grew up with these guys, you know? They been my partners for years, since before they went to the can. So they got this little beef, and I gotta go along with them. Okay?"

"Fuck them, Jilly. I'm not giving them the name of anybody."

"Let's just take it easy, okay, Don? Let's go in and talk it over, try to work it out."

Jilly was the made guy, the boss of this crew. I had rubbed these other guys the wrong way, and they had gone first to Jilly and put the beef in with him, which was the right way to do it. He had to respect their wishes because of the proper order—he had known them longer than he knew me, even though he had faith and trust in me. It was their beef, but it was his responsibility to get it resolved one way or the other. He was handling it the proper way. He came to me and talked to me first.

Then, when I hard-nosed it, said no right up front (I couldn't give in right away, I had to string it out and play the game), he said we had to sit down and talk about it. When you sit down, everybody puts their cards on the table and airs their beefs out. And Jilly had to lean toward them in granting their request about getting somebody to vouch for me in Florida. At that point I wasn't worried; because things were being handled in the right way, according to the rules.

We went back in the store. I went over to Patsy and said, "You got a beef?"

"You say you pulled off all those scores down in Miami before you came here," Patsy said. "But we don't know nothing about that. And you seem to want to say a lot around here. So Frankie and me wanna know somebody you did those jobs with, so we can check you out."

"You don't need to check me out," I said. "I been around here five-six months. Jilly and the other guys are satisfied. I don't have to satisfy you just because you were in the can."

"Yeah, you do," he said. "Let's go in the back and sit down."

Everybody walked into the back room. Patsy sat down behind the desk. "You could be anybody or anything," he said. "Maybe you're a stoolie. So we want to check you out, and we need the name of somebody to vouch for you."

"I'm not giving you any name."

Patsy opened a desk drawer and took out a .32 automatic and laid it on the desk in front of him. "You don't leave here until you give me a name."

"I'm not giving up the name of somebody just to satisfy your curiosity," I said. "You don't know me? I don't know you. How do I know you're not a stoolie?"

"You got a fucking smart mouth. You don't give me

a name, the only way you leave here is rolled up in a rug," he said.

"You do what you gotta do, because I ain't giving you a name."

It was getting pretty tense in there. Jilly tried to be a mediator. "Don, it's no big deal. Just let him contact somebody. Then everybody feels better and we forget about it."

I knew all along, from the time he pushed it to the gun, that I would give him a name. Because once he went that far in front of everybody, he wouldn't back off. But even among fellow crooks you don't ever give up a source or contact easily. You have to show them that you're a stand-up guy, that you're careful and tough in protecting people you've done jobs with. So I was making it difficult for them. I acted as if I were really torn, mulling it over.

Then I said, "Okay, as a favor to Jilly, I'm gonna give you a name. You can check with this guy. But if anything happens to this guy, I'm gonna hold you responsible. I'll come after you."

I gave him the name of a guy in Miami.

He said, "Everybody sit tight. I'm gonna go and see if we can contact somebody down there that knows this guy of yours." He left the room and shut the door.

I was nervous about the name I gave him. It was the name of an informant, a thief in Miami who was an informant for another agent down there. It had been part of my setup when I was going undercover. I had told this other agent to tell his informant than if anybody ever asked about Don Brasco, the informant should say that he and Brasco had done some scores together, and that Brasco was a good guy. The informant didn't even know who Don Brasco was, just that he should vouch for him if the circumstance came up.

So now I had a couple of worries. That had been seven months before. I wasn't absolutely sure that the informant got the message, and if he had been told, would he remember now, seven months later? If the informant blew it now, I was going to get whacked, no doubt about it. The other guys in the crew here didn't

care; they were on the fence. But Patsy or his pal
Frankie would kill me, both because of the animosity
between us and because they had taken it too far to
back down.

While Patsy was gone, I just sat around with the
other guys playing gin and bullshitting as if everything
were normal. Nobody mentioned the problem. But I
was thinking hard about how the hell I was going to
get out of there at least to make a phone call.

After a couple of hours I figured everybody had
relaxed, so I said, "I'm gonna go out and get some
coffee and rolls. I'll take orders for anybody."

"You ain't going anywhere," Frankie says, "until
Patsy comes back."

"What are we here, children?" I say. "I got no
reason to take off. But it's lunchtime."

"Sit down," Frankie says.

If it came to it, I would have to bust out of there
somehow, because I was not just going to sit there and
take a bullet behind my ear. There was a door out to
the front, which I figured Patsy had locked when he
went out. There was a back door, which was nailed
shut, never used. And there were four windows, all
barred. I didn't have many options. I could make a
move for the gun on the desk; that was about it. But I
wouldn't do anything until Patsy came back with whatever the word was, because I might luck out. And if I
could stick with it and be lucky, I would be in that
much more solid with the Colombo crew.

We sat there for hours. Everybody but me was
smoking. We all sat and breathed that crap, played
cards, and bullshitted.

It was maybe four-thirty when Patsy came back.
Instantly I could see I was okay—he had a look on his
face that said I had beaten him again.

He said, "Okay, we got an answer, and your guy
okayed you."

Everybody relaxed. Everybody but me. With what
had gone down, I couldn't let that be the end of it.
You can't go through all that and then just say, "I'm
glad you found out I'm okay, and thank you very
much." The language of the street is strength; that's

all they understand. I had been called. I had to save some face, show everybody they couldn't mess with me. I had to clear the air. I had to smack somebody.

The gun was still lying there. But now we were all standing up, starting to move around and relax. I wanted to take Patsy first. But Frankie was the one between me and the gun. I circled around, casually edging over to him. I slugged him and he went down. Patsy jumped on me and I belted him a few times. Then the rest of the crew jumped in and wrestled us apart. I had counted on the crew breaking it up before it got out of hand, so I could make my point before the two of them got at me at once.

Patsy was sitting on the floor, staring up at me.

"You fucking punks," I said. "Next time you see me, you better walk the other way."

Guido, the toughest of all of them, stepped in front of me and looked at everybody else. "That's the end of it about Don," he said. "I don't want to hear nothing else from nobody about Don not being okay."

Sally's club was a place where everybody tended to let their hair down during the long Tuesday lunches. They would bullshit about scores, about guys they had beefs with, about things that got fucked up. They would like to laugh and break each other's chops.

The next lunch at Sally's, the matter of the fugazy diamonds was good for ball busting. They called me "Don the jeweler" and said I probably thought all diamonds were fake. They got on Patsy for getting so high on a fake diamond. "Patsy's gonna get some real diamonds someday," somebody said. "But he can't show them to Don, because Don'll say they're fake and Patsy won't know the difference." Everybody laughed.

Patsy and Frankie didn't mess with me after that, even though we continued to be involved with each other. They treated me with some respect. Later on, ironically, Patsy turned informant and was put in the federal Witness Protection Program.

*   *   *

I had met Anthony Mirra in March of 1977. He invited me downtown to Little Italy. He had a little food joint called the Bus Stop Luncheonette at 115 Madison Street. We used to hang out there, or across the street at a dive called the Holiday Bar.

Mirra also introduced me to Benjamin "Lefty Guns" Ruggiero, like himself a soldier in the Bonnano family. Like Mirra, Lefty was known as a hit man. He had a social club at 43 Madison Street, just up the street from Mirra's Bus Stop Luncheonette. Mirra used to hang out there. He introduced me to Lefty on the sidewalk outside the club. "Don, this is Lefty, a friend of mine. Lefty, Don."

Lefty was in his early fifties, about my height—six feet—lean, and slightly stoop-shouldered. He had a narrow face and intense eyes.

Mirra turned away to talk to somebody else. Lefty eyed me. "Where you from?"

He had a cigarette-raspy voice, hyper. "California," I said. "Spent a lot of time between there and Miami. Now I'm living up at Ninety-first and Third."

"How long you known Tony?"

"Couple months. Mainly the last few months I've been hanging out in Brooklyn, 15th Avenue. With a guy named Jilly."

"I know Jilly," Lefty said.

Prior to that introduction, I was never invited into Lefty's club, and you can't go in without permission when you're not connected. From that time on, I would go down to Lefty's almost every day to meet Mirra. So I got to know Lefty.

I then began dividing my time between Mirra, Lefty, and the Bonanno guys in Little Italy, and Jilly and the Colombos in Brooklyn. Since I wasn't officially connected to anybody, it was permissible, if not encouraged, to move between two groups. But it was also a lot to handle when you're trying to stay sharp on every detail.

My time became triply divided with Sun Apple. The "Sun" part of Sun Apple was not proceeding as well as the "Apple" part. Agent Joe Fitzgerald had set himself up with an identity, an apartment, and the rest, just as I had, and we did basically the same thing. Fitz was doing a good job working the street in the Miami area, and he fingered a lot of fugitives for arrest. But for whatever reasons, the operation there didn't catch on as readily. Most of the guys Fitz was able to get involved with were guys that were chased out of New York, small-time dopers, credit-card scammers, and the like. No real heavyweights.

Now that I had some credentials with both the Colombo and Bonanno people, we thought that maybe I could help stimulate some contacts in Miami. So from time to time I would go down there and hang out with Fitz, letting people know that I was "connected around Madison Street" and in Brooklyn.

I had a dual role, hanging out with Fitz. First was to help him if I could, by being a connected guy from New York who he could point to for credibility. Second was to build up my own credentials. I would tell people in New York that I was going down to Miami to pull some sort of job. I would be seen down there hanging out in the right places. Word always gets back. So you always had to stay in character.

One time we were at an after-hours joint named Sammy's, where a lot of wiseguys hung out. We were at the bar. Fitz was talking to a couple of women to his right. I was sitting on his left, at the *L* of the bar, and around the corner of the *L* were three guys talking together. One of them was drunk, and I recognized him as a half-ass wiseguy from New York.

This drunk starts hollering at me. "Hey, you! Hey, you, I know you."

I ignore him, and he reaches over and grabs my arm. "Hey, I'm talking to you!" he says. "I know you from somewhere. Who you with?"

"I'm with him," I say, pointing to Fitz.

Not only is he drunk, but he is also saying things he shouldn't be saying around wiseguys, asking things he shouldn't be asking—such as about what family I was with. I signal to the two guys with him. "Your friend is letting the booze talk," I say. "He's out of line, so I suggest you quiet him down." They shrug.

I call the bartender over. "I want you to know that this guy is out of line here," I say. "And you're a witness to what he's saying, if anything happens."

The drunk keeps it up. "I know you from New York. Don't turn away from me. Who you with?"

I lean over to Fitz. "He grabs me again, I'm gonna have to clock him," I say.

"No problem," Fitz says. He is standing there, all 6'5" of him. "When you're ready, let me know, I'll take care of those other two guys."

The drunk grabs me by the shoulder. "Hey! I'm talking to you!"

"Okay, Fitz," I say. I reach over and belt the drunk, and he slides off the stool. At the same time Fitz clocks the second guy, and then the third guy, one right after the other. All three of them sink to the floor.

Everybody in the joint turns away. Where wiseguys are concerned, nobody wants to know anything.

I say to the bartender, "You saw and you heard, right?"

"Yeah," he says.

"So if anything comes down regarding this, just say how this guy was out of line. Fitz knows how to reach me and my people in New York."

It turned out the guy was a member of the Lucchese family. Word did get right back to New York. Everything was smoothed over. It helped my image.

Fitz and I cruised the Miami-area hangouts that had been identified as likely places for contacts: Sneaky Pete's, Charley Brown's Steak Joint, the Executive Club, Tony Roma's, Gold Coast up in Fort Lauderdale.

But we weren't able to lure the big-timers into conversation. For several months I went back and forth between the Colombos and the Bonannos, between New York and Florida.

Fitz and I were out one night in a nightclub near Fort Lauderdale. We were sitting at the bar. Fitz introduced me to a lot of people he knew in there. "This is Don from New York." Guys were going into the john to snort coke. I was just sitting at the bar bullshitting with a couple of half-ass wiseguys and their girlfriends.

Then this one guy comes out of the john and comes over to me holding this little open vial. He holds it out to me and says, "Here, Don, have a snort."

I smack his arm, sending the bottle flying and the cocaine spraying all over the place. I grab him by the lapels and hoist him. "I don't do that stuff," I say, "and you had no business offering it to me. Don't *ever* offer it to me again. I make money off it, but I don't use it. I keep my head clear at all times."

"But look what you did," he whines, "all my stuff!"

"Write it off to experience," I say. "You wanna fuck up your head, that's up to you. Don't bring it around me."

I didn't do these things to be a tough guy. But with things like drinking and drugs, you can't be a fence-sitter around these guys. If you smoke a joint or take a snort the first time—maybe just to show that you're a regular guy—or if you say, "Maybe later," it gives the impression that you do drugs. If you're a fence-sitter, then you're in a bind. You just invite people to keep offering it to you. And if you say, "Not now," and then keep refusing and refusing and putting it off, they begin to wonder: What's up with this guy? But if you draw the line right in the beginning—I don't do it; I ain't ever gonna do it—then that's it, nobody cares anymore.

A lot of people have the misconception that mob guys are all big drinkers or dopers. Some of them are—a greater proportion of young guys do drugs than older guys. But so many guys don't do anything that you don't stand out by saying no—it's no big deal. Tony Mirra killed twenty or thirty people, and he drank only club soda.

The thing is, even though it's a fake world for you as an undercover agent, it's a real world for the people that you're dealing with. And you have to abide by the rules in that world. And those rules include how you establish your own standards, credibility, and individuality. I know one or two guys that drank or did drugs while they were undercover just because they thought they had to do that to blend in or show they were tough guys. It was an enormous mistake. You can't compromise your own standards and personality. Smart wiseguys will see right through your act. You look like somebody that has no mind of his own, hence no strength.

I don't use drugs, and I wasn't going to start using them then just for an undercover role. How could I tell my kids not to use dope if I was out there sniffing coke just for the job?

And there's another reason, very practical. As an FBI agent, someday down the line I was going to be in court testifying on all these cases we were making. I was not going to lie. And I was not going to tarnish my credibility and risk failing on convictions by taking drugs or getting drunk or doing anything that would suggest I lacked commitment or character.

This line of thinking is not arrived at on the spur of the moment. I didn't think it over when the guy offered me the coke. I acted spontaneously, because I had sorted all this out in my head and established my priorities and standards before I ever went out on the job.

In any event, I accomplished what I wanted to. While later on I would get involved in drug transactions, nobody ever again offered me drugs for my personal use.

I was down in Miami one time working with Fitz for a week. I had told Jilly and his guys that I would be down there. But I didn't call them back with a telephone number where I could be reached.

As it turned out, they had tried to find me because they wanted me in on a big job they were going to pull down there.

They had connections in Florida. Guido told me that he had been dealing drugs in Florida for nine years, especially in the Key West area, where he had the fix in with the police department and the district attorney's office. Vinnie told me that he had a friend who owned a nursery on Staten Island where he was growing a big marijuana crop, and that when it was harvested in August, Guido would take it to Florida for sale.

In this instance they had information about a house in Fort Lauderdale where they could pull off an easy $250,000 cash score. It was a four-man job. When they couldn't locate me, Jilly joined Guido and Patsy and Frankie. When I got back to New York, they filled me in on what had happened. They had pulled off the job, and it had been a disaster.

The information their Florida tipster gave them was that an elderly lady kept the cash and diamonds in a safe. Guido bought safecracking tools for the job in Miami. They went to the house, flashed their detective shields to the lady, and said they were on an investigation and needed to come in. They handcuffed the lady. But there was no safe. And there was no quarter of a million in cash.

What they found were bullet holes in the ceiling, bank books showing that a huge deposit was made the day before in a safe-deposit box, and a little cash lying around. By the time they accounted for plane fare and tools and other expenses, they came out of the job with about $600 apiece.

Their information had been good, but late. Later their tipster filled in the story. The lady's husband had died and left the quarter mill. He had promised a large chunk of that to his nephew. But the widow didn't like the nephew and didn't want to give him the money. The nephew came to collect. He tried to frighten the lady. He pulled out a gun and fired two bullets into the ceiling. But she didn't give up the money. The next day she put it all in a safe-deposit box. That was the day before Guido and Jilly went there to steal it.

"If I'd've known all this ahead of time," Guido told me, "I never would have pulled the job."

Jilly got 1,200 ladies' and children's watches from a job at the airport. He brought samples into the store. As usual, he offered me a piece or all of the load if I could find a market. He gave me a sample to show, a Diantvs.

Meanwhile he had located a potential buyer. A couple of guys were interested in part of the load. The next afternoon, we were in the back room when these two guys walked in.

I recognized one of them as a guy I had arrested two years earlier on a hijacking charge, back before I went undercover and I was on the Truck and Hijack Squad.

I had worked on the street only a couple of months up in New York. So it wasn't as if I had arrested thousands of people. When you arrest somebody like that, you usually remember him. I remembered the face; I remembered the name: Joe. Just like the crook, he usually remembers the cop that arrests him. It's just something that stays with you. There we were.

I was introduced. Joe knew the other guys but not me. I watched his face. No reaction. I wasn't going to excuse myself and leave, because something might click with this guy, and if it did, I wanted to see the reaction so I would know. If I left and something clicked with this guy, I could come back to an ambush. I watched his face, his eyes, his hands.

They talked about the watches, the prices. I decided to get the guy in conversation. Sometimes if a guy's nervous about you, he can hide it in his expression, just avoid you. I figured if I talked to him, I could get a reaction—either he would talk easy or he would try to avoid conversation with me. I had to be sure, because there was a good chance I would run into this guy again.

"By the way," I said, "you got any use for men's digitals?" I had one and showed it to him.

"Looks like a good watch," he said. "How much?"

"You buy enough, you can have them for twenty each."

"Let me check it out, get back to you. Where can I reach you?"

"I'm right here every day," I said.

The conversation was okay. There was no hitch in his reactions. They chatted a few more minutes and left. The whole thing took maybe twenty minutes. The guy simply hadn't made me. Those situations occur from time to time, and there's nothing you can do about them, except be on your toes.

A couple days later I asked Jilly, "Joe and that other guy, did they buy the watches?"

He said, "Yeah, they took some of mine, but they didn't have any market for yours."

From time to time somebody in Jilly's crew would ask me if I had any good outlets for marijuana or coke. I was noncommittal. At that time I wasn't trying to milk the drug side, other than to report back whatever I saw and heard. The FBI wasn't so much into the drug business then. We didn't want to get involved in any small drug transactions because we couldn't get authority to buy drugs without making a bust. We were still operating on a buy-bust standard, meaning that if we made a buy, we had to make a bust, and that would have blown my whole operation. So in order not to complicate the long-range plans for my operation, I pretty much had to steer clear of drug deals.

Guido came up to me at the store. "You got plans for today?" he asked.

"No, I'm just gonna hang out. I got nothing to do," I said.

"Take a ride with me. I gotta go to Jersey."

We took Jilly's car, a blue 1976 Coupe de Ville. We drove across the Verrazano Narrows Bridge to Staten Island. We drove around Staten Island for a while, then recrossed the bridge back to Brooklyn.

I said, "I thought you said you had to go to Jersey?"

"I do," he said. "I gotta meet a guy."

We drove up the Brooklyn-Queens Expressway, crossed the Brooklyn Bridge to Manhattan, and headed north on the FDR Drive. Obviously Guido had just been cleaning himself, making sure nobody was following him, with the run to Staten Island. We crossed the George Washington Bridge into Jersey. We took the Palisades Parkway north.

A little after noon we got to Montvale, New Jersey. At the intersection of Summit Avenue and Spring Valley Road, Guido stopped to make a call at a phone booth. He got back in the car and we just sat there.

"We wait," he said.

About a half hour later a black Oldsmobile pulled up beside us. The driver motioned for us to follow him. We followed him north for a few minutes, across the Jersey line into New York. We pulled into a busy shopping center in Pearl River. Guido and the other driver got out and talked. The other guy was about 6′, 180, with a black mustache. Guido signaled for me to get out of the car.

The guy opened his trunk. There were four plain brown cardboard boxes in there. We transferred the boxes to Guido's trunk.

Guido asked, "How much is in there?"

"You got ninety-eight pounds," the guy said. "That's what you gotta pay me for."

We got back in the car and headed for Brooklyn.

"Colombian," Guido said, referring to the marijuana in the trunk. "We should get $275 a pound. On consignment. I got access to another 175 pounds. The guy said he could also supply us with coke, but not on consignment. Money up front for blow."

I unloaded the boxes and put them in the back of Jilly's store. The next day when I came in, the boxes were gone. They didn't keep drugs in the store. Guido handed me a little sample bag. It was uncleaned—stalks, leaves, seeds. "Think you can move some of this?" he said.

"I don't know," I said. "I never moved any of this stuff through my people. I'll ask around."

I held on to the sample for a couple of days, then gave it back. "Nobody I talked to could use it," I said.

None of these guys used drugs themselves, so far as I could see. To them it was strictly a matter of business. If these guys had been dopers, it might have been a different story. They really might have tested me. But the fact was that the way you proved yourself with these guys was by making scores, making money.

According to the Mafia mythology, there was supposed to be a code against dealing drugs. In the old days there wasn't a huge amount of money to be made in drugs, and they didn't do it. Now that's where the money is, forget any so-called code. Like anything else with the Mafia, if there's money to be made, they're going to do it.

One morning Jilly was sitting at the desk in the back room, scribbling on some papers.

"Gotta fill out these applications," he said.

The application was for a loan from the Small Business Administration. He told me that they had a guy in the SBA who approved loans. So Jilly would fill out an application with all fake stuff, any kind of junk information: Joe Crap the Ragman, phony business, phony address. Then he'd send it in and this guy would approve it. At that time the SBA was going strong; there was all kinds of money. So if the application looked decent and the amount requested was not so exorbitant as to attract anybody's attention, they wouldn't do any big check on it. So Jilly would ask for like $20,000. The guy they owned on the inside would approve it, get the $20,000, take five off the top for himself, and pass on $15,000 to Jilly.

The great thing about it was you didn't have to pay it back. Since everything on the application was bogus, how would they ever find you? Jilly pulled this off a couple of times.

Another day I got to the club and Jilly wasn't there. I asked Vinnie, "Where is everybody?"

"Jilly and Guido got a contract," he said, "and they're out looking for the guy they gotta hit."

You don't ask questions about a hit. If they want you to know, they'll tell you. But my job was to get information if possible. When Jilly came back, I asked him, "Where were you guys?"

"Me and Guido had to look for somebody," he said.

"Anything going on?" I asked, as if it might be some kind of score.

He proceeded to talk about an upcoming hijacking. I tried to wrangle the conversation back to the guy they were looking for, but he wouldn't talk about it. It wasn't unusual that he wouldn't tell me. Who was I? At the time I was just a guy who had been hanging around a few months, let alone an FBI agent. You don't just tell anybody if you have a piece of work to do.

I don't know if that particular hit came off or not. Whacking somebody is something that you don't talk about. In my years with the Mafia guys sometimes they would would sit around and discuss how much work they'd done in the past—"work" meaning hits. But ordinarily they never discussed openly any particular individual they hit, or an upcoming one. If something went wrong, they might sit around later and laugh about it.

One time I was hanging out with Lefty Ruggiero at his social club in Little Italy, and he and a bunch of guys were laughing about a job. They had gotten a contract to hit a guy. They tailed this guy for a week, looking for the right opportunity. Then they were told the contract's off, don't hit the guy. And it turned out it was the wrong guy they were following. They would have hit the wrong guy. To them it was the funniest thing in the world. "What the fuck you think of that? We're following the guy for a week and it's not even the right guy—ha, ha, ha! We're out every fucking night following this jerk-off. Piece a fucking luck for him, right? Ha, ha, ha!"

On the Fourth of July weekend Jilly had a cookout for everybody. He had a house down at the Jersey Shore, in Seaside Heights, a block from the beach, and he had all the guys down with their wives and girlfriends.

I went to Fretta's, the Italian meat market in Little Italy, and bought sausages and cold cuts and cheeses and took it down there for the cookout.

I wasn't married, of course. Supposedly I had a couple of girlfriends here and there, but I never brought any of them around. The guys used to get on me sometimes about never bringing a girl around, but I told them there wasn't anybody I cared enough about.

I always wear an Irish Claddagh ring that my wife gave me. It has hands holding a heart, and a crown on it, symbolizing love, friendship, and loyalty. Nobody had ever mentioned the ring.

We were sitting outside at this picnic table, and one of the guys' girlfriends says, "That's a nice ring you got on, Don. That's an Irish Claddagh ring, isn't it?"

"Yeah."

"Aren't those rings for love? Aren't they used as wedding rings?"

"Yeah, sometimes," I say. One of the guys asks about it, and I go into the history and so forth.

Then she says, "Well, what are you wearing it for? I didn't think you were married or anything."

"No, I'm not. But one of the few girls I was ever in love with gave it to me. Then a couple months later she jilted me. I keep wearing it because I don't ever want to forget her."

One of the guys looks puzzled. He says, "You sure you're not married?"

"Why?"

"Because I just can't figure it out. You mean, you loved that girl so much that you keep wearing that ring after she jilted you?"

"Sure, why not?"

"I just didn't think you were the type of guy that could love anybody. You know, the way that you're here, you're there, you got no allegiance, no ties to anybody."

"Well, there always comes a time in somebody's life when there's a girl that you love, somebody that's special, so I'd rather remember it than forget about it. I just want to wear the ring, that's all. What's the difference to anybody else?"

The only time I take the ring off is when I work out lifting weights. I wore it during the whole operation. And that was the only time anybody ever mentioned it.

What with hanging out with Jilly's Colombo crew and with Mirra and Ruggiero's Bonanno crews and going to Florida to work with Joe Fitz on Sun Apple, I wasn't getting home much at all. I missed the school sports seasons and watching my daughters cheerlead. I missed two of the girls' birthdays. I wasn't home for my birthday, either. I wasn't home for our sixteenth wedding anniversary—to celebrate, my wife went out with a couple named Howard and Gail who had been close friends of hers for a year before I even met them. I was home maybe two or three nights a month.

And when I *was* home, I was a little harried, trying to make up for lost family time but unable to put mob business out of my mind completely.

I managed to make it to my younger brother's wedding. It was a regular big Italian wedding, lots of cash and checks. After the wedding the bride and groom were leaving directly for their honeymoon. They didn't want to take all this money with them. He asked me to take care of it until they got back. "Who could be safer to leave all this with," he said, "than my brother the FBI agent?"

I put this big envelope of cash and checks under the front seat of my car and headed back to New York City.

A week later my brother asked me for the envelope. It wasn't in my apartment. It wasn't anywhere. It was still under the front seat of my car. I had been all over the place since then, to different neighborhoods in the city. My car had been parked on streets and in garages. I had totally forgotten about the money.

None of my family knew the depth of my involvement. My brother later told me that he began to suspect that I was into something heavy when I forgot about his money. The distractions of my job were causing friction in my family.

The situation was tolerable because it was temporary. A few months undercover. But now we had passed the six-month limit to the operation. I hadn't reached the big fences. But unexpectedly I was getting deeper into the mob, with my association with Bonanno members Mirra and Ruggiero in Little Italy and their introduction of me to others. My undercover assignment was extended indefinitely.

Physically I was often feeling tired. But the daily challenge stimulated me. I felt good about how things were going.

* * *

All this time I was trying to remember everything. Since I didn't take any notes—didn't dare to take any notes or write anything down, even in my apartment—I had to remember. Anything of a criminal nature discussed in conversation, any new guy that came through the clubs, the different deals and scores and the different guys involved and amounts of everything—I had to try to remember it all. Eventually federal court cases would depend on the accuracy and credibility of my memory.

It was a matter of concentration. That and little tricks. Like remembering license-plate numbers or serial numbers on weapons in series of threes. The frustration always was that I couldn't ask a lot of questions, which is one of the things I was trained to do as an FBI agent. A lot of the things I had to remember were things I overheard, and I couldn't ask for these things to be repeated, or for what I thought I heard to be confirmed. When swag came in and out, I couldn't ask to look it over more closely, or where it came from, or who it was going to. I had to hope those facts were volunteered. I had to be just a hang-around guy who wasn't more interested than was good for him.

Concentrating on conversations was draining. Most of the talk was idle, simplistic bullshit about the most mundane things—getting a haircut or a new pair of Bally shoes; how the Mets or Giants were doing; how the Chinese and Puerto Ricans were ruining neighborhoods; how much better a Cadillac was than a Lincoln; how we ought to drop the bomb on Iran; how we ought to burn rapists, each guy would gladly strap the perverts in and pull the switch himself. Most of these guys, after all, were just uneducated guys who grew up in these same neighborhoods.

But they were street-smart, and the thread of the business ran through everything all the time, and the business was stealing and hits and Mafia politics—who was up, who was down, who was gone. Somebody might be talking about a great place to buy steaks at a cut rate and in virtually the same sentence mention a hit, or somebody new getting made, or a politician they had in their pocket. These tidbits would lace conversation continually but unpredictably, and they flew by. If I wasn't always ready, I would miss something I needed to remember. And I couldn't stop them and say, "What was that about paying off the police chief somewhere?"

What's more, to be above suspicion I had to adapt my conversational style to theirs. Occasionally I would change the subject or wander away from the table purposely, right in the middle of a discussion about something criminal that might be of interest to the government—precisely to suggest that I wasn't particularly interested. Then I would hope the talk would come around that way again or that I could lead it back, get at it later or in another way. It was a necessary gambit for the long term.

And then I would have to remember facts and names and faces and numbers until I could call in a report to my contact agent.

That's why when I would get home for my one day or evening in two or three weeks, it would be difficult to adjust and focus deserved attention on my family. Especially when they didn't know what I was doing and we couldn't talk about it.

One hot August afternoon I was in the store when they came in from a job. Jilly, Guido, Patsy, Frankie, and a couple of other guys, one of them named Sonny. Jilly was nervous as hell. I had never seen him so nervous.

"We hit this house in Bayonne this morning," he told me. "The guy was a big guy [I wasn't sure whether he meant physically big or important] and I thought I was gonna have to shoot the motherfucker because he wouldn't open the safe. I had my gun on him, and I said I was gonna shoot him if he didn't open it up or if he tried anything. I really thought I was gonna have to shoot him. Finally he opened it and we handcuffed him and the woman and taped his mouth shut."

He was visibly shaken, and I didn't know why, because he'd been out on any number of similar jobs.

They had opened a black attaché case on the desk in the back room. Without making a point of sticking my nose into it, I could see jewelry—rings and earrings and neck chains—some U.S. Savings Bonds, plastic bags of coins like from a collection, a bunch of nude photographs of a man, and a man's wig.

Also in the case were sets of handcuffs of the type you can buy in a police supply house, several New York Police Department badges they probably stole someplace, and four handguns.

"We posed as cops to get in," Patsy said. "Tell him about the priest."

Sonny said, "I was in the getaway car across the street from the house, with the motor running. I happened to be in front of a church. I'm sitting there waiting for the guys to come out, and this priest comes walking by. And he stops to chat! 'Isn't it a lovely day,' this priest is saying to me. And he goes on about it. I can't get rid of him. I don't know how the guys are gonna come out of the house, running or what, and this priest is telling me about the birds and the sky. *I* couldn't leave. Finally he said good-bye and walked away. I could still see him when the guys came out."

Jilly handed me a small bunch of things. "Get rid of this junk, will you? Toss it in a dumpster in Manhattan when you go back."

It was stuff from the robbery they didn't want, and didn't want found in the neighborhood: a pink purse, a broach and matching earrings, the nude photos, a U.S. passport.

What I wanted was the guns. They were stolen property that we could trace back to the score and tie Jilly's crew to it. And we always wanted to get guns off the street.

"If you want to move those guns," I said to Jilly, "I got a guy that I sold a few guns to from my burglaries, so maybe he'd be interested in these."

"We should get $300 apiece for them," he said.

"I'll see what I can do."

He gave me the guns: a Smith & Wesson .45; a Smith & Wesson .357 Highway Patrolman; a Rohm .38 Special revolver; a Ruger .22 automatic. Whatever else the owner was, he was not a legitimate guy. Two of the guns had the serial numbers filed off. They were stolen guns before Jilly's guys got ahold of them. Generally, filing the numbers off doesn't cause us too much of a problem. Most of the time the thieves don't file deep enough to remove all evidence from the stamping process. Our laboratory guys can bring the numbers back up with acid.

The next day I put them in a paper bag and walked over to Central Park at Ninetieth St. My contact agent, Steve Bursey, was waiting for me. I handed him the bag. We decided we would try to get by with offering Jilly $800 for the guns. You never give them all that they ask in a deal. First, it's government money, and we don't want to throw out more than we have to. Second, you want to let them know that you're hard-nosed and not a mark.

The next day I went back to the club and told them that my man offered me $800.

"That's not enough," Patsy said. "You said you could get twelve hundred bucks."

"I said I'd try," I said. "The guy is firm at eight hundred."

"No good."

With some deals I would have just said okay and given the stuff back. But not with the guns. I didn't want to give the guns back. "Look, I got the guns, I got eight hundred on me. You want it or you don't." I tossed the money down on the desk, trusting to their greed when they saw the green. There was some squabbling.

"We could have got more somewhere else," Patsy said.

"Hey, if you can get more, take the fucking guns and bring them somewhere else. But who's gonna give you more than two hundred apiece for guns that are probably registered and have been stolen and the numbers filed off? You think I didn't push for all I could get? There's eight hundred of my own money. You want the deal, I'll just collect from him."

"Okay," Jilly said. He picked the money up and gave $100 each to Guido, Frankie, and Patsy as their share, and $100 to me for peddling the guns.

I handed in my $100 to Agent Bursey. So the guns cost the FBI $700.

Guido was bitching about a bunch of people that had recently been made in the Colombo family. He mentioned both Allie Boy Persico and Jerry Lang. Allie Boy was Alphonse Persico, the son of Carmine "The Snake" Persico—sometimes referred to as Junior—who was the boss of the Colombo family. Jerry Lang was Gennaro Langella, who some years later would become underboss of the Colombo family and acting boss when Carmine The Snake went to prison.

"I've done more work than half the guys that were made," Guido said, meaning that he had been in on more hits, which is one of the prime considerations in getting made, "and I ain't got my badge. That kid Allie Boy is just a wiseass punk. He never did a bit of work to earn his badge. The only reason he got made is because his old man is boss."

"You better shut up," Jilly said. "People walking in and out of the store all the time, we don't know who hears what. We're gonna be history from that kind of talk about the boss's son."

I was standing outside Lefty Ruggiero's social club on Madison Street in Little Italy when Tony Mirra came by and told me to drive him to Brooklyn.

That set off an alarm in my gut. Although it was known that I was moving between crews of two different families, that kind of freewheeling eventually draws suspicion. Pretty soon, if you don't commit to somebody, they think you can't be trusted. Suddenly Mirra, a Bonanno guy and a mean bastard, wants me to go with him to Brooklyn where I have been hanging out with Colombo guys. Was he taking me there for some kind of confrontation?

In the car Mirra said he had an appointment with The Snake.

Recollections came rushing into my head. The guy in Jilly's that I recognized as somebody I had once arrested—had he known me, after all? Guido's remarks about Allie Boy Persico—had those remarks about his son gotten back to The Snake? The recollections didn't make me feel good. Was I going to be grilled about Jilly's crew, things I had heard, what I was doing there?

If The Snake had heard about the complaints, was I going to be pressured to rat out the people doing the complaining? If I was pressured for information, would it be some kind of test?

My mind was racing as we cruised over the Brooklyn Bridge. I tried to sort out the possibilities and options. I definitely would not rat anybody out. That was for sure. If I turned rat on anybody to save my own skin, I would have to pull out of the operation, anyway, because my credibility would be blown. So if I was pressured to rat anybody out, I would just take the heat and see what happened. If they were testing my reliability, I would pass the test, and that would put me in solid.

Unless, of course, they really wanted me to talk, and decided to hit me if I didn't. They could whack me out over there and dump me in the Gowanus Canal where I wouldn't be found until I was unrecognizable. Nobody would know.

Mirra was silent. We drove to Third Avenue and Carroll Street in the Park Slope section of Brooklyn, not far from Prospect Park. We parked and waited. Carmine Persico drove up in a white Rolls-Royce convertible with New Jersey plates—444-FLA. I recognized him from pictures. A sturdy guy in his middle forties, with thinning hair, a long neck, baggy eyes, and a fleshy nose and mouth. He and a much younger man, maybe in his early twenties, got out of the Rolls and talked to Mirra for a few minutes.

When Mirra got back in the car, he said, "That was his son with him, Allie Boy. He just got straightened out."

"Straightened out" means made. I didn't say anything.

"Tommy LaBella's supposed to be the Colombo boss," Mirra said, "but that's in name only, because he's so old and sick. The Snake is the real boss. I had to talk to him about a shylock business we're trying to put together with him."

A shylock business between the Bonanno and Colombo families was all it was. I was so primed, I actually felt a letdown. Given the options, I'll take a letdown.

You could never relax with these guys, because you never knew what would be heavy-duty and what would be light.

I was getting itchy. Jilly's crew seemed to be a dead end. One of my functions was to gather evidence to make cases directly. Another was to gather intelligence that the government might use in other investigations. At the time you hear or see things, you can't always know how important they are, which way the information might be used, or whether it might be useless. You're reluctant to ignore anything, but you can't recall and report everything. You have to make choices on who and what to focus your concentration upon. How effective your choices turn out to be depends upon experience, instinct, and luck.

By midsummer of 1977, we had enough information on hijackings, burglaries, and robberies to bust up Jilly's crew any day in the week. But I wasn't moving up. I was making more inroads with Mirra and Ruggiero and the wiseguys in Little Italy than I was with the fences in Brooklyn.

I began to think, instead of concentrating on fences, what about a direct shot at the Mafia?

I brought this up in a telephone conversation with my supervisor, Guy Berada. It intrigued us both. We even risked a rare meeting in person, for lunch at a Third Avenue Manhattan restaurant called Cockeyed Clams, near my apartment.

We reevaluated our goals. The more we thought about it, the more we thought, if I get hooked up with a fence, that's all I'm hooked up with. But the Mafia had a structure and hierarchy; if I could get hooked up with wiseguys, I had a chance at a significant penetration of the mob itself.

It would mean a greater commitment from the Bureau, an increase in risks and pressures. So far as we knew, the FBI had never planted one of its own agents in the Mafia.

Finally the opportunities outweighed all other considerations. It was worth a shot to abandon the fence operation in Brooklyn and "go downtown," throw in with the wiseguys in Little Italy.

I would continue to operate alone, without surveillance. Little Italy is a tight neighborhood, like a separate world. You couldn't park a van with one-way glass on a street down there without getting made in five minutes. I would continue to operate without using hidden tape recorders or transmitters because I was still new, and there was always the danger of getting patted down. The Bureau had informants in Little Italy. They wouldn't know who I was, I wouldn't know who they were. I didn't want to risk acting different around somebody because I knew he was an informant, or having somebody act different around me.

Having made the decision, I couldn't just abruptly drop out of the Brooklyn scene. I still had to use the Brooklyn guys as backup for credibility. In all likelihood, sooner or later the downtown guys would check me out with the Brooklyn crew, and I didn't want any of Jilly's guys to say I just disappeared one day. I wanted to ease out gradually.

I hung out more and more with Mirra and Ruggiero, less and less with Jilly's crew. Gradually it got to where I was just phoning in to Jilly once in a while. By August I was full-time around Little Italy.

Jilly stayed loyal. Agents routinely show up to talk to wiseguys like Jilly, show pictures of people they're interested in, see if you have anything to say, let you know they're keeping tabs on you. One such time, agents came out to talk to him. They showed him several pictures, including a picture of me. These agents didn't know who I really was. They told him that I was a jewel thief and burglar, that they had information that I was hanging out around there, and they wanted to know what he knew about me.

Jilly wouldn't acknowledge whether he knew me or

not. Even though I wasn't around there anymore, he wouldn't give up anything about me.

Two years later Jilly got whacked. He was driving his car near his apartment. He stopped for a red light and some guy on a motorcycle pulled up beside him and pumped a couple of .38 slugs into him. It was a regular mob hit. Our information was that they thought Jilly was talking. But he wasn't.

7

TONY MIRRA

J Edgar Hoover didn't want his FBI agents to work undercover because it could be a dirty job that could end up tainting the agents. Times have changed. Undercover work is now a crucial tool in law enforcement.

Informants are valuable but unreliable. They are crooks buying their life-style or freedom with information, and they may lie or exaggerate to get a better deal. A government agent working undercover, sworn and paid to uphold the law, is more trustworthy, more credible, before a jury. But it's a risky business. You can get dirty, you can get killed.

Not every agent can work undercover. You have to have a strong personality. Strong means disciplined, controlled, confident. It doesn't mean loud or abrasive or conspicuous. It means your personality can withstand the extraordinary challenges and temptations that routinely go with the work. It means you have an ego strong enough to sustain you from within, when nobody but you knows what you're really doing and thinking.

It means you don't forget who you are, not for a

day, not for a minute. You are an FBI agent making a case.

You have to be an individualist who doesn't mind working alone. Really alone, more alone than being by yourself. You're with badguys continually, pretending to be one of them, cultivating them, laughing at their jokes, keeping feelings and opinions and fears to yourself, just like your true identity. You do this all day, every day. You don't leave this life every once in a while to share stories with friends or family about what's been going on undercover. You have nobody to talk to about what you're experiencing, except your contact agent. I talked to my contact agent for a few minutes by telephone maybe a couple of times a week. I saw him for a few minutes once a month, to pick up my spending money.

While you are pretending to be somebody else, there are the same personality conflicts you would find anywhere. There are guys you like and don't like, guys who like you and don't like you and will continually try to bust your balls. You have to override your natural inclinations for association. You cultivate whoever can help you make a case. You're not a patsy, but you swallow your gripes and control your temper.

You have to make difficult decisions on your own and often right on the spot—which way to go and how far; what risks to take. You have to accept the embarrassment and danger of being wrong and making mistakes, because you have nobody to hide behind on the street, and you are always open to second-guessing from your superiors. In my case that meant even the top FBI bosses in Washington.

You have to be street-smart, even cocky sometimes. Every good undercover agent I have known grew up on the street, like I did, and was a good street agent before becoming an undercover agent. On the street you learn what's what and who's who. You learn how to read situations and handle yourself. You can't fake the ability. It shows.

You have to be disciplined to work, be a self-starter. The law-enforcement business basically has a conservative atmosphere. Employees are used to rules and regulations. In the FBI, nobody is hired as an under-cover agent. You're brought in as a regular agent. You go to work in a tie and jacket. You sign in and you sign out.

After several years, take a regular agent and put him in an undercover capacity. Suddenly nobody tells him when to go to work. Nobody tells him what kind of clothes to wear. He dresses like the badguys. Maybe he drives a Cadillac or Mercedes. Chances are he has his own apartment, regardless of whether he's married or not, and he comes and goes as he pleases. He has money to spend.

This life-style is provided by the FBI. It's all Holly-wood, phony. But all the guys around you have Cad-dies and pinkie rings and broads and cash, and it's easy to forget that you're not one of them. If you don't have a strong personality and ego, a sense of pride in yourself, you're going to be overcome by all this, consumed by the role you're playing. The major failure among guys working undercover for any law-enforcement agency is that they fall in love with the role. They become the role. They forget who they are.

I grew up in a city, an Italian, knowing what the Mafia was. As a teenager I played cards, shot craps, played pool, went to the track, hung around social clubs. I knew that some card and crap games were run by the mob, and some social clubs were mob social clubs. I knew some guys who were mob guys. I knew that maybe the bookie wasn't a made guy, but his boss was, the guy who ran the whole operation. I knew some of them were killers. Even as a kid I knew guys that were here today, gone tomorrow, never seen again, and I knew what had happened.

I knew how wiseguys acted. I knew the mentality. I knew things to do and not to do. Keep your mouth shut at certain times. Don't get involved in things that don't concern you. Walk away from conversations and situations that aren't your business, before anybody asks you to take a hike. You handle yourself right in those situations, that's how you get credibility on the street. They say to themselves, "Hey, this guy's been around."

It helped me in my undercover role, knowing this stuff going in.

Growing up in that environment, I could have gone the wiseguy route. I knew guys that did. It happened that my mother and father were straight, and I grew up with their values. I grew up as a guy who would work for a living, raise a family, obey the laws. Other guys became badguys.

I don't moralize about that. Because of how and where I grew up, the Mafia held no big mystique for me. I didn't go into this job as any crusade against the Mafia. I might be saying to myself, "These fuckers, they're killing people. They're lying and stealing. They're badguys, and I don't like badguys." But I don't have to overcome a moralistic contempt that could get in the way of my job. I'm not a social worker, I'm an FBI agent. If my field as an agent had been civil rights or terrorists, I would have gone at it the same way—done my job to the best of my ability.

If you're a badguy, my job is to put you in the can. Simple as that.

The Mafia is not primarily an organization of murderers. First and foremost, the Mafia is made up of thieves. It is driven by greed and controlled by fear. Working undercover, I was learning how tough these guys really were, how tough they really weren't, and how the toughest among them feared their superiors.

It wasn't the toughness of an individual that caused the fear so much. It was the structure. It was the system of hierarchy, rules, and penalties that can terrify the toughest wiseguy in the business. The more potent toughness is in the ability to enforce the rules.

Everything is done to make money. Some violations may be excused if you're a good money-maker. Murder is secondary, the tool of enforcement, the threat. You can be as frail as was old Carlo Gambino—the last real Godfather, Boss of Bosses—before he died in 1976, but if by a simple yes or no, a nod or a shake of the head, or a waggle of the finger you have the power of death over anybody in your organization, there isn't a gorilla on the street who won't shake in his Bally shoes before you.

The five major Mafia families are based in New York: Gambino, Lucchese, Genovese, Colombo, Bonanno. Joe Bonanno took over the family in 1931. He was forced into retirement in the mid-1960s and now lives in ill health in Tucson, Arizona. The Bonanno boss when I went undercover was Carmine Galante.

The Gambino family was run by Big Paul Castellano; the Lucchese by Anthony "Tony Ducks" Corallo; the Genovese by Anthony "Fat Tony" Salerno; the Colombo by Tommy LaBella. Each boss has absolute authority over his family.

The Commission, on which sit the bosses of the families, resolves interfamily disputes or matters that transcend the interests of a single family, or allows for cooperative ventures, such as controlling the concrete industry in New York or skimming the take from the Las Vegas casinos. A transcendent matter may be whether the boss of a family should be hit. The Commission has to approve the execution of any boss by either a faction of his own family or by anybody else.

Beneath each boss in a family, each level of the chain of command requires total respect from those below. Each family has an underboss; a consiglieri (counselor), who mediates disputes and advises the boss; and a number of captains. Under each captain are the soldiers, the lowest level of made guys.

Then there are a lot of "connected" guys who are associated with the made guys but are not themselves made. In any family there may be, say, two hundred made guys and ten times as many connected guys. If you are a connected guy, in partnership with some soldier or captain, you are subject to many of the same rules as everybody else in the family. You have to give respect, you have to share your profits. But they don't necessarily share with you. And you are not entitled to the same respect and protection given to made guys.

In spite of how much I knew about the Mafia—both from growing up and from research—I was learning a lot. It was different being on the scene, being part of it, experiencing it firsthand. As with any law-enforcement agency, we knew a lot more than we could prove in court. So what I could come up with firsthand, on the scene, was crucial.

I was already identifying a lot of guys in the Colombo and Bonanno families, and pinpointing their ranks. I was learning that more hijacks were "give-ups" than regular hijackings. Whenever you pulled a score, you had to give a cut of it to whoever you were responsible to above you in the chain of command. You had to report to your captain or boss on everything you did. Despite these rules, though, there was more swindling of one another going on in crews than we had thought.

Along with the strict chain of command and the requirement for respect for those above you, there was a strict code of discipline. The consequence for not adhering to the rules of profit sharing and respect was not getting kicked out of the Mafia, it was being whacked out.

I was learning how it felt to be a part of this system. I was learning to act accordingly. I was becoming ever more known and trusted, was in on their plans and activities, and so had to start abiding by the rules of the mob.

It was amazing that I had been accepted at all. Everybody around me had grown up in these neighborhoods, been known forever. I was a newcomer. So far they had bought my stories and style. And I had been lucky. When you're an FBI agent running with thieves and killers, no amount of skill is itself enough to keep you alive and effective. You've got to get the breaks too.

I was in at the bottom. The only people lower than me by Mafia reckoning were ordinary citizens with nine-to-five jobs and no mob connections.

Anthony Mirra was the nastiest, most intimidating guy I met in the Mafia. He went about 6'2", 210 pounds. He was a good money-maker and a stone-cold killer. He was moody and unpredictable. You never knew what might set him off. And when he snapped, he might do anything.

Mirra was a knife man. It was common for mobsters to carry knives instead of guns, because they were often rousted by cops and didn't want to be caught with guns on them. Being caught carrying an unregistered pistol in New York means prison. They carried folding knives with long blades. I carried one. But it was not common for everybody to use their knives the way Mirra did. I was often told, "If you ever get into an argument with him, make sure you stay an arm's length away, because he will stick you." Even among mafiosi, Mirra was far from normal.

He was always in trouble, either with the law or with other wiseguys. He was totally obnoxious, he insulted everybody. He was widely despised but just as widely feared. A lot of people just tried to stay out of his way.

"Mirra's problem," Lefty Ruggiero told me, "is that he's always abusing somebody."

But for me he was a step up from Jilly's crew in importance. He accepted me, and I started hanging out with him, dividing my time between him and Jilly's Brooklyn crew. I would go to Little Italy for a couple of hours in the morning, then head over to Brooklyn for a while, then come back to bounce around with Mirra at night. We'd hit discos like Cecil's, Hippopotamus, or Ibis.

Mirra never spent his own money. Everything was "on the arm"—free with him. One of the first times I was with him we were at Hippopotamus. A lot of wiseguys hanging out there came over to talk to him. We were at the bar half the night, not paying for anything.

When we got up to leave, I put $25 down on the bar.

"Take that fucking money off the bar," Mirra growled at me in his deep voice. "Nobody pays for nothing when they're with me."

"Geez, Tony, just a tip for the bartender," I said. "That's how I operate."

He jabbed a finger in my chest. "You operate how I tell you to operate. Pick it up."

"Okay, Tony," I said, and I pocketed the bills. I wanted to avoid a big argument with him, and possible consequences. But it was not easy, letting somebody like that talk to you like that.

Mirra told me that Hippopotamus was owned by Aniello Dellacroce, the underboss of the Gambino family. Mirra introduced me to Aniello's son, Armond, who he said ran the place.

Armond had an illegal "after-hours" place at 11 West Fifty-sixth Street, with blackjack and dice tables and a roulette wheel. I went there with Mirra a few times. It was a comfortable, carpeted place, free food and booze, all kinds of girls waiting on you while you gambled. It opened at two or three in the morning and ran until maybe eight or nine.

Aniello Dellacroce died of cancer in 1985, while under indictment on RICO charges; soon after that, Armond pled guilty to federal racketeering charges, but he disappeared before sentencing and at this writing is still a fugitive.

We were at a bar in Fort Lee, New Jersey. Tony was talking to some guy on the other side of him and I was listening. I moved my elbow and knocked over my drink, spilling it on the guy on my other side. "Sorry," I say.

" 'Sorry' don't clean my coat," the guy says. "Why don't you assholes go back to New York where you belong."

"Hey, I said I'm sorry." I get a bar rag from the bartender and wipe it up.

Now this guy gets a drink, puts it on the bar, and knocks it over on me. "Take your dumb ass back across the river," he says.

Nothing's going to appease this guy. I see Tony listening to this, getting that cuckoo look in his eye, his hand in his jacket pocket.

My theory is, you don't get into an argument because you don't know what will develop—some guy pulls a gun or goes outside and brings back twenty guys. Plus Mirra may be on the verge of pulling out his knife to stick this guy. I have to end it quick.

I say, "You wanna step outside?"

"Yeah." He gets up off his stool, and I give him a shot right there, because I'm not going outside. Another guy jumps in, Mirra smacks him. The first guy comes at me again, I clock him with a bottle.

I say to Mirra, "Let's get the fuck outa here."

"Yeah, let's go," he says.

We scram before the cops come.

"Why didn't you just stick the cocksucker?" Tony says. "I was gonna do it for you."

Embarrassed? Yeah, I was. Here I am an FBI agent, a thirty-eight-year-old man, getting into a bar fight. I didn't even want to *be* in that joint with Anthony Mirra. But because I was, that's the kind of thing that can happen. And when it does, the best thing you can do is handle it quick so it doesn't get out of control. I don't believe in arguing.

Often on Friday and Saturday nights we hung out at Cecil's. I learned that Cecil's was one of the joints Mirra had muscled in on. The owners paid him a weekly cut, a salary for the privilege of having him around. Sometimes he'd tell me to watch the bartenders and manager to make sure they weren't clipping the joint.

If he didn't make $5,000 there on a weekend, he went cuckoo. One Friday night, out of the blue he decided he wasn't making enough money out of the joint, so everybody would be charged five dollars at the door. The manager and I tried to talk him out of it, because you couldn't just suddenly change the policy on the regular clientele, but Mirra wanted the money.

"Tonight everybody gets charged a fin," he said. "Everybody."

He told the kid at the door to collect, and sent me over there to make sure everybody paid.

Customers complained, but they paid. Then three guys came to the door with three girls. "We don't pay no charges," one of them said. They started to elbow their way past the kid at the door.

I recognized the guys as wiseguys, friends of Mirra's.

But I felt like busting some balls. I stepped in front of
them. "Everybody that comes in tonight pays five
bucks," I said.

"We don't pay."

"Then you don't come in."

"Who the fuck are you? Who you with?"

The question meant, What mob crew was I with? I
played dumb. "I'm here by myself."

"You know who I am?"

"I don't wanna know. But if you're some kind of
big-time operator, you ought to be able to come up
with thirty bucks for you and your girlfriends."

"I wanna see Tony Mirra!"

"You wanna see Tony, give me five bucks, you can
go right in and see him."

Now the guys are very embarrassed in front of their
girlfriends, and they start a ruckus, shouting and shov-
ing. Mirra comes over.

"These guys don't wanna pay the five bucks, Tony,"
I say.

"Not *these* guys, you fucking idiot," he says.

"Tony, I'm just doing what you told me to do. You
didn't say wiseguys come in free."

"These guys get in."

"You guys get in," I say to the bunch, giving them a
big smile.

"You're a crazy bastard," Mirra says to me.

With a guy like Mirra, you had to allow yourself a
little fun every once in a while, otherwise you would
go wacko.

I was sitting at the bar at Cecil's. A friend of Mirra's,
a guy I didn't know well, came up behind me to pat
me on the back and say hello. He ran his hand down
my back.

"What the fuck you doing?" I said as softly as I
could manage. He grunted and walked away. I knew
what he was doing. He was checking me for a wire. I
saw him talking to Mirra.

Later I was in the men's room washing my hands.
When I turned around, I bumped into this same guy.
He quickly slid his hands down the sides of my jacket.

I pushed him away. "I think you got the wrong guy, pal," I said. I just left him standing there.

Nobody could get close to Mirra. The only family he was close to was his mother. You could never get him to talk about anything personal. One day you might ask him, "How's your mother, Tony?" He might say, "Okay." Another day you ask him, and he might answer, "What the fuck you so nosy about?"

He was always hustling broads. Women were attracted to him, even though he treated them like dirt. He was never married, but he had a load of girlfriends, everything from bimbos to movie stars. When he wasn't hustling them, he was abusing them. He was just totally obnoxious. When a woman at Cecil's complained that her umbrella had been stolen out of the coatroom, he said to her, "You think I care about a fucking umbrella? The thing for you to do about it is to get the fuck out of here and don't come back."

Then there was a time down at the South Street Seaport restoration project when one of the many street vendors, an old woman selling jewelry, was waiting to use the pay phone Mirra was tying up. Wiseguys spend their lives on the telephone. Mirra had been tying up the phone for about a half hour, making one call after another. When this old woman asked him politely if she could please use the phone, because that was the only phone in the area for the vendors to use, and they used it for business, Mirra said, "Listen, you fucking cunt, I'm using this phone. When I'm finished, I'm finished. Shut your fucking mouth or I'll cut you."

He was telling a bunch of guys about this very big movie actress he was seeing. "I got her to give me a blow job while another guy was fucking her and she was jerking off another guy," he said. I must have winced or groaned or something, because he said to me, "Aw, what's the difference? She was so strung out on dope, she didn't know what she was doing. Don't act like a fucking fruitcake."

The Feast of San Gennaro is the biggest annual street festival in Little Italy, taking over Mulberry

Street for two weeks in September. It's a big tourist thing; people come from all over the country. It's a religious festival, but on the street it's all controlled by the mob. All five families are involved. Different captains each have a certain portion of a block that is his, where there may be five or six booths. You can't just go to the church and say you want a booth at such-and-such a place. That is controlled by the mob captains. Anybody that puts a booth in your section has to kick back to you. The more powerful captains control the sections closer to the center of the feast. And captains control the supplies. One captain might have control of all the sausage that comes in, another controls the beer. In other words, if you have a booth and want to sell beer, you go to the captain or his representative and say you want beer at your booth. He'll send a guy to you that will provide beer. So they get a cut of everything. You have to pay for the space the booth occupies, and you have to pay a certain amount off the top as a nightly fee.

During the Feast of San Gennaro everybody goes down and hangs around on the street, all the wiseguys. That's the big thing to do. Eat food from the various carts. Some of the people with the carts and booths were itinerant carnival types, but a lot of them were neighborhood people that had had booths there for years.

The day before the feast began in 1977, Mirra had met this girl who had a merchandise stand at South Street Seaport adjacent to the Fulton Fish Market, and he was hustling her.

"I got her a slot at the feast," he told me. "Drive me down there. I told her I'd help carry her stuff over to the feast this afternoon so she could set up."

I drove him down to South Street. She was nice-looking and pleasant. But there was something about her. We helped her pack up and drove her to Mulberry Street.

Mirra says, "I'll see you tonight, hon," and we left.

I say, "How well you know that lady, Tony?"

"I just met her. I figure I'll grab her tonight after the feast, spend a hot night."

"You sure?"

"Who the fuck you talking to?" he says.

Later that night Tony took off for his date. I was in a coffee shop when he came stomping in.

"You knew she was a fucking lezzie!" he hollers. "And you didn't tell me, you cocksucker! Son of a bitch. I went through all the trouble of getting her a booth at the feast. Know what I told her? I told her, 'Don't come back to that fucking booth tomorrow!' "

Psychologists could probably have had a field day with Mirra. For my part, he was a dangerous and necessary pain in the ass. He got on me for not hustling broads myself, or bringing any around. I just said I had a girlfriend in Jersey and one in California, but I kept that part of my life separate.

Married mob guys typically have girlfriends. They're not discreet about it. Other than that, there was much less skirt chasing than I expected. Women were always around and available, because they gravitated to these guys. Maybe they'd hook up with them later. But most evenings they just wanted to go out and have some drinks and talk over schemes with the other guys.

My personal rule was that under no circumstances would I have anything to do with any women hanging around the mob. Regardless of morality, that kind of thing will come back to haunt you when you testify in court against these guys. By saying I had a girlfriend someplace else, the heat was off me. Occasionally, just so I seemed normal, I would bring somebody around for dinner, a woman who I had maybe met in my neighborhood. I'd show her a nice evening with the mob guys, take her home and drop her off, and that was that.

At that feast in 1977, a bunch of us were sitting in a coffee shop on Mulberry Street at one A.M., Lefty and a couple other guys and a couple local girls. One girl was sitting next to me. Suddenly she's rubbing my leg under the table. She says, "Where you going when you leave here?"

"Over to see my girl in Jersey."

"Why don't you stay in the city tonight?"

This girl is the daughter of a wiseguy, and her father is in the coffee shop. I have to be careful not to insult her because she might tell her old man that I'm grabbing *her* leg or something, and then I'm history—you don't do that to a wiseguy's daughter.

"I'm pretty true to my girl," I say. "I promised I was coming over. I'd rather not lie to her."

"How come you never bring her around?"

"No reason to."

"Well, if you ever get the urge to go out, give me a call."

"Okay, I will. Sometime when I don't have to lie." I squirmed out of that one.

One of Mirra's operations was coin machines. He dealt in slots, peanut vending machines, game machines, pinball machines. He had them installed all over the city in stores, luncheonettes, clubs, after-hours places. Slot machines, since they were illegal, would be installed in back rooms. He would take me along on his route when he collected the money from the machines and when he got new business.

To collect, he just went in, opened the machines with a key, counted the money, and gave the store owner his cut—$25 or whatever it was. He would put the rest in a paper bag and out we would go. His route produced maybe $2,000 a week.

To get a new customer Mirra would walk into a place, tell the owner he was Tony and that the store needed one of his machines. Often the owner would recognize him or the name and say something like, "Oh, yeah, Tony, I was just thinking of calling you to get a machine in here." If the guy didn't think he was interested at first, Mirra would say, "In the next twenty-four hours, check around, ask about Tony down on Mulberry Street. Then I'll come back and see if you've changed your mind."

Invariably the owner had changed his mind when we came back.

He was trying to get his slot machines into Atlantic City. He said the family had five hundred slots in a warehouse, and he was just waiting for his lawyers to

come up with a way to get access for them along the
boardwalk.

Mirra says to me, "Drive me uptown."

"What's the problem?"

"I got to meet a guy that owes me money."

He was collecting on one of his shylock loans.

We drive to a restaurant on First Avenue. We go in
and stand at the bar. Pretty soon this guy walks in,
tough-looking, about thirty. He comes over to Mirra
and starts to open his mouth.

"Don't," Mirra says, holding up his hand. "Don't
mention anybody's name or I'm gonna smack you
right here."

Mob protocol is that if the guy says he talked to
another wiseguy about the situation, mentions another wiseguy's name, then Mirra would first have to
talk to the other wiseguy. So he wasn't giving this guy
a chance to mention anybody's name.

Mirra says, "Just answer the question I ask you.
Where's my fucking money?"

"Geez, Tony, you're gonna get it, I'm just having a
hard time, but I'll have it for you, you know—"

"I heard this now a couple weeks," Mirra says.
"But it don't happen. Let's take a walk."

Now I'm worried. If Mirra takes him out, this guy
could end up in the alley next door. Mirra would beat
him up or stab him. It was one of those situations
where, as an agent, I had to intercede. But at the
same time I had to maintain my role.

I say, "Hey, Tony, why don't you let me talk to the
guy, save you the aggravation. I'll take him out for a
walk."

He nods to me and shoves the guy toward the door.

I take him outside. I figure at least I can buy some
time, let Tony cool down. I say, "Look, I just saved
you. I don't want to see you get killed, but next time it
ain't gonna be that easy. When we go back in there,
you say, 'Tony, can I meet you tomorrow and give you
the money?' And you better have it for him tomorrow, because I might not be around tomorrow. And
you act scared, like I gave you a couple smacks, be-

cause that's what I'm supposed to do. You don't act right, I'll stab you myself, because I put my ass on the line with him."

This tough guy is practically licking my hand because of his fear of Mirra.

We go back in, and the guy goes right up to Mirra and says, "Tony, I'll give you the money tomorrow, meet you anywhere you want, okay? Okay?"

"The kid convinced you?" (Mirra sometimes called me "the kid.") "Tomorrow. Right here."

I was always on edge with Mirra. He was always in arguments with somebody. You never knew what might set him off, turn him into a cuckoo bird. He had no real allegiance to anybody. He was always in trouble with the law, which gave him a bad reputation on the street. I didn't want to get tied up with Mirra, because you never knew when he would go back in the can. He was almost fifty years old, and he had spent more than half his life in jail.

He was valuable for introducing me to people. He introduced me to his captain, Mickey Zaffarano. Zaffarano handled porn theaters and national porn-film distribution for the Bonanno family. He owned several pornography movie theaters in Times Square and around the country. His office was at Forty-eighth and Broadway—Times Square—upstairs from one of his theaters, the Pussycat. Mirra had me drive him up to Zaffarano's office a couple of times. Zaffarano also came down to Madison Street once in a while. He was a big, good-looking guy, tall and heavyset.

Zaffarano eventually got caught up in the FBI sting operation called "Mi-Porn" out of Miami. When the agents went up to his office to arrest him, he started running away through the halls, and in the course of his run he dropped dead of a heart attack.

Lefty Ruggierro had a little storefront social club similar to dozens of others in Little Italy. Coffee, booze, card tables, TV. Downstairs was another room for more serious card games. Members only. Men only. Associates of Lefty and the Bonanno family only. It was a place to hang out.

In the back of the room was a phone and table, a place to take bets. Lefty was a bookie. Sometimes Mirra wasn't there and I would bullshit with Lefty, chat about sports and what teams were hot to bet on. I began placing a few bets on baseball and horses, and on football when the pro exhibition season started—$50 to $100 just to help me be accepted. We started to develop a relationship. Lefty started calling me Donnie instead of Don, and that's what everybody called me from then on.

The daily routine at Lefty's was not much different from what it was at Jilly's in Brooklyn, except that it was more of a real social club, not a store. Guys talked about the sports book, the numbers business, who owed what to whom, what scores were coming up. They groused about money. It didn't matter how much anybody made or anybody had; they always groused about it. They were always talking about squeezing another nickel out of somebody.

After about two weeks Lefty asked me how I made money. By then I felt comfortable, not like I was rushing anything, so I told him I was a jewel thief and burglar.

"My son-in-law Marco is in that line," he said. "Maybe you guys can get some things going together."

"I usually work alone, Lefty," I said. "But if there's a good score and I like it, that's always a possibility."

For a while it was like a testing period. I just bided my time and didn't push my nose into anything. Lefty started hitting me up for loans every now and then. He needed to pick up some clothes or some furniture, or whatever. I would lend him $300, $125. Sometimes he'd pay me back a fraction of it. I never thought he needed the money. I knew it was part of the hustle. You squeeze money out from whoever you can. Also, my lending him money was an indication that I was making money. So as not to seem like a patsy, I'd never give him all he asked for. He'd say he needed $500, I'd give him $200.

"Donnie, I need that thousand we talked about.

You gonna be able to come up with that thousand for me?"

"A grand's a lot for me right now, Lefty."

"Yeah, but, see, I gotta pick up seventeen hundred bucks worth of clothes from this guy. What I'll do, you give me the thousand, I'll pay you back two hundred on that three-fifty I owe you."

That kind of cycle went on with everybody. It didn't necessarily mean guys were broke. It was just that everybody did everything possible to avoid using his own money.

In those days I was still moving around. I would stop down at Lefty's at maybe ten o'clock in the morning, hang around the club for an hour or two, have some coffee, read the papers, listen in on whatever conversations were going on, listen to some of the betting action going on over the telephone in the back. Then I'd go to Brooklyn and hang around Jilly's for a couple of hours. Then in the evening I would hook up with Mirra, maybe meet him at Cecil's, and hit the night spots.

Lefty suggested I come down to the club some nights. There were crap games or three-card monte games in the neighborhood. Some of them were heavy-duty. There would be regular games in a couple rooms upstairs from Fretta's, the meat market on Mulberry Street. Or they'd move around to different empty lofts. They'd move the games every week or two, just to keep on the safe side. They were pretty safe, anyway, in that neighborhood, as far as trouble from the cops was concerned, but you didn't want to shove it in anybody's face. Mainly I'd just watch. Guys could be winning or losing $100,000. Too steep for me on an FBI budget.

Lefty ran the bookmaking operation for Nicky Marangello, the underboss of the Bonanno family. One day he asked me to drive him uptown, to an address on lower Fifth Avenue. "I gotta see one of my biggest bettors," Lefty said. "This guy makes men's clothes, mostly shirts, up on the fourth floor. He put down $175,000 this weekend. I gotta collect."

I gathered that in this instance Lefty collected between $5,000 and $10,000. "That's a good week for me with him," Lefty said. "One week last season I dropped sixteen grand in football bets to this guy." He began regularly having me drive him around to make collections and payoffs on the betting operation. Sometimes he would meet somebody at the Biondi Coffee House on Mulberry Street to pick up money to pay off the bettors. His fortunes varied widely in the betting business.

"Couple weeks ago I got beat thirteen grand for the week," he said. "Last week I booked fifty-two grand and my losses were only seventeen-fifty."

One afternoon he had to run off somewhere, and he asked me, "You want to handle the phone while I'm gone?"

So I started taking bets over the phone for Lefty.

Lefty was very different from Mirra. He talked a lot and was excitable. He had a big reputation as a killer, but on a daily social basis he wasn't as likely to inflict damage. Lefty and Mirra were both soldiers but under different captains. Mirra was under Zaffarano (until he died). Lefty was under Mike Sabella.

Sabella owned a prominent restaurant on Mulberry Street, CaSa Bella. Occasionally we went there for dinner. Lefty introduced me to Sabella, a short, paunchy man with baggy eyes. "Mike, this is Donnie, a friend of mine."

One time during the Feast of San Gennaro, Lefty and I and Mike Sabella were sitting in a club across the street from CaSa Bella, which Mike usually closed during the feast because he hated tourists.

Jimmy Roselli, the Italian singer, had his car parked out on the street. He opened the trunk, and it was filled with his records. He started hawking his own records out of his car trunk right there at the feast.

Mike couldn't believe it. He went outside and said to Roselli, "Put the fucking trunk down because you're fucking embarrassing me by trying to sell your fucking records here on the street!"

Roselli closed the trunk immediately.

"He'll act different from now on," Lefty says.

Nicky Marangello, the underboss, stopped by Lefty's club regularly. Called Nicky Glasses or Little Nicky or Nicky Cigars, Marangello was a small man with slicked-back hair, thick glasses, and a sharp nose. He never smiled. Because of his thick glasses, he seemed always to be staring. Lefty introduced me to him. "Nicky, this is Donnie, a friend of mine." I wasn't invited to join in conversation, so I would walk away while they talked.

Marangello had his own social club, called Toyland. It was Mirra who first took me to Toyland, at 94 Hester Street, on the outskirts of Little Italy and Chinatown. Toyland wasn't the same kind of social club as Lefty's.

The first time Mirra asked me to drive him there, he told me, "Toyland is Nicky's office. You don't go there unless you've got business there, unless he wants you there, or somebody like me or Lefty sends you there. You don't hang out there. Nicky is usually there from about twelve-thirty to about four or five in the afternoon, Monday through Friday. You take care of your business with Nicky and then you leave."

On the door was "Toyland Social Club" in painted script, and under that, "Members Only." The room inside had a few card tables, a counter, a coffee machine—it looked typical for the little social clubs all around the neighborhood that were hangouts for wiseguys and connected guys. But it wasn't social. Guys talked to Nicky one at a time. Others waited outside.

That was where I first heard about the "zips." Mirra pointed out some of the guys hanging around Toyland, and he referred to them as "zips." He said the zips were Sicilians being brought into the country to distribute heroin and carry out hits for Carmine "Lilo" Galante, the boss of the Bonanno family. This operation, Mirra said, was strictly in the hands of Galante. The zips were effective because, although they were in the family, they were unknown in this country—no police records. They were set up in pizza parlors, where they received and distributed heroin, laundered money, and waited for any other assignments from Galante.

The zips, Mirra said, were clannish and secretive. They hung out mainly by themselves in the area of Knickerbocker Avenue in Brooklyn. They were, he said, the meanest killers in the business. Unlike the American Mafia, zips would kill cops and judges.

Two of those he pointed out were Salvatore Catalano and Caesar Bonventre. Bonventre was lean and stylish. Catalano was chunky and narrow-eyed.

This was the first solid information I got on what was going on with the Sicilians. We knew there were Sicilians showing up, some coming into the country legally, some smuggled through Canada. But we didn't know who was behind it, or what these Sicilians were being brought in for.

It's an example of the importance of intelligence information even when you're not making a particular case at the time. I was then primarily intent on working my way into the Bonanno family. When I first came across the zips with Mirra, I didn't even know what I was on to. I just picked up the information and passed it on. Several years later my information on the Sicilians was put together with other intelligence, and a full-scale investigation was launched. It resulted in the huge Pizza Connection case in New York in 1986—the largest international heroin-smuggling case ever.

Eventually Lefty started sending me to Toyland to report on weekly bookmaking operations to Marangello. There was no chitchat. I would deliver the figures, how much we won over the weekend, how much we got hit for, what the total "handle" was—the total taken in. Maybe I'd answer a couple of questions. Then I'd leave. But I noticed that Marangello was looking me over.

Other people were looking me over, too, though I didn't know it then. In separate operations, both the New York Police Department and the FBI had Toyland and CaSa Bella under surveillance during this time for other investigations. I showed up in their surveillance photographs. They had no idea who I really was. The NYPD identified me as Don Brasco, an associate of the Bonanno organized crime family.

Lefty and Mirra had once been partners, but now they hated each other. Each of them saw me as a potential good money-earner, so jealousy developed.

"Why you so friendly with that fuck Lefty?" Mirra would ask me. "He can't do nothing for you."

"That Mirra's a crazy rat bastard," Lefty would say. "He's nothing but trouble. You shouldn't be spending time with him."

It was a dangerous game, being in the middle between those two guys. With each of them bad-mouthing the other to me, and each wanting me to drop the other guy, I was in a squeeze, too much in the spotlight. Eventually I would have to choose.

Mirra was a better money-maker than Lefty. He told me that in the four months he'd lately been out of jail, he'd made more than $200,000. He roamed wider and had more varied contacts. But he was crazy. People around him acted like they were his friends because they feared him. But everybody hated him. Even Lefty's captain, Mike Sabella, hated Mirra. Lefty wasn't as volatile as Mirra and had more loyalty toward friends. Lefty also had good contacts. And I could see that Lefty commanded more respect from other wiseguys, because of his loyalty and the fact that he wasn't so troublesome. I thought it would probably be more effective to concentrate on Lefty.

As it turned out, I didn't have to choose.

One afternoon I walked into the club and Lefty was on the phone. "Hey, Donnie, somebody here wants to talk to you."

I thought, Who the hell would be calling me down here? It was Jilly. "Lefty was asking me about you," Jilly said. "I put in a good word."

After the call I asked Lefty what that was all about.

"Jilly says you ain't no leech. He says you keep busy and earn good, and nobody over there had to carry you."

"So?"

"So I'm happy to hear it."

A few days later he said, "Donnie, I put in a claim on you. I went on record with Mike and Nicky. You're my partner now."

"Hey, Lefty, that's great," I said.

"Now, Donnie, this means that you have to start really listening to me, going by the rules. I'm responsible for you. You're responsible to me. I hope everything you say about yourself is true. Because if you fuck up, we're both gonna go bye-bye."

Suddenly everything was changed. I couldn't be so loosey-goosey anymore, come and go as I pleased, pretend ignorance. I couldn't make excuses about not belonging to anybody or not knowing the rules.

Lefty began what he called his "schooling" of me. It began right away and never stopped.

Lefty was fastidious. He told me to shave off my mustache and cut my hair. "No real wiseguys wear mustaches," he said, "except some of the old mustache petes. You gotta look neat, dress right, which means at night you throw on a sport jacket and slacks."

He told me I have to show respect to all family members. "That's the most important thing," he said, "respect. The worst thing you can do is embarrass a wiseguy. If you embarrass a captain or a boss, forget about it. You're history."

When you were around a captain or a boss, you didn't speak or join in the conversation unless asked to.

"Now, when a wiseguy introduces you to another wiseguy, he will say, 'Donnie is a friend of *mine.*' That means Donnie is okay, and you can talk in front of him if you want, but he's not a made guy, so you may not want to talk about certain business or family matters in front of him. That's the way I introduce you, see. When a wiseguy is introducing another made guy, he will say, 'He's a friend of *ours.*' That means you can talk business in front of him, because he's a member of La Cosa Nostra."

He told me that my activities had to be cleared

through him. If I wanted to travel out of town, I had to get permission from him, and I had to keep in constant contact with him. Any proceeds I made had to be split with him.

"When you talk on the phone," he told me, "you don't talk direct about what's going on. You talk around it, throw me a curve—just give me a hint about what you're talking about. Because all the phones are tapped, you know."

Like most mobsters, he was paranoid. "There's agents everywhere," he said. One time we were out on the sidewalk and he pointed down the street at a school. "See up on that roof there?" There were some TV antennas. "Agents put them up there. If they're listening, they can hear every fucking word we say."

You didn't use last names unless absolutely necessary.

You didn't mess with a wiseguy's wife or girlfriend.

You always took the wiseguy's side of a dispute with a non-wiseguy, even if the wiseguy was wrong.

Since I was now a connected guy, but not a wiseguy, I was not to argue or talk back to a wiseguy or to raise my hands to one. "When you're not a wiseguy," Lefty said, "the wiseguy is always right and you're always wrong. It don't matter what. Don't forget that, Donnie. Because no other wiseguy is gonna side with you against another wiseguy."

You observed the code of silence about the family. You didn't put business "on the street."

"You keep your nose clean and don't fuck up," he said, "and obey the rules and be a good earner, maybe you'll get proposed for membership one day."

Occasionally I was still spending time with Tony Mirra. Lefty whined about it, but as long as I split with him any proceeds of anything I did with Mirra, it was okay. Mirra was a late-night person, anyway, and Lefty was not, so I could manage them both. I didn't want to cut myself off totally from Mirra unless and until I had to.

I was out bouncing with Mirra and a couple other wiseguys and their girlfriends. About four in the morning we went for breakfast. Suddenly Mirra turns ob-

noxious with the waitress, bitching about cold eggs
and bad service. He cranks it up, getting nastier, making a scene.

Finally I say quietly, "Hey, Tony, it's not her fault,
she's doing the best she can."

That sets him off worse. He leans across the table
and says, "You shut the fuck up. You don't ever tell
me what to say or not to say or how to act."

"I don't mean to, Tony. I just thought maybe you
could ease up on her."

Then he launches into a tirade in front of everybody. "You fucking jerk-off. You're nothing, you know
that? You got no power, you got no say. You think
that fuck Lefty's gonna protect you? You're with me
here, and you keep your fucking mouth shut if you
want to keep breathing."

I had to shut up because it was only going to get
worse and go totally out of control. So I say, "Tony,
you're right. I probably was out of line."

But inside I was seething. I'm on the job here at
four o'clock in the morning doing the best I can in my
role, tired, missing my family, and I have to take this
shit in front of people in a restaurant. I had never
allowed anybody else to talk to me like that in my life.

When I got back to my apartment, I grew angrier
about it. I knew the rules: If you're not a wiseguy, you
don't talk back to a wiseguy, you don't raise your
hands to a wiseguy. But this wasn't the first time he
had dressed me down in front of people. I couldn't let
him continue to walk all over me just because he was
Anthony Mirra.

I risked seeming like a patsy. This guy is talking to
me like I'm a nitwit, and on the street you have to
command a measure of respect no matter who you
are.

But I had to be careful, because I was still consoli-
dating my position with the Bonanno family, and any
wrong move could blow all the previous months of
effort. I had to straighten this situation out with Mirra,
but it had to be just him and me, not in front of
witnesses. I had to let him save some face.

I had to confront him and hope I could keep the

situation under control. If it came to a fight, I was a loser either way. If I beat him, I'm a loser because for sure I'm going to get whacked by him sometime soon afterward. If he beat me up or cut me, then I would be a pussy in everybody's eyes.

The next day I find him at his luncheonette on Madison Street. I say, "Tony, let's take a walk."

We walk up Madison Street. Outwardly I'm casual. But inside the adrenaline is pumping. There are people on the street, but that won't help me if it goes bad. I am thinking about his temper and his knife.

I say, "Tony, I realize that you're a wiseguy and I'm not, and that you command a certain respect for being a wiseguy."

"Yeah," he says.

"But I'm telling you now, don't ever embarrass me in front of people again. Because I'm not just some fucking Joe Scumbag on the street. And if you keep doing it, one of these days, Tony, I'm gonna get you for it. And it'll be when no one else is around."

I wait for his reaction. We keep walking.

"Ah, you're okay with me," he says at last. "I like you."

"Then don't embarrass me. As far as I'm concerned, right now everything's forgotten, nothing ever happened, we have a new start."

That was the end of the conversation. He peeled off and went back to his luncheonette. He never mentioned anything about it, but there was an edge between us after that. He never forgot.

He offered me a job. Mirra wanted me to handle his slot-machine route, make the collections. "I'll give you three hundred bucks a week," he said.

That was strange. I knew he respected my abilities, but I couldn't be sure what was cooking in that off-the-wall mind of his. There was no way I could take the job, because if I did, I'd be married to the guy, under his thumb, like an errand boy—which is what everybody was to Mirra. I'd be looking over my shoulder all the time.

I said, "Look, Tony, I'd be happy to help you now and then, you know. But I got some things going, and three hundred a week just wouldn't be worth my while to get tied up."

"Fine," he said.

I told Lefty about the job offer. "You did the right thing, Donnie," he said. "Anybody that gets hooked up with that cocksucker ends up getting fucked over or whacked."

Not long after that, Mirra went on the lam. He snuck out of town in a Volkswagen. He was wanted by the state on another narcotics rap. They caught up with him after about three months, and Mirra was back in the can.

He was sentenced to eight and a half years in New York's Riker's Island Prison. Lefty said, "See how tough he is with those niggers out there."

I was through with Mirra—for a while.

Besides the bookmaking operation, there were all kinds of scams and schemes around. Little ones and big ones. These guys might pull off a $100,000 score one day, rob a parking meter the day after. Anything where there's a dime to be ripped off.

The key was in the number of scams. Two hundred dollars isn't a lot, but if you're hitting up fifty scams for $200 apiece, you're making some money. We had counterfeit credit cards and stolen credit cards. You could always beat those once or twice before it got hot. They would go in with these cards and buy a lot of electronic equipment that they could sell.

A guy named Nick the Greek regularly supplied Lefty with manifests of cargo ships docked over in Jersey. Lefty would have stuff stolen to order. He showed me the manifests so I could check through them and see if I wanted to buy anything—radios, luggage, clothes. He and his crew could provide all kinds of phony documents. He had a guy in the Department of Motor Vehicles who supplied him with blank drivers' licenses. You just had to type in the information. One guy paid Lefty $350 for six phony New York State drivers' licenses and six phony Social Security cards.

For settling a beef between owners of a company at

the Fulton Fish Market, Lefty and two of his associates were given twenty percent of the ownership, plus a salary of $5,000 a month. "It's a shame," he told me after meeting with the other owners at his club, "that my shares couldn't be put in my name." Wiseguys didn't like to show income or ownership of anything. The cars they drive are almost always registered to somebody else. Lefty didn't file tax returns.

A typical scam was how we worked cashier's checks. Lefty told me he had access to cashier's checks from a bank in upstate New York. "We got a vice-president up there that will authorize cashing the checks when anybody calls him up," he said. The checks would be used to "buy" merchandise, which we could then resell.

He introduced me to a guy named Larry, who used to own a bar on Seventy-first Street. Larry was the contact on the deal. Larry said he had sat down with some friends of his in the banking business and figured out the best way to work the scam.

He had the stamp machine to certify the checks. He had several guys besides me to pass them. He had eight checks and provided us with a list of eight names, which were the names to be used on the checks. He provided New York State drivers' licenses and Social Security cards for IDs on the eight names. Bank accounts had been opened in these names. There just wasn't money in them to cover these bogus checks. When a business would call the bank for verification, giving the name on the check, this vice-president would okay the check. In order to pull this off before the bank caught up with the scheme, all the checks had to be cashed within one week. If we worked it at maximum efficiency, the checks could be worth $500,000.

Larry had a list of stores where we could buy merchandise with the checks, stores innocent of the scheme but places Larry knew could accept cashier's checks. I was supposed to use the name and ID papers of "John Martin," and be working for a company named Outlet Stores. In case the merchant wanted to verify that Outlet Stores existed, Larry gave me a number for him to call, where someone would answer "Showroom, Outlet Stores."

I was to go into a store and select the merchandise I wanted to buy, then tell the merchant I would be back with a cashier's check in the proper amount. Then I would call a number to reach a guy named Nick. I would give Nick the name of the store and the amount, and Nick would fill in the check and stamp it "certified."

The guys passing the checks would be spread out in the New York–New Jersey area. I was directed to go to a certain store on Orchard Street, in New York's lower east side, and buy around $4,000 worth of clothes.

I went to the store, picked out $2,660 worth of men's clothes, and told the salesman I would be back shortly with a certified check. I left the store and called Nick.

Nick said to meet him at Lefty's club in an hour. Nick handed me the check, marked with a blue "certified" stamp.

We went back to the store, picked up the clothes, and loaded them in the trunk of his car. Other of his guys would take care of selling the stuff from all the purchases of all the guys.

A week later Larry met me at Lefty's. He said that he had had trouble getting rid of the clothes I had bought and that he had finally gotten $1,100 for them. After expenses he had $600 left. "I had to give the banker his cut, see," Larry said. "And then the other two main guys, they hammered me for a bigger cut. You know."

Lefty was disgusted. "Forget about it," he said. "Just give us what you got for us, and don't come back around here no more."

Half of the $600 was Larry's, so he gave me $300. I had to split my end, as always, with Lefty.

I came out of this whole big deal with $150, which I passed on to my contact agent.

After the operation the FBI reimbursed the stores.

Lefty introduced me to a guy named "Fort Lee Jimmy" Capasso (because he was from Fort Lee, New Jersey), a capo in the Bonanno family and a partner of Nicky Marangello. One day I was waiting around in front of Toyland when Fort Lee Jimmy came over and said, "Donnie, like to talk to you."

He was in his fifties, always seemed like a decent guy.

He took me aside. He says, "Donnie, you seem like a pretty sharp guy. I just want to give you a piece of advice. This business we're in, you get old fast, and a lot of things you do now you can't do when you get older. Lot of these guys you see around make a lot of money, then they get older, fifty or sixty, and they're broke because they didn't save anything. And now they can't make so many good moves anymore. So my advice is, Donnie, find somebody you can really trust. Every time you pull a score, take some of that money and give it to that friend and have them keep it for you. And make the rule with that friend that he won't give you any of that money until you like retire. You can't go to this guy tomorrow and ask for a grand or two, because he won't give it to you—that's the rule you've set up. Just keep doing that over the years, so when you get older and can't be out stealing every day, you got yourself a nice little stash. You don't have to worry about being old and broke, like a lot of these guys."

He was recommending a little Mafia IRA, back in 1977.

8

LEFTY

Like most wiseguys, Lefty Guns Ruggiero still lived in the same neighborhood where he was born and raised.

He lived in a big old apartment complex called Knickerbocker Village on Monroe Street, a few blocks south of Little Italy. A lot of wiseguys lived in there, including Tony Mirra. Lefty invited me up there often.

Lefty's apartment was a small one-bedroom on the eighth floor, overlooking the interior courtyard of the complex. He loved tropical fish and had several tanks of them. He had a big color TV and a VCR, and a cable connection into which he had tapped illegally, like all the wiseguys, so it was free.

He didn't have air-conditioning. Lefty hated air-conditioning. On the hottest, most humid days, he wouldn't let me turn it on even in the car. He chain-smoked English Ovals, which made the air everywhere he was worse—especially for a nonsmoker like me.

He was a great cook, any kind of food. I would go over there to eat a couple of times a week.

Lefty had been divorced for a long time. His girlfriend, Louise, was a nice girl from the neighborhood. I got along good with Louise. She put up with a lot. Lefty had no sensitivity and sometimes treated her badly, just like he treated everybody else. But at the same time he was protective of her and quite faithful. She had a full-time job as a secretary.

When Louise's mother died, she asked me to come to the wake. I didn't know her mother, but I was complimented to think that Louise liked me well enough to include me. I remember it was raining like hell when I went to the wake. It was dreary and sad, and put me in a strange mood, sharing this kind of time with somebody who thinks you're somebody else.

You develop feelings for people, even in this job. It's easy to accept deceiving the badguys, because that's the game. Knowing that for five or six years you're deceiving others in their world who are not badguys, who don't know what's going on, who just happened to be born to or married to badguys, that's tougher on your mind. Some of those people develop feelings for you too. While you are allowing this to happen, you know that in the end, they are going to be hurt by what you are doing. And they don't even know who you really are.

Lefty had had four grown kids. I got quite close to Lefty's kids, really became a friend to them. They would come to me with their problems. His youngest daughter, in her mid-twenties, lived with his ex-wife in the building and worked at a hospital. She was a hard worker. Every year she had a booth at the Feast of San Gennaro, where she sold soft drinks and fruits. His son, Tommy, who was about twenty-eight, also lived in the building. He was a thief and had done some work for the family. Basically he was a free-lancer. But he also had problems with heroin. He was an on-and-off junkie.

Lefty was continually asking me to talk to Tommy, get him straightened out. He wanted me to help keep him off drugs and to get him to settle down to work. Sometimes Tommy and I would be in Lefty's club in the early afternoon watching our favorite soap operas, like *All My Children*. Lefty would come in and see that and throw a fit. "Turn off them fucking soap boxes!" he would bark. "You should be out stealing and looking for business. Come on, Donnie, get Tommy busy out on the street."

Two of Lefty's daughters were married to wiseguys. One had the misfortune to be married to Marco.

I met Marco at the Bus Stop Luncheonette, Mirra's place. Besides being a jewel thief, Marco was supposed to be an expert safe-and-lock man. He was also a drug dealer and a loudmouth. Other than a few conversations about jewels, I never had much to do with Marco. He lived a flashy life, vacationed in Florida where he had a big boat. He boasted that he could move all the dope that anybody could provide him with.

When I met Marco, he was worried about his partner, Billy Paradise. "Billy has turned stoolie," Marco said. "Billy could put me away twenty-two times if he ratted me out about the jobs we pulled."

Lefty was also worried about Billy Paradise. "We gotta think about having that guy whacked," he said. "I'd like to take him on my boat and throw him to the fishes. I ever tell you that story, Donnie, about the guy that thought I was gonna whack him on my boat?"

"No."

"One day I asked this guy to come out with me in

my boat, you know, in the East River, my speedboat. He came along, but he kept watching me, wouldn't turn his back to me. Finally I asked him what the hell was the matter. He said he was afraid that I thought maybe he had turned stoolie and I was gonna shoot him and throw him overboard. I said, 'You dumb bastard. If I wanted you whacked, I wouldn't have bothered bringing you out in my boat. I would have hit you downstairs at the club while you were playing cards and rolled you up in a rug and dumped you in the river right at South Street. That's what we do with stoolies,' I told him."

He was looking at me. I didn't know if he was just telling me a story, or if he was giving me a message about what happens to informants.

"Well, I hope this guy Paradise don't rat anybody out," I said.

One day Marco just disappeared. The word was he got into skimming drug profits that were supposed to go to the organization. He was never found. Word on the street was that the contract had gone to Lefty, to whack his own son-in-law. But Lefty never said anything about it.

Louise knew what kind of business Lefty was in, that he came and went when he wanted to, like all the wiseguys do. They seemed to have a comfortable relationship. Lefty talked openly in front of her, but without swearing. That's a thing about wiseguys. You can go out and kill somebody, but don't swear in front of a female. And if a female swears, she's a *puttana*—a whore. "If Louise said 'fuck,' I'd throw her out the window," he said.

In September they decided to get married. Lefty asked me to be best man. The wedding was at City Hall. They were all dressed up. Lefty was so nervous that he forgot to pick up the license. The ceremony was at five P.M., and the license bureau was closed. The judge got his clerk to go down and get the license.

I gave them $200 as a wedding gift. We went to CaSa Bella to celebrate. Maybe ten people. Mike came over and sat down with us to have a drink. Then we went uptown to Château Madrid, Lefty's favorite place, where we saw a floor show with flamenco dancing.

"You ever do a hit on anybody, Donnie?" Lefty asked.

"I never had a contract, if that's what you mean. I killed a couple guys. One guy in a fight, another guy that fucked me out of a score and we got into a beef."

"That ain't a hit."

"If you kill somebody, you kill somebody, what's the difference?"

"No, Donnie, you don't understand. It ain't that simple. That's why I gotta school you. Hitting a guy on a contract is a lot different than whacking a guy over a beef. On a beef, you got a rage about the guy. But on a contract you might have no feelings one way or another about the guy, it might not even concern you why the guy's getting hit. You got to be able to do it just like a professional job, with no emotion at all. You think you could do that?"

"I don't see why not."

"Yeah, well, we'll see. Lot of guys think it's easy, then they freeze up and can't do it. Next time I get a contract, I'll take you with me, show you how to do it. Generally you use a .22. A .22 doesn't make a clean hole like some bigger calibers. Just right behind the ear. A .22 ricochets around your skull, tears everything up. Next contract I get, I'll take you along."

What would I do if and when that situation came up? As an agent, I can't allow a hit to go through, can't condone it, certainly can't participate in it, if I know it's going to happen. But I could find myself in the situation all of a sudden. I didn't always know where we were going or why, and it wasn't appropriate to ask.

If a hit is going down and I'm on the scene, do I risk trying to stop it and maybe getting killed myself? My decision was that if it came to it, if the target was a wiseguy and it came down to whether it was him or me, it was going to be him that got whacked. If it was an ordinary citizen, then I would take the risk and try to stop it.

*   *   *

By midsummer of 1977, I was really becoming accepted and trusted and could move around easily. I knew most of the regular wiseguys down on Mulberry Street, not only Bonannos but guys from other crews. I was given the familiar hugs and kisses on the cheek that wiseguys exchange. I could come and go in any of the joints I wanted. I could move in and out. A lot of times we would hang out at 116 Madison Street, the Holiday Bar, a place so dingy that I would only drink beer or club soda out of a bottle, I wouldn't touch a glass. Social clubs, coffee shops, CaSa Bella. We would hang around, play gin, and everybody would tell war stories to each other and bust balls.

I met guys like Al Walker, Tony Mirra's uncle, whose real name was Al Embarrato. Mirra's nephew, Joey D'Amico, who went by the name of "Joe Moak." Big Willie Ravielo who ran the numbers in Harlem for Nicky Marangello; Joey Massino, a beefy, broad-shouldered, potbellied man who was rising quickly through the ranks; Nicky Santora, who had served time for bookmaking and aspired to be a partner with Lefty; the Chilli brothers, Joe and Jerry.

And then there were Frankie Fish, Porkie, Bobby Smash, Louie Ha Ha, Bobby Badheart (because he wore a pacemaker), Joe Red, and so on.

Real names didn't mean anything to these guys. They didn't introduce by last names. I knew guys that had been hanging out together for five or ten years and didn't know each other's last names. Nobody cares. You were introduced by a first name or a nickname. If you don't volunteer somebody's last name, nobody'll ask you. That's just the code. The feeling is, if you wanted me to know a name, you would have told me.

The reason I knew guys' last names was through our own FBI identification. I always tried to get some kind of ID on everybody that came through the scene, even if it was just a nickname. You never knew who might turn out to be important somewhere down the road, or in some other investigation.

I told Lefty I had a girlfriend in Jersey and that sometimes when he called my apartment and I wasn't there, I was probably with her. Over a period of time the topic of my girlfriend came up a lot. I never volunteered a name. He never asked what her name was. Nobody did.

All through 1977, Lefty didn't tell me his last name. I *knew* his name, of course, but he didn't tell me. I didn't tell him mine. I knew him as Lefty and Bennie. He knew me as Donnie. I used to go to his house on Sundays or at night and eat with him and Louise. I'd watch TV with them. I'd lie on the couch and fall asleep. He never told me his last name or asked me mine. The first time we traveled together and checked into a hotel, he said, "What name do you want me to put down for you?" That was how he found out my name was Brasco. And the first time I had to check him in someplace, that was when I asked him what his last name was.

All during this time I was passing on to the Bureau more intelligence about the structure of the Bonanno family and other families: how they operated, who was who and what rank, information on the Mafia nation-wide, intelligence we've never had before from an agent on the inside. I was continuing to pick up information on the Sicilian mafiosi that were being brought over, how Galante and Carlo Gambino were collaborating on setting them up in pizza-parlor businesses in the East and the Midwest and leaving them there until the bosses needed them to do something. How these "zips" were being used as heroin couriers and hit men.

To ease the tension I used to try to run every day, and lift weights at the health club in my apartment building. I didn't know any wiseguys at the time who were doing that. It was okay, I was just considered a health nut. On most Sundays I would try to go to Mass. Wiseguys didn't do that, either.

Lefty was treating me like we were pretty close. He saw me as a good earner. I didn't portray myself as somebody having a big bank account or big business because I didn't want to get tagged as a mark. I wanted to get tagged as a working thief. I portrayed myself just like they were—you make a score, you live good for two or three weeks, then you're back to scrounging again. He saw just enough money come out of me to suggest that I could make a lot. He needed that, because he was in trouble.

"I owe a lot of fucking money," he told me. "I'm in hock a hundred and sixty thousand to Nicky. I can't get no place with that debt hanging over my head. It's like I'm spinning my wheels. We gotta make some money."

Unlike most wiseguys, Lefty had not served time in prison. He had been arrested many times for extortion and theft but had always beaten the rap. Lefty's real problem was that he was a degenerate gambler. If he made $2,000 one day, he would blow $3,000 at the track the next day. I knew him to lose as much as $10,000 in one day at the track or an OTB (Off-Track Betting) parlor. If he went through that and had $2 left, he'd bet that too. He preferred bookies because at OTB, if you win, you pay them a percentage right off the top; with bookies you don't pay them anything if you win, and they pay better odds than the state does.

I'm the world's worst gambler. I couldn't win at craps, at cards, or at the track. I wouldn't bet on anything ever if it weren't for this job. But Lefty was worse. He had no more skill, his luck was just as bad, but he was the typical gambling addict. The big killing was just around the corner.

Sometimes we'd pop down to Florida for a little vacation. We'd hit the dog tracks and the horse tracks. He didn't know much about the dogs. We might win or lose $100 or $200. Mostly we lost. He didn't know much about the horses, either. We didn't get inside tips. Lefty would just handicap by the program.

One time we were at Hialeah and we went for the "pick six." For the first five races we invested a couple of thousand on long shots and won every time. The sixth race was worth about $30,000 if we picked right. So we figured that in this last race we'd bet the favorite, to be safer. The favorite lost. So we blew a shot at $30,000.

His reaction was: "Finally we bet the chalk horse, the fucking horse loses. That other horse hadda come from nowhere. Thirty fucking thousand we coulda won."

"Well, we only lost a couple grand," I said.

"Ain't the question, Donnie. The point is, we had it right in our fucking hands!"

His problem was so bad that it had delayed his becoming a made guy. He told me that when I first met him, he wasn't made yet, and that was because he hadn't paid off his gambling debts. He whittled them down some, and because of that he was able to get made shortly after I met him, in the summer of 1977.

But now he was in hock again for this huge amount, and that meant that everything he made from the bookmaking or anything else, Marangello was taking Lefty's piece right off the top to apply to the debt, and Lefty never had anything, except what he could hide. The nature of the game was that everybody always pled poverty, anyway, so you could never be sure whether Lefty was broke or not.

I brought around just enough money to convince Lefty that I was a good earner, with potential that he could develop. Together we could make our fortune, as Lefty saw it.

He encouraged me about my future in the mob.

"The thing is, Donnie, you gotta keep your nose clean. You gotta be a good earner and don't get into trouble, don't offend, don't insult anybody, and you're gonna be a made guy someday. Now, the only thing is, they might give you a contract to go out and whack somebody. But don't worry about it. Like I told you, I'll show you how. You got the makings, Donnie. You handle yourself right, keep your nose clean, keep on the good side of people, I'll propose you for membership."

Lefty says, "Come on, we got to go up to Sabella's."

It's a hot July night. We go to CaSa Bella but we don't go in. There are five or six other guys standing outside on the sidewalk, guys I recognize as being under Mike Sabella. We stand on the sidewalk with these other guys.

I ask Lefty, "Why the hell are we standing here?"

"We're out here to make sure nothing happens to the Old Man. He's in there."

The Old Man is Carmine Galante, the boss of the Bonanno family. He just recently got out of prison. I look in the restaurant window and I can see him sitting at the table reserved for big shots; he's hawk-nosed, almost bald, has a big cigar in his mouth. Sabella and a few others are seated with him.

"What's the big deal?" I say. "What's gonna happen to him?"

"Things are going on," he says. "There's a lot of things you don't know, Donnie. Things I can't talk about."

"Well, why can't we go inside and make sure nothing happens to him in there, where at least we could sit down?"

"Donnie, Donnie, listen to me. You don't understand nothing sometimes. In the first place, Lilo don't sit down with anybody except captains or above—bosses. He don't sit down with soldiers or below, like me and you. He doesn't have anybody around him except people he wants. You can't even talk to this guy. You got to go through somebody higher, somebody that can talk to him. He don't want nobody in the restaurant except those people in there, and that's it."

"Okay, if you say so."

"You don't know how mean this guy is, Donnie," Lefty goes on quietly. "Lilo is a mean son of a bitch, a tyrant. That's just me telling you, it don't go no further. Lot of people hate him. They feel he's only out for himself. He's the only one making any money. There's only a few people that he's close to. And mainly that's the zips, like Caesar and those that you see around Toyland. Those guys are always with him. He brought them over from Sicily, and he uses them for different pieces of work and for dealing all that junk. They're as mean as he is. You can't trust those bastard zips. Nobody can. Except the Old Man. He can trust them because he brought them over here and he can control them. Everybody else has to steer clear of him. There's a lot of people out there who would like to see him get whacked. That's why we're here."

This happened a few times, Lefty and I going down to CaSa Bella to stand guard outside while Carmine Galante held meetings inside. Lefty was nervous, out there on the sidewalk. He and the other guards, except me, were carrying guns in their waistbands under their shirts. He watched people and cars going by. He watched windows across the street.

I wasn't comfortable, either. Here I was, an FBI agent, worried about getting whacked on this sidewalk on Mulberry Street because I was trusted enough by these mobsters to be standing guard over the feared boss of the Bonanno family.

Every few days I would call in to my contact agent. There was a special telephone line installed in the New York office for my calls only, and it would be answered by my contact agent. I would give him a rundown on what had been going on and what was coming up. Sometimes, for other operations, he would ask me to find out what's going on at this or that club, who's showing up or what's being discussed. If I needed anything checked out—like a name or what a guy was into—he would take care of that for me. Any information I gave him that was noteworthy and that might be useful as evidence would be typed up as what we call "302s." Once in a while the contact agent would bring along a handful of these reports for me to initial.

Once or twice a month, depending upon my circumstances, I met with a contact agent to get an envelope of cash for me to live and operate on. We would meet only briefly, usually just a couple of minutes. Often we met at museums—like the Guggenheim or the Metropolitan on Fifth Avenue. We would just be browsing, looking at the exhibits, he'd slip me the money. Sometimes we met on a bench in Central Park. Sometimes at a coffee shop.

We were approaching the end of 1977, and I had been undercover now for more than a year. The Bureau was about to close down the "Sun" part of Sun Apple in Florida, just settle for what Joe Fitz had been able to get so far without risking him down there any longer for minimal gains.

Once in a while my supervisor asked me how I felt, if I wanted to go a little longer. I felt fine. I wanted to keep right on going.

There were a couple of new considerations. I now had a good foothold with Lefty and the Bonannos. I was in pretty solid. The Bureau had started other undercover operations around the country. We could use my new mob credentials to establish credibility of other undercover agents in some of these other operations. I could be brought around to vouch for these other agents—attest that they were "good" badguys. Badguy targets of these other operations could check me out: I'm a friend of Lefty's in New York.

It would be easier for me to do this if I wasn't based in New York City, under Lefty's thumb and eye on a day-to-day basis. If I moved someplace else while remaining Lefty's partner, I could more easily slip around to these other undercover operations without having to ask permission to go out of town and without having Lefty knowing of my every move and questioning me about it. Also, conceivably I could bring Lefty out to these other operations, introduce him, hope that he might horn in, establish a link with the Bonannos that would form a conspiracy under the law.

I could still regularly come back to New York for two or three weeks at a time, continue to develop my association with Lefty, and maintain the partnership.

The other consideration was my family. Earlier I hadn't been too concerned about protection of my family. I would get home to our house in New Jersey maybe one night every ten days or two weeks. I was always careful and covered my tracks. But by the fall of 1977, I was beginning to think that if I continued to get deeper into the mob, eventually my family was going to have to move away. There was always the chance of momentary carelessness that could be disastrous. I knew I was under surveillance by cops because I was being followed. Three or four times I was stopped and searched—for no apparent reason. Suppose I didn't shake them off my tail sometime and they followed me right to my house? Or what if Lefty or some other wiseguy decided to follow me?

It was time to get my family out of there. That would eliminate that problem. And if I was going to be transferred out to another area, we might as well combine the two.

Through December and into January, I discussed this with my supervisor. He took the matter to headquarters. It was a pretty simple proposition. We decided to make the moves on February 1.

My family was used to moving. We had already moved four times for my job. But now my daughters were at an age where attachments to friends and boyfriends were more important. We had close relatives in New Jersey. When we moved back there for my earlier transfer to the New York office, we had supposed we would be staying. Nobody wanted to move again. My wife understood that it was necessary, without knowing the details. We didn't have big discussions about it, because I didn't present it as a choice. I was being transferred. They still didn't know how deeply involved I was with the Mafia. They didn't know the move had to do with their safety.

The FBI then had fifty-two offices throughout the country. They gave us the choice of five areas in which to relocate. As far as my work was concerned, where we lived didn't matter because I would still be assigned to the New York case, and otherwise I would be roaming to different parts of the country. My wife and I picked an area.

I managed to get home late Christmas Eve and spend most of Christmas Day at home. In January, my wife and I took a trip to find a new house. We found one right away—smaller than our house in Jersey but in a pleasant neighborhood. The next week we put our New Jersey house up for sale. I had a friend who was a mover. I told him we needed to move and that he shouldn't talk about it.

There were lots of family tears shed over the move. Nobody wanted to stand in the way of the work I was doing, but neither did anybody really know what I was doing. Had my family known more, they might have been more tolerant of my situation. But if that would have decreased the weight on me, it would have been at the cost of more fear to them.

For me and my colleagues in the Bureau, there had been no expectation that this job would go on so long. Now there was no guess at how long it would continue. What started with the idea of getting to fences had become penetrating the Mafia in Little Italy and now had evolved to me representing the mob in other places. It could have been mind-boggling except for the fact that we didn't know where we were headed, and so we had no good perspective on where we were. The only certainty was that to continue at all I had to continue full-out. Donnie Brasco had the momentum.

The FBI had a couple of situations in San Diego and Los Angeles that they wanted me to look into. I told Lefty I had decided to go back to California—where I had supposedly spent a lot of my earlier jewel-thief life—for a while. "You know, Left," I said, "I'm not making all that much money here right now. Why don't I go out there and start making some good scores, you know, and come back and forth? You could even come out there, hang out for a couple weeks, see if we couldn't get something going."

He thought that was a good idea. So I took off for California.

In L.A., we had an agent going by the undercover name of Larry Keaton. Larry was a longtime friend of mine. He was trying to get in tight with some thieves who were engaged in all kinds of property crimes: thefts of stocks and bonds, checks, cars—the whole spectrum. These badguys were not necessarily Mafia, but some of them were ex-New Yorkers, and naturally they were respectful of wiseguys and connected guys.

They liked to hang out at a particular restaurant, and Larry would mix with them, trying to get in deeper. It happened that a bartender from a New York restaurant came out on vacation, and he hung out at this L.A. restaurant and was friendly with some of these badguys. Larry didn't know anything about this bartender. He thought maybe he was a badguy too. Since the bartender was from New York, Larry thought it was just possible I might know him.

It so happened that I did. It was a coincidence that on occasion Lefty and I went to La Maganette, a restaurant on Third Avenue and Fifty-fifth Street—not a Bonanno hangout, just a place where he and I and a couple other guys would go have a couple drinks and eat. We got to know this bartender, Johnny. Johnny wasn't himself a badguy, wasn't into anything, but like a lot bartenders, he knew who was who. He knew who Lefty was, and that as Lefty's partner I was a connected guy. So this was a chance for me to give Larry some credibility with these badguys.

I went to this L.A. restaurant where Larry was hanging out and saw Johnny there. "Hey, Johnny," I said, "how you doing?"

"Donnie, how you been? What're you doing out here?"

"Hanging out, looking around." Larry was in the group, so obviously he had already met Johnny. "I see you know Larry here. Larry's a friend of mine. We may be working on a deal together."

We chatted a little while, and the job was done. I knew that Johnny would tell the badguys there that I was a connected guy back in New York, and that Larry was a friend of mine, so he was all right.

On and off I would hook up with Larry like that to help him gain credibility. Sometimes we'd go to the track with some badguys, things like that. I was just somebody to introduce. I never worked on his cases. He took it from there. He started making a bunch of cases. It was the type of operation where the government was continually arresting people as Larry brought in the evidence. Eventually he had to testify in court several times and got a load of convictions.

In the middle of this, Larry had occasion to come to New York to pursue yet another case of stolen stocks. I was also back in New York at that time, on one of my regular trips. Larry called Johnny the bartender to tell him he would be coming in. They set up a meet at P. J. Clarke's, on Third Avenue because that's where Johnny liked to hang out in the afternoon.

So I hooked up with Larry and we went down to P. J. Clarke's together. Johnny had a table in the back of the room with a bunch of people. We joined them.

Johnny introduced us around, and we were sitting there an hour or so.

Now, Larry is black. That means that in some badguy situations he was conspicuous. But he was smooth enough to make it work.

I see a guy headed for our table. Suddenly Larry whispers to me, "Let's get outa here. Back door, quick." He stands up and says to Johnny, "I just forgot, we got an appointment."

I hustle Larry out the side door.

"Pretty close," Larry says. "Did you see that guy coming toward our table, the guy in the suit? He was a defense attorney from L.A. He's seen me testify in court."

"I got us covered from this end," I say, "with Lefty, just in case."

"Good," he says. "And I'm outa here tomorrow, anyway."

This kind of situation—a chance discovery or somebody reporting back on you—can happen at any minute of any day. You can't wait for it to happen and then think of a way to protect yourself. You have to lay groundwork to cover yourself ahead of time—all the time. I knew Lefty would get a call on this.

From the time I began in California, I stayed in virtual daily touch with Lefty. He didn't know how to reach me directly. I said I was always moving around. While Lefty was schooling me, I was also schooling him about me. I wanted him to get used to the fact that I was unpredictable. I would be vague about what I was doing, where I was. When I needed to cover myself, he would already be used to my style.

I had a couple of "hello" phones where he could leave messages, and I called him. In this case, after meeting Larry and Johnny out there, I had called Lefty and told him about running into Johnny in California. "Guess who I bumped into in L.A.," I had told him. "Johnny. He was out there on vacation, seeing a bunch of guys. He was with this one guy named Larry who was into some kind of stocks-and-bonds deal. In fact, I think I'm going to look into that. I think we can make some money there."

That's what I had told Lefty. Because even without this surprise at P. J. Clarke's, I knew that sometime when I was with Lefty at La Maganette, the bartender Johnny was going to say something like, "How's that guy Larry in L.A.?" And then Lefty was going to say, "Who's Larry?"

So this way I had already introduced the name to Lefty. I had also suggested that Larry was hanging around with Johnny rather than with me—just enough of an offhand twist to protect Larry and me.

Sure enough, the next day Lefty grabbed me at the club.

"Hey, Donnie, that guy you were with in L.A., what's the story on him?"

"Larry? That's the guy I told you about that I met through Johnny the bartender. The wheeler-dealer I told you I was trying to do a stocks-and-bonds deal with. What are you upset about?"

"I'll tell you what I'm upset about. I got a call from Johnny. I wanna know the whole story, what you were doing with that guy at P. J. Clarke's."

"Hey, Left, all I know is, I meet this guy Larry in L.A. He tells me he's got some stolen stock deals going. He's coming to New York, and we plan to hook up. So we're at P. J.'s, and he's got this three o'clock appointment at the Sheraton, for us to meet this guy on the stock deal. So we leave P. J.'s and go to the Sheraton. The guy doesn't show. So I say, 'Well, too bad.' And I leave. That's it. What's the matter?"

"I'll tell you what's the matter, you jerk-off. That guy's a fucking federal agent! Johnny said a guy came in while you were there, some lawyer, and he seen you guys leaving the table, and he says to Johnny, 'I seen that guy testifying in court, he's a fucking agent.' That's what he told Johnny. Johnny tells me you're hanging around with a fucking federal agent!"

"Hey, Left, that's hard to believe. But, anyway, I don't care what he is, he doesn't know anything about me. I didn't tell him anything about us or anything else. All he knows is I might be interested in a deal. He doesn't even know where to find me. Nothing to worry about, Left."

"Maybe Johnny's full of shit, Donnie. I don't know. But stay away from this guy, Larry. Understand? Just in case. Don't have nothing to do with him. Donnie, sometimes I think you're not too careful."

"Don't worry about it, Left."

So I couldn't do anything more with Larry in the Los Angeles area. But he had his operation well under control. His cases eventually brought in some two hundred thieves, and the government recovered $42 million in stolen property.

If Larry hadn't spotted that lawyer coming into P. J. Clarke's, my whole Mafia project might have ended right there.

Anyplace I traveled, I tried to touch base or make contact with any wiseguys that I knew of in the area—Bonanno guys or any others that I had met. That established me as a guy with connections, a guy good at freewheeling around the country, a guy with things going on. The more places I was seen, the more times I was recognized by wiseguys, the better my credentials.

Back in California, the Bureau had their eye on some restaurants and nightclubs in the San Diego and La Jolla area and wanted to know if they were mobbed up. I went to these places just to size them up first so I could talk intelligently about them.

Then I called Lefty. I told him I was hitting a few joints out there, trying to line some things up, and that it looked like I had found a couple of places where some wiseguys hung out or had a piece of.

"Why don't you come out here, Left? Maybe we can get something going. If these joints aren't already wiseguy joints, maybe we could do something to move in on one of them. And also, it's nice out here—nice weather, the ocean."

"I never been to San Diego. Is it like Miami?"

I booked us a room at the Sheraton, right on the water. I picked him up at the airport and carried his bags—catered to him the way anybody in the organization is supposed to treat their superior. I told him I had made a score recently and gave him his end.

During the day we toured San Diego, just the two of us, because neither one of us knew anybody in San Diego. Lefty was impressed. "Nice ocean," he said. "Nice city. Clean. Not like New York. The people dress different."

I took him to the San Diego Zoo. "This place is amazing," Lefty said. "Think of the Bronx Zoo. Look how they really take care of this place. Donnie, San Diego is the kind of place where you can walk around and not be afraid of getting mugged."

Everything he saw, he evaluated in terms of how it would go in New York, how much money you could make. "Can you imagine if we had this in New York, Donnie?" he'd say about some kind of store or vending operation or location. "We'd make a fortune." Everything was a scheme or a scam.

Evenings we went to the joints the Bureau had targeted. I watched Lefty operate.

He would get into innocuous conversations with the managers or maître d's: Nice place. How long you been in business? How'd you find dependable suppliers? Looks like you keep everything running real smooth. Anybody give you troubles with a place like this—the city or unions or anybody?

He'd size the place up, look for little things. He pointed out to me things he was seeing. Maybe there's a guy hanging around the cash register not doing anything. See who talks to him. See if there's a guy sitting at a certain table all the time, no meal in front of him, like he's just waiting to talk to people. And people go over one at a time and sit down and have conversation with him and then leave. Watch how people treat him. See how the waitresses treat the guy. An ordinary citizen could look at this and not see anything. A wiseguy sees things if there are wiseguy things to see: how a person acts, carries himself, talks; what deference is paid to him.

We confirmed the Bureau's suspicions. In one place Lefty knew a couple of the guys involved. Each of the others, he said, looked like they were either mob operations or mob-connected.

"We can't fuck around with these places, Donnie," Lefty said, "because they're already mobbed up."

To do my job better and to stay alive, I was working at picking these things up. I was adjusting my demeanor and the way I looked at things. So that I could ask the right questions and see the right things, I was learning not only how to act like a wiseguy, but also how to think like a wiseguy. When Lefty and I bounced around to different spots, I began to see the same things he did, pick up things the way he did. Like wiseguys, I was learning not to volunteer that I didn't know things. Keep your mouth shut and absorb as fast as possible. The key is, you act like you know, so that by the time they find out you didn't, you do.

Lefty was the epitome of the wiseguy. He was at it twenty-four hours a day, scheming. On the street, in wiseguy situations, he was savvy and sharp and tough. That's why he got a lot of respect from wiseguys. But you take him off his turf and you find out he's just a small-town guy in some ways, unsophisticated about the rest of the world.

One afternoon we're sitting in the lounge of a hotel, and there is this really nice-looking woman across the room who keeps looking at me.

"That lady can't take her eyes off you, Donnie," Lefty says. "Why don't you invite her over to the table?"

I smile, she smiles. "Lefty, she's probably a hooker."

"Naw, Donnie, you're nuts. She's too nice. Good clothes. Hookers don't dress like that."

"Left, this is California. People dress different."

"Not hookers. She's probably a regular business lady. Come on, Donnie, she thinks you're a good-looking guy, and she'd like to get to know you. Invite her over."

The only way to stop Lefty when he got onto something was to do what he said. So I ask the waitress to invite the woman to our table. She comes over and sits down. Lefty doesn't want to be in the way of this sweet flirtation, so right away he says, "Well, I think I'll go up and take a little nap," and he leaves.

I chat with the lady, and it doesn't take five minutes to find out that she is a hooker. I go up to the room and tell Lefty. "I can't believe it!" he says. "She didn't have all the makeup or the short skirt or anything. How you supposed to tell?" He laughs. "Hey, Donnie, you got to watch yourself out here. You'll lose all your New York instincts."

Although he traveled a lot on mob business, he was used to somebody booking his flights. When he had to join me someplace, he wanted me to book his flights. I found out why one time when he had to book his own flight. He got intimidated and called me. "Donnie, at the airline they wanna know when I'm coming back."

"We don't know. Just tell them you want an open return."

"What's an open return?"

"That means you'll have the return ticket already paid for and in your hands, but you just won't have a date on it. Then when you're ready to go back, you just call the airline and tell them the date you want to fly."

"You can do that?"

Lefty stayed about a week that first trip, then he wanted me to come back to New York with him. I told him I couldn't because I had a potential big score that I had to look into. That pacified him. That meant money for him.

What I really had to do was go to Milwaukee. The Bureau had set up an operation there to bag the Milwaukee Mafia family, but it was slow getting off the ground. They contacted me to see if I had any ideas.

The undercover agent working the case went by the name of Tony Conte. Tony was a friend, a tough street agent. The boss of the Milwaukee family—which was answerable to the Chicago mob, rather than New York—was Frank Balistrieri. We knew that Balistrieri controlled all the vending-machine business in the city. The Bureau wanted to show that it was done illegally through hidden ownerships and mob muscle. The idea was for Conte to set up his own vending-machine business and try to get his machines into various stores and bars and clubs. Then if Balistrieri tried to muscle him out of business, we could make an extortion case.

Conte had set up his fake personal background, opened a small office in Milwaukee, applied to the city for a vending license, bought a couple of machines. And he went around to the clubs and bars trying to solicit business. But he hadn't made any inroads.

The problem was, Balistrieri had the city tied up so tight that nobody would accept any of Conte's machines. The places that Conte went refused his machines because they already had machines that belonged to Frank Balistrieri. Nobody wanted to move Balistrieri's machines out to put Conte's in.

After a month or so he still hadn't been able to install any of his machines, and nobody had approached him to warn him off. So he called me and asked if there was any possibility that I might get some of my New York contacts involved. If I could get somebody from New York interested in Conte's vending business, then they might try to form a partnership with Balistrieri.

So I made a trip to Milwaukee. I checked into a motel and called Conte. He came over with the case agent, Mike Potkonjak. It didn't matter if Conte was seen with me, because he was operating undercover, anyway, so nobody out there knew who he really was. And only the case agent in Milwaukee knew who I was. They filled me in on the operation—exactly what Conte had done so far.

It sounded feasible to me. I said I would try to introduce the idea to Lefty and see what happened.

I went to New York. I had given up my apartment, so on these visits now I took a room either at the Holiday Inn on Route 80 on the Jersey side of the George Washington Bridge, or at the Sheraton Centre on Seventh Avenue. It was just a place to sleep, anyway. Most of the time I was with Lefty. He was always after me to come back to New York to stay; he didn't like me being in California. Partly it was because he missed me, partly it was because he really thought California was for lying on the beach and hustling broads and getting your brains scrambled. He was always after me to take an apartment in Knickerbocker Village, where he lived. In fact, eventually he had it all set up for me to take an apartment and just keep it for my visits.

Whenever I was coming in, he'd say, "What do you want to eat when we get home?" Because he would cook for me and his wife, Louise. He would go out and buy special veal cutlets from the best outlet. Or maybe he'd make lasagna from scratch. Or if we decided to eat out, we'd wait for Louise to get home from work, then go to a Chinese restaurant. He liked to talk to me about his kids, his grandchildren, any problems he was having with Mike Sabella or anybody else.

On this trip I planted the seed for Milwaukee.

For everything I did, every operation with Lefty, I first laid a foundation, introduced the matter in casual conversation, and dropped it. Brought it up again, dropped it. Then finally brought it up and made it stick. On Milwaukee I didn't want to lay it all out at once, about having a friend out there who's trying to get into the vending business and is having trouble, etc. Because I figured I was going to be cultivating Lefty for other operations down the line, and I didn't want him to say, "Hey, how come you always got a friend in trouble someplace?"

We're just shooting the breeze about California, and I say, "You know what, Left, I ran into a guy that I knew ten years ago in Baltimore. We pulled a few jobs together back in those days. Now he tells me he's been semi-legit for all these years since, and now he's about to go into business. I think he's going into the vending-machine business."

"Oh, yeah?" Lefty says. "Tough racket." That's all he says.

I didn't even tell him where it was. I just let him swallow that first mention, let him digest it. Conte was ready to move in Milwaukee. I had started priming Lefty. In coming weeks I would mention it again in little ways. All we needed now were the right circumstances. I went back to California.

The Bureau had come up with some more places they wanted checked out. "You know, Left," I said over the telephone, "I really like California. You ought to give it a chance. You're always talking about how you'd like to open up a bar of your own somewhere. I've got a line on a couple places out here. Why don't you come out for a little vacation; we'll look these places over."

So in May, Lefty came out to San Diego again. I showed him a good time. We went to the track a few times, and we looked into a couple of bars and restaurants.

Then I got a break on Milwaukee.

Lefty got a call from his daughter. His son, Tommy, had been arrested for armed robbery in Manhattan. Apparently he had tried to stick up some guy who was carrying a bunch of diamonds in the midtown diamond district. Cops chased him; he fired some shots.

The fact that Tommy had committed a robbery and shot at cops and been caught was no big deal. That's part of the game, to get arrested and spend time in jail. A wiseguy doesn't worry about his kid being in jail like a citizen would. What made it a big deal was that it turned out that the guy he robbed was a connected guy with another family.

Lefty was very upset. "Can you believe it?" he says to me. "That dumb shit Tommy. This guy is connected to a heavyweight. There's gonna be a sitdown over this, Donnie. I just hope I can work something out so Tommy don't get whacked out over this. Donnie, I need a thousand right away. Where can we come up with a grand?"

He was hitting on me for money to take to the sitdown so he could patch things over with a payoff. That didn't mean he didn't have the money. It was another instance of a wiseguy avoiding using his own money if at all possible—even when his son's life was in danger. He knew I didn't have the money either—or that I would be as reluctant as he was to part with my own.

But it was an opening for me. Typically money was the key. These guys, money is their whole life, scamming people, getting money from somebody for free. They're never going to go to a bank for a loan.

I say, "Hey, maybe we could call that guy—remember that old friend I told you about, the one I knew in Baltimore? If he's got money to open a vending-machine business, maybe we can get something from him. It's worth a shot."

"Yeah, try that," Lefty says.

I went to my room and called Tony Conte in Milwaukee. "Tony, I think we got the opening. We might have to come up with some bread for Lefty." I explained the situation. I never intended to give Lefty all he asked for. "Maybe we can get away with five hundred."

"That's no big deal," Tony said. "Let's do it."

We always had to consider the value when we laid out relatively big taxpayer bucks. But here we were talking about the possibility of getting to a major crime boss, what the hell's $500?

I went back and told Lefty that Tony said he would lend us the money. And I dropped another seed: "Tony's got quite a few bucks, I think, to invest in this vending-machine business he wants to start."

All that concerned him was that the guy would lend him the G-note. "All right," he said with his customary gratitude, "we gotta get back to New York right away and get this straightened out about my kid."

We flew back to New York the next day. Lefty had to make a lot of phone calls and go to a couple sitdowns to try to settle the beef. He told them that Tommy didn't know who the guy was, didn't know he was connected, that he had just gotten a tip from somebody that the guy was carrying diamonds. So it was all just a big mistake. It cost Lefty five grand, just as a pacifier, to settle that beef.

"What about that guy with the money?" Lefty asked me. "When you gonna get that grand for me?"

It was time to set the Milwaukee hook.

9

MILWAUKEE

"What about that grand you were gonna get for me from that guy?" Lefty asks. "When you gonna get it?"

We were eating a delicious dinner of veal cutlets in his apartment.

"I'm gonna call the guy, but I wanted to talk to you first. There may be some money in it. He says he's just been a working stiff at a factory for several years, and he's saved up quite a bit. Now he wants to go into the vending-machine business. His wife gave him a load of money for it, to go with what he saved. But he's running into some problems. I figure if we could help him out, maybe we could get a piece of the business or something."

"The guy's all right?"

"He was all right when I knew him in Baltimore. I never had any problems with him." Whenever I introduced another agent in, my escape hatch was that I never vouched for him one hundred percent—I knew the guy, he was all right to me, you draw your own conclusions. In case anything went wrong down the line, that protected me and the operation.

"Where'd you say he was?"

"Milwaukee."

"Milwaukee! Is he connected?"

"No. He don't know anything about the mob."

Lefty slaps his fork down. "He's crazy, Donnie. Doesn't the fucking guy know you can't operate a vending business anywhere without connections? Especially Milwaukee. They're crazy out there. It ain't like in New York, Donnie, where they may just throw you a beating to chase you out. Out there they're vicious. They answer to Chicago, you know. They blow people up. Donnie, if this guy's a friend of yours, you better tell him to get the hell out of that town. Why don't you tell him to move the business back to Baltimore? Baltimore's controlled by the crews from Philly and Jersey. They're easier to deal with."

"The guy's been living out there for a while, Lefty. He's got his family there and everything. He doesn't want to leave."

"Tell him to forget about it. How much money does the guy have?"

"Something like a hundred, two hundred grand."

That touches his soul. "You said his name is Tony? Look, you better let me talk to him. You go out there and get Tony and bring him back. With the thousand he said he'd give me. I actually need more than a grand, Donnie, so tell him to bring two. And we'll talk."

I went out to Milwaukee and met with Tony and the case agent, Mike Potkonjak. They filled me in on the extent of Frank Balistrieri's stranglehold on Milwaukee. The main thing we would try to do was get New York into a meeting with Balistrieri so as maybe to become business partners, with Conte's Best Vending Company the business.

In the years I was under, I would never collaborate with or introduce another agent into an operation unless I knew him ahead of time and trusted his skills and toughness completely. Every agent I introduced in had been a top street agent before going undercover. We are trusting each other with our lives.

Conte was experienced on the street but inexperienced with the mob. He was an unpretentious Midwestern guy who could, if he wanted to, give the appearance of being a hick. Tough as he was, he was no city slicker.

Conte and I went over the situation very carefully. We spent time discussing how to act, when to talk and not to talk, and so forth. I stressed: Don't try to impress upon Lefty that you know anything about the mob. We're going to play this realistically—you're ignorant about the Mafia. Naturally you know there's a mob. You know that I'm mobbed up. But even though you're supposed to be Italian (he was not), you didn't grow up with the mob, so you don't know how everything works. You don't know what it means to talk out of turn. You don't know what the proper channels are. You don't know the rules. You don't know anybody, you don't know about being connected, you don't know about protocol. That way you'll get away with more. If you make a mistake, we fall back on your ignorance.

I was the intermediary in fact and in fiction, the buffer. But he was the guy with the vending-machine business. He would deal with Lefty on the business matters.

As always with undercover agents, we would use our undercover names when dealing with each other even in private. Tony and Donnie. That way you never slip out of character.

We flew into New York at night and drove down to Monroe Street, near Lefty's. I called him from the phone booth on the corner of Cherry and Monroe. "We're downstairs," I tell Lefty. "Come on down, I want you to meet this guy. I got some bread for you."

"Leave the guy in the car. You just stay by the phone and I'll be right down."

He comes down. I hand him the cash.

"It's only five hundred," I say.

"Donnie, you said you was coming up with a thousand. I was counting on a thousand."

"He had to pay for the plane fare and everything, Left. He said that's all he could come up with on short notice. The guy promises a thousand, he shows up with five hundred. What do you want me to do, Left? It's better than nothing."

Down the block, under a streetlight, Conte is leaning against the car, looking around at the sights. He is wearing white shoes and a white belt. He is an avid golfer.

Lefty glances at him. "All right. I don't want to see this guy right now. Tomorrow you come by the house.

You can fill me in on the background, and we'll go from there."

Conte and I were staying at the Sheraton Centre. That night I told Conte, "I think we got him."

The next day around noon we headed down to Little Italy. Conte had never been there. He wanted to go to Vincent's Clam Bar on Mott Street to try some calamari and scungilli. I dropped him off and went to Lefty's.

Lefty was more interested now because Conte had actually come to New York to see him and had actually given him some money. I gave Lefty the rundown on Conte's situation in Milwaukee.

"Milwaukee is bad," he says. "If this guy doesn't get connected, there's a good chance they'll kill him out there. But if he's got the kind of money you say he has, maybe we can work something out. If we do this, we got to give Mike a cut, then we got to give the people in Milwaukee a cut, so we got to make sure he's got the money and he's willing to give up the money. How much would he be willing to give us a week if we get him the shot to operate his business out there?"

"I don't know, Left. You got to talk to him about that."

"Okay, meet me tonight seven-thirty at La Maganette, and I'll talk to him. Where is he now?"

"Vincent's. He wanted some calamari."

"Donnie, you crazy bastard. If he's dressed anything like he was last night, he looks like a fucking hoosier. They'll think he's a cop or something at Vincent's, and he'll get himself whacked. Go down and get him out of there."

That night we went to La Maganette. I introduced Conte to Johnny the bartender. Then Lefty came in. He ignored Conte. Conte was at one side of me; Lefty went to the other side to talk to me.

These preliminaries are all part of the protocol about not talking directly to a new guy from the outside until it is time for proper introductions. Lefty asked me if I had explained to Conte about how things would work if we became partners with him, and I said I had mentioned it.

"Okay, let me talk to him," Lefty said.

After introductions Lefty says, "Did Donnie tell you about how tough it is to open that business in Milwaukee?"

"Yeah," Conte says. "But I don't want to move. Milwaukee's a nice small town. I feel comfortable there, with my family, friends. And the vending people out there don't service the machines very well. Eventually I can pull together a couple hundred grand. I think with hard work I could develop a real good business."

"You're not connected with anybody out there?"

"I don't know anybody special. I'm trying to do this on my own."

"Tony, I'm surprised they let you get this far without muscling in on you. I'm surprised they haven't killed you already. They're a crazy bunch, Tony. They can't be controlled by New York or anyone else. They're controlled from Chicago. You know Gene Autry, the singing cowboy actor? A few years ago he tried to open a restaurant in Chicago without permission. He was advised against it by the Chicago mob. He did it, anyway. On the night of the opening the Chicago guys came in. They told all the customers and waitresses and bartenders and everybody to leave. They used three bombs and blew up the entire place. Autry went back to the West Coast. Now, Tony, you sure you know what you wanna do?"

Tony looks shocked. "Hey, I don't want to get involved in any rough stuff. Screw it, Lefty, if somebody's going to get killed, I'll just take what I can get from it and get out, just quit my business rather than get into that stuff."

"Now hold on, hold on. I didn't say it was impossible. See, you come to me in the nick of time. Don't be rash. How much money you got invested so far?"

"I got about twenty grand tied up in the business, another thirty grand on hand."

"If you quit now, how much would you get back out of it?"

"Probably eight to ten grand by selling my truck and machines."

"So it wouldn't pay you to quit. See, if I get involved, you're safe. Understand? Once my name is in there. Now, I want to contact another guy, my boss, and run it down to him. If he's interested, I'll come out to Milwaukee and look everything over. Then if I like it and he likes it, he will go to the Old Man about it, who is in prison. If he likes it, we contact the people who have the power in Milwaukee. If they're interested, there would have to be a sitdown with them. It's their town. They might say that they don't want you out there. Then you have to pack up and leave. Or they might like the idea and then go partners with us—you run the business and they're fifty-fifty partners. Or they could just tell you to get out of town but still give you back your whole twenty-grand investment out of respect to the New York family. Understand?"

"It's pretty complicated, Lefty. All I know is, I don't want to take a big loss, but I don't want to get killed, either. I'll give it a try if you think you can help me out."

"Good. You let me worry about all this here. Now, there's one thing. I need twenty-five hundred up front. I give fifteen hundred of that to my boss, Mike. Then I got travel expenses and all that. Understand?"

"That's a lot of up-front money for me right now, Lefty, because the business isn't going."

"That's just for good faith. You keep your business and your life, that's a good investment. You'll have peace of mind, Tony."

"Okay. I have to go home to get the money."

"I'll have Donnie go back out there with you, look the whole thing over. Because you can't afford to let much time go by on this here."

When we're leaving the bar, Lefty says quietly to me, "Make sure he has what he says, Donnie, and that he does what he says."

I went out to Milwaukee with Conte. Lefty, as a made guy, would have to have his captain's permission to check out something in somebody else's territory. As a connected guy with the Bonanno family, I could go out on Lefty's permission alone. It's a very delicate situation when you're dealing between two families, especially when you're trying to go into another family's territory and open a business that that family has a sole lock on. If you don't do things right, you start a war and get people killed.

The Milwaukee boss might be tempted into a deal like this because he might appreciate having another good man out on the street working for him, and he might like having a good link to New York. There's always a chance you'll want a favor done.

Lefty had not mentioned the name of Balistrieri, so we proceeded as if we didn't know who the power was.

By now Conte had a two-room office at 1531 North Farwell Avenue, a neighborhood of apartment buildings and bars. He had business cards. "THE BEST VENDING CO. Prompt Service is the 'Best' Way. Anthony Conte, President." He took me around to neighborhood bars and restaurants and clubs where Balistrieri had his vending machines. We wanted to be seen together giving the impression that we were doing what we were supposed to be doing, in case Lefty or anybody else checked up or asked questions.

He told the owners how he was starting a new business and wanted to bring in his machines. The owners of the places said they didn't want to change companies. Some of them said they didn't want any trouble with the company they already had. Nobody mentioned Balistrieri, but we knew what they were talking about. After a couple of days I called Lefty and told him the situation looked good. I told him that Conte had an office, a truck, a few machines, some good potential outlets.

He said he would get permission from Mike Sabella and come out right away. "Did you send the twenty-five hundred?" Lefty asked. "Because I got to give Mike fifteen hundred before I come."

To send a soldier into another family's territory, Sabella had to get permission from Bonanno boss Carmine Galante. Galante was back in prison for parole violation. As a known mobster, Sabella couldn't be on the visitor's list. Somebody on the visitor's list was the courier for information back and forth between Galante and his captains. Word came from Galante that permission was granted for Lefty to visit Milwaukee.

In Milwaukee, we recorded Lefty for the first time. For his Milwaukee operation, code-named Timber, Conte's car was wired with a Nagra tape recorder. I never had my car wired in New York because of how my dashboard had been taken apart by the Colombo guys in Brooklyn. Recording of conversations by the FBI is not done lightly. When an agent makes a recording, he must turn it in to the FBI and have it logged as an official document. Even if there turns out to be nothing important said, once the recording is made, the cassette must be dated and initialed by the agent. And subsequently, when a case comes to trial, the tape is made accessible to defense attorneys.

On the night of June 21, Tony and I picked up Lefty at Chicago's O'Hare Airport and drove him to Milwaukee. Lefty and I checked in at the Best Western Midway Motor Lodge on South Howell Avenue. The next morning the three of us met for breakfast prior to taking a tour of the city so Lefty could assess the town and the possibilities.

"My people are checking this whole thing out," Lefty told Conte, "who's who up here and everything. And my boss is gonna be entertaining people in New York now, who he's sending for."

Lefty and Mike Sabella had begun the long, careful process of getting the Milwaukee and New York mob families together. Nothing is done directly. You go through friends of friends. In New York, Sabella was reaching out for the network of Bonanno people and intermediaries that would lead properly to the Balistrieri people in Milwaukee. There would be a lot of wining and dining at CaSa Bella, Lefty pointed out, and that would cost money. It would cost Conte money.

Lefty begins instructing Conte right away. "First thing is you got to get a beeper. See what doctors got? That's a beeper. Every successful businessman has it.

It's the most fantastic thing going. You're in the car, you got that on you, a machine goes bad someplace and they try to reach you, you pull over to the side and make your call. You don't lose three or four hours. Also, I need to be able to reach you twenty-four hours a day. Call the telephone company and tell them you want a beeper and they'll fix it all up."

"I'll call them right away," Conte says.

Lefty takes out a pen and scribbles on a napkin. "Now, I'm gonna give you five numbers where I can be reached day and night. If anybody bothers you, anybody approaches you, you throw a name at them. You tell them you got a partner in New York, on Mulberry Street, and he's very well connected."

He hands the napkin to Conte.

We ride around the business and industrial areas of the city. Conte points out the strips of motels, bars, and restaurants where he figures he should get business. "Look at the bars here," Lefty says. "It's like Hoboken."

"They like their beer here," Conte says. "All these places got machines already, but they're not happy with them. But they don't want to change."

"Let me explain something to you," Lefty says. "I know the machine racket better than the back of my hand. I been in that racket for thirty years. This town is connected, you better believe it. When you put your machines in, anybody approaches you, first little beef you get, you say I got a partner in New York. But it ain't gonna be the owner that approaches you. He'll be a working man. You say to the guy you want a name. You say you're being very nice about it, if he'll give you a name, then you will contact your partner in New York and give him that name and everything will be straightened out. You listening, Donnie?"

"I'm listening."

"Because this is important, this here. Tony, you tell the guy, 'Don't be foolish and make a mistake.' If he tells you to get your fucking machine out, you say, 'Hey, look, don't make a mistake in telling me things like that. Because it's only a two-hour ride from New York, and my man won't stand for it.' You tell him

your man is very reputable, known in the five bor-
oughs, known all over the country. Jesus Christ Al-
mighty, I'm known all over the fucking world. You
say, 'I'll have my man up here in two hours.' And you
show the guy you got a beeper, too, you can be
reached twenty hours a day. They come up with a
name, we'll meet. You're out of the picture and they
can't make a move until it's all checked out."

"When you start talking to your people and these
people here," Tony says, "I'm out of place. I know I
can't do that, I won't even try. I'll let you do it. With
the ordinary chump on the street, I can bust heads as
well as anybody else, but . . ."

"That don't cut no ice. Wiseguys only need to know
what car you're driving and where you live. Donnie
understands all this. I'm just giving you an idea of it."

"I feel better now," Tony says.

"From what I see here, Tony, this ain't no small
town. Forget about it. There's fucking money in this
town—you can see it. There's room here for everybody. Maybe one or two syndicates have got this, and
they gotta honor me. First thing I would tell the guy
who approaches you with any beef, 'What, are you
crazy? You can't take a living away from me. That's
the law of the land. Wiseguys are known all over the
world.' Our main guy says, 'No matter where you go
in this world, give me one day's notice and I'll get you
somebody to see.' He's in the can now."

"What's it look like with him?" I ask, referring to
Carmine Galante.

"On the twenty-ninth he'll find out if he does twenty
more months or they gotta release him. They're not
gonna release him. He's gotta go back to Atlanta. I
gotta send him cigars. He smokes the best Cuban
cigars. He calls Mike every night. He asks Mike about
me. He says, 'How's Mike's bad boy doing?' Mike
tells him I'm in Milwaukee. The Old Man's got a lot of
confidence in Mike. He's got lemon groves in Miami,
and mansions. He's got men all over the country. So I
gotta take care of Mike, you understand? Like with
that money you sent. Because he's gonna be entertaining a lot of people on this here. Whatever expenses he

goes through, he's gotta get back. My man don't come up with no money. This is your project. He says you take care of it."

We went by Conte's still bare office. "Don't go crazy fixing it up," Lefty says. "Just an indoor-outdoor rug, desk, phone, and your beeper. You gotta go around to the places. Go to the bartenders, give them your card. You tell them that if they can see their way clear to put one of your machines in there, there's a nice Christmas bonus in it for them, a good week's pay. And tell the guy maybe you'll throw in an extra fifty bucks a week. And you're partners with the guy fifty-fifty on the machines. Try to get partners with the owner of the joint, buy in, and you got your machines in there. Leave your cards. Don't stay long, just one drink in each joint. How many machines you got?"

"None. They're ordered. You got to buy ten, initial purchase. They average about two thousand apiece. My truck's supposed to be delivered in two weeks. Mechanized lift on the back. To drive it I got a kid I used to work with."

"Is he reliable? You know this guy, right?"

"Very reliable. I know him four or five years."

He wanted Conte to invest in buying a bar and grill, building up credit. "See, in New York City you can buy any fifty-grand joint with seventy-five hundred bucks and financing. So over here, how much could a gin mill cost? Say a neighborhood bar and grill is worth fifteen grand. So you put two grand down and finance the rest. And you put your machines in there. You ain't getting fifty percent on your machines no more, you're getting a hundred."

"Businesses are going good here, they don't want to sell," Tony says.

"Listen to me. I don't care where we go in the world, a lot of business people are in trouble for gambling, with taxes and stuff. Gambling is . . . forget about it, I know about gambling. In Vegas you got two type of crowds. You got the Texans. You got the Arabs. And you got the Japanese. Now, Atlantic City's gonna be—forget about it when New York City opens up. Jews cater to wiseguys. The thing about a Jewish person, he'll give you fifteen percent of the money he makes, as long as he's got the peace of mind. So the point is, over here you're liable to catch a guy that's a gambler, in debt to shylocks, and wants to get out of his gin-mill business. That's where you step in. He sells to you."

"You're thinking bigger than me," Conte says.

"My mind works overtime. I'm thinking about the opportunity you got in front of you. Business is good, somebody approaches you and wants to give you thirty grand for the joint. You take that thirty grand and buy a fifty-grand joint, build that up and sell it for eighty."

"Geez, I don't know, Lefty. I don't know how to make all these deals."

"That's why I'm instructing you, if you'll just pay attention to me. Tony, you got right now sixty grand to invest. With that you can get a hundred grand in credit. That's a hundred and sixty grand without you lifting a finger, that you're worth. When you got a joint, maybe you take in a partner, and you take four hundred bucks a week out of the joint, without even working there. So if you get ten or twelve joints like that, that's five grand a week. You're not even there working for it. Your machines are there, and you're getting one hundred percent for them. What the fuck, in five years time you got yourself a million dollars. Am I wrong or right, Donnie?"

"Right."

"First thing you know, you got forty or fifty gin mills in this town. Then I might move out here. Or if they need me in New York, I could still come out here weekends."

"They tell me some places to make a deal to get a machine in you got to pay the liquor license, six hundred bucks a year," Conte says.

"That's all right, forget about it. Let me tell you something. Once you pay it, you got him. Jesus Christ can't stop you. Remember that there. Donnie, I wish to hell you could stay here, give Tony a hand, answer questions he can't answer, 'cause he ain't got the head for it."

I had told Lefty I was going back to California to
visit my "injured girlfriend." I was getting desperate
to get home to see my family. Lefty resented it anytime I said I wanted to go to California. So now I had
come up with the story that my girlfriend had been in
a car crash. So he had to agree to let me go. "Monday
I'll come back," I say, "just three days. I'll keep in
touch with Tony every day from L.A."

"It ain't the question, keeping in touch. Question of
what are you gonna do out in L.A.?"

"Once I see that she's all right and everything . . ."

"Donnie, let's not kid ourselves. She lasted this
long, she's gonna be all right. Let's hope she's not
disfigured. I happen to like that girl." (He had never
met her, of course.) "Listen, she can't go back to
work for a couple weeks, right? So why don't you
bring her over here and help Tony set it up? Use your
noggin, Donnie. She's going on a plane, she'll be
happy. And you got the most beautiful place, this is
gorgeous over here. So you spend a week or two out
here."

"That's what I'll do, then."

"The thing is, Donnie, I can't see you laying out
there because the girl's in the hospital. Don't get me
wrong. It's just that it's ridiculous."

When Lefty spotted a situation and a mark, energy
poured out of him. Conte was handling him perfectly,
using just the right touch of innocence to suck him in.

"Once everything is set out over here," Lefty says,
"then we can branch out someplace else. Because
Mike is very sincere. You know what he likes about
me? I was on the balls of my ass when I gave him my
speedboat. I coulda sold it, he knew it."

"Does he like the speedboat?" I ask.

"Forget about it. It goes seventy-two on the water.
Imagine going seventy-two miles on the water. It's a
fucking jet. *Shooo!* I would like to take that boat to
New York from here."

"How would you do that, Left?"

"Hug the shoreline. Tell me one thing. I seen all
kinds of land where we drive. Where's the ocean around
here?"

"There's no ocean," Tony says. "There's the lake."

"There's no ocean in this town, Milwaukee?"

"A lake."

"I don't like lakes. I like the ocean."

"This is a pretty big lake, Lefty."

"Let's go see that lake."

We drive down to the shore of Lake Michigan.

"That's a *lake*?" Lefty gapes. "That looks like a fucking ocean. Look at the boats out there! Ships! How the fuck can that be a lake if them kind of things go in there?"

"It's a big lake," Tony says. "Ships can come in from Europe through the Saint Lawrence Seaway."

"I don't believe it. You ever see anything like this, Donnie? What's the name of this lake?"

"Lake Michigan. On the other side is Michigan, maybe fifty miles away."

"You sure it's not the ocean and they just call it something else? Un-fucking-believable. Now let's get a fucking pair of trunks, because we're gonna sit outside by the pool; we're going to iron this whole fucking thing out."

Lefty needed a "cabana set," which meant that somebody else was to provide it. "My waist is thirty-three," he told Conte, "and I wear a 9½D shoe." Conte went over to the Southridge Shopping Center and bought the items for Lefty. We sat by the pool at the motel. Lefty drank his usual white-wine spritzers, and chain-smoked his usual English Ovals, as he had been doing all day in the car.

"The town is nice," Lefty says, "I like it. I gotta tell them when I go back, I'm all for this project. I'll get a green light all the way through. This is easy living, Tony. It's a clean town. You can breathe the air here. You're gonna be very successful out here. You're gonna make it. You're gonna be very contented."

"You don't know me yet," Conte says. "When you know me, you'll find out that I make a plan, I work it hard until I get what I want. You'll find out someday."

"I ain't saying different," Lefty says. "Now, as soon as I go back, I'll probably have to shoot right back here again to meet the people over here who he is finding out about by entertaining in his restaurant over there."

The next morning Tony and Lefty dropped me off at the Milwaukee Airport for my trip to "California" to see my "injured girlfriend." Tony took Lefty on to O'Hare for his trip back to New York.

"You think Donnie might end up marrying this girl?" Tony asked.

"I know he's crazy about her," Lefty said. "But Donnie ain't the type to settle down."

I hadn't been home in three weeks. When I called to say I was coming home, my wife told me that the house across the street from ours had burned to the ground. There had been a strong wind and sparks had gone everywhere. She had been out helping people water down nearby roofs where the embers were landing, including ours. Everybody had been scared to death.

It was Friday, June 23. She would pick me up at the airport as always. My flight was due in at 3:45 P.M. She never made it.

10

THE ACCIDENT

I arrived at the airport that served my new hometown. My wife was not at the gate. I was met by another agent whom I knew only slightly. He said, "Your wife has been in an accident." He said it was a head-on car crash; both drivers were women, similar in appearance except that one was younger. The younger one had been killed. He wasn't sure which one that was. He said other stuff, but that's all I remember.

We went to the hospital. My wife had not been killed. She was in intensive care, in critical condition, attached to machines and tubes. Her eyes were covered with bandages. Both her corneas had been lacerated. Her face was a web of gashes. She had a collapsed lung, a broken wrist, a broken collarbone. She was hooked up to a lung machine. She couldn't see. She could barely talk. She squeezed my hand.

My daughters were there. The youngest, who was nine, had gotten sick at the sight of her mother and gone into the bathroom to throw up. I hugged the others, who were fifteen and thirteen, and tried to smile and act like everything was okay.

My wife told me that on her way to the airport a car coming toward her had veered out to pass another car stopped in that lane and hit her head-on. My wife climbed out of the car somehow and ran to the side of the road, afraid the cars were going to blow up. She heard bubbling in her chest, and as a nurse she knew that her lung was punctured. There were two women who had witnessed the accident. She asked if she could please lay her head down in the lap of one of them, because it would help her breathe. Her contact lenses had been smashed into her eyes. She thought she had lost at least one of her eyes. She told the women that in her car was a notebook and her husband's flight number. She asked them to call the FBI and ask for an agent to pick me up at the airport and to call a friend's house where the girls were staying. And then the ambulance came and she was brought to the hospital.

She was in terrible pain and scared. When I saw her, she didn't know that the other driver was dead, and I couldn't bring myself to tell her. Her friend Ginny was there. I went out in the hall. Later my wife said that Ginny had told her I was crying, and she said, "I told Ginny, 'I'm sorry I missed that, I've never seen Joe cry.'"

I stayed with her at the hospital. My youngest daughter couldn't bear to visit her because she was so mutilated. She sent notes instead.

The next day my two older daughters were leaving

to drive home. My fifteen-year-old had just gotten her driver's permit. Within sight of the hospital they were broadsided by another car that ran a stop sign. They were brought back to the emergency room by ambulance.

The nurses in the emergency room already knew them from their mother's accident. The nurse called upstairs for me. I told my wife I was going to get a Coke and take a walk. In her condition I couldn't tell her right then that the kids had been in an accident. But she knew something was wrong. "Why aren't they coming to visit me tonight?" she asked. "They've got a lot of homework," I said. "I told them to stay home."

Our girls were not seriously hurt, just bruises and stitches. They were treated and released. My wife's parents had flown in the night of her accident, and so were on hand to help take care of their injured granddaughters as well.

I started thinking, What the hell's going on here? What have I done wrong? I had been on this job since the summer of 1976. Now it is the summer of 1978. Two years and I haven't been home two months. And everything could have been wiped out in the last two days.

I wish my circumstances allowed me to describe my family more completely, what they looked like, their relatives and friends, where we lived. At least to use their names.

Actually they changed their names—their last name. They dropped Pistone and adopted a new name. We never traveled under Pistone, anyway, and I used different names for everything, so it wasn't such a big deal. Also, the girls had always been teased about their last name—Yellowrock, Wetstone, etc. So they were happy to be rid of Pistone. And my feeling was, they would probably eventually get married and change their last names, anyway.

But I used various names, just to make it a little more difficult for anybody ever to trace me. That got to be a pain for everybody but me. Sometimes my wife would get confused at an airline counter when she couldn't remember which name she was supposed to be using that day. Or when she went to pick up things I had left at the cleaners, she often had to try several names before she came up with the one that I had left the clothes under.

My long absences were bothering my family more and more. "What kind of marriage is it," my wife would say over the phone, "when the husband is never home?" The fact is, if we hadn't had so strong a marriage, it probably wouldn't have survived these years.

The way she coped with it was to develop a life of her own, even more independent of me—almost, she would say, as if she didn't have a husband. It was not in her nature to brood or to feel sorry for herself. The family had moved to its present home only a few months before, and it had not been easy. My wife was recovering from major surgery she had undergone shortly before the move. And in the first weeks after the move, the kids were having trouble adjusting. They wouldn't go to school. I offered advice, support, whatever, mostly over the phone. My wife dealt with it all on the scene. Friends included her in everything, with or without me. She encouraged our daughters to have kids over, and she cooked for bunches of teenagers all the time. She went out with our oldest daughter— just girls out on the town having a good time.

Her way of avoiding worry about me was to maintain a semblance of normalcy in the home. The hardest thing for her, she would tell me, was that when I went undercover, she had to start taking care of all the bills. That was the one thing she had never done, and she hated it.

She kept so occupied, she said, that she could go for long periods without ever thinking about being alone. Except that when I would call, she'd turn angry. Frustrations would pour out, sometimes in strange ways. She had focused so totally on the household that she would want to talk about that. The lawn mower wouldn't start. The washing machine was broken. I've only got five minutes to talk, I would say, I don't want to talk about that stuff. "To me," she would say, "this is the real stuff, right here at home. I can't see any further right now than what's bothering me here." Sometimes we would yell at each other.

The telephone became our link, our lifeline. When I called, I wanted to talk to everybody in turn. My wife always filled me in on everything that was going on with the kids. That was important. Often there were problems—school, discipline, personal—and my wife would tell me about them over the telephone and I'd try to straighten things out. But more often than not, I couldn't straighten things out over the telephone. There'd be crying and screaming and everything. Everybody would be upset, and all I could do was put my two cents in. The kids were upset that I was away so much. I couldn't defend myself very well, except to say that I had a job to do. Their mother would try to make them understand about my dedication to the job. What did they care about how dedicated I was? They were kids. They wanted their father home.

Sometimes when frustrations got bad, my wife would holler at me something like, "Either get out of this job or I'm getting divorced." She never meant it. I knew that. But the kids didn't know that, and sometimes they overheard it.

My youngest daughter sometimes pretended that we were divorced. Some of her friends had divorced parents. So she would play this game in her mind that she was a kid from a broken home. Somehow that made it easier for her to get along during some of the tough times, especially when they moved into a new area.

Then when I did come home, they would resent me. My wife said to me, "I get so excited when you're coming home, I really can't wait. Then when you get here, I get furious. It's bad enough you being gone for long periods of time. But then when you come home, you want to run the show again. You're home a couple of hours and you want to become boss. You want to run the show. But *I'm* running it. I'm used to doing things my own way around here."

I couldn't help walking into the house and wanting to be the head of the household, and she couldn't help her resentments of that. Sometimes it would take us a couple of days to get reacclimated to each other. A lot of the times we didn't *have* two days. Sometimes we had only one. Sometimes we had half a day or just a night. She clung to her own system, and I was sometimes an outsider. She found herself even resenting having me crowd her in her bed. So she bought a king-size bed to be able to sprawl like she was used to.

As the girls were growing up, they had more outside activities. I would get home to find one or two or all of them going out. I would say, "Aren't you going to stay home with me?"

They would say, "You never stay home with us." Or, "We can't count on you being here, so we can't make appointments around you, Dad."

Sometimes I would get home for a day and would have to leave the next morning before they were up. I didn't always say when I was going. My youngest daughter cried when I got home and cried when I left.

I had frustrations too. If I came home for a day and a night and found out there was a problem, I would have to try to straighten things out instantly—there was no time to take time. I would try to make rules. My daughters would tell me that I was like a visitor and had no right to make rules. Sometimes I just seemed to get on people's nerves.

Over time the girls developed the habit of going to their mother with everything they wanted to talk about. They went to her first. They told her everything. As understandable as that was, it hurt me.

They came more and more to resent the job, and the FBI. "What you're doing is not a job for a married man with a family," my wife would say. "They don't care about us. They don't care about you."

My wife was in the hospital for eleven days. And then when she came home, she was nearly helpless. For a long time she couldn't see well. She had to wear special dark glasses, and even a satin sleep mask at night, because light was agony to her eyes. There were still pieces of glass embedded under her skin. She would need plastic surgery, but first she would have to heal for a year. The cast on her arm allowed her fingers to move. But sometimes when she was holding something, like a cup or a glass, it would just suddenly drop from her hand. Things like that would bother her.

My wife was always self-reliant, energetic, optimistic. She was athletic, always playing tennis, doing aerobics, on the go. She was always doing things for everybody else. And now, suddenly, she couldn't do things for herself. Her spirits were down. I wouldn't say she was depressed. In the thirty years I've known her I've never seen her depressed. But now she was down, not able to do ordinary things.

For the first time our daughters saw her in this almost helpless state. They started getting on me harder about not being home more. I wanted to be home more. But what could I say?

When my wife came home from the hospital, I stayed one more week. We all had a pretty good time, given the circumstances. It was the most time we had all spent together in years. We had outdoor barbecues and everything. I had fun with the girls. It was going to take a while for my wife to heal. Her eyes were still extremely sensitive to light, so she had to keep them covered most of the time. But at least we were together.

My wife is basically a pretty understanding person. But this was a bad time. She wanted me to quit the undercover job. I could see her point of view. It had come up before: "You're just away too much at one time. It wouldn't be too bad if you were gone a day or two, but you're gone three weeks at a time, then you come home for one or two days."

But I had come too far. By now, quitting wouldn't involve just me. I had brought Lefty around to other operations, and the people running those operations were depending on me to keep their operations going. If I backed out now, a lot of people would be left holding the bag. Quitting was something I couldn't do.

She knew I was working with the mob. I gave her a few more details, some of the circumstances in Milwaukee, to try to ease the tension a little bit, to show that my being away weeks at a time couldn't be helped.

She knew of Tony Conte because she had talked with him on the phone a few times. I explained to her that if I pulled out, Lefty and the others in New York would stop working with Conte.

I didn't talk to anybody else about these concerns. Nobody. Because nobody else but me was going to make the decision to leave the job or stay. I didn't feel it concerned anybody else. No matter what anybody said to me, the decision was going to be mine. I had to stay on the job.

I was in touch with Lefty throughout this time, by telephone. I had left a California "hello phone" number where supposedly he could reach me. He left messages, I called him back.

I told him my girlfriend was fine and that everything ought to get moving again in Milwaukee after the Fourth of July holidays.

He was busy spreading Tony Conte's money around and trying to arrange for a sitdown with the Milwaukee mob. Mike Sabella was entertaining people. Sabella had borrowed $200,000 for a major renovation of CaSa Bella, but the contractor had quit on him. "He's in trouble there," Lefty said, "that cocksucker contractor."

One day he said to me, "You see that *David Suskind Show* last night? They had two informers, you know, paid by the government. On TV. You know, guys that already cooperated, and now the government gave them a different identification and put them out there. They said they got 2,250 informers and half of them are in the San Diego and L.A. area."

"Wow."

"So these guys, some guy that's writing a book accidentally cracked it out about them. So now they're ratted out, and guys are looking to get rid of all these guys."

"Whack 'em out, right?"

"Yup. They don't give a fuck, the government. So these two stool pigeons say anybody that becomes a government informer is fucking crazy. Unbelievable. How's your girl?"

Over a period of time I got so I could understand

just about everything Lefty said. Two guys in the
federal Witness Protection Program had been accidentally exposed, so now they had bared their resentments about the government's carelessness over TV,
and that the mob was looking for all these protected
informants.

"My girl's good. Everything's all right."

"Why can't your girl come into New York or Milwaukee with you?"

"She's working. She don't get vacation now."

"Well, you gotta get back out there and get the
groundwork. And once you get that, you're gonna
stay there a long time."

"Yeah, I know. We gotta start making some ends
out there. When are you going out there, after the
Fourth?"

"When I'm gonna get out there, I don't know. I'm
feuding with the wife now. We had a fight about she
wants to go away somewhere for a vacation. I gotta go
reach out for people for late this afternoon. Tonight I
got an appointment. Tomorrow night I got an appointment. I got meetings in Philadelphia."

"Mike likes this Milwaukee deal, right?"

"Right. No question about it. I'll tell you something: Everything's green lights."

Lefty had been given the full go-ahead by a message
from Carmine Galante in prison. While he was arranging for the sitdown, I went back to Milwaukee. For
the first couple of days I didn't tell Lefty because I
wanted some time with Conte to go over things without having to account to Lefty for every minute of
every day. Then Conte and I hit some more spots,
trying to place machines, and again ran into a stone
wall. But we were gathering evidence of the case, and
by being seen by more and more people, we were
establishing more credibility as guys trying to hustle a
buck. We were also insuring that word got back to the
Balistrieri people that we were out there pushing a
vending-machine business.

We made a visit to Pioneer Sales and Service, a
vending-machine wholesaler in Menomonee Falls, to

look over the various machines available. Along with
Conte and me was Conte's "employee" that he had
told Lefty about. The "employee" was another undercover agent who went by the name of Steve Greca.
Conte told the president of the company that he wanted
to buy machines for distribution in the Milwaukee
area, and that he would also be interested in purchas-
ing any vending routes that became available. He told
him that Best Vending was a serious, licensed operation, not fly-by-night, and he showed the guy the city
and state licenses for the business. The president said
he would be happy to cooperate with Best Vending,
and he gave us a tour of the place, showing us the
various machines, and handed us a mess of brochures.

Just to give the impression that we were moving the
business along, I called Lefty and told him that Conte
had ordered some machines—when in fact he hadn't.

The mob blew up a guy in Milwaukee. Somebody
put a bomb under the car of a guy named Augie
Palmisano. The murder was in the newspapers, plus
our people came up with some information about it.
Palmisano was with the Balistrieri family, and the mob
suspected he was an informant. The word was that
guys were starting to put remote-controlled starters in
their cars.

The killing made Conte and me a little nervous.

Lefty called and told Conte, "I got a meeting tonight with those people from Chicago at my man's
place. We reached out, you know. I might have to fly
out there later to get a proper introduction. That's the
way they do it. We didn't sleep on this thing. I've been
with people every day. But everything is fine. No
problems whatsoever."

"I'm glad to hear that," Conte says, "because they're
playing kind of rough around here. Did Donnie tell
you about they're blowing guys up here?"

"Forget about it," Lefty says. "Doesn't mean shit.
They're blowing guys up because they done something
wrong."

"Yeah, but I wanna make sure I don't do nothing
wrong."

"You're not doing nothing wrong."

"Okay."

"Let me tell you something," Lefty says. "Once you start rolling, I'll be there with you for the first ten days. When I get it set up and I come out to Chicago, you gotta meet the people. Understand? Once I get the proper introduction, I'll have dinner with you and them. There's no problem over here. We're in like Flynn. Put Donnie on the phone."

I take the phone.

"Donnie," he says, "he didn't sound too enthused what we're doing here. He's worried about people bombing out there."

"He's enthused, but he's nervous. He doesn't know what's going on."

"I don't blame him for being nervous," Lefty says. "But that's got nothing to do with us. The guy might have been a stool pigeon. The guy could have been anything. Tell him not to worry about anything. And to keep near that beeper, because I might have to reach him anytime now, now things are moving."

"Donnie, is Tony there with you?"

"Yeah, Lefty."

"Tell Tony, where's Rockford?"

"Rockford, Illinois?"

"Yeah."

I ask Conte where Rockford is. "He says it's about ten miles outside of Chicago, Left. Why?"

"Some people are making some phone calls and I got to go out there, to see people out there. They will set up an appointment for me. I gotta wait for a call. He's gonna make a call to this place Rockford, wherever that is. He's gonna give my name and when I'm coming out. And I gotta lay the cards on the table what I'm doing there. That's the whole thing in a nutshell. Mike entertained six of them last week. He didn't give me the bill. He ain't worried about it."

"Everything at Mike's went all right?"

"Everything is perfect. The guy kissed me on both cheeks. We can do anything. I stood with them about an hour and a half, then I excused myself. Because

Mike was still with them. They were bullshitting about old times. Tell Tony to keep near the beeper."

A guy had a pizza joint next door to Lefty's social club. Lefty decided he didn't like him anymore, so he beat him up and threw him off the street. The guy was an ordinary citizen, and he now wanted $2,000 cash for damages. Lefty said if he didn't come up with the money, the guy would press charges and Lefty could face six months in the can. Mike Sabella thought Lefty should take over the joint and make it his own pizza parlor. Also, Lefty was still getting muscled over the jam his son got into when he tried to rob a guy for diamonds and the guy turned out to be connected. They were leaning on him for $3,500 more.

So, while pushing the matter of the sitdown on Milwaukee, Lefty was poor-mouthing as always.

"Some people wanna meet me tomorrow at Newark Airport," Lefty told Conte over the phone, never giving Conte as much information as he would give me, his partner. "Here's the situation now. You see, we're broke. I have no goddamn money. You understand? Now I got to entertain these people. I ain't even got a car to get out there tomorrow. And then I gotta come out there where you are by plane. You gotta get me a reservation. Now, I gotta see if I can scheme tomorrow morning for some bread someplace and a car to get there. And when I do come out where you are, you gotta meet me and we'll go see these people out there, because they're gonna have to know you better than they know me. Because you're representing me. Understand?"

"Yeah."

"But the question is, I got exactly twenty-three bucks in my pocket. How the fuck do I get out there tomorrow?"

"Maybe we could do a car-rental deal," Conte said, stringing him out.

"This guy tomorrow is giving us names. Bosses. They're the main guys, you know. They're looking to help our situation over there. One hand washes the other. I gotta entertain this guy all day. The guy is eighty-one years old. He's a heavyweight. The guy owns hotels out there at Newark Airport. How do I entertain these people all day with twenty-three bucks?"

"Well, I'll have to send you some bread," Conte says finally.

"Yeah, but I'm embarrassed because Donnie says you don't feel too enthused about all this here, how we're breaking our ass over here."

"Hey, I never said I wasn't enthused. Certainly I'm enthused."

"Let me tell you something. That's why I got mad at Donnie. Guy's a jerk-off. Says you weren't enthused. I says, 'Don't you think he's gonna meet these people?' Because when you see these people, forget about it. And you're gonna sit down with these people with me."

"I don't want nothing to happen to me," Conte says. "I do what you tell me, right?"

"Right. There's no problem. Where is Donnie now?"

"He's out."

"I don't understand this frigging guy. He's out. See, the question is, if Donnie wasn't gonna do nothing out there with you, he shoulda been in with me. Now he could run around with me. But here I'm stranded by myself."

"I'll send you a grand in the morning, Western Union."

"Make it as early as possible. And tell that guy Donnie not to do nothing but stay by you. I will definitely have to come right out there after I see these people tomorrow. You're gonna sit down with these people and me. We're gonna entertain them people, you and I and Donnie. Take them to dinner. We'll get everything straight. And everything that you listen to, you know from the ground floor in. Everything that's going on. And we got no problem. You stay by that beep. The first beep you get from New York, I'll tell you what plane I'm taking and everything."

The man he was to meet at a motel near Newark Airport was Tony Riela, an aging Bonanno captain with contacts to Chicago. It was Riela that had kissed him on both cheeks at CaSa Bella. The understanding was, Riela would make the calls to Chicago to set up a meeting. The Chicago people would call people in Rockford. And those people would make the introductions to Balistrieri in Milwaukee.

Lefty had a successful meeting in Newark. The day after, he called to announce that he was coming to Milwaukee for the sitdown. It was now July 24. More than a month had gone by so far in arranging for the meet. He gave Conte the flight information and told him to write it all down. "Get me that same room in that same Best Western, right? Them people come from right in that town. I'll explain everything when I see you. Where's Donnie?"

Conte hands me the phone.

"He wrote everything down?" Lefty says.

"Yeah, he got it all."

"Listen to me carefully."

"I'm listening."

"Don't let it go any further."

"Okay."

"I got me a sitdown with the two main guys in that town where you are now. I can't get no names until I get out there. When I get there, I gotta make a phone call back into New York at six o'clock, tell them where I am, what room number. They call the Chicago guy. He's gonna come and pick me up. They're gonna take me away. They're gonna talk to me. And they're gonna check this guy out completely."

"Okay."

"I hope he's all right."

"Yeah, Tony's all right."

"I mean, I don't wanna get him scared by saying that, and I representing him."

"Right."

"They wanted to know if he was a local guy. I said, definitely a local guy."

"Yeah."

"Now, once they call me, I'll be on standby there. When I call New York and they call back, it might take a day, might take two hours. In other words, I cannot move away from that room. We'll have to eat and drink and sleep there. Understand?"

"Yeah, we wait."

"They'll send representatives down to pick me up and they'll take me to go with these people. We all go—me, you, and him. But I go into a separate room with them for the first conversation at the table. I represent the situation. They cause him a table. When everything is all right, then I call him in, I introduce them after the first conversation."

"Okay."

"Now, the money he sent me. I went for already five hundred on my phone. My plane I'm taking first-class is two-hundred-thirty something. And we gotta entertain them people after I get through introducing them. And I dropped two-fifty at the Newark Airport, with all them people. Because it took me four hours. But I ain't worried about that. The most important thing is that the main one comes from that town and everything is beautiful. Not to go further. But they told me, I sit down with them alone. And then they're gonna check him out. So as long as we got a peace of mind there."

"Yeah, there's no problem with Tony."

"Good enough."

Lefty flew out. We went to our room at the Midway Motor Lodge. Lefty called New York and told them what room he was in. New York was to call the Chicago–Rockford people and tell them what room Lefty was in. Then somebody would call and say they were on the way to pick us up. We just had to sit and wait for the phone call.

Lefty had said we might end up waiting any amount of time, even days. That's what happened. We couldn't leave the hotel. Conte came to hang around with us during the day. We had a first-floor room. We sat around the indoor pool. We played cards. We shot the breeze. We ate breakfast, lunch, dinner. At night we hung around the lounge and listened to the band.

Lefty briefed Conte on the upcoming sitdown. Conte now belonged to the Bonannos, so the Milwaukee boss couldn't steal him or the vending plans. The options the Milwaukee boss had were: yes, you can stay and do what you want; yes, you can stay and I'm your partner; or no, I don't want you here. The Bonannos had to abide by his decision.

"I tell them that you're out of Baltimore, you're here three years. I know you from Baltimore. You're going into a pinball business. You're buying a route. You won't disrespect nobody. I'm involved in it, my money. You're like our representative out here. We don't want no problems. Because we can handle our own problems. You open the doors for us, we appreciate it, and if you got somebody's relative that wants to come in with us, most likely they will. That's all. Like Mike, my man, says, 'Short and sweet.' "

"I just tell them that some of it's your money and some of it's my money?"

"You don't tell him anything. You don't do no talking."

"I meant if they ask."

"No, they don't ask you nothing. They can't ask you. They have no right to ask you. They take my word for everything I say to them. Because I'm not asking them to put nothing up."

"I'll be glad when this is over," Conte says.

"Sure, you'll have peace of mind."

One day went by. Two days. Just sitting and waiting. I thought, What the hell am I doing here? My wife is home trying to cope with recovering while I'm sitting around a damn motel twiddling my thumbs. Finally on the third day I said, "Left, I'm not sitting around here any more waiting for this phone call. We might be waiting another week. I gotta get back and see my girl. She's not doing too good."

"What are you talking about?" he snaps. "We gotta wait for this here. I thought you said your girl was working."

"She was, but she had a relapse. I'll just shoot out there for a day or so, then shoot right back here."

"What the fuck are you talking about, Donnie? This is the most important thing we got right here. We got a sitdown coming up. You're putting your girl before what we got here."

"Hey, Left, I gotta. She's got nobody out there, she's in bad shape. Just a day or two, I'll come right back."

"Unbelievable, you put her first. That's the trouble with you, Donnie. You fucking take off anytime you feel like it. She ain't gonna die. What are you worrying about?"

That really ticked me off. I flew home.

The next day they got the call.

Three guys came to pick them up: Joe Zito, the old man from Rockford who was the main contact, and two guys named Charlie and Phil. They had Conte and Lefty follow them downtown to a dinner theater named Center Stage, which was owned by Frank Balistrieri. There they were introduced to Frank's brother, Peter, and Steve DiSalvo, who was Frank's right-hand man. Then to drive to the sitdown, Conte suggested that the Rockford guys ride with him and Lefty. They followed Peter and Steve to Snug's Restaurant, in the Shorecrest Hotel on North Prospect. These, too, were Frank's places.

At Snug's they had the sitdown with Frank Balistrieri, the boss of Milwaukee; his brother, Peter; Steve DiSalvo; and the three Rockford guys.

Lefty gave them the rundown before calling Conte in. When Lefty introduced Conte, Frank Balistrieri started to laugh.

Conte called me to tell me about it. It seems that Balistrieri didn't know Conte was hooked up with New York, didn't associate him with Lefty and the sitdown. He had Conte and me stalked out because we were trying to start a vending-machine company and move into Frank's town. He had two guys watching the office during the time we were waiting with Lefty at the motel.

"Frank Balistrieri pointed at me," Conte said, "and he said, 'We was gonna hit you. We thought you was the G.' "

"G" is the government. His first thought had been that Conte was an agent. Because if he and the guy he was with—me—had been tough guys trying to muscle in on his territory, Frank would have heard of us somewhere. Whatever we were, he had guys out right then looking for us. Those two guys had been watching the office waiting for us to come back during the time we were fortunately waiting with Lefty at the motel. So Balistrieri laughed when he was introduced to Conte and said he better call his guys off.

"When he said he had been planning to have me hit," Conte told me, "I got so nervous that I was afraid to light a cigarette because I didn't want these guys to see my hand shake. I still didn't know if I was out of the woods. Man, we could have been dead."

He said "we" because if they hit him and I was with him at the time, naturally they would have hit me too.

"First thing I'm gonna do," Conte said, "is put a remote starter in my Cadillac."

After the sitdown, Conte and Lefty took Joe Zito and his two pals back to the Center Stage where their car was. Conte had maneuvered them into riding to and from the sitdown in his car because it was wired.

Lefty says, "It was a real pleasure meeting you people. Like I said, one day next week we'll spend the whole day together with you over there."

"And don't forget when you come back home, call Tony," one of them says. "Tony said he wanted this thing right. He was so anxious, he's been calling to see if it's all right."

That Tony was Tony Riela in Newark.

"He's on top of the situation," Lefty says. "Same thing what we do in New York. If anybody comes in or wants something done, we don't rest until it's done. That's the way it's supposed to work. Frank gave me satisfaction, didn't he?"

"Definitely."

"Forget about it."

"What's your first name again?"

"Tony."

"And your last name?"

"Conte."

"Conte?"

"C-O-N-T-E."

"Oh, Italiano. Frank was checking you out."

"Don't laugh," Lefty says. "They were looking for you."

"Every move you made," the guy says, "they knew already, every move. The machines, how you paid for them, they knew."

"A few months, they grab you."

They laugh. Conte says, "I don't think it was too funny."

"I said few months. Maybe a week, maybe two weeks, you know. You got plenty time on his hands to grab you."

"Oh, yeah," Lefty says. "In this business we always have plenty of time."

"Ah, Benny and you know each other, Tony?"

"Yeah, sure," says Lefty, who is sometimes called Benny. "If I didn't know him, would I bring him in?"

"Tony, you born out east?"

"Yeah. Baltimore."

"Baltimore."

After they dropped the trio off, Conte headed his car toward Lefty's motel.

Lefty lets out a sigh. "Oh, was you in trouble. You were gone. They gonna bury you. Oooh. Good thing I made this trip. Wow."

"I told you I was scared," Conte says.

"Yeah, you had it right. They were laying for you. That cocksucker gave you up, that jukebox guy. That motherfucker."

"The day we talked to that vending company."

"Yeah. They thought you were a fucking agent. They were gonna fucking bury you in a minute. They had guys on you. Okay, let me tell you this deal now. I gotta come back out here next week. We're gonna merge with them. We're gonna go far, big. He says to me, 'Lefty, you're my guy.' He's gonna call New York. Now you're gonna work with them. You got a green light. You got a partner that's gonna come up with the money. How much you wanna go—forty cash?—he puts up forty cash too. Because he don't want no problem with my people. He puts a guy with you with books and everything. I'm your partner. He wants to take me around and introduce me to his men. You come around with me. Don't ask no fucking questions. You're just a working man and that's it. And you'll make a ton of fucking money."

They rode in silence for some moments.

"They had your fucking joint spotted," Lefty says. "Good thing I was out here or they fucking break up our business."

"Yeah. You remember about two days ago, I had the feeling you saved my life?"

"That's right, I did. The guy says, 'Who the fuck is he to come into my town? I own this town,' he says."

"Can you imagine what would've happened if I tried this on my own?" Conte says.

"Yeah. They were looking for you now. They didn't know I represented you. In other words, if you hung in your store, they box you in and that's it."

"The way he looked at me when he first met me. He said, 'I been looking for you.' "

"He was hot. Now you got a big thing. That's a boss, you know. Not many people like you ever get to meet a boss. In New York you can't sit down with a boss. Forget about it. But now you're gonna have one of the biggest operations in the country. Jesus Christ can't touch you, because I represent you."

"But if I knew in the beginning what I know now," Conte says, "I wouldn't have even done it."

Lefty was grousing all the time because I wasn't in Milwaukee. The fact is, I took my wife on a vacation. She couldn't fly, because of her lung. Her eyes were still sore. Her arm was still in a cast for her shattered wrist. Otherwise she was coming along well. We drove nine hours to get to this particular beach where we could lie in the sand for a few days. I was on the phone with Lefty and Conte for several hours every day. She said it wasn't very companionable of me to go away and be on the phone all the time when we were together on our first vacation in years.

I was gone only ten days, but Lefty was frustrated by my lack of concentration on the Milwaukee scene. He thought I was in California. Conte's story had been to tell him I had lined up a score. The last time I had lined up a big score as an excuse for being away, I had disappointed Lefty with a few hundred dollars instead of several thousand. I told him I had been cheated on my end of the score.

"It's a ridiculous thing what you're doing out there," Lefty says. "The other guy tells me you got some other score or something out there. Forget about it. They're making a fool out of you. You said you didn't make enough the last one, you got cheated. Forget about it, cancel it out, because you're in on the ground floor over here. What are you laughing about? There must be something wrong, pal. I think your girl has got you fucked up. That's the trouble with you, Donnie. All right, take your girl with you. What the hell, I don't care."

"No, I'm laughing at him, at Tony. He was telling me about when he walked into it at the sitdown, you know, and the guy said . . ."

"All right, listen, don't worry about that. Everything's taken care of."

"If I run into that guy, Left, I don't wanna have them start blasting somebody."

"No, no, you're like Allstate, pal. It's all straightened out. He's well satisfied. Everything's beautiful out there."

Frank Balistrieri's lawyers, who were his sons Joe and John, would be drawing up papers for the partnership, Lefty said. The partnership would not include the Balistrieri name. Somebody else's name would be put on the papers. Balistrieri would be a hidden partner. Tony Conte would be his beard, putting machines in, buying up routes and maybe other businesses as well. Their split would be fifty-fifty with Conte. Lefty would get his end out of Conte's split.

"One thing, Donnie," Lefty says. "Tony's gotta get rid of that guy Steve that works for him. Frank said that. He said no outsiders can be involved, not even as a hired hand. And I can't vouch for this guy, and you can't vouch for this guy, and so only Tony can vouch for this guy, and that ain't good enough. Tony can just give him a week's pay and tell him to look for another job."

So agent "Steve Greca" had to leave the operation.

On that basis, the marriage was formed between the Balistrieri family and the Bonanno family in New York. This was a coup for us, the FBI agents. We were now into two Mafia families. And we were actually in partnership with a boss.

"Now, what's on your mind about coming into Milwaukee?" Lefty asks.

"Well, what are you gonna do?"

"I gotta come out there, but I'm short. I dropped $500 at the airport today, I went over there. Diner's Club turned Louise down for a credit card. I got hit with a subpoena today. The agents grabbed me 3:10 this afternoon outside the club. Grand jury for the little guy, my man Nicky. For the fifteenth of August."

Nicky was Nicky Marangello, the Bonanno underboss.

"What the hell they doing with him?" I ask.

"Nothing. They got nothing on the guy. Ain't got nothing to do with me. I'm not under investigation. I'll take the Fifth and be in and out. Forget about that. Donnie, listen to me. You're not up-to-date. See, it's so ticklish now. Don't be insulted when I tell you I gotta ease you in. When I go back out there, I'm gonna introduce you as my representative for when I'm not there, and I'm gonna say you're my blood. These people are heavyweights out there. And the guy out there, he's under the impression that you don't wanna come in."

"Tony? Oh, no, I'll be there."

"We're gonna set you up with a bar and grill out there. And get an apartment near the office."

"Okay."

"Now listen. You gotta give me a number where I can reach you."

"I ain't got one."

"Listen, pal, don't tell me you ain't got one. You're laying up someplace. I don't understand you. You live in a hotel? You sleep in subways?"

"I'm at her house, but she's got no phone. She wasn't paying her bills, so they disconnected it."

"My schedule is not like yours, Donnie. Because I gotta account for myself. You make me laugh."

11

FRANK BALISTRIERI

I rejoined Conte. We worked the vending business just enough to make it look real. We ordered a few machines and placed them in four or five bars and restaurants. We spent most of our time pushing the investigation.

Our case was that by forcing Conte into a secret partnership in order to do business in Milwaukee, and by forcing other businessmen out, Balistrieri was committing extortion and creating a monopoly and interfering with interstate commerce.

We wanted to see what else we could get on him. We had information, for example, that he had a big bookmaking operation, that he was involved in skimming the take at the Las Vegas casinos, that he was involved with illegal union activities. There was always a chance you could clear up some murder cases. Things like that.

Lefty flew in for a Friday night meeting with Balistrieri to "ease me in." The three of us drove to Snug's, Frank's large, busy restaurant.

Lefty's instructions were: Let Balistrieri initiate conversation. This is a social function, so don't discuss business. Frank might not want the others to know that he's in business with us. Only answer his questions. Don't get inquisitive about anything.

"Donnie," Lefty says, "do me one favor. I love you. I'd rather do five years than lose your friendship. Do everything right over here because you can name your own ticket, believe me."

Tony and I went to the bar to await being summoned. Lefty was taken directly to Balistrieri's table, near the large front window, where there was a lot of fuss made over him and the usual kissing of cheeks.

After an hour we were escorted to the table by the maître d'. Frank Balistrieri, in his early sixties, was short and pudgy, with a jowly face and black, slicked-back hair. He was immaculately dressed in a dark blue suit, like an old-time Mafia guy out of the movies.

Tony had already met him at the sitdown. Lefty introduced me. "Frank, this is Donnie. He's with me, and he's with Mike." Frank introduced those around the table. Among the half dozen was his right-hand man, Steven DiSalvo, short, hard-looking, with just a monk's-fringe of hair around the ears.

Frank ordered bottles of $70 wine. He talked with Lefty about various New York Bonanno people he knew, like our boss, Carmine Galante, whom he called by his nickname, Lilo. He had some education, wasn't a "dese-and-dose" type.

When he started telling us about an incident regarding a vending business in Fort Lauderdale, Florida, where he had a piece, his face and voice turned mean, and he put a fist on the table. He said he had been down there during the past week to collect his end. The guy with the business had put $45,000 in cash on the table. Frank said he swatted the money off the table and told the guy, "Wipe your ass with forty-five grand. My end is at least a quarter million." He needed somebody like Lefty, he said, to take care of the vending business in Florida, straighten people out.

I thought, This guy could lull you to sleep, but he is nobody to mess with.

Out of the blue, Frank invited us to his home for dinner the next night, Saturday.

When we left the restaurant, Lefty was ecstatic. "Donnie, you remember when we used to have to stand outside Sabella's joint when Lilo was inside? We couldn't even go inside the joint. He'd come out and he wouldn't even say hello to you. Tony, in New York you can't even sit at the same table with a boss. And here we're sitting down with a fucking boss, and tomorrow night we're going to his house for dinner. Tell him, Donnie, would this ever happen in New York? Never."

"He's right, Tony," I said.

"But listen. He can be moody, nasty. Frank can be maybe Jekyll and Hyde, a man who can be a fucking animal. He don't forget. He don't like that guy from Rockford, that Phil, because he played him for a sucker once, years ago. That's why the call to Rockford came through Chicago, for my introduction, because Chicago was hoping to heal that there between Rockford and Milwaukee."

"What do those guys in Rockford control, Left?" I ask.

"That's it, only Rockford. This guy here controls. He's more in charge than anybody else."

"Even though those guys are older out there in Rockford?"

"What do you mean, older? Age? There's no age limit on this here. Mike says this guy's the biggest man in the Midwest. He didn't get what he's got just by staying in Milwaukee. He owns Kansas City. Cleveland and Detroit belong to Frank. I just found that out. He's on a plane every day. He stays here one, two days a week. This guy has a limousine he uses for his mother once a week to go to church. A 1978 limousine *parked*, Donnie. This town, there's nothing you can do, you gotta go through him. He's got every union."

"Does he ever come to New York for anything, Left?"

"Once, twice a year, that's all. In and out. Who he's gotta see, mostly he goes to the West Coast, does his business out there. Like Vegas."

"Has Frank got any say back in New York?"

"He's got say all over the *world*. Mostly that's all over this country. You kidding me? They got the Commission. They settle everything. He was on it. The last war, him and the Chicago boss kicked Joe Bonanno out. He knows all the bosses. When he used to go to New York, he'd go to the Old Man's house, Gambino's. Equal boss."

"How's he get along with Lilo?"

"They love each other," Lefty says. "I'm a-scared of him sometimes. Tony, let him do the fucking talking. You just blend into the situation."

"I did something wrong?" Tony says.

"You told that one guy at the table, 'Where do you come from?' That shook me up. They don't like that. Never ask anybody where they're from. Because, why you asking? You a cop? That got me fucking chilled to my fucking death. I'm glad that went over Frank's head. Because he could turn around and say, 'Who the fuck are you to ask my friends where they come from?' God forbid you get into a conversation."

"Okay," Tony says. "Now I know. I'm learning."

"Lemme tell you something, Tony. By next summer you'll be so polished in the underworld field that you won't need me. And I'm gonna turn around and say I'm very proud of you. But we ain't talking about that. Tony, we gotta emphasize to Frank that we're getting spots for machines, we're going after routes, taking over companies, easing other guys out. You can't be lax in this field. That's a tough guy there. Not somebody like that mutt, Anthony Mirra. He's got a real empire here, Frank has. So far the people are very nice. You know that Steve DiSalvo, Frank's guy you met at the table? I'm impressed by him. He's got almost as many hits as I do."

Frank Balistrieri, alone, drove us to his house in his black Cadillac. Lefty gave me a look—he couldn't believe a boss would go anywhere alone, let alone drive himself.

On the way Frank told us, "I've got a good crew, but they're older, kind of set in their ways. I could use some younger guys that I could trust to take over a couple of my clubs and other businesses. Younger guys would be able to relate to the ways of today's business world."

"If you need anything done," Lefty pipes up, "Donnie and Tony can do it. You can trust them. They're good with people. They're at your disposal, Frank, if you need them."

It was only about a ten-minute drive to his lakefront Colonial-style home. The people from the night before were joined by Frank's brother, Peter. Peter was a little taller, less intense than his brother, the boss. "I wouldn't be in his position for all the tea in China," he said. "I couldn't take the heat."

We were introduced to Frank's wife. She and another lady did the cooking and serving.

Frank sat at the head of the table, Lefty at his right hand. The women didn't sit with us, just served. It was a fine five-course dinner with veal as the main course. Bottles of Château Lafitte wine were continuously replenished on the table. Later came Louis XIII brandy.

Frank talked about the old days. At one time he owned seven clubs in downtown Milwaukee and promoted boxing matches, many of which were setups, fixed. He said that when he travels nowadays, he flies by private jet and does not move in or out of major airports, and that he always travels under an alias—currently "Lenny Frank."

The mood got warm and relaxed. But Conte and I had to maintain concentration and composure, choose our words and actions carefully so as not to offend. This was a boss's house.

On the next evening, Sunday, there was to be a big "Icebreaker" banquet to kick off the Italian Golf Tournament, a charity event. He said he had not attended for several years because he was enemies with the guy who once headed the committee, Louis Fazio. "But now he's dead," Frank said. "Five times thirty-eight." He laughed, but it was no joke. Thirty-eight, as in caliber. So he planned to attend this banquet as a surprise and "have some fun." He invited us to come along as his guests.

His brother Peter said, "I owe some aggravation to some people too. I wouldn't mind throwing a scare into some of them."

Lefty smiled. "A little violence never hurt anybody," he said.

Our group arrived late at the Grand Ballroom of the Marc Plaza Hotel for the Icebreaker Banquet.

When we appeared in the door, the maître d' and the chairman of the banquet committee came running over, full of apologies to Frank that there was no table ready for him—they had not known that he was coming.

There were no empty tables, and everybody had started eating their fruit cocktails. Waiters started scurrying around. People were already looking at us and whispering. Obviously they knew who Frank Balistrieri was. There was a table right in front of the stage where they would have the ceremonies. The maître d' told these people they would have to move to accommodate us. Nobody complained. A new table was set up for us. Then they brought us in and sat us down. Waiters were all over us, two or three catering to our table alone.

After the meal a steady stream of people came over and paid homage. "Frank, you're looking good. . . . Nice to see you here, Frank. . . ." I had never seen anything like this. It was unreal.

Frank played his power to the hilt. "This is Leftie and Donnie, my good friends from New York. This is Tony, my good friend from Baltimore. . . ." He would introduce these people to us, then immediately ignore them and resume talking to us, leaving them standing there with the color draining from their faces.

Carmen Basilio, the former boxer and one of the guests of honor, and Johnny Desmond, who sang at the event, came over to be introduced.

After the ceremonies were over, Frank said, "Let's go over to the snitch's place."

That was the Peppercorn, a lounge and restaurant in the downtown Athletic Club. The Peppercorn was operated by a guy Frank said he hated "because he's a snitch."

The place was jammed, mostly with people who had come over from the banquet. We stayed in the bar. More people came over to pay their respects to Frank.

Frank and Steve DiSalvo started telling us about stool pigeons.

"There's so many fucking stool pigeons," Steve says, "that you can't kill them all. You need Castro's army to kill all the stool pigeons in Milwaukee. Around here, how you can tell the stoolies is, they all have remote starters in their cars."

Conte had recently put a remote-control starter in his car.

Frank said he couldn't understand how people could turn against their own. "No witness ever lived to testify against me."

Steve says to me, "I been trying to get Frank, instead of running his own book, to charge all the other bookies in town $1,000 a week just to operate. Because it's a pain in the ass with so many stoolies, a headache. Let them run their book, charge them, and leave your own guys out of it. You can't get anybody good to run the book anymore."

Frank said that the guy who ran his day-to-day gambling operation the previous year didn't tend to business. "I don't want to have to look over somebody's shoulder all the time. I need somebody I can trust."

"Donnie can do it," Lefty jumps in. "He worked with me in my bookmaking operation, he can handle it, he knows what he's doing."

Frank looks at me. "You interested?"

"Sure I'm interested."

Frank grabs Lefty's arm. "Let's talk." They go away to a small table.

As a connected guy but not a made guy, I could be loaned out from one family to another. Lefty would get a cut of whatever I did, and he knew how big this guy's bookmaking business was.

Not only would I be handling the bookmaking for the mob boss of Milwaukee, but I had the chance to get inside the skimming operation in Las Vegas. At casinos controlled by the mob, money is skimmed right off the top as the mob's share. Balistrieri had the responsibility of collecting that skim money and distributing it to the other mob families involved around the country.

It was a sensational opening for me. But I couldn't do it. I knew that instantly. The largest part of Frank's bookmaking operation was football. The football season lasts about twenty weeks. During that season the

Special agent Joseph Pistone, operating undercover as jewel thief "Donnie Brasco," is shown in New York's Little Italy in 1977. Agent Pistone's operation was so secret that even the FBI surveillance team thought "Donnie Brasco" was an associate of the Bonanno family. As Agent Pistone infiltrated higher levels of La Costra Nostra, surveillance teams became part of his operation to document evidence against the Mafia and to protect his life. Many of the photographs on these pages are FBI surveillance shots taken without his knowledge.

These surveillance photos were taken outside the Toyland Social Club in New York, the headquarters of Bonanno family underboss Nicky Marangello and a key meeting place for top members of the Bonanno crew.

Underboss Nicky Marangello, who went by nicknames "Nicky Cigars," "Nicky Glasses," or "Little Nicky," controlled the numbers and other gambling operations for the Bonanno family.

Capo Mike Sabella (left) with one of his top soldiers and hitmen, Benjamin "Lefty Guns" Ruggiero. Ruggiero became "Donnie Brasco's" Mafia partner.

Tony Mirra (right), one of the most feared of all Bonanno soldiers, talks with Marangello. Mirra eventually became jealous of "Donnie Brasco's" rising influence, and wanted him dead.

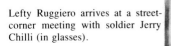

Lefty Ruggiero arrives at a street-corner meeting with soldier Jerry Chilli (in glasses).

Tony Mirra (back to camera) and Joey D'Amico (left) meet with two of the most important "zips," Caesar Bonventre and Sal Catalano (right). "Zips" were Sicilians imported to set up a huge heroin-smuggling ring operating through pizza parlors—an operation that became famous as the "Pizza Connection" case.

From left, Al Walker, big Joey Massino, an unidentified companion, and Tony Mirra. Massino eventually was put in charge of the zips, and became the heir apparent to ailing Bonanno boss Philip "Rusty" Rastelli.

Agent Pistone as "Donnie Brasco" relaxes at poolside at the Tahitian Motor Lodge in Holiday, Florida, in July 1980 with Dominick "Sonny Black" Napolitano, the top-ranking Bonanno captain.

Lefty Ruggiero emerges from a Florida motel on his way to case a potential bank job in St. Petersburg.

Bonanno boss Carmine Galante lies in a pool of blood, his cigar still clenched in his teeth, after being shotgunned to death in an ambush at a Brooklyn restaurant on July 12, 1979. As a result of the execution, Rusty Rastelli became the new Bonanno family boss, and Sonny Black was elevated to top captain.

Sonny Black emerges from a motel coffee shop with Florida boss Santo Trafficante. The two forged a new alliance between the Bonanno and Trafficante families to share gambling and other illegal activities.

rank Balistrieri, boss of the Milwaukee family. Agent Pistone set up an alliance between the Balistrieri and Bonanno families in 1978 to hare a Milwaukee vending-machine operation.

Philip "Rusty" Rastelli ran the Bonanno family for several years from a cell at the federal penitentiary in Lewisberg, Pa.

This early-morning surveillance photo shows the Motion Lounge in Brooklyn, Sonny Black's headquarters. His apartment was on the third floor, his pigeon coops on the roof.

Outside the Motion Lounge on May 14, 1981, the day Sonny Black gave "Donnie Brasco" the contract to "hit" a rival Mafia member. From left, Nicky Santora, Boobie Cerasani, Sonny Black, and Agent Pistone.

On July 28, 1981, two days after Agent Pistone ended his undercover role, FBI agents (left to right) Jerry Loar, James Kinne, and Doug Fencl emerge from Sonny Black's apartment after informing him that "Donnie Brasco" was an FBI agent.

After the agents' visit, Sonny Black went up to the roof, to his pigeon coops, where he often retreated to think in private. The revelation that the Bonanno family had been infiltrated by an FBI agent meant death sentences for those responsible for the unprecedented breach in Mafia security.

Sonny Black summoned the top members of his crew to plan strategy regarding the stunning news about "Donnie Brasco." From left: Boobie Cerasani, Nicky Santora, Lefty Ruggiero, Sonny Black.

Lefty Ruggiero, Agent Pistone's Mafia "partner" for five years, stands in the doorway of the Motion Lounge as the "Donnie Brasco" revelation sinks in.

bookmaking operation goes on seven days a week. We were now entering August, and football season was about to start.

There was no way I could be away from home now for five solid months.

By not turning it down immediately, I thought maybe I could milk a little more information out of them.

After Lefty and Frank talked for a few minutes they came over. Frank said, "Okay, you get together with Steve next Tuesday. He'll give you the whole rundown."

We left the Peppercorn at about two A.M.

Lefty explained what he and Frank had talked about. "Frank says to me, 'You know, if Donnie takes this, you gotta be responsible for him. You know the consequences.' I says I definitely do. He says, 'Once I put it on record, if this guy fucks up, you're in trouble, not him. They don't look for him. They look for you.' So I says, 'You don't have to look far. I take the full responsibility.' I told him you're my blood, Donnie, nobody had to worry about you."

Frank still had to call New York to get permission from our captain, Mike Sabella, to use me, and to go on record that Lefty was taking full responsibility if anything went wrong—such as if I was a snitch, or if I absconded with money from the book.

"I shook hands with him," Lefty says, "but that don't count. He's still gonna put it on record in New York. 'Go ahead and make your phone call,' I says. 'I'd stake my life on the man.' Tony, the responsibility I gave Donnie just now . . . if he fucks up, I'm a dead man. New York City, they only call bosses to bosses. This boss here, he calls New York, he talks to a boss. If I get sent for, I don't know what I'm getting sent for. They just say to come in. And I'd be getting killed for something I didn't even know. I'll tell you one thing. You two guys, you couldn't have any opportunity like this nowhere. You got the world at your feet. They're all afraid of him over here. They're all fucking Hoosiers."

After Lefty went to bed I got hold of Conte right away. I said, "Tony, I just can't do this." He understood and said, "Donnie, you do what you've got to do. Don't worry about it."

I called the case agent, Mike Potkonjak, and told him. He got in touch with Ralph Hill, the Assistant Special Agent in Charge in Milwaukee. Hill wanted to meet and talk it over.

This all had to be handled immediately. I was going to have to tell Lefty the next morning, before Balistrieri called New York, or my credibility would be shot. I couldn't meet with DiSalvo, get all the inside details, and then turn it down—I would look very much like a cop or a snitch.

Before dawn, Conte and I met with Hill and Potkonjak in a room at another hotel outside of town.

"I'd really like for you to go through with it," Hill says, after we'd kicked it around. "You know what you're throwing away."

"There comes a point where I've got to start thinking about my family."

Hill says, "What would it take for you to change your mind?"

They couldn't make my job easier or safer. Half facetiously I say, "More money."

He thought he could get me a raise. He called Headquarters in Washington. He explained the situation and asked that I be raised one grade, to supervisor, which would mean a couple thousand dollars more in salary.

Headquarters said no. They couldn't advance me to supervisor because I wasn't doing supervisory work, which meant either working in a Headquarters office in Washington or having a squad of men under you in the field. Hill pleaded that they not stick to technicalities, but they held firm.

That took me off the hook. I wasn't going to take the job, anyway. But if Headquarters didn't care enough to bend the rules for this opportunity when I was putting my ass on the line every day, at least I didn't have to feel guilty.

Now I had to come up with a reason that Lefty would buy. Lefty would have to come up with yet another one to give Balistrieri.

Balistrieri wouldn't be too upset because he had just that night made the offer and hadn't yet contacted New York, and I hadn't gotten involved in details. Lefty could just tell him that something came up with family business—the kind of dodge these guys use all the time because you can't question that.

One thing that I had in my favor, seen through any mob guy's eyes, was that no cop would ever turn that job down. So I would be above suspicion in that regard. Lefty would go cuckoo no matter what I said, but I could think of only one reason he would believe: simply that I would not stay cooped up in Milwaukee for twenty straight weeks, especially when it included the damn cold winter. He would scream, but he would believe it. He wouldn't tell Sabella anything because it would be embarrassing. I had been his partner for more than a year, I had never embarrassed him, we still had prospects in Milwaukee, he would get over it.

Lefty came down to the coffee shop for breakfast, still bubbling over about how much money we were going to make.

I told him I had thought it over and changed my mind, and why.

He went bananas. "You wanna be a fucking play-boy and lay around in California all the time! You worry too much about your girlfriend! You worry about getting pinched! Everything's a joke to you! We're blowing two hundred fucking grand!"

He was yelling in front of everybody in the coffee shop. When he calmed down, he said to Conte, "Tony, you get in touch with Frank. Go down there today and tell him that Donnie can't take the gambling job because Mike just called this morning and he wants him free to be back and forth to New York for another job."

He wouldn't look at me. "Go to California and don't bother me. I'm too mad to talk to you now. Go fuck with the broads on the beach and call me in a couple days when I cool down. Tony, take me to the airport."

*   *   *

Lefty had been pushing Conte to rent him a car through Best Vending and have the business pay for it. It was a typical wiseguy way of thinking: Muscle into any business that you can, get a weekly cut, and squeeze out any extra perks you can.

Conte had been stalling. Now we reconsidered. Lefty had been good for the investigation. By cultivating him and keeping him happy, we had shortcut a lot of effort. He got us a sitdown with Balistrieri, got us the partnership. If he hadn't come out to Milwaukee, Conte would be dead.

So we figured, what the hell, let's rent him a car and let him keep it for a couple of months. Conte rented him a maroon Thunderbird and drove it to New York and presented it to him.

Mike Sabella wanted to talk to me. Lefty hadn't told Mike that I had turned down the gambling job. "Don't say nothing to upset him," Lefty says. "He got enough in his mind. Work on his restaurant is gonna cost him six hundred grand now. Yesterday he smacked the contractor and almost killed him. And with the feast, there's a new guy down there from the precinct, and he ain't gonna allow no wheels down there, and Mike is blowing his top because of that."

"Wheels" were roulette wheels, a major source of profit at the Feast of San Gennaro.

We went to CaSa Bella. Mike told me, "Don't advertise what we got going in Milwaukee, because we don't want everybody in New York to know about it. Permission came from Lilo and Nicky, and we want to keep it between bosses. Frank has Fort Lauderdale sewed up. We'd like to get into that action, through Frank. We don't want any other crews fucking up our deal."

He wanted to keep all the information among just Lefty, himself as our captain, boss Carmine Galante, and underboss Nicky Marangello.

Then suddenly everything changed. The Balistrieris started avoiding Conte. They weren't giving him leads on routes to buy. They weren't returning his calls.

There was no explanation. Conte and I went to see John Balistrieri, Frank's son and lawyer, to try to dope out what the hang-up was.

We met with John at his office. Conte did the talking because this involved his business. He didn't bring up the problem directly, just tried to sense the situation. He reiterated Lefty's invitations to all of them to come to the Feast of San Gennaro and be wined and dined by the New York crew. John was courteous. He said his father was tied up with some kind of grand jury matter lately, but he was sure his father wanted to come if he could get free, and they'd get back to us.

John seemed friendly, but he didn't say what we wanted to hear, which was why they had retreated from business dealings with Conte. And they didn't get back to us.

Lefty's reaction was, "Maybe Frank's just got his balls twisted over that grand jury. They were gonna bury him. Then twenty-three guys went in there and took the Fifth. Maybe that's what's been taking his mind up. But listen, you should've never gave up that goddamn bookmaking thing with him. And that would've only been a start, for chrissake. Then he starts sending you around to Vegas and Florida and Kansas collecting money. You messed the whole thing up. You should've listened to me. We would've been on easy street."

The situation with Balistrieri didn't improve. Nobody would return Lefty's calls now, either. And finally Mike got involved, putting out inquiries through channels. Nothing. Even his calls were not returned.

Two weeks later, in early September, Conte got a letter from Balistrieri's lawyer-sons dissolving the partnership with Conte.

Lefty called me back to New York. We met at Lynn's, a restaurant on East Seventy-first Street.

"It don't make no sense to me," Lefty says. "Maybe they think he's a shady character. Maybe they're afraid to put money in his hand because he's a swindler. They won't even pick up a phone for nobody over there, understand? This is an introduction through you. What is the story on this gentleman? I can't explain this situation to anybody. You gotta tell me what the story is."

"I don't know what to tell you, Left. I knew the guy ten years ago, he was okay."

"Maybe he's a ladies' man. Listen, Donnie, last time he was in New York, he brought that car in, I took him to a joint, he bought drinks for three ladies in there. I lectured him about that. Now I hear that he made a play for one of Frank's girlfriends out there, in one of his joints. Is that true, Donnie?"

"How the hell do I know, Left? I ain't with him night and day. I never saw him do anything."

"You know the way Mike feels about somebody that insults a wiseguy's wife or girlfriend: That's worse than being a rat or a pimp. Mike and I are embarrassed now because we introduced him to Frank. I'm in jeopardy over here. And you brought him in. You got to do something about this, Donnie."

"What you want me to do?"

"You say you knew him in Baltimore. Go to Baltimore and check him out. Find people who knew him. Maybe he's a snitch. We don't know who the hell he is. If you check him out okay, maybe we can still salvage the situation out there."

So I went to Baltimore. Of course, I didn't do anything. I hung out for a few days, then went back to New York.

I told Lefty I had found a few guys who knew Conte in the old days, that he'd never done anything wrong as far as they knew, that he wasn't a "wire"—which is a snitch or informant—he never got out of line with the ladies, didn't insult people.

"All right," Lefty says, "now we gotta get this guy in here and talk to him. Go out to Milwaukee. Bring him in."

I went to Milwaukee. Conte and I analyzed the whole matter. We tried to think like wiseguys think.

Two families had put a business together through a sitdown. Now Balistrieri had canceled the agreement without explanation and hadn't returned phone calls from a top Bonanno captain for more than a month. That was a major discourtesy, meaning he had a major cause. Something had spooked Balistrieri. Conte could get whacked at any time.

We were convinced that for whatever reason, the partnership was finished, Balistrieri wasn't coming back in. So there was no need to continue with a vending business.

But Conte and I couldn't just fold it up, either. A citizen like Conte can't retire from doing business with a mob guy. Once a guy like Lefty gets his hooks into you, he's going to keep draining you. You run the business, he's your partner and gets fifty percent. Or you're going to sell everything and he'll take fifty percent of that. If you say no to those alternatives, I get a call, as Lefty's man on the scene, and he tells me to work this guy over, do a number on him. You always have to pay a price for getting out.

At this same time Lefty was pushing for money for a score. There was a load of Betamax videocassette recorders that he could take for $15,000. He could make $18,000 in ten days. But he didn't have the money. Mike had agreed to lend him $5,000 for ten days, at a price of $2,000. Lefty wanted Conte to invest the rest, $10,000.

We needed to buy some time both to come up with a safe evacuation plan and to avoid Conte having to cough up ten grand. So Conte faked a heart attack.

He checked into St. Luke's Hospital, complaining of chest pains. They hooked him up to all the machines and gave him medication. Nobody at the hospital was clued in, because you never clue anybody in if you don't have to—you never know who's legit and who's not. Also, we knew that Lefty would call to check up.

I called Lefty to tell him about the heart attack. Lefty called the hospital and said he was Conte's cousin and wanted to verify that he was a patient.

After a few days of tests, Conte checked out. Lefty was mad when Conte was in the hospital, and he was mad when he got out. Lefty pushed for the $10,000. Conte said he was broke because he had $6,000 in doctor bills.

"He's so fucking full of shit," Lefty groans to me. "We fall down in the street with an attack—what doctor bills? Three days in the hospital, six thousand bucks? What's he think he's talking to, a moron?"

"He says he can't come up with the money, Left. The only money he's got now is his wife's money."

"Oh, suddenly it's his wife's money? He's telling fifteen different stories. He says to me, 'You didn't come out here and help me with these guys when we had this problem.' I said, 'I didn't tell you to go to bed with different people's women.' Mike is blowing his top now. First of all, he says, the guy bullshit you that he's got a heart attack. And second of all, he ain't sending you nothing. This guy's throwing the towel in, so you might as well sell everything over there."

"I think he's gonna just keep trying to operate his business."

"What, without me? I'll make one phone call. They'll take it all away from him. Then he's going to run to the cops and then that's the end of him. Donnie, we'd of finished this Betamax deal in ten days. And we'd have had winter money, all three of us. The guy's sick in the coconut, boy."

The first idea to extricate Conte and close up the vending operation was that he would just take off and disappear. Whoa, I said, we can't just do it like that, because then you're really putting the heat on me. I'm in enough trouble already, for bringing him in. We have to have a reason for him to take off. He has to be eased out in such a way as to protect my credibility and my ass, because I will still be out there as Donnie Brasco. So, talking it over with Potkonjak, we came up with the idea that Conte would pull a big score and then decide to keep his end all to himself and not split with Lefty and me. I could back up that reasoning.

It would be a two-stage disappearance. We hatched a story that Conte had a really big score coming up in December with some old friends in Chicago. An art score, because that required special contacts and special outlets that would be harder to check up on. After the score he would have to lie low for a time while the art was disposed of. Then he would surface, say the score had been a big success and that he would have to leave again soon to pick up his cut to divvy up with

Lefty and me. At that point he would disappear for good.

A week before Thanksgiving, Conte called Lefty and told him he had this score coming up.

I was with Conte in Milwaukee all during this critical period. Lefty called me the next day. His spirits were raised. "He's got a big one coming up for next month. He said the three of us will get off."

"Is that right?"

"He said we'll be all right for a whole solid year, living like a king."

In the next weeks Lefty anticipated big money. He changed his social club into a candy store and had his daughter run it. He started a bookmaking business with me and two other partners—each was supposed to chip in $2,500. We looked around the neighborhood at various bars we might buy. He started work on another club that he and I were going to run as a fish-and-chips joint a couple of doors from the candy store. In mid-December we went down to Miami Beach for a few days, staying at the Thunderbird and hanging out at the lounge there and at the Diplomat and at a place called the Top Hat, enjoying the company of a lot of wiseguys that we knew.

Lefty had kept the rental car long enough, so before Christmas, our agents stole it back. Lefty had parked it in a lot, the agents went in and hooked it—just like I used to do. One of the guys drove it back to Milwaukee and stashed it until the operation was over.

"Fucking Puerto Ricans!" Lefty said. "They musta seen the Christmas presents in the back seat, that's why they took it." He filed a report with the police.

By the New Year, Lefty was desperate for money. His Betamax deal had gone sour. He was about to be thrown out of the partnership in the new numbers business because he couldn't come up with his share. He owed $25,000, and Mike Sabella was squeezing him for it.

Then—a total coincidence—Lefty saw an item in the paper about a $3 million art heist in Chicago. "That's it," he said, "that's the one. That's got to be him."

His end of that score, he figured, depending on the other splits, had to be at least a quarter million.

The first week in February, Conte called Lefty and told him he made the score, but he couldn't pick up his end in Chicago for another week. Lefty told me to bring Conte in right away for a sitdown with Sabella.

Joined by Conte's "girlfriend," an agent going by the undercover name of Sherry, we flew into New York and went first to Lefty's apartment. Lefty took Conte and me into his bedroom.

"Okay, listen to me now," Lefty says. "We're going over to Mike's joint, and you pay careful attention to everything Mike says, because this went right to the top, and there were a lot of bosses involved in the Milwaukee situation."

Lefty brought Louise. The five of us went to CaSa Bella.

We went into the bar and were greeted by Mike. Mike and Lefty talked alone for a few minutes, then called Conte and me over.

Mike asked Conte for a complete rundown on the Milwaukee situation, start to finish. He listened without saying a word.

Then Mike says, "I found out what the situation is and I can tell you in three words: They don't want New York people in Milwaukee. That guy went ahead and shook your hand and made the agreement when he didn't have the authority. Now, Tony, I don't talk to a citizen like you. I'm making an exception here. Milwaukee is responsible to Chicago, and Chicago is responsible to New York. Milwaukee has no authority to make an agreement like that without getting permission from the people they're responsible to."

"I understand," Conte says.

"What you don't understand, Tony, is they are all responsible to New York. Across the street is the boss of bosses. Last Wednesday there was a sitdown there, and Chicago and Milwaukee came in. He made a decision in our favor."

Since the Bonanno boss, Carmine Galante, was still in prison, we assumed the decision was made by Genovese boss Funzi Tieri, who was the reigning chief of the Commission. The decision, Mike explained, was that Conte could resume his vending business in Milwaukee and that Balistrieri could again become partners if he wished, but if he didn't want to become partners again, he still couldn't hinder Conte in any way. If Balistrieri did hinder him, he should immediately contact Lefty. The decision went our way because Balistrieri had made the initial mistake.

"If I had made a mistake," Conte says, "I would be man enough to go to the individual and apologize."

Both Lefty and Mike vigorously shake their heads. "A boss doesn't admit he make a mistake," Mike says. "The only out he had, because he had made the mistake, was to dissolve the partnership without explanation."

Mike pushed his chair back from the table—the sitdown was over.

We rejoined Sherry and Louise.

Lefty was glowing. "I feel good tonight for the first time since before the holidays. Lemme tell you something. Because of the situation out there, I didn't get invited to one Christmas party or wedding or wake or nothing. I didn't even get a Christmas bonus due to the fact of that there, and how it made me look. Now I feel good."

The restaurant's strolling guitarist came by our table. Louise requested the theme from *The Godfather*. The guy sang it in Italian and then in English.

"This restaurant just reopened a few days ago from remodeling," Lefty says. "See all that marble? He went for six hundred grand. All from Italy. You know what he had shipped in with the shipments of marble? Junk, heroin."

Lefty wanted to go up to Château Madrid and catch the floor show. He told Conte that Mike should get $1,000 for his recent efforts. "Mike'll make out a tab, and give him your American Express."

Since Mike had to pay taxes on that, Lefty said to add on taxes and tip so that Mike would be able to keep $1,000.

As we were leaving, Mike pulled me and Lefty aside.

"You still vouching for this guy, Donnie?" Mike asks.

"Yeah, Mike, as much as I did before."

"Okay, I'm holding you responsible."

Lefty says, "Now, he's gotta go back and pick up that money? You fly back with him. And then you don't leave his side. You go with him to pick up the money, and then you come back in here with him and that money."

"Okay, Lefty, that's what I'll do."

We headed uptown on the FDR Drive. Lefty pointed out some of the sights to Conte and Sherry.

"Right over there," Lefty says, pointing to the East River, "that's where we dump the bodies. One time some wiseguys dumped two bodies in there. Couple cops from the Seventh Precinct happened to see the bodies dumped. They didn't want to be bothered with it. So they took their little boat out and dragged the bodies down the river to the next precinct so they wouldn't have to investigate the case."

The next morning Conte and I went down to see Lefty. Lefty presented Conte with an itemized bill for all services to date, totaling $31,500—$17,500 of which was for Nicky Marangello, the underboss.

"Nicky was very strong for us at the sitdown with the bosses," Lefty says. "And listen. I'm asking Mike for permission to take youse, one at a time, out on a contract job with me so you'll have the experience, and you can get on the list for being made wiseguys."

On the flight to Milwaukee, Conte and I assessed the whole situation. The bosses had had this big sitdown and decided after all that Conte was free to run his business in Milwaukee and share with Lefty. What did the FBI need a vending-machine business for? We had accomplished all we needed with that. All told in this operation, we had laid out about $50,000. That included gifts for Balistrieri, and "loans" and cuts from "scores" to Lefty and other wiseguys. For about the salary of one agent, we had enough violations we believed to bring down the Balistrieri crime family. But we didn't need to spend any more. And if we spent any more time in Milwaukee, there was a good chance that Balistrieri would consider us thorns in his side and have us whacked. We were in agreement. It was time to close up Operation Timber.

Now was the time for Conte to take off—just as if he had grabbed the money from the score and wasn't going to share it. And I would try to fade the heat off me.

We checked into the Marriott Inn. The next morning, February 7, Conte and I were supposed to drive to Chicago together to pick up his end of the score, then fly straight back to New York with the money. We set it up with the case agent for Conte to disappear. That morning he left; his job in Milwaukee was over.

Later, over the telephone, I told Lefty that we had changed our plans. At about nine A.M., I said, we had packed the car with our clothes and everything, ready to leave, and then he got a call from the guy he was supposed to meet—"the guy with the jewelry," as we put it in code. The guy said Conte couldn't bring anybody with him, he had to come alone or he would not get his end. So I said, Conte had gone alone. But his plan was to come right back and pick me up. Now it was late afternoon. He hadn't showed, I hadn't heard from him. I was afraid something went wrong.

"Maybe they killed him," Lefty says.

"Hey, please, Left."

"Listen, you stay put. Don't go out to eat or nothing."

"Lefty, where the hell am I gonna go? It's snowing like a bastard here. Cold as hell. I got forty bucks in my pocket. I got the clothes on my back. Everything else went with him in the car. He took the plane tickets for the flight back to New York. I'm stranded here."

"He seem worried about anything?"

"He was in a great mood. He said he was glad we had the meeting with Mike and that we could go ahead with the business. He was glad that you're not pissed at him anymore."

"I'm blowing my top here. You weren't supposed to leave his side. That's why you're there. Call me in an hour."

I called an hour later.

"Nothing, Left. You think he got pinched?"

"I don't think he got pinched. Maybe it's his heart, he's in the hospital. Who knows? If you would've been concentrating on what you're supposed to do, this wouldn't't've happened. When you come back, you have to go into five years' probation over here with these guys. They'll make you come down every day, every night. You make one mistake, you get chased out."

"All right."

"All right nothing. You gotta listen. You stay put. Now you're stuck there, no clothes. Good thing you can order food in the room. He knows all this. He's gotta come back. That guy called me up again fifteen minutes ago."

"Mike?"

"He says, 'What do you mean you don't know what's going on?' I says, 'Well, he got tied up out there.' You put me in fucking mean positions with these guys."

"Maybe he was scared."

"Why should he be scared?"

"I don't know."

"You don't even know how to talk to people, feel people out. I mean, you don't know nothing. I'll tell you one thing. There ain't a punk in the street that hangs out with a wiseguy could get away with what you two guys done. Forget about it. Youse won't last five minutes in the city of New York. Because you got different ways of thinking. And nothing bothers you. What are you laughing at?"

"I'm not laughing. I'm coughing. I got a cold. It's freezing here."

"Don't go to sleep, because every hour on the hour we're gonna call."

An hour later I say, "I think this guy got clipped."

"What makes you say a thing like that?"

"The guy's all happy about going and everything, got all my clothes in the car. It takes four hours to drive down there and back. It's not like him. He would've called."

"I don't believe he's got clipped. Now don't start getting me crazy. I say he got hung up in Chicago."

All night long it goes on. The next morning I say, "Lefty, listen. I just got a phone call. Guy says, 'Is Tony there?' I say he stepped out for a minute. Guy says, 'I'm a friend of his. I was supposed to meet him yesterday in Chicago and he never showed up, and I wondered if you know where he is.' Probably the jeweler guy. He never got to him."

"Then you listen to the radio over there. Go downstairs and buy the papers. Because nothing happened to this guy. Because it'd be a big splash out there. They publicize everything. Ain't you got a television? Leave the news on all the time."

"But he's in Chicago, right? This is Milwaukee. That's a hundred miles away."

"So Milwaukee ain't got news? Anything goes on in Chicago, Milwaukee gets."

"Maybe the law doesn't know about it."

"Let me tell you something. That's Tony checking on if you're still there. He put a guy on the phone."

"Why would he be checking?"

"I don't know what's in the back of his head."

An hour later I tell Lefty, "The guy called back. He said, 'Don't wait around for your friend because he's not coming back.' "

"Why would he say that?"

"How the hell do I know? I'm just sitting here answering the phone. It's twenty-four hours already."

"He's not coming back," Lefty says. "Because this is Tony in Chicago making that call! Getting his friend to do that. But not even have the decency to say your clothes are at the airport or something, right?"

"Just said not to wait for my friend."

"You'll get a phone call in a couple hours to see if you left. Next time he calls you, you say, 'You tell fucking Tony just to leave my fucking plane ticket and my fucking clothes at the airport. We don't give a fuck if he never comes back into New York.' Open your mouth, Donnie. Talk like me. See what he says."

"All right."

After a pause he says, "Could this fucking guy be a fucking agent?"

"Who?"

"Tony."

"I don't know, Left."

"I know you don't know! That's your famous words. I'm so fucking mad. I don't even wanna get mad at you right now. I'm fifty-two, and I'm willing to spend the rest of my life in jail over this, because I'm gonna do what I gotta do with this son of a bitch because he fucked me pretty good. I'm facing shame in this neighborhood. The only way I can redeem myself is by doing what I gotta do with this guy. I take an oath on my dead father on this thing."

"We'll get it squared away, Left."

"Ain't the question, get it squared away. I can track this guy down anyplace I want. I took three photos of him in Chicago. I'm getting a thousand made up. I'll ship them out throughout the country—Phoenix, Minneapolis, Chicago. When I put word out on this fucking motherfucker, forget about it. So he lays up six months to a year. That don't mean shit. He's gotta come out of the woodwork. And when he does, nobody gonna touch him until you and I get out there. I'm giving my fucking life's work to this guy. He embarrassed me."

"He embarrassed me too."

"Forget about you. I can't go on Mulberry Street because I implicated myself with a jerk-off."

"He's probably got the money stashed somewhere by now," I say.

"I don't care about the money no more. Only thing I care about now is I'm gonna track this guy down and get satisfaction."

"I think the guy got whacked, Left, I'm telling you. He's not gonna go for twenty-four hours and not call."

"I don't believe it's a hit. If they're gonna set him up, they'll set him up in Milwaukee. I figure Tony don't wanna come up with this bread."

"But if it was one of the guys he pulled that job with," I say, "somebody that wanted his end, too, then you can kiss it all good-bye."

"I ain't kissing anything good-bye. If there's no write-up about this guy, and he don't come in, we'll track him down no matter where the fuck he goes. It's the two phone calls you got I don't like. It doesn't make sense. Because nobody advertises that they're doing this. They ain't gonna call up. What do they give a fuck about you? Donnie, you're gonna do something now. You're gonna rent a car. Use your credit card. Go two places. The airport in Milwaukee, then Chicago and that airport. The car has gotta be in the airport. If his car's in the airport, then you know he took off without us."

"I find the car, then what?"

"Then I come out there. We'll break the trunk to see if his body's in there or your clothes is in there."

I allowed six hours for the round trip to Chicago and a check of the airports. All day I sat in the motel room watching television inside and the snow outside, not ordering anything from room service, not answering the phone—as if I weren't there.

That night I called Lefty. I told him I went to the airports, I didn't find his car. But in Chicago I had described the car to the parking-lot attendants and asked if they saw it. One of them said he did see a white Cadillac like that the night before. He said the cops were towing it out, and he heard them talking about blood on the seat. "I think the guy got whacked, Left."

"I don't think he got whacked. Something's fishy."

"Left, I can't keep hanging around here. I got no money. I got the same clothes on I had on two days ago. I got to jump the bill and get out of here."

"All right. Come in. Lay low. Don't let Mike see you. I tell you this, Donnie. If I didn't love you how much I love you, you'd be fucking dead. Mike don't love you like I do."

I left Milwaukee. I still had to face the music back in New York. I still didn't know what had spooked Frank Balistrieri. But if we had covered our tracks as well as I thought, I might get punished, but I wouldn't get whacked.

12

SONNY BLACK

I wasn't punished. I wasn't put on probation. Mike Sabella gave me the cold shoulder, but since I wasn't a made guy, I was excused for a couple of errors in judgment. Lefty never let me forget how I let Conte and $200,000 get away. For a few months I moved around the country, ostensibly checking out scores for Lefty and me.

I was in Miami in July when Lefty called and told me to go out and buy the New York papers. "You'll be in for a big surprise," he said.

Carmine Galante had been hit. The Bonanno family boss had been out of Atlanta federal prison for only a few months. When I used to stand guard for him with Lefty outside CaSa Bella, I worried about getting whacked. Now there was Galante himself on the front page, lying dead on his back in a pool of blood, his cigar still clenched between his teeth. He had been shotgunned to death by three men while having lunch in the rear courtyard of Joe and Mary's Italian American Restaurant on Knickerbocker Avenue—the street where the zips hung out—in the Bushwick section of Brooklyn. The restaurant owner and a friend were also killed. Two other guys were identified as having been with Galante at the lunch: Galante's bodyguards, Baldo Amato and Caesar Bonventre, two of the "zips" I had seen around the Toyland Social Club. They had fled after the shooting.

I called Lefty. "Wow," I said.

"There's gonna be big changes."

"Well, where do we stand with everybody?"

"I can't talk over the phone. Come in right away."

When a boss gets killed, that's not the end of it. If one faction got permission from the Commission to take out a boss, rival factions, or those loyal to the dead boss, must be brought into line or wiped out. There will be a winning side and a losing side. Sometimes it takes years before one side wins and the killing stops. I didn't know how the factions lined up and which side Lefty would end up with now. Lefty had hated Galante, but you couldn't go just by that. Supposedly the zips were Galante's chosen people. But two of his prime zips were with him when he got whacked, and that said setup. So I didn't know where anybody stood, which means I didn't know where I stood, either.

I met Lefty on Madison Street, outside the candy store.

"Rusty Rastelli is the new boss," Lefty says, "even though he's still in the can. We're gonna be under Sonny Black. He was made captain. He's taking over Mike's crew."

Dominick "Sonny Black" Napolitano was with the Brooklyn Bonanno crew. I had seen him around once or twice, but for the most part the Brooklyn guys hang out in Brooklyn, the Manhattan crew in Manhattan. Sonny had been in prison for hijacking most of the time I had been on this job.

"What about Mike?" I ask.

"Him and Nicky were both supposed to get whacked, but they got passes because a lot of people liked them. They made a deal to get knocked down instead."

Sabella and Marangello accepted demotion. Now they were just ordinary soldiers of Lefty's rank. They were lucky.

"So where does all this leave us?" I say.

"We got no problems. I thought I was gonna get whacked."

After Galante got hit, he said, he got a call from Sonny Black. Sonny, even though knowing that Lefty was under Mike Sabella, directed him to come to a midnight meeting at the Motion Lounge, Sonny's hangout at Graham and Withers Streets in Brooklyn. And Lefty wasn't to tell anybody where he was going.

"I figure they're gonna whack me, too, because I was always close to Mike," Lefty tells me. "And he's telling me I can't tell my own captain I'm going over there. But I got no choice because I know that Sonny Black is now a power. I don't know what the fuck's coming down when I drive out to Brooklyn to see Sonny."

The meeting was friendly. Sonny told him all that had happened—who'd been knocked down, who the new captains were, and so forth. Joey Massino, the fat guy I had seen hanging around social clubs, was made captain. Sal Catalano, another Toyland guy, was made street boss of the zips, the imported Sicilians. And Caesar Bonventre, the slick young zip who was with Galante when he got whacked, was made captain—at twenty-eight, the youngest in the family. Sonny gave Lefty a choice to go with him or with Joey Massino. But Sonny wanted him.

"So I says, 'Yeah, I'll be with you.' "

In mob business you ask questions about aspects that pertain only to you. Normal curiosity is not normal curiosity for a wiseguy. A wiseguy does not go around asking who clipped the boss. Look too curious and you draw attention to yourself. If the cops did break something, the first thing everybody thinks is that there was an informant. I didn't want anybody saying, "Why was Donnie so curious about everything?"

I didn't go out of my way to learn what intelligence the FBI might have been getting about the murder from informants. I didn't want to know more than I could logically know as a connected guy. It could be just as risky to know too much as to know too little. I didn't want the burden of having to sort out what I should know from what I shouldn't.

The murder of a boss doesn't get talked about much on the street. Business policy doesn't change. There's only one policy in the mob: You earn money and you kick your money upstairs. Only the personalities change, and ordinary wiseguys or connected guys don't have anything to say about that. You go about your business while the power is sorted out by leaders of the factions.

"When Rusty gets out of the can," Lefty said, "things are gonna be different."

He liked Philip "Rusty" Rastelli. They were old buddies. I had never seen Rastelli because he had been in the can since 1975 for extortion.

It was strange walking down Mulberry Street past CaSa Bella and realizing that Mike Sabella was no longer a power.

For a time, Lefty said, nobody would be making any big moves. He was back to his check scams and numbers rackets. He decided that our fish-and-chips place would become a fast-food fried-chicken takeout place instead and, with his daughter running it, would be a steady source of income from the projects nearby. He wanted to buy the bar on the corner, but for that we would have had to come up with $60,000, and there was no way the Bureau wanted to get into that kind of money, and no way I wanted to be tied down running a bar.

Meanwhile I had some freedom to move around and contribute to other operations. Other agents could introduce me as a connected guy and a friend of theirs from New York, and that would enhance their credibility with the badguys they were working on. I told Lefty I had to start making some bigger money, so I wanted to check out a few things here and there. I worked short stints on various Bureau undercover investigations, ranging from New England to the Southwest. Some of these operations are continuing, some came to nothing. Some I can't talk about.

Larry Keaton, the agent working out of L.A., had an operation going on in a suburban town involving a gang of blacks engaged in political corruption, gambling, and drug dealing. He wanted to show these guys that he had mob connections. He wanted me to come out to Las Vegas and pose as a Mafia member representing a boss. He had another guy lined up to play the part of the boss.

My supposed role was to see if these guys had

projects worthy of putting before the boss. And if they did, I was to prepare them for meeting the boss, tell them how to act.

I went out to the Desert Inn where we had a big suite. These four guys arrived, tough, slick-looking dudes dressed in the latest outfits. We arranged the guys around the room and I told them how to sit. One guy put his feet up on the coffee table and I kicked them off. "You think you can talk to a boss with your feet up that way?" I say. "You got no respect for furniture?" I tell another guy, "Don't slouch on the sofa that way! Sit up and look like you're interested in meeting a boss."

"See," Larry says, "this guy ain't fucking around. You misbehave in front of the boss when he comes in, you're gonna get me in a jam. Because everything here is a reflection on me."

Everybody now is sitting up straight and tall and paying attention. I go at them one at a time. "You, what's your name again? What's your gig?" They tell me they move some coke, some marijuana, run a gambling place. I say, "We have to be assured that you guys can guarantee protection with the local politicians and sheriffs." I start to draw them out on what they can do, because I have to justify taking the boss's time. They say, "We got some politicians in town, the sheriff." They really want to convince me they are worthy of meeting the boss. They give me names, dates, amounts, plans.

"Hey! Slow down," I say. "When the boss comes in, you have to talk slow, make everything clear, because he doesn't want to have to ask for anything to be repeated, and he's not used to talking to blacks or hearing black street talk."

Also, we had the room bugged and wanted to make sure we got everything.

I said that when he comes in here, they should show respect, stand up. They should not expect to shake hands. Nobody touches the boss. They shouldn't speak unless they're asked to speak. They shouldn't expect the boss to speak to them because the boss doesn't speak directly to ordinary citizens. The boss is only coming here as a favor to Larry because he thinks a lot of him. We got everybody all tensed up, concentrating on doing everything right, sitting straight, talking slowly and clearly.

Then I went into the next room to get the boss.

The boss, an agent going by the name of Steve, was perfect. He was dressed up in a black suit with a white tie and a white carnation in his lapel. Stocky guy, dark face, heavy five-o'clock shadow. He looked like Frank Nitty from the old *Untouchables* TV show.

I make a big production of bringing him in, pulling out a chair for him to sit down.

"Okay, Donald," the boss says, "introduce me to the gentlemen."

One by one I introduce them. I say that I told the boss the whole thing, and he's very pleased that you guys are dedicated in this, and capable of making the scores, because he thinks a lot of Larry. He doesn't want to put Larry in any position that's going to be adverse for him.

Oh, no, they say, we wouldn't do that.

Steve the boss doesn't say a word. He just nods. I ask if they have any questions they want to ask the boss. No, no, no. Then I say to Steve, "Boss, anything you want to say to these gentlemen?"

He says, "Just tell them that I'm glad everything's going to work out."

I repeat his words, then say, "Okay, that's it." And I walk the boss out.

The whole thing took maybe forty minutes.

I didn't have anything more to do with that case. Larry got them all convicted.

Lefty and I spent a lot of time around Miami—vacationing, losing money at Hialeah or the dog tracks, looking for deals. Miami was considered more or less open territory, like Las Vegas, where the different mob families could operate so long as nobody stepped on anybody else's toes. Lefty was always scheming about how to crack into Florida where the big money was. He was always on the lookout for a bar or lounge to buy, once we made a big score and had some cash.

"That's how you make a fortune," he would say, "grab yourself a good lounge."

We would often stay at the Deauville or the Thunderbird where a lot of the wiseguys that he knew stayed. He introduced me to wiseguys here and there, including some Bonanno guys that lived in the area. The Deauville was a favorite of Lefty's because the manager, a straight guy named Nick, was a friend of his. Lefty always talked to him about getting a lounge or a game room going in one of the hotels, and Nick was always keeping his eye open.

Lefty and I were in Miami in August when a bunch of guys came down from New York for a vacation with their wives or girlfriends. They kept talking about how nice it would be to have a boat and go for a sea cruise. Lefty, who missed having a boat of his own, was always yearning to get on the water.

This was during the time that the undercover sting operation that became known as ABSCAM was under way. Eventually several Congressmen would be caught taking bribes from agents posing as rich Arabs. For the operation the FBI was using a boat to entertain their targets. Called the *Left Hand*, it was a white Chinese-made yacht, one of only two or three such models in the world. It had a full-time captain on board.

I happened to know the agent working ABSCAM. His undercover name was Tony Devita. I got in touch with him and explained what I had—a bunch of wiseguys and their ladies who would be very impressed if I could take them out on that boat. I asked him if ABSCAM was going to break anytime soon, and if not, if the boat could be available. He assured me that nothing would break publicly on the case for a long time. He found an open date in the schedule and set it up for us to use the *Left Hand*.

I told the guys that a girl I had been fooling around with up in Fort Lauderdale had introduced me to her rich brother, who owned a fancy boat. The brother was living in California but kept the boat at Pier 66 in Fort Lauderdale. She introduced me to her brother when he was visiting, and we hit it off. He put me in touch with the captain and said if I ever wanted to use the boat, I was welcome. So I had reserved the boat for a day.

Everybody was excited. There were about a dozen of us, including Lefty and one of the bartenders from 116, the Holiday Bar. We went out and bought Italian cold cuts and bread and olives and pickles and side dishes. The women made up sandwiches. We stuffed coolers full of beer and wine and sodas. We piled into our cars and headed up to Pier 66.

They went nuts when they saw the boat—especially Lefty, because he was proud of how his partner could produce for the crew. "What a fucking boat!" he says. "Donnie, you did some fucking job getting a boat like this." Everybody was oohing and aahing as we went on board.

"Where's your broad?" Lefty asks me. "The one with the brother?"

"She couldn't make it."

I did, however, bring along another guy. As a favor to another agent running another operation, I introduced an undercover policeman into my Mafia crowd. The cop's undercover name was Rocky. Bringing Rocky along on the cruise helped establish him with some of the badguys he might be running across in his operation.

Out on the ocean we went. We cruised around all day, ate and drank and had a wonderful time. A couple of the people had cameras, and everybody enjoyed posing with everybody else.

Then we came back and pulled into the slip where the boat was docked, and we ate and drank some more. "Never been on a boat that big," people were saying. "Like a fucking ship! You could go to the Bahamas on it!"

It was a great day. Afterward I just put ABSCAM and the boat out of my mind.

Lefty brought his wife, Louise, down to Miami. I went with them to the Thunderbird for dinner and the show. We arrived late, so even though we were tight with the maître d', we had to sit at a table right in front of the stage because the joint was packed.

A comedian comes on. I think he was from Australia. He starts working the crowd, cracking jokes at people sitting near the stage, and pretty soon he is focusing on us.

Lefty waves the guy off. "Don't bother us over here."

The comedian thinks he has a live one to banter with, so he goes at Lefty with wisecracks.

"I'm telling you, go take your microphone over there." Lefty points to the other end of the stage.

The guys keeps it up. All of a sudden Lefty goes up on the stage, grabs the mike from the guy, walks it to the far side, plunks it down, and walks back to the guy. "Now that's the last time I'm gonna tell you."

Lefty says to me, "If this guy comes back here, you go up and drag him off the fucking stage."

The guy stays over there but throws a few more barbs at our table. The crowd reacts like this is all part of the act.

When the show ends, Lefty says to me, "Go talk to that guy so he don't come back over here next show."

I catch up with the guy and grab his arm. "Hey, pal, next time you're told something, you listen. We walk in here again, you just make like you don't even know we're here."

"Listen," he says, pulling away, "this is what I do with the audience all the time, and I'm not changing my act just because you don't like it."

I give him a right-hand shot to the stomach, which doubles him over, and start dragging him out toward the back.

The manager has reached us by now. "Donnie, what's the matter?"

"You saw us try to tell this guy to leave us alone."

"Yeah, I was trying to catch his eye. Sorry about it."

I let the guy walk away. Next day he was fired.

Lefty got a phone call from a New Jersey wiseguy, one of Sam "The Plumber" DeCavalcante's guys, who was responsible for hiring this comedian. He apologized for what had happened and invited us all back down to the place that night for dinner.

We went for dinner. Everything was on the house from this guy, and he kept apologizing over and over.

"Forget about it," Lefty says. "The guy was a mutt, that's all. Donnie straightened him out."

Chuck, the undercover agent who had the record business and put on concerts back in the beginning of my operation, was working on an operation in Miami on banks that were laundering drug money for Colombian and Cuban customers. The FBI code name was Bancoshares. The mob is always looking for ways to launder money. Chuck thought maybe I could lure the Bonannos in.

I told Lefty about it and suggested that maybe we could steer some customers down there and get a cut. He decided we should go down and meet with the brains behind the scheme. Chuck couldn't meet with Lefty because he had met him years before when he was a "straight-up" agent—not undercover—in New York City. We brought in Nicholas J. Lore, an agent who had been working in California and has since retired from the F.B.I. to live there. He would pose as a big-shot free-lancer who was the brains behind everything—the guy who put the deals together with all the banks.

I told Lefty that coincidentally, Nick was the guy who owned the boat we went out on, the brother of the woman I knew. It was no more than putting a flesh-and-blood person into the story, instead of just a name, to add reality.

We came down for the meeting with Nick. Lefty was impressed with Nick's access to big money. Nick wined and dined us at a joint on Key Biscayne. He introduced Lefty to "Tony Fernandez," an agent who was supposedly his middleman in dealing with the banks. Tony was working with the president of a Miami bank—a Cuban who was deeply involved in laundering drug money through his bank.

Lefty wanted to get a piece of the banker's action on money laundering by bringing in contacts from New York. He also wanted to get going on some cocaine smuggling. At that time you could buy a key—

kilogram—of coke in Colombia for $5,000 to $6,000 and sell it in New York for maybe $45,000. But his attitude on drugs was: To hell with middlemen and cutting profits up with anybody, let's do it ourselves and keep it to ourselves. Donnie himself can go to Colombia and get the loads. "I don't need nobody in New York City," Lefty says. "Donnie comes in with it, nobody knows his business." Not splitting with the family could get you rich, killed, or both. But since we were dealing with people who weren't wiseguys—not even Americans—Lefty figured it was worth a shot.

Fernandez put the proposition to this Cuban banker that he do business with Lefty and me, wiseguys from New York. The banker readily agreed and set up a meeting for us at his bank to work out details.

Lefty and I went with Fernandez to this banker's office. The banker preferred to speak Spanish, so Fernandez was the translator. We sat down and began asking about details of prices and so forth, how the operation would proceed. Suddenly the banker became evasive. He didn't know anything about the drug business. He didn't know anything about money laundering. Clearly there would be no deal, and Lefty and I quickly lost patience with this guy's tap dancing—I wanted the banker busted, Lefty wanted big cocaine bucks.

We left. We couldn't figure out what spooked this guy. Maybe Lefty, who can be a very intimidating wiseguy, had made him nervous.

It wasn't Lefty. It was me. Later Fernandez went back to ask him what went wrong. The banker said, "I look in those eyes of Donnie and they're killer eyes. If something goes wrong in Colombia or anywhere, he'll come back and kill me. I don't want to have anything to do with that Donnie."

Lefty laughed. "I'm the fucking mob killer, and he's afraid of you."

But it wasn't funny to him that we had blown a drug connection in Colombia. Lefty told Nick, "Somebody should sit this banker down and explain to him how you can't make promises and then back out on it and waste our time. That's not the way Italians do things."

* * *

An agent going by the name of Tony Rossi was in Florida trying to infiltrate the gambling business that might lead to a connection with the Santo Trafficante family. Trafficante, who had been operating out of Tampa for twenty-five years, was the biggest Mafia don in Florida. He ran gambling casinos in Havana until Castro came to power, and achieved a lot of public notoriety when he admitted participating in a CIA plot to assassinate Castro during the Kennedy administration.

Rossi got a job as an enforcer, a strong-arm guy protecting card games. After a few weeks of this Rossi and the supervisor, Tony Daniels, decided that this wasn't moving fast enough.

Tony Conte joined Rossi, adding his experience from the Project Timber operation in Milwaukee. They came up with the idea of opening a nightclub. The operation using the nightclub as a way to get to Trafficante was code-named Project Coldwater.

Four case agents worked as contacts for the undercover agents: Jim Kinne, Jackie Case, Bill Garner, and Mike Lunsford. In the fall of 1979, they rented a club in Holiday, in Pasco County, forty miles northwest of Tampa, on busy U.S. Route 19. It was an octagonal building on five acres that had been a tennis club, with six tennis courts. They named it King's Court.

Rossi was established as "owner." So that King's Court didn't have to deal with the liquor authority, it was a private "bottle club" that you could join for a membership fee of $25. People brought their own bottles and left them in little lockers behind the bar. They paid for setups.

Rossie and Conte hired a manager for the tennis courts, and bartenders, waitresses, a piano player, and a club manager. Nobody knew it was an FBI operation. The club was all redecorated, new bar, new drapes, new oak tables, and padded oak chairs. The front door had a peephole, and signs saying: KING'S COURT PRIVATE LOUNGE; NO BLUE JEANS: MEMBERS AND GUESTS RING BELL TO ENTER.

They started running poker games out of a back room in the club, the house taking five percent. They paid off a member of the Pasco County Sheriff's Department for protection. They managed to entice in some local hoods who pulled small swag deals, drug deals. A couple of the guys that came in had garbage-collection businesses, so they came up with the idea of starting a Cartmen's Association by which members would control that business in the area and keep newcomers out.

Some half-assed wiseguys began hanging out there—ex–Chicago guys, ex–New York guys. They indicated that they had big connections, maybe leading to Trafficante. But nothing happened.

Conte suggested that maybe I could bring the Bonannos in, like we had done in Milwaukee, and get something going with Trafficante. A liaison with the Florida boss, allowing them to operate in the area, would be just as interesting to the Bonannos as it was to us. We might facilitate a sitdown with Trafficante as we had with Milwaukee. Of course, Conte had to pull out of it. He was leaving, anyway. His past had caught up with him.

All of a sudden, on an October day, word came down from FBI Headquarters that I was to pull out, end the Donnie Brasco role. The Bureau had found out what had spooked Frank Balistrieri in Milwaukee: Balistrieri had learned that Tony Conte was an agent. By mob rules, Balistrieri's next move should have been to tell the Bonannos in New York. It was just another quick step to them implicating me.

The decision had been made at the top without consulting me. I had to talk them out of it. I was certain that I had laid enough groundwork to continue.

I flew to Chicago to meet with Mike Potkonjak who had been the case agent for Project Timber. I presented my case.

Evidently Balistrieri had not yet passed on his information to New York. We had to assume that eventually he would. Then what would happen?

It was true that there wouldn't necessarily be any

warnings if New York got the word and they decided
to ice me. But I didn't think it would happen. It was
true also that I had brought Conte in. But I had been
very careful to vouch for him only to a certain extent.
If Lefty questioned me, I would say, "Look, like I told
you, he and I did some things ten years ago and I had
no complaints. So maybe he was an agent ten years
ago—so what? I didn't know about it then, I don't
know anything more now." Lefty would believe me.
Plus, Lefty was in a box. In order to convince Balistrieri
of Conte's reliability, Lefty had told Balistrieri that he
himself knew Conte, that Conte was a friend of *his*.
And further, at the Icebreaker Banquet, Balistrieri
had introduced Conte as *his* friend from Baltimore.

Potkonjak was on my side. So was the guy I trusted
most in the whole outfit, an old friend, Jules Bonavolonta, coordinator of the Organized Crime Program
in New York. But the matter was very intense. We
had to work quickly, and all by telephone. We convinced Jimmy Nelson at Headquarters, who was the
supervisor on Project Timber and with whom I had
worked earlier in New York.

They went to work on the very top levels at Headquarters. Finally everybody came around. I was allowed to continue as Donnie Brasco. But there would
remain a lot of concern in Washington. Every once in
a while after that, people got nervous for my safety
and thought I should come out. To their credit they
were convinced, time after time, that I should stay
under—that I could survive, that the stuff we were
getting was better and better.

I was pretty sure I was right. But from then on this
circumstance was always in the back of my mind.
Every time I was called in for a meeting with anybody
in the family, I wondered whether it might be because
Balistrieri had finally passed on his information, and
my number had come up.

My wife and daughters flew in to New Jersey to
spend the Christmas holidays with relatives.

The day of Christmas Eve is when all the mob guys
go around and pay their respects to other wiseguys at

all the social clubs. You have a drink with everybody you know. Lefty and I hit all the spots, including CaSa Bella and other restaurants where guys hung out.

Christmas Eve I went to Lefty's apartment and had dinner with him and Louise. They had a little Christmas tree on the table. Lefty and I exchanged presents—a couple of shirts for him, a couple of shirts for me.

At about eleven o'clock I went back to Jersey "to see my girl."

Christmas Day, I went back down to Little Italy to spend the day with Lefty. We cruised around again to the different spots and hung out. At about four P.M., he packed it in for the day, and I went back to Jersey to spend the rest of Christmas with my family.

The day after Christmas, we were all back on the job, hanging out and hustling.

Lefty had finally gotten his son Tommy cleaned up and off drugs. He had sent him to a rehabilitation center in Hawaii. Then he had gotten him a job at the Fulton Fish Market. Tommy was living with a girl and they had a child.

I walk into 116 one afternoon and Lefty is there, steaming. He tells me that Tommy's girlfriend called him and said that Tommy hasn't been coming home, hasn't been giving her money to buy food and necessities for the child. It looked like maybe Tommy was back on junk.

Lefty was seething because Tommy wasn't taking care of his baby.

"Donnie, he's supposed to meet me here so I can talk to him. He ain't showing up. I want you to go find him. I want you to throw him a fucking beating. Then bring him back here."

I couldn't beat up his kid, so I stalled for time. "What's the problem?"

"I just told you the fucking problem."

"Yeah, but, I mean, is it drugs or the broad or what?"

"Donnie, just find him, do a number, bring him here to me."

Luckily Tommy walks into the bar and comes over.

Lefty lights into him, reads him the riot act about taking care of the child. Tommy tries to explain something, but Lefty won't hear it. He just wants to ream his son out.

From the fall of 1979 through February of 1980, I gradually cultivated Lefty about King's Court. I told him a guy I had known from Pittsburgh had come into the Tampa area as a strong-arm, then had opened up a nightclub, and he wasn't connected with anybody, and he was getting hassled by half-ass wiseguys. There was a possibility that we could move in. Lefty was interested. He wanted me to keep looking it over. Meanwhile Rossi was introducing me to people as his New York connection.

Finally I called Lefty and told him that I was convinced we could make a good score by becoming partners with this guy, and that now was the time to lay claim to the place before anybody else jumped in.

"How much money can we get from this guy, Donnie?" Lefty asks me. "We gotta get at least five grand on my first trip because first I gotta get permission from Sonny to come down, and if he gives me the okay, I gotta give him twenty-five hundred, then out of the other twenty-five hundred I give you your end."

"Yeah, I'll make sure."

But I tell Rossi, "Tony, we aren't giving him five grand up front. Most we give him is two grand. He'll push, but don't worry about it."

Rossi and I had the same relative roles as Conte and I had had in Milwaukee. I was the mob representative, he was the local businessman—though in his role he wasn't as "straight" as Conte. I would handle Lefty or any of the other New York wiseguys.

In March, Lefty made his first trip down to King's Court. Rossi and I picked him up and took him to Pappas Restaurant, a popular Greek place in Tarpon Springs.

"Donnie," Lefty says, "tell Tony to tell me what the situation is."

I ask Rossi to tell him. He tells Lefty about the club, the card games, the half-ass wiseguys around the

club. He says that a guy named Jimmy East, a captain
in the Lucchese family, has given him permission to
operate games in the area. And that a couple of
ex–New York guys named Jo-Jo Fitapelli and Jimmy
Acquafredda did some jobs around the club and talked
about having heavyweight contacts and were trying to
get a garbagemen's monopoly going.

"I'm disgusted with these guys," Rossi says. "They
talk about being New York wiseguys, but they don't
come up with anything. I want to get some things
going—maybe over in Orlando, too, because I got a
D.A. in my pocket. But I don't want these guys to
move in on me because they can't produce."

"Anybody else invested money in your club?" Lefty
asks.

"It's all my own fucking money."

"You got no partners?"

"No partners. I'm on my own."

"Since nobody put up any money and you got no
partners," Lefty says, "that means you and I can form
a partnership. Anybody asks, you say I invested fifteen grand in this joint."

The rule is, once a wiseguy puts money into a club
or operation, he is a partner and no other wiseguy can
muscle in, because he'd be taking the earnings from
another wiseguy. That's the protection you have with
a wiseguy partner, the "peace of mind" you pay for.

We went down to King's Court and sat at Rossi's
round table in the back. Waitresses knew never to seat
anybody else at that table unless they were invited
over. Behind it were French doors leading to the rear
tennis courts. Rossi pointed out Acquafredda sitting at
the bar.

Lefty says, "Tony, you go tell him that you would
like him to meet a very dear friend of yours, Lefty, a
wiseguy from New York City."

Rossi brings Acquafredda over to the table and
introduces him. Supposedly he is a tough guy, but his
face is flushed and he seems nervous when he sits
down opposite Lefty. Acquafredda says that he knew
Rusty Rastelli and some of the other guys on the crew,
and that he has a Cartmen's Association going.

"I'm here for a few days," Lefty says, "to visit my old friend Tony here, my partner. I just put a bundle of money into this club. Tony can tell you about that. I'll come down here once in a while to make sure everything goes smooth. I got sixteen guys in my crew in the Miami–Lauderdale area, they'll be keeping an eye on things too. Any problems about the club, I can be contacted in New York."

Acquafredda nods respectfully and returns to the bar.

Jo-Jo is on duty at the door, which has a peephole and a buzzer for entry. Lefty tells Rossi to bring him over.

I knew from my first visits that Jo-Jo was interested in making a move soon on the club. I could tell he was disturbed that with my connections I might interfere with his plan.

After introductions Jo-Jo says he has a cousin in New York who has recently become a made member of the Lucchese family, and this cousin is planning to come down to the club next week to look it over.

"Since I'm Tony's partner," Lefty says calmly, "there's no reason for your cousin to come down unless it's for a vacation. If he wants to talk about anything regarding this club here, he can contact me on Madison Street or Mulberry Street. Just ask for Lefty, everybody knows me."

Fitapelli nods and goes back to the door.

"You won't be bothered now by nobody," Lefty says to Rossi. He turns to me. "Okay, Donnie, let's talk about money. Tell Tony how much money is he gonna give me."

I start to ask Tony, but Lefty says, "No, Donnie, take him outside."

We go through the French doors.

"What the hell is going on?" Rossi asks.

"This is the way things are done." I explain that Lefty's thinking—like a lot of wiseguys—is that if he doesn't hear extortion or a conspiracy being discussed, he can't be breaking those laws. "On the money, we're gonna go back in and I'll tell him your answer, then he's gonna want something else, and we're gonna walk outside again. But we won't give him all he wants. Stick to the two grand, no matter what he says."

We go back in and sit down, Rossi right across the table from Lefty. I say, "Lefty, I know I told you he was gonna give you five grand, but he only has two."

"I told Sonny five, Donnie. I got to split with him, and I got to spread this around when I make appointments to see people regarding this situation. Talk to him."

"Lefty, he says all he's got is two. Maybe he can come up with another thousand by the time you leave."

"Donnie, tell Tony how much he makes a week and how much of that he's willing to give me as his partner."

We go outside. Whatever we say he makes in a week, Lefty's going to take half. We don't want to give Lefty too much or too little. Eventually when the cases are tried in court, we don't want it to look like we were just throwing taxpayers' money at these wiseguys. But we have to give him enough to keep him interested. The enticement is the money. You have to show that this is an attractive deal, that the club is a big potential money-maker. If we played it right, I knew Lefty would bring Sonny Black down and we'd have a good chance of getting something going with Santo Trafficante. We stay outside enjoying ourselves long enough to have discussed this.

Back at the table, I say, "Lefty, he takes five hundred a week, and he says he'll give you two-fifty a week."

"Okay, tell him that I'll accept two-fifty a week, which he should mail every Wednesday so I get it by Friday, plus the two thousand, plus a grand before I leave."

I repeat all that, the partnership is made, and the conversation becomes more normal. "You got peace of mind now," he says to Rossi. Lefty says he will contact "the right people" to clear the way for Rossi to expand operations into Orlando and other parts of Florida. He wants to know how much the club makes on the card games.

"We just started gambling," Rossi says. "The last game netted two hundred and forty-seven bucks."

"No, no, that ain't nothing, that there. What you do is, the game is a twenty-dollar limit with three raises, and that would bring eight hundred to a thousand bucks a night cut for the house. So we gotta get that going."

Lefty also wanted the club expanded outside: an Olympic-size swimming pool, four racquet-ball courts, fifteen cabanas, a lot of landscaping.

"Get an architecture out here," Lefty says, "to draw up the plans. Go call one up."

"First thing in the morning," Rossi says, because now it's two A.M.

"Naw, get one now. Check the Yellow Pages, find a home phone. Tell him you're Tony, owner of the King's Court. He'll know you. Tell him you'll buy him a steak dinner and throw him a hundred dollars. He'll come right over."

I say, "Left, you think there will be any problems with Santo Trafficante, with us operating here in the Tampa area?"

"Don't worry about it. You just concentrate on building up this business here."

I went back with Lefty to the room at the Best Western Tahitian Motor Lodge on Route 19. He was still moaning about not getting $5,000.

"Left," I say, "let's not pressure the guy right from the beginning because we got a good thing going."

"Okay. But, Donnie, you gotta make sure that if Sonny ever says anything, you tell him that's all I got, because I don't want him thinking that I'm holding out on him."

"I'll back you up."

He dialed a number on the room phone. "Sonny? Everything here is all right. I am satisfied with the situation here."

Lefty went back to New York. A week later, the day after Easter, Sonny sent him back down to dictate an official partnership agreement. The agreement, back-dated for a month to preclude any challenge from another family, stated that they were fifty-fifty partners, that the second partner had invested $15,000 in the club. They went to a notary. Rossi signed "E. Anthony Rossi." Lefty signed "Thomas Sbano," the name of his son.

Lefty called a member of his crew in Miami, Johnny Spaghetti, and asked him to drive to Holiday to look the operation over. In case both Lefty and I were in New York and Rossi got into a beef with somebody, Johnny Spaghetti could shoot up from Miami and settle things.

Johnny Spaghetti got there that afternoon. A big, rough-and-tough type, about 6', 220 pounds, with silver hair. He used to work on the docks in New York until he hurt his back. He started getting workman's compensation, moved to Miami, and continued to do jobs for the family. Lefty told Rossi to give Spaghetti $40 for gas expenses for the trip from Miami.

That night we went to the Derby Lane greyhound track on the outskirts of Tampa. Rossi gave Lefty his $250 weekly salary plus his $200 cut from recent card games. Lefty lost it all to the dogs.

At the motel coffee shop the next morning, Lefty said I should talk to Rossi about the rest of the original $5,000 he was supposed to get. "Tell him he's gonna have peace of mind for the two thousand more. Tell him, Donnie, that if it wasn't for you being involved and being my partner, I would have walked away from the deal when he couldn't come up with the five grand. I need another two thousand to put this whole thing together up in New York, Donnie."

That night Rossi and I discussed it and decided it was worth it. Lefty had Sonny interested—what's another $2,000 when it's going to lead us to putting Sonny Black together with Santo Trafficante?

13

KING'S COURT

We were establishing ourselves and King's Court as part of the local underworld scene. Rossi was taking me around and letting people know that I was his New York guy. I had to prove myself right away to both New York and Florida people so that I could have freedom to operate.

He took me to a restaurant called Joe Pete's River Boat. Joe Pete was an ex–New Yorker, a half-ass tough guy who bragged about his connections and his Italian food. He also ran a gambling operation.

We sat down in the restaurant and were eating when Joe Pete came over from the bar. "Tony, how you been? Good to see you."

Rossi says, "Joe, like you to meet Donnie. He's my new partner. He's from New York."

"Oh, yeah?" Joe Pete says. He went into the who-do-you-know-that-I-know game.

I had a cold, and my voice was hoarse. Rossi and I kept eating.

Joe Pete says, "Geez, Donnie, you don't sound too good."

"I don't feel too good. Maybe it's from your food."

"What do you mean?"

"I felt good until I started eating your fucking food. Now I feel like I'm gonna die from this meal."

He got very offended. "Why you say a thing like that?"

"I say what I gotta say. Your fucking food, I feel like I'm gonna die from it."

He got up. "Maybe you might die from something else."

"Naw, just the food."

We got a reputation. Out of the local woodwork came drug deals, swag deals, connections.

Jo-Jo Fitapelli and Jimmy Acquafredda were acquainting Rossi with means of recruiting and keeping members in the Cartmen's Association.

"You need a little muscle," Acquafredda says. "If you scare somebody where you pound him and put a scar on his fucking head—you know, mentally—he'll stay if you scare him the right way."

Rossi said he didn't think scare tactics would work with some of the area garbage collectors.

Acquafredda persisted. "And you get an outlaw truck and send it out to compete with nonmembers. And if you have a member that you don't like, kick him out of the association, go after him, and run him out of the business."

Lefty called from New York. He said that Sonny was very happy with how things were going with King's Court. He loved the architectural plans for enlargement. He was so happy with the prospects that he was coming down to see it for himself on April 6.

Meeting Sonny Black was going to be a big test for me, more of a challenge than Balistrieri had been in Milwaukee. I was better-known now, considered more experienced and responsible, with fewer excuses for making mistakes. My scam got bigger and better all the time, I had more to protect, and I had to keep my confidence up to match it. Sonny was a very important captain in New York. He had a reputation for being unusually tough and savvy, even for a Mafia capo.

Lefty had vouched for me, and surely Sonny had checked me out with guys on Mulberry Street. Still, he would have to buy me face-to-face. If I didn't convince Sonny Black that I was who I said I was, if I didn't give him the right impression, if I gave him any doubts at all, the whole case would come to a halt. If I played my part right, I might gain direct access to him without having to go through Lefty or anybody else, as I had had to with Mike Sabella.

Rossi and I met them at the airport. Lefty, Sonny, and Sonny's girlfriend, Judy. Lefty and I shook hands and kissed each other on the cheek. Lefty says, "Sonny, Donnie." Sonny and I kissed each other. I say, "Sonny, this is Tony, he's with me. Tony, Sonny." Sonny shook Rossi's hand.

We took them to Malio's Restaurant in Tampa for dinner and then to King's Court.

Sonny, in his late forties, was a sturdy 5'7", about 170 pounds, with a powerfully developed chest and arms. On his right arm was a tattoo of a panther. He was swarthy, with hair he dyed jet-black—hence his nickname. His face was fleshy, with rings under the eyes that made him look, depending upon his mood, either tired or menacing. When he fixed his dark eyes on you, either in anger or to give an order, he could freeze anybody. Everything dark about him got darker, and nothing was soft. Yet in contrast to Lefty, Sonny had a laid-back style. He radiated confidence, control, and power, but not arrogance. He was younger than Mike Sabella, more observant, harder. He noticed everything. I paid close attention to everything he said. He had a reputation for personal loyalty, a guy who would kill you in a minute if you crossed him.

After a tour of King's Court, Sonny took me aside to a table apart from the others.

"Donnie, before I came here, I did some checking. Talked to some guys from downtown that know you. They say good things about you. Lefty says good things about you. They tell me you're the kind of guy, you do your business and keep your mouth shut and don't bother people and don't make a scene about anything. You're a good earner and you're not flamboyant. I like that. From now on you can report to me. You don't have to report to Lefty."

"I'm flattered."

"What do you want to do down here?"

"Maybe some bookmaking and shylocking."

"Good. Our people in New York will back it. You

want me to send somebody down to help you start the loan-sharking operation?"

"I don't think so. I got a guy I brought in, Chico, to oversee things here. I trust him." "Chico" was an undercover agent we had made the general overseer of the club so that Rossi and I could be free to go back and forth to New York when we needed to.

"How much do you need to start a shylock operation?"

"Maybe twenty-five grand."

"What's the vig rate down here?"

Vigorish is the interest on shylock loans. "Tony says it's four or five points, depending on the customer and the size of the loan. We'd also like to move into Orlando."

"When we're ready here, then we can go into Orlando. I got somebody looking into Orlando. I like what I see here so far, the club layout. It looks like we can make a lot of money here. Donnie, remember this: We can all earn. When we're doing business among friends, we all share everything equally and we don't try to cheat each other. We got an army up in New York behind us. Nobody can bother us as long as we conduct ourselves in the proper manner."

Sonny's approach to me—telling me I could report to him—put me in a difficult position. If I had been a legitimate badguy, I would have jumped at the chance to hook up directly to a captain and rise up the ladder. But as an agent, I couldn't jeopardize the operation. If Lefty got angry with me, he could have engineered a squelch of the whole King's Court deal. On the one hand, I couldn't appear to be defying Sonny. On the other hand, I had to stay loyal to Lefty. I had to tell him about Sonny's approach before he heard it from somebody else. And I had to tell him in such a way that I would be protected if my words got back to Sonny. Whatever Sonny heard about me had to include that I was a stand-up guy.

First thing the next morning I sat Lefty down and told him what Sonny had said. "But I'm still going to be loyal to you," I say. "Anything that I do with

Sonny, I'm gonna run it by you, because you and me started together."

"I'm happy you say that," Lefty says. "But who does this guy think he is if he thinks he can take you away from me? He ain't got no right to you."

The next day we all lounged around the pool at the Tahitian, and Sonny continued to encourage plans. He suggested that a good way to work the bookmaking and shylocking was by using a coffee truck that delivered to construction sites. The driver could run the business right out of the truck. He wanted us to have a Las Vegas Night, a popular event where the gambling is supposedly for charity.

"Once we have a Vegas Night," Sonny says, "then it becomes ours. Nobody else can have it. Start lining it up. I'll send wheels and stuff down from New York."

I am an avid reader. In this job especially, I was an avid newspaper reader. I read whatever newspapers I could get my hands on. The guys would say "Give Donnie the newspapers and he sits in a corner and he's happy all day."

But I wasn't always reading just to read. It was a good cover. While I was reading the *New York Post* or *The New York Times* or the *Daily News* from cover to cover, I was listening to their conversations. I was seeming to read so my listening was not obvious.

When I was away from New York, whether I was in Milwaukee or California or Florida, Lefty always would bring me the *New York Post* and the *Daily News* for that day. He never missed. He would get off a plane, and the first thing he'd do was hand me those newspapers.

One time I picked him up at the Tampa airport and we were driving to the hotel. It dawned on me that he hadn't given me anything. "Left, where are my newspapers?"

"You won't fucking believe what happened, Donnie. I'm sitting there on the plane reading the *Daily News,* and there's this Indian sitting next to me."

"What do you mean, Indian?"

"One of them guys with the towels on their head."

"Oh, you don't mean an American Indian, you mean a guy from India."

"He's a fucking Indian, I don't know where he's from. Got a big towel on his head. Don't matter where he's from. He's an Indian."

"So what about the newspapers?"

"I'm reading the paper, reading an article about Ted Kennedy. This guy's leaning over all the time, looking at the paper. He says, 'What do you think of Ted Kennedy?' I ignore him. He don't even speak English, broken English. He repeats it. I say, 'Hey, Charlie, do I know you? What the fuck you care what I think about Ted Kennedy?'

"I finish reading the *News* and put it down and start reading the *Post*. This guy touches the paper, Donnie! He starts leafing through my *Daily News*. When I put the *Post* down, he touches that too. I wouldn't bring these papers to you after that towel-head touches them."

"Left, nine million people touch that newspaper."

"Donnie, I don't know what this Indian's got. He could have any disease. I wouldn't let you touch the same newspaper as this Indian. I left those fucking newspapers right on the plane."

Everyplace we went, Lefty had Rossi pick up the tab. Lefty would bring guests for dinner, Rossi would have to pick up the tab. Rossi went to the mall to pick up some shaving stuff, Lefty would join him, pile the cart high with poolside gear and toiletries, and Rossi would pay at the checkout.

It was Lefty's birthday. You always exchange birthday and Christmas presents with guys you're close to in the crew. It's expected. This day I don't say anything. I don't even wish him happy birthday. I just let him stew.

All day he's asking me, "Donnie, didn't you forget something today? Isn't something supposed to happen today?"

"Nothing I can think of. Everything's under control."

Finally, at ten o'clock that night, he and Rossi and I are sitting at our round table at the club and Lefty is grumpy. I say, "Lefty! I forgot! It's your birthday!"

"Hey, that's right." He grins.

I lean over and give him a kiss and hand him an envelope. In it, wrapped in tissue, are seven diamonds, confiscated by the FBI. "This is from Tony and me. Happy birthday!"

He opens it. "Aw, Donnie, you didn't have to do this. What a great present! I'll give one to my wife, one to each daughter, one to each grandchild."

"Tony and me figured you're worth it."

"Aw, gee." He gives me a big hug and kiss. "What's Tony giving me?"

Rossi is sitting right there.

"The diamonds are from both of us," I say.

"Donnie, I can't tell you, that's the nicest present. That's why I love you. You make mistakes, but times like this are just— What about Tony, he forget?"

"Lefty, we both are giving you this."

"Is Tony gonna give me anything?"

Finally Rossi gets up, goes into the office, puts three $100 bills in an envelope, comes back, and gives it to Lefty. "Happy birthday, Lefty," he says.

"Aw, Tony, you didn't have to do this. You could have shared with Donnie and both give me the diamonds, that would have been enough."

We decided to hold our first Las Vegas Night on Friday, May 9. Sonny sent down a roulette wheel, blackjack tables, cards, dice, and so on, by the Airborne Airfreight Company. The sender on the bill was "Danny Manzo, Italian Veterans Club, 415 Graham Ave, Brooklyn N.Y." We made up a sign announcing the event and saying that proceeds would go to the Italian-American War Veterans Club.

Captain Joseph Donahue of the Pasco County Sheriff's Office made one of his regular visits to the club. As usual, he was not in uniform and came during the afternoon when the club was closed. Donahue was in his early sixties. He liked to brag that he had been a cop in New York City for sixteen years, something we could never confirm.

Rossi told him we were planning a Vegas Night. Donahue assured him he would keep everything under control. If a deputy did show up, Rossi asked him, could he be barred at the door, since this is a private club? Donahue said that a deputy couldn't be kept out but that no locked rooms could be searched without a warrant. Donahue said that he would stay on duty during Las Vegas Night to make sure there was no trouble.

Rossi gave him $200 for the visit.

We set up the club as a game room. In another room we had a long table with a free buffet—cold cuts, salads. Sonny came down with Lefty and a couple of pros Sonny provided to work the games. Maybe two hundred people came to that first Vegas Night. Rossi had paid off the cop, Donahue, $400 to make sure we weren't hassled. Everything was going smoothly until a couple of sharpshooters tried to hustle an old guy running one of the crap tables.

We had imported a couple of old-timers from Miami to run the tables. These guys were good at running street games, but they weren't used to the complexities of the real Las Vegas crap table. So these two customers are trying to bulldoze the old guy, whose name was Ricky.

Ricky comes over to me. "Donnie, a couple of guys working together are murdering us at the table. To be honest with you, I can't handle this table as well as I thought I could. They're too fast for me, and I know they're cheating."

I walk over to take a look. I know these two Greek guys, a couple of heavy-hitting gamblers. I see that they are claiming bets they didn't make and intimidating Ricky. So I intervene.

I step in front of these guys and speak so that the whole club can get the message. Also, I know that Sonny's eyes are on me, and this is the first time he's seen me in action.

"You guys are trying to burn this table," I say. "This is an honest game. You got a fair shot at cleaning house. But I'm telling you now, you don't come in here and fuck with any of our people or our games. Because you do it one more time, I will personally carry you out of here. And before I carry you through the door, I will take all the money you got in your pockets."

"Oh, no, we weren't trying to do anything . . . just got on a hot streak . . . playing it straight."

"You can stay at the table. Wherever I am in the club, I'll be watching you."

They stayed. I had caught them early, and they had already pocketed a couple grand off the table. Now Ricky went back at them. He recovered it all.

We went all night. Sonny was pleased with the crowd and the performance and the few G's that he walked away with. It would help lead to a meeting with Santo Trafficante. He said we should make a deal with owners of other clubs that we'd run Vegas Nights in their clubs, and they could keep the liquor sales and a piece of the Vegas money.

Sonny wanted us to try a lot of things. He asked me if I had any cocaine or marijuana connections in the area, because he wanted to increase his sources. "I used to have some contacts in Miami," I said, "but lately I haven't been fucking around with dope. Two or three months ago I was getting it for forty-eight grand a key, but I don't know what it would be now, or whether I could get back with the same people."

He said that his man Bobby in Orlando had cars to transport drugs to New York. He wanted us to keep our eyes open for outlets for plywood, paint, and counterfeit designer jeans that he had access to. He wanted me to check around and see if a numbers business would be a good idea, and if it was, he could send a guy down from New York to run it.

"I've already got a book set up for the football season," I say.

"I'm gonna talk to Rusty about putting some family money in here," Sonny says. "Rusty knows about your work here. I want to bring Stevie down to look at it because he's handling the money for the family. It'll probably take a couple of weeks to get it. You'll have to pay it back at one and a half points."

Steve "Stevie Beef" Cannone was the consiglieri of

the Bonanno family. Naturally I would welcome a chance to meet him.

Sonny said he had a deal going in New York where he had to put up $400,000 for loads of some semiprecious metals that would bring him $1 million. "The guy that owns some factories that produce this stuff is supposed to be giving up these loads to me. He promised a load and he didn't come through with it. I burned down one of his factories. I'll burn down another building every time he fucks me around with a load."

When we were alone, Sonny says, "What's going on with Lefty? There's something wrong between him and Rossi."

The night before Las Vegas Night, we had all gone out to eat, and Lefty had invited some of the hostesses from the club. He ordered several bottles of expensive wine. Then he stuck Rossi with the tab. Sonny didn't like that. He wouldn't say anything at the dinner because he's not going to embarrass a wiseguy in front of citizens. Also, he wanted the facts first.

But I have to be careful about what I say. Anytime I am brought into a situation between wiseguys, it is like walking on eggshells. I don't want to offend or insult anybody, because I want to keep the operation going. But I have to act like a stand-up wiseguy. Here's a captain asking me about one of the top wiseguys in his crew. I don't want him to think I give up a guy right away. On the other hand, maybe it's a good time to put a clamp on Lefty's bleeding of Rossi. I lay it off on Rossi.

"Well, Sonny, Rossi's been complaining to me that Lefty's bleeding him too much. He doesn't mind the two hundred and and fifty bucks a week. But all the other stuff—meals, trips."

"Tell Rossi that other than the two fifty, he doesn't give Lefty any more money. You tell him that he's only to answer to me."

"Okay, I'll tell him."

I didn't say anything to Lefty. If Rossi and I were legitimate badguys, I would have followed Sonny's instructions to the letter. But I was walking a thread here because I didn't want Lefty to dump Rossi, which he could have done easily, just by lying to Sonny about him. He could say to me, "He don't want to give me any more money? Fine, I'll just tell Sonny *x*, *y*, and *z*, and Rossi's finished." I couldn't appear to be ignoring Sonny's directive, either. Rossi and I would just have to make it seem that Lefty had backed off on the money thing.

Sonny was joined in Holiday by his right-hand man, John "Boobie" Cerasani, who came down from New York. I had known about Boobie since 1978 because he used to come around Lefty's. Boobie was taller and leaner than Sonny, balding at the temples, with a hawklike face. He was quiet and smart, a chess lover. He was one mean fucker, very closemouthed, a hard guy to get to know. If you got him to talk to you, he was all right. Sonny wasn't close to a lot of people. Boobie was his confidant, capable of doing whatever was needed, which included watching Sonny's back. "I trust Boobie," Sonny says, "and that's it."

Sonny called me from New York. He asked me if I knew anything about paintings. I said I didn't. He said they had burglarized a Brooklyn warehouse where the Shah of Iran had stored various kinds of expensive artworks and he needed somebody to fence the stuff right away.

"Chico has some contacts," I say. Sonny had met Chico, the agent who was managing the club. "I'll ask him if he's interested and get back to you."

The Shah had been in the news lately because of his ouster from Iran and his illness. We tried to find out if there had been a report of such a burglary, and there had been none.

I called Sonny back and told him that Chico was interested but couldn't get up there for a couple of days. Sonny was impatient. He didn't know anything about dealing this kind of stuff and didn't want it lying around. We didn't want to make it look like we were too anxious, that Chico had nothing to do. Sonny said he'd wait.

Chico hooked up with another agent from Chicago

who posed as a shady art dealer, and they flew to New York.

Sonny picked them up at La Guardia Airport and, after making some quick turns to clean off possible tails, took them to Staten Island where the stolen artwork was stashed. The stuff looked impressive—trays and relics of gold, good paintings. Chico took Polaroid pictures of everything, explaining that it was necessary to study the photos and check out the goods for "provenance"— to prove their authenticity.

A few days passed. Still there was no report of any theft. Chico passed word to Sonny that his man couldn't find a buyer right now. Sonny started to sell some pieces off. There was nothing we could do. The FBI couldn't seize the goods without revealing our operation.

Sonny came to Florida to pursue some contacts that might lead to an introduction to Trafficante.

Rossi and I were having breakfast with Sonny in the coffee shop at the Tahitian. Sonny brought up the matter of the Shah's artwork.

"We took over a hundred grand," he says, "and they didn't even know it was missing."

But then they had tried to burglarize the town house owned by the Shah's sister on Beekman Place, one of Manhattan's most exclusive neighborhoods. They had a man who supposedly had taken care of the security guards. Sonny waited in the car while a couple others went upstairs to pull the job. He heard a shot and took off.

He went back to his club in Brooklyn. Soon the burglary team showed up. One of them had shot himself in the hand. There had been a scuffle with a guard, and the whole thing was blown. Sonny sent the guy to their regular doctor around the corner, then gave him $500 and told him to get lost for a couple of weeks.

"It was fucking close to a billion-dollar score," Sonny says. "I don't even want to talk about it."

But there was hope because the Shah, who was in Egypt, was fatally ill and would die soon. And when he did, Sonny wanted us to shoot up to New York because they were going to hit that warehouse again.

"You come running right down, brother," Sonny says. "Take a fucking fast jet. We'll get all this guy's stuff when it comes from Egypt."

But when the Shah died a few weeks later, Boobie called me and told me that the whole thing was on hold.

Angelo Bruno, the longtime boss of Philadelphia, had been hit—the second major boss to be rubbed out in a year. He was sitting in his car when somebody put a shotgun behind his ear. I asked Lefty about it.

"Bruno wanted all of Atlantic City," he says. "He already had all the services at the casinos, but then he wanted all the gambling. You can't have all of Atlantic City. The Gambinos got interests there. Trafficante's got interests. Santo gave Bruno a piece of Florida in exchange for a piece of Atlantic City. We got interests over there. See, when you do things with people, you share. Especially whatever you do in the family, Donnie, you share with your people. In our family, the reason Lilo got whacked is that he wouldn't share his drug business with anybody else in the family."

"Is that right?"

"Hey, listen carefully, Donnie. If they can hit a boss, nobody's immune."

14

COLDWATER

The FBI had had Santo Trafficante under surveillance for some time. With the prospect of bringing the Bonannos together with Trafficante, Project Coldwater continued that surveillance and added electronic devices at King's Court. The club had hidden videotape cameras that could monitor the office and the private round table in the main room that Rossi used. There were bugs in the chandelier over the round table and in the telephone. Rossi's car had a Nagra tape recorder hidden in the trunk.

I moved into a one-bedroom, second-floor apartment in a complex of four-story buildings called Holiday Park Apartments directly across Route 19 from King's Court, where Rossi also had an apartment. From my window I could see King's Court. My telephone was wired for recording. Earlier in the Mafia operation, in Milwaukee or Florida, when I had wanted to record a conversation over a phone, I had done it with a simple suction-cup microphone attached to the handset and a regular tape recorder. Now that I had an apartment, I would have visitors, so I couldn't have any recording devices lying around. A recorder was hidden inside the wall and hooked directly into the telephone line.

On occasion, Rossi or I would wear a "wire," either a Nagra tape recorder or a T-4 transmitter.

The Nagra I used was four-by-six inches, three quarters of an inch thick, and used a three-hour tape. It recorded only, with no playback capability. The microphone, about the size of a pencil-tip eraser, was on a long wire so that you could hide it anywhere on your body. The recorder had an on-off switch. Prior to using it, you could test it to see that the tape was rolling. But without pulling the tape and putting it on a playback machine, you could not test it for recording.

The T-4 transmitter was half the size of the Nagra recorder—$3\frac{1}{2} \times 2$ inches, a quarter inch thick. It had no recording capability of its own. It transmitted sound to monitoring agents positioned in the vicinity who could listen and record. There was no on-off switch. It had a small flexible antenna, one to two inches long, with a tiny bulb on the end, which was the microphone. When you screwed on the antenna, the transmitter was turned on. Fresh batteries lasted about four hours. You could test the transmitter ahead of time by getting a monitoring agent on the phone and asking him if he was picking up your radio transmissions. But as with the Nagra recorder, once you were out on the job, there was no way of telling whether the system was working.

An advantage of the Nagra was that you could record a conversation anywhere without backup agents. The advantages of the transmitter were its smaller size for concealment purposes, and the fact that when you were using it, there were monitoring agents nearby getting direct communications from the transmitter. With a transmitter, if a situation went bad and the undercover agent was in immediate danger, the other agents could be on the scene in moments. With a Nagra you could get in trouble and nobody would know.

But whereas you could record anywhere with a Nagra, in the city the transmitter had a broadcast reach of maybe two blocks. Steel structures could interfere with transmission, as could atmospheric conditions or passing vehicles. The surveillance team could lose you or get out of range. One danger was that it was possible for a T-4 transmission to be picked up and broadcast back over a television set. You could be sitting in a room chatting with a couple of wiseguys when suddenly the TV is broadcasting your conversation back at you. Everybody in the room knows that somebody is wearing a wire.

A disadvantage to any recording or transmitting device was that you risked your life using it. To be caught wearing a wire was usually a death sentence. Also, they didn't always work. It looks easy in the movies. Just tape the device to your body, go in, and record the incriminating conversation. In reality the devices, while they are supposed to be at or near state-of-the-art in technology, are not infallible. There is always a compromise in efficiency when you try to make things small.

We undercover agents were not always given the equipment with the ultimate in advanced secret technology—stuff that spies may have. Eventually we testify in court, and we have to reveal the details of the electronics equipment we used in the investigation. Spies don't go to court, so what they use won't be revealed. Electronic stuff that the government wants to keep secret will not be given to undercover agents to use in making cases that go to court.

All these devices have delicate recording capabilities. That means that they pick up *all* sound. A device hidden on your body will pick up your own belches, the rustling of your clothing, and everything else in a room or nearby—conversations, shuffling of feet and chairs, radios and TVs, air-conditioners, street noise. Because of their paranoia that there are bugs planted everywhere, mob guys, whether in hotel rooms or cars or wherever, always turn on the TV or radio to cover the conversation.

Then, if everything else is just right, you still can't insist that people talk about what you want them to talk about when you want them to talk about it. Our rules governing recording and transmissions were that once you've turned a device on, you leave it on for an entire conversation, and that conversation—recorded over the telephone or on the scene or by other agents monitoring your transmissions—is turned in as evidence. It doesn't matter whether the conversation turns out to be irrelevant or whether it contains irrelevant sections; the whole thing is provided to the courts. While only relevant parts of conversations may be presented as testimony, the entire conversations are available to the defense attorneys so that they can't claim we were being unfairly selective—trying to distort conversations—in what we recorded on the scene.

You turn on the recorder or transmitter prior to arriving at the scene. It may be hours before the conversation gets around to what you want to hear. Tapes run out. Batteries run down.

You have almost no control over conditions. You can't test on the scene for sound levels. You can't arrange people as you would like to for recording. You can't ask them to raise their voices. You can't control extraneous sounds that muddy the reception. You might go through hours of conversation laying the groundwork for the conversation you want. Finally he's telling you everything you want to know. Then when they play the tapes at the Bureau, you got only half the conversation or maybe nothing—you don't know that until it's over. You can't reconstruct that conversation. You can't go back to the badguy and say, "You remember that conversation we had yesterday? Let's talk about that again, and this time let's not walk by that same building because there's too much steel in it. . . . And let's not walk too fast because the car that's recording this is getting out of range." Or, "Let's go over it again because last time the batteries were bad or the spindles were worn or the tape was dragging."

That kind of frustration was to me more of a burden, more pressure than all the other undercover work.

I didn't like carrying any device. It was difficult to hide anything. I was in solid with these guys, and there was always the traditional hugging and kissing of cheeks. There was horseplay, wrestling around. I was with these guys day and night. With Lefty it was twenty-four hours a day. I stayed in hotel rooms with him, changed clothes in the rooms, stripped to swimming trunks to go sit around the pool.

When I did use a recorder or transmitter, I never taped one to my body. The only time I did that was way back in 1975, at the beginning of the heavy-equipment theft operation. I carried the Nagra or T-4 loose, usually in my jacket pocket. With the Nagra I preferred not to risk running the microphone up under my clothes, so usually I wrapped the cord around the machine and stuck the whole thing in my pocket. When I wasn't going to be wearing a jacket, I would put the Nagra in my cowboy boot. Then I would have to run the microphone cord up under my clothes and tape the mike to my chest.

I never wanted to keep the devices around. There was always a chance somebody would bust into your apartment or car. So when I wanted to use one, I made arrangements to meet the case agent somewhere for a pickup, and afterward for a drop.

The obvious overall advantage to wearing a wire is that you may get a crucial conversation that makes a case. That's what makes it worth the risk. It was up to me whether I wanted to wear a wire or not in any situation. Altogether, beginning with Project Coldwater, I probably wore a wire a dozen times.

Sonny was pushing for an introduction to Trafficante. He sent Lefty down to Holiday on a mission to try to set up an introduction through intermediaries. We thought Lefty might talk about important people and procedures. It was too hot for a jacket. I put a Nagra in my cowboy boot.

He had told me that we were going to fly to Miami to meet the son-in-law of Meyer Lansky, the notorious mob mastermind of money and gambling businesses, who supposedly was a friend of Trafficante's.

At breakfast I say, "I'm still not clear why we're going down there."

"Because I wanna see this guy," Lefty says. "He's in Miami Beach. He's gonna introduce me to that guy there who's going to introduce me to the main guy over here."

Lefty was complaining as usual about Rossi not giving him enough money. Rossi had booked his round-trip flight from New York but had not offered to pay for his trip from Holiday to Miami, or for expenses he might incur.

"Just sit him down and explain to him what's going on," I say.

"That's your job to tell him. This thing here is his idea."

"I know it's his idea, but he hasn't made any fucking money yet, either."

"I don't need this aggravation. Just tell him we're going to see Meyer Lansky's son-in-law. Just tell him he's got to give me the money."

Lefty had sent Rossi over to the club to look for his Tampa–New York return-flight ticket. He said he had lost it somewhere. But he hadn't lost it. He confided to me that he wanted to test Rossi's reaction.

When Sonny had been down to see the club earlier, he had noticed that Rossi's car had Pennsylvania tags and told Lefty he was suspicious about that. Lefty asked me, and I explained that it was a rented car, so the tags are whatever the car has on it when you pick it up.

But Lefty wanted to check him out a little more. Rossi had booked the New York–Tampa round-trip flight for Lefty on his American Express card. By pretending to lose the ticket, Lefty wanted to see how Rossi reacted. If he was an agent, Lefty reasoned, he would get nervous because he would probably have to account for the ticket to his office, plus he would be worried that somebody "in the underworld business" might meanwhile find the ticket and check out the American Express number to see if it was a government number.

When I had a chance, I clued Rossi in so he could end the search. He told Lefty he would just cancel the ticket and order another one.

We went to the club. Rossi says, "Nothing for nothing, Lefty, but just so I understand, you want me to pay for your ticket to Miami, right?"

"Well, who we going down there to see? I'm gonna see this guy in order to make a move out here. I'm not gonna make this move for myself. Once this guy gives you the green light, you can go anyplace you wanna go. That's his father-in-law. I meet the old man, he calls this guy over here, and then I get a proper introduction. Now, you gotta give me my regular two-fifty to take back to New York. And a buck and a half to entertain this guy over there."

"In other words," Rossi says, "you're gonna meet with old man Santo."

"No, he's over *here*. Gonna meet first old man Meyer Lansky. See, you can't get an introduction to this man over here unless *he* sends you over here. He makes one phone call in front of me: 'Hello, how are you? A dear friend of mine, he's gonna visit you such-and-such a day at three o'clock.' Now I go here. I explain what I'm gonna do in this town. And this is the moves I want to make. I say, 'Do we have your blessings, or do we have to go further with it?' Most likely he'll say, 'You got my blessings.' That's the proper way of doing things. You can't do it no other way. Now we clear all the middlemen out, all the bullshitters. Now you do what you fucking want in this fucking town. Ain't nobody can approach you and say, 'Hey you, what are you doing here?' Know what you tell them? 'Go see this fellow—*if* you can see him, which I doubt.' "

"So you're arranging a meeting," Rossi says, drawing him out to get it on the tape, "with Santo."

"That's it, I'm making a whole fucking move. Listen. We stood three days in a fucking room—Donnie could tell you—in Chicago. Three days they made me lay in. Finally: 'Come on, get in the limousine, let's go.' I didn't know where the fuck I was going, but I got in the limousine. They took me to a big, big fucking cabaret. It was closed. It was the off-season. 'Wait here.' And from there went to a fucking restaurant. 'Wait here.' Then the main guy come out. He said, 'Come on, let's go in the office. You're well recommended.' And that was it."

I say, "He wants to make sure that when we make these moves, we get protection from anybody that wants to come in."

"I *know* that," Lefty says.

"Not you, Left. I'm not talking to you. *Tony's* got to know it."

"The thing is, Lefty," Rossi says, "nothing for nothing, but I gotta start earning."

"Just a minute," Lefty says. "Are we opening the doors for you right now? Another thing, we gotta get a tent for here. Free food, free drinks. Gambling in the tent. Why should you lose a Friday night business in the club? That's the biggest mistake you made. And what about a Sunday afternoon?"

"We gotta operate in the bigger cities," Rossi says, "like Orlando."

"They own Orlando too. That's the first thing I'm gonna get is Orlando."

"And Tampa," Rossi says.

"He *owns* Tampa. This is what the fuck I'm making a move for. I was with the fucking people all day yesterday, in New York."

"Don't misunderstand," Rossi says. "I'm not trying

to be disrespectful. I got a lot of respect for you. But I got to work hard in my life. Stealing ain't easy today."

"Well, let me tell you something, my man. Just a starting point. You just caught the off-season. You got the football season. Donnie's going out and help you. You're gonna have a lot of fucking action over here. You can't close on Sundays, though, because Sunday's your biggest fucking day."

"But you still can't go on betting on the fucking come, you know," Rossi says. "Eventually you got to start earning. And the big money is still not here."

"It's in Tampa," Lefty says. "And what the fuck you think we're going to fucking Miami for? You think I like to ride in motherfucking planes? I don't like restaurants, for number one. I don't like traveling in a suitcase, for number two. Donnie knows what I like. Fucking weekends I'm home watching fucking TV, me and my wife. I don't even want to go to a fucking joint. I don't even go to Mike's no more because I'm sick and tired of a fucking joint."

"You understand what I'm saying."

"I understand. All right, Donnie, go get your clothes. Let's get the fuck out of here, do what we got to do. You know what I would like, Tony? I can make it myself. A nice cold spritzer."

Johnny Spaghetti picked us up at the airport in Miami and took us to Joe Puma's Restaurant, Little Italy, at 1025 E. Hallandale Beach Boulevard in Hallandale, just outside Miami. Joe Puma was a Bonanno guy who had been under Mike Sabella until the Galante hit, then was put under Phil "Philly Lucky" Giaccone. Lefty wanted me to meet Puma and Steve Maruca, another made guy. Maruca had recently been released from prison. He was more intimidating than Puma. He was a rugged-looking guy, about 6'2", with a big voice and big hands.

Puma and Maruca were both under Philly Lucky. There was nothing wrong with us getting together with guys under another captain, but with the unstable circumstances of the Bonanno family at the time, I didn't know what was up with Lefty wanting me to meet these guys, what it might mean, who was on what side in the factions maneuvering for control under Rusty Rastelli. But I knew that Puma and Maruca were important in the family.

Lefty was exploring another route to Trafficante, through a relative of Santo Trafficante's. Supposedly he would introduce Lefty to the relative, who would introduce him to Santo.

Neither of the meetings came off. Both guys were out of town.

Sonny called and told me that he and Boobie were flying down for Memorial Day weekend. I call Lefty to tell him. That set him off about his turf.

"What do you mean, Sonny's coming down tomorrow?"

"I don't know. I asked him if he had talked to you, because I wanted to make sure you knew about it. He said, 'Don't worry, there's no problem with Lefty, I'll see him tomorrow before we go.' "

"I don't believe this fucking guy over here. This is my fucking operation."

"Left, I'm gonna be with you, you know that."

"Ain't the question. Why's he coming down there?"

"Maybe he wants to come down for a vacation."

"Don't give me that fucking bullshit, maybe he wants. He ain't supposed to be in that town without me. Who's paying for his fucking plane fare?"

"I guess we are, but he said he'll straighten it out tomorrow."

"Don't con me, pal."

"That's what he said."

"Who the fuck are you to accept confirmation on his plane ticket?"

"Lefty, I'm gonna argue with him?"

"Yeah, you cocksucker."

I hang up on him.

He calls right back. "You fucking motherfucker! You don't hang up on me!"

I can imagine his veins bulging. "Don't ever call me cocksucker, Lefty."

"I call you what I want! I call you a cocksucker, a—"

I hang up.

He calls right back. "Lemme talk to Tony."

I give the phone to Tony.

"That fucking son of a bitch cocksucker better understand who he's talking to, Tony. Nobody treats me that way, hanging up. You better talk to that guy."

"Lefty, I don't know what you're talking about," Tony says.

"Lemme talk to Donnie."

I get back on the phone and he resumes.

"I told you nobody goes on the expense sheet. You tell that motherfucker Tony that he owes me $500 and he sends me $500 tomorrow. I'm gonna shoot that motherfucker in the head. There's something wrong over here, pal. I'm going to Brooklyn tomorrow and I'll have all the answers. Who's your fucking boss?"

"You are."

"I'm your boss. I'll get the answers in Brooklyn before he leaves. I want you by the phone at the club, twelve o'clock. Make sure that other motherfucker's on the extension phone. I want both you guys on the phone when I call."

"I'll make sure he's there."

"When I get through with Sonny, right then and there, if he can't give me the right answers, I'm gonna tell you something."

"What?"

"Ain't nobody knows that I got three fucking grenades. Ain't no motherfucker could ever live after I get through with them. If this guy gives me the wrong answers tomorrow, I'll blow the fuck everybody up."

"Lefty."

Sonny and Boobie came down. They sat with Rossi and me in the lounge at the Tahitian. I had a Nagra in my boot.

"I don't want to get caught in the middle with Lefty," I say.

"I spoke to him," Sonny says. "See, when I say to you, 'Don't say nothing,' don't say nothing. Lefty

stood up for me when I was away. And I'd never do
nothing to hurt him. He'll go all the way with you.
He's a tremendous guy, a dynamite guy, but he tends
to dramatize. He called me back after he talked to
you. He was fucking whacked. Now, I don't have to
tell nobody what I'm doing. So you don't tell him
nothing. I'll tell him what I want him to know. I'm
never telling him what conversations take place. He
knows me too long. I never do nothing underhanded.
If I take down any money from here, he gets his end
and he goes home to sleep."

"He's done a lot for me, too, in six years," I say,
"but I don't want to have arguments with him over
you. Anything we do, I'm always gonna give him a
piece of my end. I don't want him to think that I'm
fucking him."

"Donnie, you know the story with this crew. When
I went away, they put me on the clothesline."

"I know." When Sonny was in the can, his crew had
deserted him. He was separated from his wife, but he
had four kids he wanted taken care of. Money supposed to go to his family wasn't paid.

"They didn't want to bother with me, this crew,"
Sonny says. "They were afraid. But when the boss
told him to keep his fucking mouth shut about me, he
stood up. So now I come back home, the whole fucking story changes. Now we got all the power. So I
brought him right back."

"He's a stand-up guy. There ain't no two ways about
it."

"But you can't tell him nothing. He gets them two
fucking wines in him and then—well, he's trying to
help you, but he's hurting you. Now, see, everything is
politics. Five years ago, I give you my word of honor,
I'm gonna put two guns in my fucking pocket for
whoever calls me. But today you can't do it. Today
you gotta sit back and just go step by step."

"That's right," Rossi and I say.

"You got all the kids coming around today, you
know, and they're stronger than lions. And all these
old guys, they got a brain of a seventy- or eighty-year-
old person. A seventy-year-old brain can't compare

with mine, because where he's got like twenty more years experience in his day, I got like fifty more years experience in my day. And we're living in my day, not their day anymore. That's what they fail to understand."

"That's right," we say.

"Like, who thought jeans were gonna be good? A young kid thought of jeans and look at the fucking money jeans are making. These old-timers will never wear a pair of jeans in their life. Their brain stopped. I'll show you men that will go through a fucking tank for you, and I gotta give them a hundred, two hundred a week, and they ain't earning a dime. All these big puffers with their cigars and pinkie rings, they're taking down all the money. It's gotta change."

"Yeah," Boobie says. He is looking around at some of the people passing through. "Those blondes is with somebody down here or what?"

"They're just around," I say, "far as I know."

Rossi left the table for a few minutes. Sonny opened up more around me because Rossi was still considered an outsider.

I told Sonny that "our friend, the cop" had introduced Tony to a guy who owned shrimp boats and used them to bring in cocaine and marijuana.

"The deputy gave you this guy as a connection?" Sonny asks.

"Yeah. The deputy was with this guy a while back, protecting him for hauling marijuana. This guy does everything. We just met him, you understand. I told Tony, 'Let this guy do all the talking. We don't want it to look like we're too anxious to do business. We just let him keep telling us what he wants to do.' He said he was gonna come and see us a couple of months ago, but he wanted to make sure we were okay."

"I don't want to talk to Tony about it," Sonny says. "If we do anything with this guy, you arrange it. We'll take one piece and put it out on the street. Take us seven days. Whatever money we get, we'll send up. Tell him the smoke is good because there ain't that much involved. See, I got an army of cars to go back and forth from Orlando. Now, what we're dealing with is a tremendous amount of trust in people. I only talk to you because you're good, and you talk to me."

"Right."

"Down the line, these motherfuckers are weak. So don't talk to nobody. I always talk alone, because the only way there is to get caught is talking with two other people. Because now there is a strict law. In other words, me and you are talking like now. They can't pinch him over there for conspiracy with us because there's just two of us. But there's a lot of guys got five or ten years. We don't trust nobody. We gotta get sneaky. Because the sneakier we are, the smarter we are."

A few days earlier, Donahue, the deputy sheriff, brought up the matter of dog-racing tracks with Rossi. He wanted to know if Rossi's people might be interested. Some politicians would have to be bribed. I brought it up with Sonny. "The cop told Tony his people are gonna come up with the bread, and they got a lock in Tallahassee, which is the state capital, for the license. He wants to help him put it together and for protection, so nobody else is gonna muscle in on it."

"We could definitely protect this guy, down to the track. We gotta bring in another family, because that family controls over there."

"That's what I think he's looking for."

"Yeah, I'll get that. Meanwhile I'll come out with my top guns. Let's hear what Tony's got to say." He waves for Tony to return to the table. "We're talking about the dog track."

Rossi nods. "He guaranteed that he's got two investors around here, and each will put up a million dollars. But what he wants is protection, all what it takes in order to put this thing together."

"What kind of help does he want? Protection from what?"

"He came to me because, you know, you couldn't run a track here in Florida without Trafficante's permission. That never came up directly. That's what I read into it. He thinks I could, you know, reach out."

"Yeah, well, that's no problem. But who knows

anything about putting a track together? That's what we gotta find out. What is he actually looking for?"

"Sonny, all I do is listen. I didn't say yes, no, nothing. There's three dog tracks now, each one is open four months, so they're all working with each other. Now, you put in this other track, you're gonna have problems with those other three tracks unless there's somebody there that controls it. So what he's really looking for is the permission."

"Or somebody," I say, "that can go sit down with the guy in Tampa."

"All right. I'll lay it down to him when I see this guy, see what he says. If the guy says, 'All right, go ahead,' then youse go ahead, nobody will ever bother us. But if he says, 'Listen, I got three, what do I need four for?' Then forget about it. Because you gotta show him respect. The deputy was happy with that four hundred we gave him?"

"Oh, yeah," Rossi says. "I give him money all along—two hundred, three hundred."

"I mean, for that one night."

"The Vegas Night? Oh, yeah."

"We should tell him that we'd like to get another one in a few weeks time. I'll bring the crew down, two guys for the crap table. This way maybe this time we could take down some real money."

Phone calls home were not satisfying. "When are you coming home? Why aren't you coming home?"

I would talk to each of the girls, ask about school, whether they were keeping the horses fed—they had three horses now that they kept in a barn down the road. Mainly they wanted to know when I was coming home. My wife would say, "Joe, tell me some of the things you're doing. Knowing where you are, picturing you doing something, that makes me feel more comfortable about it, helps keep my mind clear."

I would tell her a little bit. If the kids were afraid for me, I'd say, "There's nothing to be afraid of. These guys are so stupid, they couldn't find their way out of a paper bag."

Bills, household problems, teenager problems—I

couldn't do anything about any of it. So much had been going on, guys coming and going in Florida, that I hadn't been home in seven weeks.

I got home for my oldest daughter's graduation, the first weekend in June. I was a stranger. A month earlier my wife had fallen while mowing the grass and sliced open her ankle, requiring six stitches. She hadn't mentioned it. My daughters had gotten into a couple of bad habits—nothing disastrous, just frustrating because I wasn't there to deal with it. At one point when I was by myself, I put my fist through the bedroom door.

My wife produced a nice brunch party for my daughter's graduation. My mother was there; her mother was there. I wasn't in sync. I wasn't conversational. I was missing a lot of years.

Afterward my wife said, "It was your daughter's graduation. You should have just forgotten for a while and been happy and put a different face on."

I had to get back to Florida because Sonny and Lefty were coming down. They had arranged a sit-down with Trafficante. I had been home for three days. "You've been in a horrible mood the whole time," my wife said. She didn't ask what was wrong. I wouldn't have known what to answer.

Tuesday morning, June 3, she drove me to the airport. It was our nineteenth wedding anniversary.

When I got to Tampa, I called to apologize for my mood.

Sonny came down with his girlfriend, Judy, and Lefty, and checked into the Tahitian Motor Lodge. Sonny had to wait for a call. Trafficante would say when and where they would meet. We hung around the pool.

The next day he got the call. He was to meet Trafficante that night at eight. He wanted me to pick him up at six forty-five. "I like to get there early," Sonny says, "and get the feel of the place, look it over to make sure it's not a setup or there aren't any cops."

A top Bonanno captain was meeting with the biggest boss in Florida. The FBI put a surveillance team on.

I took Rossi's car because it was wired with a Nagra in the trunk. I picked Sonny up. Lefty was not with him.

"We're going to Pappas," he says, indicating the restaurant in Tarpon Springs. "He didn't even say the name. He didn't have to. He just said 'I feel like eating Greek tonight.' I said, 'I know the place you mean.' "

At about seven-fifteen we went into the restaurant. We sat at the bar and had a drink. Sonny scanned the place casually.

"How's this guy gonna know you?" I ask.

"I met him up in New York last week. I been trying to set this up all along. He was up there. Stevie knew him from years ago. Stevie introduced me to him."

At about seven-thirty, Sonny says, "Okay, Donnie, you leave, go back to the club, and I'll call you when it's time to pick me up."

I walked out. Going through the parking lot, I passed right by Trafficante and another man heading toward the restaurant. Trafficante was such a quiet-looking old gentleman, shoulders slightly hunched, calm old face. It was odd to think of him as what he really was.

Sonny called at ten o'clock. I met him in the lounge at the restaurant. We had a drink before we left. I didn't say anything about having seen Trafficante.

"He's a dynamite guy," Sonny says. "He likes me. We got whatever we want. All the doors are open to us in Florida now, just so we do things properly. A fifty-fifty split. If we fuck up, Donnie, the old man will shut every door on us. One of the things we should start looking at, he said, was bingo. He's big in bingo, but he doesn't have any in Pasco County. Big money in that."

In the car, Sonny unwound. "It was a feeling-out conversation," he says. "I told him, 'Listen, I'm no sophisticated person. I'm a street person all my life.' I says, 'I love the streets, you know. I don't know nothing about nothing, about gambling or anything.' I says, 'Me, I just like to go in the street, rob who the fuck I gotta rob.' "

"What did he say?"

"He laughed."

"He probably likes you because you're honest."

"I really respect the man. You show that when you talk."

"It was a stroke of luck that you met him in New York last week."

"You know what I told Stevie before? I went down to see him and I says, 'Hey, Stevie, you gotta come to Florida. I'm telling you now. I never asked you for a motherfucking thing, I'm always alongside you. If you don't come to fucking Florida with me, I ain't even gonna fucking come around here no more—just leave me the fuck alone and I'll do my own thing.' And I got up and walked out. He called me the next day. He says, 'Look how lucky we are—the guy is here. We reached right out,' he says."

"Is that right?"

"He says, 'What are you getting mad at me for? I would have come with you,' he says."

"So the guy tonight, nice guy to talk to, huh?"

"It's like me and you talking already, Donnie."

"That's great."

"He was saying stories, you know, about other people. He says other people think like—take this Bruno, for instance, from Philadelphia—he says because you wasn't born there, Bruno don't wanna open up the door for you. 'That's the wrong thing,' he says. 'Like, you come here, I was born here,' he says, 'you got something. We'll work together,' he says."

"Well, everybody is gonna be making the money, right?"

"Right, bro."

We were both happy for the same reason, more or less. I felt deeply satisfied for having engineered a second marriage between two Mafia families.

The next day, Trafficante's man, Benny Husick, a short, white-haired guy, came to see Sonny about the bingo operation. Afterward Sonny said that Benny ran Trafficante's bingo parlors. He said that we would start looking for sites with Benny, and that we had to get a building of 8,000 to 10,000 square feet, with air-conditioning. An old supermarket was perfect. He said that we would supply the location and half the money to open it up; Trafficante would supply the equipment and know-how and the other half of the money. We should dream up the name of a charity as sponsoring organization, but the word *Italian* should not be included. Some kind of disabled war veterans group was good, and you could hire a disabled guy to sit near the door to make it look real.

I started to fill Lefty in on what Sonny had told me about how the sitdown with Trafficante came about, but he knew all about it.

"He was up there in New York," Lefty says. "What's the matter, who do you think made all these fucking moves in New York? I did it, not him. Both of us know him."

"I didn't think you could sit down with a guy like Trafficante, Left."

"Uh-huh. Don't underestimate your goomba."

Sonny handed me $5,000—fifty $100 bills—to "put on the street" for the loan-sharking operation. He instructed us to "keep the vig," or interest, and reinvest the capital until it was built into $60,000 to $80,000. Then the split would be me, him, Boobie, and Lefty, with Rossi getting a smaller share.

"For the time being," he says, "don't make no loans of more than five hundred bucks. You send two hundred a month to Steve to pay back the family."

Rossi and I recorded the series year and serial numbers of the bills and turned the money over to the case agents.

Sonny, Judy, and Boobie came down for the Fourth of July weekend. On July 4, Sonny had another meeting with Trafficante. Rossi and I drove Sonny over to Britton Plaza in Tampa, where Trafficante had one of his bingo parlors which his man Husick wanted to show us. Husick took Sonny to the meeting. After his meeting Sonny joined us at the Jack-in-the-Box restaurant.

He was in good spirits. He said that Trafficante liked the dog-track idea, and he told Sonny that he would line up an attorney and an architect. They would be "straight people," so we shouldn't discuss mob business with them, Trafficante had told him.

"We gotta get things going," Sonny says, "because the old man is expecting things to happen. There's so much fucking money in Florida that if the old man dies, I'll move right down here and take over the whole state." He said he was giving up fifteen soldiers in New York, assigning them to other capos, so he could concentrate "on the big stuff in the Florida operation."

We took a breather. Sonny, Boobie, and I drove out of town to where they had water slides. They give you a little mat to sit on and you climb the stairs fifty or sixty feet in the air and slide down this thing, maybe going twenty miles per hour, and you splash into a big pool at the bottom. We went down every which way—on our bellies, on our backs, making "trains" by locking hands and ankles with each other. We must have spent three or four hours going down the water slides, laughing like kids, taunting each other on who could go fastest.

On Sunday, Sonny, Judy, Rossi, and I took a ride to Orlando so that Sonny could scout the area where he wanted to set up bingo and bookmaking operations, now with the support of the Trafficante organization. Earlier Rossi had said that he had a top Orange County official in his pocket, so Sonny assumed we were under his protection also—Orlando was an easy mark.

Then we went to Disney World. It was the first time Sonny had been anyplace like that. We spent the rest of the day, went on all the rides, visited the museums and exhibits, fooled around. We went to a shooting gallery where they had rifles and moving targets. Sonny was a pretty good shot. But Rossi and I were knocking the hell out of everything. "You guys are fucking better shots than I am," he says. "Where'd you learn to shoot like that?"

He could relax easier than Lefty could. Lefty was Mafia twenty-four hours a day. Mafia business was always intertwined with everything Lefty did with me. He would never let his guard down. Despite the fact that Sonny was more powerful and more dangerous, it was a relief to be with him. In restaurants or in public, he was a gentleman, not a loudmouth. I didn't have to carry his bags. Away from mob business, Sonny was just a regular street guy who could laugh and break chops. No business was discussed when we were having a good time.

His girlfriend, Judy, was a good kid, a straight girl, sharp. She didn't know much about what he did. He never involved her in anything of the business. She was his main girlfriend. He had met her when she was tending bar at CaSa Bella. She was another one of those outsiders that I was sorry about, because of what would happen down the line.

At a roadside stand, Sonny saw little baby palm trees in pots. He decided he wanted some back in Brooklyn, to plant outdoors. "Palm trees would look great up there," he says. "It would knock people out."

"Palm trees are for tropical climates," I say. "They won't last the winter in Brooklyn."

"As long as they live through the summertime," he says, "what's the difference? Nothing lives forever."

So we bought five or six and shipped them Federal Express to Brooklyn.

Sonny wasn't any good at tennis, but he loved to play. He would take the court at King's Court in his black socks. Rossi and I would play doubles against him and Boobie. Sonny would run around whacking at the ball and hollering at us, "I'm gonna kill you!"

Sometimes he and I would arm-wrestle. Sonny lifted weights. So did I. He was strong, but I had the advantage of leverage, being taller and having longer arms. We would be sitting around the pool or someplace when he would challenge me. He could never beat

me. It drove him nuts. I never saw him challenge
anybody else. But he never stopped challenging me.

One day Sonny brought a bottle of pills to the club.
The pills were called Zooms and they were supposed
to enhance your sex life. Sonny gave the bottle to
Chico. "These were made by the virgin nuns of Peru,"
he tells Chico. "They keep your pecker hard. You're
gonna love them. Give one to Donnie to try too. Let
all the guys try it."

Chico took the bottle home. We knew they were
just some caffeine concoction. The next day Chico
came into the club. "Wow, they were sensational,
those Zooms," he says to Sonny.

"Great, right?" Sonny says. "You give one to
Donnie?"

"Naw, I took them all," Chico says, "all twenty."

"You took them all! You must be crazy!"

"The thing is, I just can't get it to go down now. I
push on it and slap it, it won't go down."

"You crazy bastard! You can't use Zooms like they
was a fucking toy! They come from Peru! You're lucky
you're alive!"

Since we were now dealing with Trafficante, we
wanted to keep King's Court clean, relatively. We
didn't want to attract more attention than necessary to
the club as a gambling place. So we opened up another club for the card games. It was just a small
store, at 1227 Dixie Highway, a couple of miles away.
Sonny gave me $500 for the security deposit. We took
the card tables out of the back room of King's Court
and sent them off down there, with the poker dealers,
and that's where the nightly games continued.

"We gotta do things right," Sonny says. "The old
man says he has five hundred men down here and
they're not pulling their weight. He's looking for new
blood in this state, and that's us."

Rossi had met a guy named Teddy who was a book-
maker in the area. Teddy wanted to run the football
book for us. We arranged for him to meet Sonny. The
five of us—Teddy, me, Rossi, Sonny, and Lefty—sat
around the pool at the Tahitian. Teddy said he ran a

big-time book. Sonny grilled him. He asked him how long he had been booking, how much action he was taking, how he ran the business, everything.

After Teddy left, Sonny says, "I don't want to do business with this guy. He thinks he's too sharp. I think he'd end up trying to fuck us, and then I'd end up having to kill him. For now, let Jo-Jo take the bets over the phone, and Chico can handle payments and collections."

Sonny was shuttling between New York and Florida for meetings with Trafficante, solidifying his position. On August 8, he and Lefty came down. Sonny called me at the apartment and said for me and Rossi to be at the coffee shop at the Tahitian at three-thirty in the afternoon. "That guy is coming," he says.

I decided to carry a transmitter.

I met our contact and picked up the transmitter. Rossi and I tested it in my apartment. Rossi put in a call to agent Mike Lunsford, who was on location. I spoke into the transmitter. Lunsford couldn't hear anything coming over the radio. We tried it again and again as time drew short. Lunsford wasn't picking up anything.

Rossi says, "What the fuck we got all this fancy equipment for if it doesn't work?"

It's hard to explain to anybody how it makes you feel. You risk your life and exposure of the operation by carrying this piece of equipment. You go through maybe a whole day or night with this on you. You think you've got some dynamite conversations. But nothing came in on the receiver, or all you got on your tape was beeps and noises, or just silence. It was good equipment. Maybe it was used a lot before they gave it to you. There's no way to know when it's going to malfunction.

If I got caught with a transmitter, the first thing these guys would think is that I was an informant. If you're a cop or an agent, maybe they'll think twice because you're doing your job. I had been with these guys four years now. There's no way they would believe I was an agent. They would think I just turned and went bad. No leeway. They would kill me.

So here I was about to go out with Sonny Black, who was going to meet with Santo Trafficante, and I had a piece-of-shit transmitter. It was better to find out ahead of time. But the more Rossi and I tried to make it work and the more we talked about it, the more aggravated we got.

Finally I wound up and threw the transmitter at the wall. It hit right next to the window and clanked down on the floor, bent and sprung. "At least nobody else will get stuck with this piece-of-shit transmitter," I say.

Rossi and I went to the coffee shop. Sonny was sitting at a table with Trafficante and Husick. He motioned for us to sit at another table by ourselves. Husick came over and wanted us to take him to look at a potential bingo site on Ridge Road in New Port Richey. When we came back, Sonny and Trafficante were still talking. Sonny told us to sit at the counter.

Half an hour later Sonny came over and told Rossi to make dinner reservations for three at the Bon Appetit restaurant in Dunedin. "You guys go up to Lefty's room," he says.

Lefty's room was next to Sonny's. Lefty was lying on the bed watching TV. Rossi got on the phone as instructed. I was standing in the doorway.

Sonny and Trafficante came walking by. Sonny motioned for me to come into his room. Inside, he introduced me.

"Donnie, this is Santo. Santo, Donnie." Santo looked at me with narrow eyes through thick glasses. I shook hands with my second Mafia boss.

15

DRUGS AND GUNS

Sonny wanted me to come to New York to update him on all the various rackets we supposedly had under way—bingo, numbers, gambling. I went to his neighborhood for the first time.

The Withers Italian-American War Veterans Club, Inc., Sonny's private social club, was at 415 Graham Avenue, at the corner of Graham and Withers Street in the Greenpoint section of Brooklyn. The neighborhood was quiet, safe, and clean, mostly small shops and storefront businesses in two-story or three-story apartment buildings. It was similar to the neighborhood in the Bensonhurst section to the south, where I had been involved four years earlier with Jilly's crew and the Colombos. One of the main similarities was that both neighborhoods gave you the feeling that outsiders would be noticed quickly.

The Withers club had a big front room with a small bar and a few card tables, and a back room with a desk, telephones, a sink, and the men's room.

Diagonally across the intersection, at 420 Graham Street, was the Motion Lounge, another private hangout for Sonny and his crew. There was no sign at the front door. The exterior wall of the club was covered with fake fieldstone siding. The upper floor of the three-story building was sheathed with brown shingles. In the front room of the lounge was the bar, a large-screen projection TV, a pinball machine, a couple of tables. Behind the bar was a big tank of tropical fish. In the back room was a small stage, a pool table, a jukebox, a few card tables. A kitchen was off the back room.

As it was with the clubs in Little Italy, the wiseguys in Sonny's crew lounged around inside and outside during the summer. Their cars—mostly Cadillacs—were parked and double-parked on the block.

Sonny said I shouldn't bother with the expense and inconvenience of a hotel; I should stay at his apartment. That was on the top floor above the Motion Lounge, a three-story walk-up. It was a modest, utilitarian one-bedroom place. You entered into a hallway with a small kitchen to the left, a dining room ahead, and a living room with a pullout sofa bed to the right, and Sonny's bedroom off that. There were no doors. A sort of ladderlike set of stairs led up to the roof, where he kept his racing pigeons.

He didn't have air-conditioning in the apartment, because the building wasn't wired for it, and the heat that night was brutal. He kept the windows open, which looked out over the adjoining roof. I slept on the pullout couch in the living room; he slept in the bedroom.

I fell asleep on my back, sweating. I woke up. Something touched my chest. At first, in my daze, I thought it was hands, fingernails feeling for my neck—somebody was going to strangle me.

But it was claws—a rat!

I froze, afraid to open my eyes. Sleeping in the apartment of a Mafia captain didn't bother me at all. But I am terrified of mice or rats. I shudder when I see them dead or alive. If there is a mouse in my home, my wife or kids have to deal with it.

Now I was going to get bitten by a rat and die of rabies.

I held my breath while I counted down. Then I swung my hand with everything I had and swatted it across the room. The rat thudded to the floor as I hit the light switch.

It was a cat I glimpsed, leaping for the window and disappearing into the night across the rooftops.

Sonny came running in. "What the fuck happened?"

I told him. He started laughing like a son of a bitch. "Big, tough guy, scared of a fucking cat," he says. "Wait till I tell everybody this story."

I was shaking. "Sonny, you better not tell anybody this story, not anybody. If you got some fucking air-conditioning in here, we wouldn't have to leave the windows open and let any fucking animal in the world in here."

"Okay."

"Anybody could come in through that window, Sonny, it ain't safe."

"Okay, okay." He went back to his bedroom, still laughing.

At about six-thirty he woke me up. He had already been to the bakery across the street to pick up pastry and had made coffee. We sat around his kitchen table in our underwear, drinking coffee and bullshitting about the business.

He had weights and a weight bench in his bedroom. We lifted weights together.

We went up on the roof so he could show me his pigeons.

He was proud of his racing pigeons. He loved to spend time up on the roof. He had three coops. Both the roof of the building and the roof of his coops were topped with miniature white picket fences.

He told me about blending their food, adding vitamins for stamina. He explained about the different breeds, how you matched different breeds to get birds that could fly long distances. Each pigeon had a band on its leg for identification. He said there were lots of races in different cities. The pigeons would fly home to their coops. Owners had a clock that would stamp the time on the band. He said you could win up to $3,000.

He said he did some of his best thinking up on the roof taking care of his pigeons.

As a kid growing up in that same neighborhood, he told me, he was just a thief in the streets. "I didn't care about being a mob guy. I was doing good enough." But then he got to a point where he couldn't do anything without the approval of the local mob guy in his neighborhood. "So it was easier to join them than to fight them." He became a hijacker and stickup man, and eventually served time.

He talked about mob politics. The Colombo family was in bad shape because both Carmine and Allie Boy Persico were under indictment. He hinted that the power struggle was heating up within the Bonanno family.

"The whole thing is how strong you are and how much power you got and how fucking mean you are—that's what makes you rise in the mob." Sonny would repeat the theme time and time again in conversations with me up on the roof with his pigeons. "Every day is a fucking struggle, because you don't know who's looking to knock you off, especially when you become a captain or boss. Every day somebody's looking to dispose of you and take your position. You always got to be on your toes. Every fucking day is a scam day to keep your power and position."

When we were around other mob guys, it was different. Sonny acted like a captain and commanded respect. On the street and in other business situations, you could see that he was not only respected but feared. But here, when nobody else was around, we just shot the breeze like two equals. He talked about how much he loved his kids. He was very optimistic about Florida. He encouraged me to move on drug deals. He wanted us to get going on plans for another Las Vegas Night.

He gave me my own key so that I could use his apartment anytime I wanted, whether he was there or not. Sometimes he stayed at Judy's apartment on Staten Island. From then on I stayed at Sonny's almost every time I came to New York.

When I went back down to Florida, I sent Sonny a pair of ceiling fans for his apartment. He sent me a big package of canned squid, Italian bread, Italian cold cuts and cheeses, because he knew I loved those things and I couldn't get the best New York–type stuff where I was in Florida.

Sonny was not satisfied with the volume in our bookmaking and shylock business. He wanted to send somebody down from New York to run it. Rossi and I had a better idea: my friend from Philadelphia, an agent whose undercover name was Eddie Shannon. I had known Shannon since 1968, when he was a detective in the Philadelphia Police Department and I was with Naval Intelligence. He had run an undercover bookmaking business in Baltimore.

"I got a guy that could do the book," I tell Sonny. "He's not Italian, he's Irish, but he's good." I filled him in. "Next time you come down here, I'll have him come down. You can get to know him, talk to him alone. If you like the guy, fine. You make the decision. If you want him to stay with us, he'll stay, because he owes me some favors."

"Now we gotta deal with a fucking Irishman," Sonny says.

Sonny came down and spent a couple of days getting to know Eddie Shannon. Then he says, "I like the kid. He's sharp, knowledgeable. He's got a lot of loyalty to you, a stand-up guy. I like that. Get him an apartment down here and tell him to move in."

Shannon got an apartment in the same complex where Rossi and I lived, the same complex in which other agents received and monitored the microwave video transmissions from King's Court.

Rossi and I were continually working on potential drug deals. That is, we worked to line them up and then tap-danced to keep them from happening. We had to encourage drug sources by promoting our contacts and outlets, how much we could move through "our" people. We had to keep Sonny and Lefty interested by promoting the capabilities of our drug sources. But we couldn't let any big deals happen. Nor could we have any busts that would compromise our operation. So the trick was to contact sellers, drag information out of them, keep them on the hook, and keep Sonny and Lefty excited—all while keeping the two sides apart.

Our contacts were ready to provide a wide range of products. We had a local guy with coke to sell at $15,000 a pound. We had a guy peddling Quaaludes for eighty or ninety cents apiece, and grass for $230 to $240 a pound. There was a coke dealer in Cocoa

Beach. We had a guy with heroin samples from Mexico, and a twin-engined Piper Aztec he used to fly loads in. One local guy said that if we could find him a plane, he could make $1 million in two months on trips to Colombia where he could get cocaine that was ninety percent pure. He needed $25,000 front money to set it up and would charge $50,000 per trip. This same guy said he could get " 'ludes" in South America for twenty cents each. We kept talking to them all, going back and forth with prices, questions, promises, broken promises.

"In my FBI file," Lefty says to Rossi and me, "it says 'This man hates junk.' Right next to my picture."

We were talking about how many young millionaires there were in south Florida who had made their fortunes in the drug business.

Sonny was always talking about heroin, cocaine, marijuana, Quaaludes. One time he tells me, "Don't bother with the coke right now. The hard stuff and the smoke is what's selling big now in New York." He had one outlet immediately for 300 pounds of grass and another for 400 pounds. "I want a steady source that can provide a hundred pounds a week. I could net ten grand a week from the outlets I got. We'll have twenty grand to pay for the first load up front."

On the phone, one of our code phrases for drugs was "pigeon feed." Over the phone I was telling him about a new connection. He said, "Bring a sample of the pigeon feed up to New York," so he could have it checked out.

Rossi put a sample in his pocket and we flew to New York. At JFK we were met by Boobie. He introduced us to Nicky Santora. Nicky, an overweight, curly-haired, happy-go-lucky type, was in Sonny's crew.

Boobie asked if I had the sample.

"The marijuana? Tony's got it."

"I thought you were bringing heroin."

"I thought Sonny meant marijuana. We got our signals crossed, I guess."

Boobie was upset because he had a friend standing by to test the sample of heroin.

"We'll bring that on the next trip," I say.

Nicky drove us to Little Neck, on Long Island, where Sonny was staying temporarily. Nicky talked about the bookmaking business. He had just recently gotten out of jail. "I was convicted for taking four bets over the telephone," he says. "Can you imagine that?"

Sonny was staying with a guy named John Palzolla in the North Shore Apartments in Little Neck.

Sonny says, "You told me you had a sample of heroin."

"No, I didn't."

"Well, fuck it. Give the sample to Nicky. Maybe he can do something with it."

Rossi handed Nicky the small plastic bag of grass.

"The guy wants two hundred and seventy a pound," I say.

"That's high," Sonny says.

"Maybe we can get three-fifty to four hundred a pound in the city," Nicky says, looking at the stuff. "It's got a lot of seeds. I'll take it out tomorrow and shop it around to a few people."

A bunch of us met downstairs for dinner at the Chop House Restaurant, which was in the apartment building. Sonny's cousin, Carmine, was there. Nino, Frankie, Jimmy—last names weren't used. A few women came around, including one named Sabina. Sabina took a joint rolled from our grass sample and went away for an hour. When she came back, she said, "Gee, that wasn't bad stuff."

Everybody talked about what they had going. Carmine said he had a lot of fugazy jewelry available— fake Rolex watches, vermeil trinkets, gold charms. Rossi agreed to take some back to sell at the club.

John was awaiting sentencing for "Ponzi" schemes that he and his brother had conducted around the country. He said a good way to work a Ponzi scheme was to go to some rich guy who needs to put his money someplace and tell him that you have connections with a clothing manufacturer who produces a lot of overruns. And these surpluses—jeans or whatever— are available at a fraction of wholesale. If this person invests, say $5,000, you can guarantee $500 return for the first week. The return is so fantastic that more and more people invest, and they invest more and more. You give them these great interest payments, but you keep the capital. When you get enough capital, you "skip town and never see these investors again."

Doctors and professional people were the best targets, he said, because they were always looking for ways to invest their cash. Lately his most prominent victims had been chiropractors. He had pled guilty so that other "family" members wouldn't be hauled into court to testify.

Rossi and I stayed in the apartment with Sonny and John. At about two A.M., we were all getting ready to go to bed. Rossi comes out of the john in his Jockey shorts. Sonny starts rolling on the floor laughing. "Holy underwears!" he spouts whenever he can get a breath. "Holy underwears!" Rossi's Jockey shorts have holes in the back. Sonny can't control himself. "Wearing two hundred dollar slacks, hundred dollar shirts, two hundred dollar shoes, and you got fucking underwear on since you were in high school! Holy fucking underwears!"

Two days later Nicky Santora reported that he had found our marijuana price of $270 to be too high. But he said that he could do business if our source would "front" 200 pounds and wait for payment for a week.

When we went back to Florida, we contacted our source and told him the grass hadn't checked out to be as good as he said, and that the only way our people would buy it was if they would front 300 pounds and wait two weeks for payment. The guy had to think it over.

The next time Sonny came to Florida, he brought news of a shake-up in the Commission. "They knocked down Funzi Tieri," he tells me. He said the power was now Paul Castellano, Neil Dellacroce, and Joe Gallo— the top guns of the Gambino family. "They were given the power and are handling it properly," he says. "I met with Paulie the other day. I did him a big favor which nobody else could do. Paulie has an alliance now with the old man here." He meant Trafficante.

He didn't tell me what the favor was. But the

Gambinos were big in the drug business. In any case, Sonny was indicating that he was now in tight with the new boss of bosses.

He was waiting for Santo Trafficante to come to the motel. Trafficante arrived, and they went to Sonny's room. Permitted by a court order, we had his room bugged. But right away they turned up the TV volume to cover their conversation.

Sonny and I were having dinner alone. Sonny didn't wear a lot of jewelry or anything flamboyant, but he did have some nice rings. If he had a gold buckle on his belt, he would wear gold; with a silver buckle, white gold. It is common for wiseguys to wear pinkie rings. But he had one that I really liked, a white-gold horseshoe with tiny diamonds in it. I loved that ring. It was his favorite too.

"Sonny, one of these days I'm gonna get a ring like that."

"Like what?"

"That diamond horseshoe ring. I really like that ring. I always wanted one like that. But they're too expensive, and I never could get one in a score. One day I'll get lucky."

"You like it? You just got lucky. Here." He slid the ring off his finger and put it down by my hand. "It's yours."

"Hey, Sonny, I can't take that from you."

"Why not? You like it, you got it."

I really couldn't take it from him. I couldn't accept an expensive gift like that in my position. I would have to log it and turn it in just like any other evidence; otherwise, I would compromise myself in the investigation. I guess I could have taken it and then given it back when the operation was over, but if it got lost, or Sonny got whacked or something before, it would really bother me to have accepted it.

I didn't want to offend him, either, because he did it from the heart. He would do things like that, never make a big deal out of it. "I really appreciate it because I know how much you like that ring." I pushed it back across the table with my fingers. "I can't take it, but thanks."

He shrugged and slipped it back on his pinkie.

The next afternoon we're in the coffee shop at the Tahitian.

"I feel strong today," he says.

"So? What does that mean?"

"I feel strong enough to beat you at arm wrestling."

"Sonny, you never beat me. What's gonna make today any different?"

"How strong I am. Come on."

"In here?"

"Come on."

We put our elbows up on the table and go through all the gyrations of getting ready, lock our hands in.

"You ready?" He looks me in the eye.

"Yeah."

"I'm gonna beat you."

"Go ahead."

"Go!"

We strain our arms together. Then he spits in my face, I flinch, and he slams my hand down.

"I didn't tell you *how* I was gonna beat you."

Sonny had a scheme. You couldn't get really good Italian bread anywhere in the area. We asked around why that was, why the bread was so much better in New York. Nobody knew. We asked a baker, an Italian guy from New York.

"The water," he says. "The water in the New York area is the best there is. It's crucial. Something to do with how the yeast reacts. That's why you can't bake Italian bread that good anyplace else in the country."

Next thing I know, Sonny had set up a deal with this guy. He's going to bake for us. Sonny is going to get a fleet of tanker trucks, like those that deliver milk, and truck New York water down to Florida and have this guy bake our Italian bread and make a fortune.

Tony Mirra got out of prison. When he was in the can, guys kept reporting to Lefty that Mirra was calling people and was pissed off because he heard that

Lefty and I had made a ton of money in Milwaukee and were making a ton of money in Florida, and some of that should be his because he brought me around to the crew in the first place.

Lefty tells me, "I told him, 'You better have friends when you come out.' I says, 'You better stop knocking people, knocking their brains out.' "

When I was alone with Sonny at the Tahitian, he says, "I gotta ask you something, Donnie. Is Rocky a wire?"

"Hey, Sonny, I been dealing with him for over six years without any problems, and I been using him to buy and sell merchandise. No problems. That's all I can say."

"Well, Mirra branded him a wire. But, of course, that's Mirra's style."

Lefty had a lion. Some guy who raised animals in New Jersey gave Lefty a little cub. Lefty loved it. He took it with him when he drove around in the car. He kept it at the Motion Lounge, and we played with it. It was a nice little pet. Lefty never gave it a name. We just called it "lion." It stayed in the front of the club at the bar. We also had a regular house cat that stayed in the back.

After a couple of months the lion was growing into a real lion. It started leaving claw marks on the leather seats of Lefty's car, so he couldn't drive around with it anymore. It clawed you when you played with it. It got to be the size of a large dog. Pretty soon we couldn't even take it out for its usual walks. It stayed at the club during the day, but it couldn't be left there all night anymore. Sonny's cousin, Carmine, owned an empty warehouse not far away from the Motion Lounge, so Lefty would take the lion over there every night in a van. Guys would go there every day and feed it. It was costing around $200 a day to feed, because the guys were giving it prime steaks.

I was on the phone from King's Court one day, talking to Boobie at the Motion Lounge. "Lefty's across the street loading the lion in the truck," Boobie says. "We got to get the lion out from under the bar.

Somebody ratted him out. It could cost us a $10,000 fine."

Somebody in the neighborhood had spotted the lion in the club and called the police. By the time the police came, Lefty had taken the lion to the warehouse. What the cops found was the house cat sleeping on the pool table in the back room.

The cop says to Charlie the bartender, "I'm talking about a lion."

"What we got is that cat," Charlie says. "If we got a lion, that's it."

After that, the lion had to stay full-time at the warehouse.

Lefty called me in Florida. "We gotta get rid of the lion. It's tearing up the walls in the warehouse. It eats the wires. How about you take it down there? You got five acres. Just put a chain-link fence over one of the tennis courts. We'll ship it down."

"You're crazy. They're not gonna let us keep a lion in a tennis court."

One night they loaded the lion into the van and took it to a park in Queens and tied it by its leash to a bench.

Lefty called me. "Get today's *Post*. They found our lion. It escaped. They got it at the ASPCA. That lion is making some news. It's all over television. Pretty bastard."

The front page of the *New York Post* had the headline: KING OF THE JUNGLE FOUND IN QUEENS! A big picture showed the lion between two cops, one holding its leash. The story said that a man had found this six-month-old lion cub wandering outside St. Mary's Cemetery in Flushing, Queens. Nobody had the slightest idea where the lion had come from.

Some of Sonny's crew in Brooklyn were arrested, and it looked like there was a snitch involved. Lefty called to tell me everybody new was suspect.

"In other words," he tell me over the phone, "who's responsible has to die."

"They're not worried about Tony, are they?"

"Let's put it this way: You're not, I'm not, but they are. We gotta go to his background."

"Okay."

"We got Rocky around us. And what's that guy?"

"Eddie."

"Eddie, yeah. And we got Chico, right?"

"Well, Chico had another argument with his girl, and he took off." Agent Chico had left the operation.

"I don't like that. You see, that's another thing I gotta check out there. That's another thing that's no good."

"Well, this broad is driving him crazy."

"I understand that, but it's no good. You're involved in all these things. I can't account for everything. Like now, they're letting it slide about Rocky out there."

Rocky, the undercover cop I had helped introduce into the mob world for a separate operation, the one who had gone on the boat trip with us, had a car business not far from New York City. I helped Rocky set up this business as a cover. When Tony Mirra got out of prison, he started hanging out with Rocky. That put Lefty in a bind. Since I had introduced Rocky to him, Lefty felt that Rocky belonged to him and owed him a share of anything he did. At the same time, Lefty didn't want to have anything to do with Mirra.

"He's hanging out with that stool pigeon," Lefty says, meaning Mirra. "I don't know what you're gonna do with him. I don't know what's going on. This guy does something wrong, Donnie, you and I are going bye-bye. I know this guy is gonna send us to our death. I gotta talk to you about it."

It put me in a bind, too, because I didn't know what was going on with Rocky and Mirra, either.

"We're coming out tomorrow," Lefty says over the phone, a few days before Thanksgiving. "Four guys."

"Who's coming?"

"You gotta pick us up. He's gonna tell you that there." He gave me the flight information to write down and said that "he," meaning Sonny, was going to be calling me about this. "Four people. Don't ask no questions."

"Okay. All right. Uh, these guys heavyweights, or what?"

"Look, leave it alone. Just get us a couple of rooms. You gotta get us a car. Get a big four-door job. Charge it to our expense on the business."

"Okay."

"Double rooms next to each other, by the pool."

A few hours later Sonny called.

"Look, a couple of people are gonna come down there. They need the car. And only if Boobie asks you for anything, whatever you want, you give him, and then I'll make it up."

"Yeah, okay."

"Only him."

"All right."

"They'll explain to you down there."

"I was just talking to Lefty," I say, "and he said that you wanted to talk to me about some people coming down. You don't have any information, though, huh?"

"Tomorrow."

Then I called Lefty back—I kept both of them clued in to cover myself. "I just talked to him," I say, "and he said Boobie and a couple of other guys would be coming down."

"He didn't mention my name? I don't know what's on this fucking man's fucking mind. That's all he told you—Boobie's coming down with a couple of guys tomorrow. And he never mentioned my name."

"Not right off the bat, but I said I had talked to you—see, I don't want to mention anybody's name."

"Right, there's no names involved. We always doing everything right. And we can't embarrass ourselves, that's what counts, that's the goddamn thing. Now, we're not gonna tie you guys up, you understand?"

"Yeah. We'll just give you the car, you do what you gotta do."

"We'll come back, party it up, a few drinks."

"You're not gonna do nothing tomorrow night, right?"

"No, no, we're gonna just have a few drinks to-- gether. And expect us back in the future. I'll explain to you when I see you."

The next night, Rossi and I were to pick them up at the Tampa airport. We were trying to hold expenses down, especially where Lefty was concerned. I told Rossi that I wasn't going to put out any money to rent them a car. They could rent their own car.

We met Lefty, Boobie, an ex–New York cop named Dennis, and Jimmy Legs—James Episcopia—a big guy abut 6'4", with skinny arms and skinny legs and a pot-belly and a toupee.

Lefty says, "You rent a car?"

"No, my American Express line is used up. I'm overextended."

"Well, who the fuck's gonna rent the car?"

"Put it on *your* fucking card for once. Why should I get stuck with the bill? I don't even know why the fuck you're here."

Then we went to the baggage claim. I didn't pick up his bag as I always had. Everybody else got their bags, and his was still riding around. Finally he got the idea and picked up his own bag.

This happened in front of these other wiseguys, and he was very steamed. I was really going to hear about this when we were alone, but I didn't care. I was tired of Lefty.

There were times I could sit and talk enjoyably with Lefty, largely because of the genuine affection he had for me. Then there were times I could have strangled him on the spot because he embarrassed me or treated me like a piece of shit. Like, we might be at a Chinese restaurant and I'm ordering something that's not Chinese. And in front of everybody he would talk about what a fucking nitwit idiot I was. I knew this wasn't personal. He was like that with everybody. But I couldn't swallow everything all the time.

Back at the end of 1979, I had blown up at him over something. "I ain't your fucking slave," I had said. "So when we're out, don't you fucking embarrass me in front of people because I might lose my head and fucking whack you, and that's bad for me because then *I* get killed."

"But see, Donnie, you don't understand," he had said. "What I'm trying to do is to school you. You never hear me talk to Mike Sabella that way. Suppose Mike heard you talk like that? When they open the books, they won't put you up. Don't you want to be a wiseguy?"

So now, we got to the rental car ahead of the others, and he blew.

"You fucking embarrassed me in front of my friends, you cocksucker!"

"You don't like it, huh? Now you know how I feel when you embarrass me. Now I'm schooling you in *my* thoughts. I'm not a fucking peon anymore. I've made a lot of fucking money for everybody. I'm entitled to the same respect."

"Don't you think these guys noticed? Don't you think they're gonna go back and tell Sonny? Don't you think that's a black mark on you?"

"I would never embarrass Sonny, because he's a fucking boss. But, hey, if that's the way the fucking game's played, then that's the way it's played."

He sighed. "Six fucking years and you still don't know nothing."

Dennis the ex-cop and Jimmy Legs joined us in that car. Boobie rode with Rossi.

On the way to the Tahitian, Boobie asked Rossi, "How many guns do you have?"

"Three."

"Good, except I don't want any small guns like .25s."

"I've got .32 automatics."

"Those are okay. We aren't going to do anything now. We're just looking things over and running time tests, learning the streets in St. Petersburg. We'll be back next week to do this job if everything works out."

Time tests related to casing a job—the time it takes to pull something off, to get there and get out.

That night we sat at the King's Court until maybe five A.M., bullshitting, laughing. We talked about everything from the difficulty of hiring reliable waitresses, to the prime lending rate at banks, to the value of education.

Jimmy Legs says, "When I was up in Canada doing some work guarding the Old Man, I had a lot of time on my hands, so I decided to take some philosophy courses at the college up there."

Boobie asked Rossi how it was going with the fugazy jewelry he had brought down from Sonny's cousin, Carmine. We had it on display for sale. Rossi said that some of the less expensive items sold okay, but some of the heavier stuff wasn't going to go. He sold a "Rolex" watch to one of the waitresses. "It's a good-looking watch," Rossi says, "but it turned her arm green."

Lefty says privately, "Donnie, I can't tell you about this job because it's not my score. But when we're ready to do it, I'll let you know what it is. We're probably going to use your apartment to stash the loot and maybe to hole up in."

The next morning, the four of them took off in the big car. A surveillance team followed them to the St. Petersburg area but lost them in the vicinity of Route 19 and Forty-ninth Street.

That night, the seven of us went to a Greek night-club in Tarpon Springs where they had belly dancers. The girls were dancing around our table, and the guys were putting $5 and $10 bills in their bras and panties.

The guys started debating about who was the best-looking guy, which of us the girls would go for. Boobie slapped a $100 bill to his forehead, where it stuck, and said, "This is the best-looking guy."

The following day, the surveillance team stayed with them to Pinellas Park, just outside St. Pete. The agents watched them case the LandmarkTrust Bank. That bank is only a block from police headquarters.

Later that day, Lefty said they had decided against the score. "Things didn't look right," he says.

Behind the scenes, Rossi and I were dealing with one of the primary frustrations of working undercover. We couldn't get clear authorization to give these guys the guns if it came to that.

We often had difficulty getting decisions fast enough from Headquarters on what we could and couldn't do.

On the street you have to make decisions on the spot, often during conversations with a badguy. That's normal, an everyday part of undercover work. But we might need an authorization for something from Headquarters in a day, and it takes two weeks. Part of the reason for this was that we were asking for authorizations in legally sensitive, potentially controversial areas where things weren't black-and-white.

But these were crucial situations for our investigations. Often they were life-and-death situations. With myself and most of the undercover agents I talked to in the course of my whole career, the greatest frustration was that they couldn't get an answer when they needed it.

You get a deal worked out with the badguys. You ask Headquarters: "Can I do this?" Nobody wants to say yes or no, so it gets drawn out. So that puts you in the position of having to draw out your story for the badguys, keep them on the line.

You might request money or approval to make a buy. You can string a buy out for a couple of days, that's no big deal. But you can't string it out for a month. If you go weeks with excuses, that knocks down your credibility—especially if at the end of that time you can't go through with the deal. If you pull that two or three times, it gets old. The badguys are going to think, This guy's got no power, he's not worth dealing with. Word gets around the street that you're a bullshitter. Or maybe you're a snitch.

Earlier, when I was working the cashier's-check scam with Lefty, I had the okay from a U.S. Attorney—it was okay to do it as long as I made a record of the purchases so that when the case was over, we could go back and repay the merchant. Later on, another U.S. Attorney took over the case and said that he would have been opposed to what I did from the beginning and might have prosecuted *me* for carrying out the scam.

That's why an undercover agent always has in the back of his mind: Even if I keep proper records, make proper reports, follow approved procedures, and nail the badguys, is it possible that I myself might be prosecuted for something? Am I going to be prosecuted for doing my job?

In this case, with Lefty and Boobie and the others, it involved these guns.

When Sonny or Lefty had asked, I told them we had guns stashed down in Florida. I'm supposed to be connected, so naturally I have access to guns. You can't carry guns back and forth on planes, so the most convenient thing is to have guns waiting for you where you need them.

So when the guys came down to case the bank job, Boobie asked Rossi if he had guns available, and Rossi gave the right answer: Yes, we've got guns.

Then Rossi got in touch with the contact agent and asked what we should do if we were asked to give them these guns—would it be okay? The question was passed on to the U.S. Attorney. He said, "Sure, just make the guns inoperable so they can't fire." That's no big deal, it's easy to do. So then you're not on the spot, because if anything happens that these guys try to use the guns, they will misfire, and nobody will get shot with our guns.

Then Headquarters was asked. They needed time to ask the legal department. The debate went on for three days. Meanwhile Lefty's crew decided not to pull the bank job, so they didn't need the guns. Then our legal department said no.

So we had the U.S. Attorney, who was going to be prosecuting the case, saying yes. We had FBI Headquarters saying no. I work for the FBI, not the U.S. Attorney. Ordinarily I go with whatever the FBI says.

What would I have done in this case? I would have made the guns inoperable and given them to Lefty's crew. There are some decisions you have to make on your own.

Word came that FBI Director William Webster was impressed by our work and wanted to meet us, the undercover agents working Project Coldwater, in Florida, under whatever circumstances necessary to assure security.

At first I wasn't too keen on the idea. There would be a security risk to the operation, no matter what. He couldn't come to us at the club or apartments, so it involved our driving someplace. You never know who is going to see you somewhere, and anyone seeing the three of us together—Rossi, Shannon, and me—would wonder what the hell we were doing there.

But since the FBI officials setting it up were willing to let us call the shots, and since it was the Director, we decided to go ahead with it.

We set it up for midnight in Tampa at the Bay Harbor Hotel, George Steinbrenner's hotel. It was near the airport, a busy hotel, a place we went to on occasion. It was better there than farther away, because if we were spotted at some really out-of-the-way place, it would be even more suspicious.

The three of us went into the hotel lounge and had a couple of drinks. We didn't leave for the Director's room together. We went up one by one, separated from each other by a few minutes.

The Director was there with an aide, and with Tampa Case Agent Kinne, who had coordinated the meeting. Judge Webster—he's a former federal judge—is a quiet man who spoke so softly that sometimes it was difficult to hear him.

He complimented us for the Florida operation, and me for being under so long in my other operations and penetrating as deep as I had. He congratulated us for the sacrifices we were making to work undercover and carry out this dangerous assignment, and how well we were doing it. He knew the case, who the major players were. He asked for some details, but this wasn't really storytelling time, so it was brief and general. Basically he was concerned about our welfare and wanted to make sure we were getting the proper support, everything we needed from the Bureau. That's why he was there, he said; he wanted to see for himself.

We made no complaints. We were honored.

* * *

Sonny wanted me to come up to New York and bring $2,500 from our bookmaking "profits." He said they got hit bad on their football book for three weeks in a row, and he needed the money to put back on the street.

"Remember when you came in the last time you came by John's house?" he says. "Is that issue still available, the problem that you brought over?"

"I don't know. I haven't seen the guy."

"Well, see him."

"All right. What about if I can't get that stuff?"

"You don't have to get it, just so long as it's open, it's still there. I'm interested in that one issue."

Lefty called shortly afterward.

"Let me get a pencil and get these figures," he says, "because I gotta go see the guy. What we win yesterday?"

"Yesterday, eleven-sixty."

"And the other day?"

"The Thursday game? The Dallas game?"

"Yeah."

"We won twenty-four-eighty."

"So you're still up by fifteen hundred for the week."

"Yeah. Now don't forget, tell him I'm gonna take a thousand out for that guy's salary. I wanna give him some money."

"I don't know if he's gonna accept that."

"Well, I'll hold off, and then when I see Sonny Wednesday I'll explain it to him myself."

Lefty was moaning and groaning. "I don't feel good. Maybe flu. The doctor gave me a shot, ordered me home for a week. I made reservations for a chest X-ray. I ain't got no money. Nobody will even take my bets. Listen, Donnie. When you come up here with that for him, you gotta bring me a hundred and five bucks for that rental car, you know? Because that hundred and five I give to my wife. She's gotta pay the American Express card. I told him about it."

I delivered the $2,500 to Sonny and told him that the marijuana was still available. He told me that John, the guy whose apartment I stayed at the time I

delivered the sample, owed loan sharks more than
$200,000. "And since he's with me," Sonny says, "I
had to vouch for him. He owes sixty grand of that to
Carmine. I made him put up a hundred and fifty grand
in jewelry to Carmine. I tell you, if I don't stick
behind him, one of the guys is gonna fucking kill him.
He runs up all these debts, and then he lies to everybody about them."

Sonny had bought a hundred pounds of marijuana
from a Cuban in Miami and made a deal with some
people out on Long Island to sell it. He needed another hundred pounds as soon as possible. He had
made a cocaine connection in Miami, and a sample
tested out at eighty-one percent pure. He was buying
it at $47,000 a kilo. He wanted us to push our heroin
connections.

In the office at King's Court, Pete and Tom Solmo,
father and son, were trying to push their drug business
to Rossi. Two cocky, bearded guys. Rossi sat behind
the desk. Tom, the son, draped in gold necklaces and
bracelets sat in an armchair in front of the desk. Pete
stood with his arms folded, or paced and kept refilling
their glasses with wine and Scotch.

"What we really need," Rossi says, "is heroin."

"Horse is tough," Tom says. "How much marijuana
do you need?"

"If you give me a sample, I've got people coming
from New York on Wednesday and they'll let me
know."

Pete explained how a marijuana transfer would work.
"He comes down, checks into a motel. North Miami,
Hollywood, Lauderdale's fine. He gives me a call. We
go to him. He's got the bread, right? You give me the
keys to your vehicle, I give them to my man. He goes,
gets it loaded, brings it back. He comes up to the
room and gives you the keys. And that's it. Every bale
will be numbered and have the weight right on it. Use
us once, you'll see."

"My dad finances everything," Tom says. "I go and
work it all out. I know what stuff is good and what
stuff is bad. I been down to Colombia many times."

"He does all the dirty work," his dad says. "He's captained boats. He's been a runner, bringing it in small ways, bringing it in by the ton."

Rossi says, "The last I brought up to New York, he said, 'What the fuck you bringing me all these seeds for?'"

"We got stuff got no seeds," Tom says.

"You guys got a strong supply, huh?"

"Fantastic," Tom says. "We'll get you five thousand pounds every week. That's no problem."

Rossi says, "I gotta be totally up-front here. Up in New York he might say, 'We're totally overloaded here, let it go for a week, a month.' I have no way of knowing. What I'm trying to say, I guess, is I can't tell you how fast all this will be put together. You understand that I'm only like the fucking go-between."

"On this other shit," Tom says, casually taking a small plastic bag of white powder out of his jacket pocket, "it's good stuff. You don't know what you're looking at." He put the bag back in his pocket. "I don't think you know that much about the product."

"No, I don't," Rossi says. "You don't have to tell me that."

"You don't use it, you don't know it," Tom says.

"What's the price on that?" Rossi asks.

"Right there?" Tom pulls out the sample again and lays it on the desk. "This is two-twenty-five."

"What percentage is that?"

"I'd give it an eighty."

"We've had a ninety-two," Rossi says.

"How was it tested?"

"How the fuck do I know? All I'm telling you is that the guy gave it to another guy, had it tested, comes back and says, 'Tony, it's ninety-two percent.' I said, 'Is that good?' He said, 'That's terrific.'"

"You give me five minutes with your buyer, he'll buy our shit, because I do have the best stuff in town."

"You don't need to have *no* time with my buyer," Rossi says. "I just hand it to him. Your problem is when we tell you what we want and you get it, and then we come to you and it might not be the right thing."

"If he likes *that*," Tom says, waving the sample, "*that* will tell you what he's gonna get."

"What about 'ludes?"

"It depends. If you want five hundred thousand, I got 'ludes."

"What they call those, 'lemons'?"

"It depends. They're all homemade now. Usually your lemon has Valium in it. You want quantity like that, we're talking about thirty-five cents apiece. I can give your man anything he wants. Only positive request involved in this is C.O.D. I'm talking about for a start. Once it's established, I don't give a shit."

"What I don't want," Rossi says, "is jacking around."

I come into the office along with Eddie Shannon. Rossi says, "Donnie's my partner from New York. Eddie's the action guy around here. You meet Donnie before?"

"No," say both Pete and Tom.

"Down at Joe Pete's one night," I say. "You guys were both drunk."

They squirm around, embarrassed.

"They brought us a sample, Donnie," Rossi says. "They said they could supply us with whatever we needed—everything with the exception of the horse, which is what we're looking for."

"No," Tom says, "don't say without it. We got it. But it's . . . we gotta find out . . ."

"Fucking coke is nothing up there," I say. "Forget about it. You can't give coke away up there. Everybody is using the horse up there. When you gonna know about the H?"

"I don't think I want to," Tom says. "Down there, there's too many deaths. I been in battles down there. It's ridiculous. It's a pain in the ass. Now, if you want, I can take you down there and let *you* jump on the bandwagon."

"If we got an introduction," I say, "we can make it worth your while to introduce one of our guys in New York to somebody down there."

"Have to find that out," Tom says.

"I'd have to think about that real hard," says his dad.

"What about prices on the coke? Where's it from?"

Tom takes out the sample again. "Fifty-five, sixty. Either Colombia or here."

"Fifty-five grand?" Rossi says.

"To sixty," Pete says.

"What we give you, the sample," Tom says, putting the sample on the desk for Rossi, "that's what you're gonna get."

"Sounds good to me," I say.

They left the sample with us. The next day the cocaine sample was tested at the Pinellas County Sheriff's Office lab. It was less than fifteen percent pure.

The day after that, we got the father and son back in the office. Jo-Jo knew these guys, so we had him in there with us. He was pretty uncomfortable.

I say, "I don't know if you think you're fucking with some jerk-offs or what. But that sample of coke ain't even fucking fifteen percent. It's bullshit. It's been stepped on nineteen fucking times."

Pete and Tom start stammering. "Y-you think we'd pull a shot like that, Don? You think we'd do that?"

"You told us it was eighty percent," Rossi says.

"Just overnight the thought came to me," Tom says. "It was something I grabbed that night. That's why I kept it in my pocket. No way I'm gonna do that intentionally. What I'd love to do—really, I'd *love* to do this, because if what you're saying is true . . ."

"It's not *if* what we're saying is true," Rossi says, "it *is* true. Why would we tell you different? We're hoping it's *ninety* percent."

"Then somebody's gonna fall," Tom says. "This guy's never done that. I been with the guy five years, and this is the first time, believe me. I'm serious."

"It's not a question of the money," Rossi says. "It's a question of the honorability."

"Goddamn, man." Tom shakes his head while his father paces around, shaking his head too.

"Whoever gave it to you is putting you in a fucking box," Rossi says.

"Donnie, don't get us wrong," Pete says, "that we think you're jacking us off or something like that."

They are getting real edgy. Pete says, "What we wanna do is drop it. Just give the sample back."

I get up and walk over to Pete. Jo-Jo is squirming in a chair right behind me.

"Just forget it," Pete says. "I'll buy you a drink. Now." He jabs his finger at Rossi. "Now!"

"What's 'now'?" Rossi says.

"Give it back!" He throws up his hands. "All right, don't give us the sample. Done. I'm really getting pissed off."

"You can get pissed off all you want," I say. "But don't get the fucking attitude, pal, that we're trying to fuck you with a bullshit sample. Understand what I'm saying?"

I hear Jo-Jo's small voice behind me: "Donnie . . . Donnie . . ." He's trying to tug my sleeve. He's afraid somebody is going to get killed. I put my finger on Pete's chest. "How can we be fucking you when we got the sample from you? Because if I take the sample from you and I want to move it, I want good stuff, right?"

Pete backs off fast. "You ain't got good stuff there."

"That's what my man says."

"Well, no deal, no money, no nothing. Hey, we're friends."

"That's right. Because he's with *me*. He's not with anybody else."

"Of course, he's with you all the way. Your word is your man's word."

"So don't come into this fucking joint saying that we're trying to fuck you guys."

"Can I come in the joint and have a drink?"

Tom is still shaking his head. "In my heart, I can tell you, this is the first time."

"Hey, this business isn't fucking in your heart," I say. "This business is in your pocket. In your head. Not what's in your heart."

"What I mean by heart is my head. First of all, ain't nobody gonna charge you for no sample."

Rossi laughs. "Charge us for a sample? We get fucking samples of that shit every day."

At that I walk out. Tom and Pete whine behind me, "Donnie! Donnie! Come back, Donnie!"

We planned our second Las Vegas Night for December 13. Trafficante was going to supply a crew to run the games. When the time came, his people weren't available, so we postponed the gambling event to January.

Rossi and I went to New York to spend the few days before Christmas with Sonny and the crew. On December 17, he had the big Christmas party at the Motion Lounge. Each captain gives a Christmas party for his crew. Charley the bartender did all the cooking—pasta and sausage and peppers and meatballs. All the guys that belonged to Sonny's crew came. We just ate and drank and told war stories and had a good time. Rossi and I each gave Sonny $200 as our presents.

Sonny was anxious to get back to Florida to meet with "the Old Man down there to really firm things up." He said Carmine was going to put up money for an addition on the back of King's Court, a dance floor and a swimming pool. The main thing now, he said, was to get the Las Vegas Night set up. "Now we're going to start making money."

But for the next few weeks he had to stay in New York. "There's some problems I'm having in Brooklyn." The Miami cocaine deal had not come through yet, but he had bought a hundred pounds of marijuana out on Long Island, and Nicky Santora had picked it up in a rented U-Haul truck and taken it to Tony Boots's garage for temporary storage.

Antonio "Boots" Tomasulo—who always wore work boots—had a place across the street from the Motion Lounge called Capri Car Service, at 421 Graham Avenue. I never saw any car-service business go on there. It was just a cluttered place where Boots carried on activities on behalf of Sonny. He was Sonny's partner in the numbers business, did all the collecting. Sonny often used the phones in there.

Sonny said he had a carbine and several handguns

stashed away and that he might give me some of them to take down to Florida in case his crew needed them. Nicky Santora said that he had two .38 pistols wrapped in cloth that he had put in a sink drain at the Motion Lounge before he went to jail. They were still there, but he hadn't checked them. "I hope they're not all fucked up with water," he says. "I wrapped them pretty good in oil."

After the first of the year Sonny said he was moving out of the Withers social club. We would be meeting at the Motion Lounge.

Rossi went back to Florida to run King's Court, and I stayed to hang around with Sonny.

I stayed at his apartment, learned more about the pigeons, had many conversations. His estranged wife was causing him problems of some sort. He was concerned about his kids. I would spend a couple of hours a day hanging out over in Manhattan on Madison Street, at the Holiday Bar with Lefty. At night I'd go bouncing with Sonny.

Nicky Santora ran a string of go-go joints out on Long Island. One night Sonny and I had been out bouncing, and we came back to the Motion Lounge at about two A.M. Nicky and a few guys and some of the girls from his joints were partying in the back room.

"You can take your pick," Nicky says to us. "There's one that gives a great blow job."

We look the girls over while they're partying it up.

"I'll take the one that gives good head," Sonny says.

I have to come up with a good quick line here, because Sonny will take the girl upstairs, and I'm staying with him, so I would be expected to take a girl upstairs too. "I'm gonna have to beg off, bro. You go ahead. But I don't know these broads, they hang around with bikers out there at the joint, and you know how dirty they are. There's this herpes thing around, and I don't wanna risk no herpes."

"Jesus, Donnie, maybe you got a point. Nicky, those broads hang out with bikers. Get them outa here right away, hurry up."

"What's the matter?"

"Those fucking broads are gonna give us all herpals."

"Herpals?"

"Yeah. Don't touch nothing."

Nicky complained to Sonny that a guy named Curly was moving in on Nicky's go-go joints. "We had a sitdown on it yesterday," Nicky says, "and the decision was that I keep my twelve joints and the other guy that belongs to Curly keeps his ten. Now, this other guy went to one of my joints and threatened one of my girls that she had to kick back money to him in order to dance at my joint."

"Have Lefty set up an appointment for Monday between me and Curly," Sonny says, "and I'll straighten it out."

One night Sonny and Boobie and I were at Crisci's Restaurant, not far from the club, at 593 Lorimer Street. It was a favorite place of ours. They loved Sonny. Sonny and anybody with him was treated royally. We wouldn't even use menus. We'd order whatever we wanted and they'd make it.

We had a couple drinks at the bar before going to our table.

"I'm pleased with how you're conducting yourself down there," Sonny says, "what you're doing, the book, the shylocking. You're independent, don't have to be told what to do. You're not always coming and asking me for money like a lot of the guys."

"Thanks, bro."

"The books are gonna open up for membership at the end of the year. I can propose five guys, which I got already. Boobie is number one. Then I'm obligated with four other guys that are relatives of family members. But the next time the books open up, maybe next year, you're gonna be the first guy that I propose."

"Hey, Sonny, I really appreciate that. I'm honored. I'm glad you think of me that way."

"You got any drug arrests?"

"No."

"Good. The big thing now is drugs, and the cops are

always hounding you if you got drug arrests. Keep doing what you're doing, and you're the next name I put in."

"I'm really glad. That's what I was looking for, Sonny."

That was the truth. Obviously, no agent had ever become a made guy undercover in the Mafia. What I could accomplish as a made guy was unbelievable.

"Now," Sonny goes on, "have you checked Tony out completely? You can vouch for him?"

"Sure—you know, much as I can. He's a top guy, a good earner."

"If he's still working with you and earning, Donnie, I'll put his name in too. You guys deserve it."

We went to our table. We were eating escarole and beans and Italian bread. I had to take a chance and bring up again the matter of Lefty bleeding Rossi. Rossi and I had discussed it. We were still spending too much government money on Lefty's entertainment and travel. Since Sonny's last directive that we cut back on Lefty and report any problems to him, things had not improved. I was increasingly worried that Sonny himself would notice the expenses and blame *me* for not following his orders.

I wanted Sonny to know that I was keeping on top of things. And after all, I, too, was supposed to be enjoying all this money we were glomming from Rossi.

"Nothing for nothing," I say, "and I really feel uncomfortable bringing the subject up again. But Tony's getting very pissed off about spending so much on Lefty, and he's complaining to me about it all the time."

"What the fuck you want me to do, Donnie?"

By his tone I figured I'd blown this one. "Sonny, I just want you to be aware in case Rossi decides to pull out—we lose paydays with the club and his connections."

Sonny picked away at his salad. "You got two choices, Donnie. Either you handle it with Lefty or I'll handle it with Lefty. And if I handle it with Lefty and he gets smart about it, I'll chop his fucking legs off. You tell me what you want to do."

"Of course I want to handle it with Lefty, because I'm with him. I don't want anything to happen to him. I don't want to create any beef between you and Lefty or me and Lefty. Let's just leave it at this table, and it doesn't go any further, just so you're aware."

"Okay," he says, "it stays here. But if there's any more trouble, I will handle it."

16

THE RAID

As they had for the past couple of years, my wife and daughters flew in to spend the Christmas holidays with our relatives in New Jersey.

Early in the evening I went by to wish Lefty and Louise a Merry Christmas. They had their little Christmas tree on the table. I gave Lefty two shirts. He gave me a gift certificate for $100 from Leighton's, a men's clothing store on Broadway. He signed it; "Donny—To a good friend—Lefty."

Then I went over to Brooklyn and hung out at the Motion Lounge for a little while. Sonny took me into the kitchen and showed me two boxed stereo systems. He said Carmine had bought fifty of them from a truck driver. He had cut the serial numbers off the boxes. "These are for you and Tony," he says, "for Christmas for your apartments in Florida."

Then I excused myself to go spend the rest of Christmas Eve "with my girl over in Jersey."

On Christmas morning everybody met at the club. I had coffee with the crew and hung around until about three or four in the afternoon, then went to Jersey for Christmas dinner with my family.

*   *   *

Two days after Christmas, I was sitting with Lefty and Sonny in the back room of the Motion Lounge.

"Tomorrow morning," Lefty says, "we want you to take a ride to Monticello. Go to the Monticello Diner. I'll give you a number to call. Ask for Al. He'll come down and meet you. He has some guns for us."

Monticello is a two-hour drive northwest of the city, near the Catskill Mountains. I had been to the racetrack there a few times.

It was as cold as a bastard. The drive was miserable because there was snow and ice on the roads. I got to the Miss Monticello Diner by ten A.M. There was a pay phone inside. I called the number Lefty had given me and talked to Al. "This is Donnie from New York. I'll be sitting at the counter. I'm six feet tall with dark hair, and I'll be wearing a brown leather jacket."

A few minutes later the guy came in. "Donnie? Al."

Al was heavy, about 5'9" and 200 pounds, wore glasses. He sat down for a cup of coffee. He said that he was from New York but had lived in Monticello for the past five years. We chatted about the weather.

"I gotta get going back," I say.

"Come on out, I'll give you your Christmas presents."

We went out to the parking lot. He was driving a Lincoln. I memorized the license number for my report. He opened the trunk and took out a package the size and shape of a shoe box, wrapped in Christmas paper with a red ribbon on it.

"Thanks for the present," I say.

"Drive careful."

On the Palisades Parkway near the George Washington Bridge, I stopped at a service area where there were outdoor telephones. I unwrapped the package carefully, taking my time to make sure I didn't rip anything. Luckily he didn't have it taped, just tied with the ribbon.

There were four handguns, each in its own plastic bag: a .22-caliber Burgo six-shot revolver with no serial number; a .45 Colt automatic with a U.S. Army property number; a Ceska Zerojovka-Narodni Podnik automatic whose caliber I estimated at .22 or .32; a .38 Colt Cobra with a two-inch barrel.

I wrote down all the information on a slip of paper. Then I carefully rewrapped the package, sure to get all the creases just the way they had been. I went to a phone booth and called Case Agent Jerry Loar in New York and read off the information. Then I tore up the slip of paper and threw it in the trash can.

I got to Lefty's apartment at about noon. Lefty wasn't there. "I just want to leave this package for Lefty," I say to Louise. "He knows what it is." I put it under the Christmas tree.

Then I drove to Brooklyn and told Lefty that I had delivered the package.

"Good," he says. "I'll check them out, see which ones I want to keep and which ones to send down to you in Florida."

That evening a bunch of us were sitting around bullshitting about mob business. Lefty began expounding upon deals that he had pulled off, and successful businesses that he had invested in, including the King's Court, where I was his man. Then he started talking about Milwaukee.

I listened and watched him carefully. He told how he had gotten involved in a vending-machine business with me and how that deal had led to a sitdown between Milwaukee and New York. He said that the New York end of the sitdown had been arranged by Tony "Ducks" Corallo, the boss of the Lucchese family.

Lefty never mentioned Tony Conte. There was no hint that Lefty or anybody else in the room knew anything about informants or undercover agents involved in the Milwaukee operations. It was as if Tony Conte never existed.

Sonny's "Brooklyn problems" kept him from going to King's Court for New Year's Eve. I stayed in Brooklyn too. It was important for me to spend as much time with him as I could. I slept at his apartment. We took care of the pigeons together. We hung out at the club and the Motion Lounge, played gin. We went across the street for espresso at the Caffe Capri, a little shop with ornate white grillwork over the front windows and five or six small tables inside. Once in a while we'd go to Manhattan, to Little Italy, maybe take in a crap game on Mott Street.

It was obvious that I got more respect from the crew now because I was Sonny's man. I was always with Sonny when I was in New York. Guys in the crew talked more freely around me.

Sometimes when we were up on the roof with the pigeons, Sonny would lean on the railing and look out over the rooftops of the neighborhood where he had lived all his life. I wondered what he was thinking about.

He didn't mention that Tony Mirra was raising a stink over me, insisting that I belonged to him and not to Lefty and demanding a piece of King's Court. I wasn't supposed to know about this because this was mob business and I wasn't a made guy. Lefty told me as a favor. Sonny knew, but he didn't say a word.

We walked out of Peter Luger's Steak House in Brooklyn. Sonny stopped at the door for a minute to talk to someone he knew. I went on to get the car, which we had parked on the street.

A block away, a guy walked up to me. He came straight up to me and stopped right in front of me. He looked like a normal guy. Then I saw he had a knife. He stood close, like we were going to have an intimate chat, and pressed the tip of the blade against my belly.

"Gimme your money, slow."

I am more afraid of a knife than a gun, if the guy knows how to use the knife. He was welcome to my money.

Sonny came walking up from behind me and kept right on walking past us, evidently thinking I was talking to somebody I knew and it was none of his business. Suddenly he spun back and delivered a power-house right at the base of the guy's skull. The guy dropped like a stone and lay there.

"Come on, let's get out of here," Sonny says, "before you get into any more trouble."

*   *   *

A week into the new year, I went back to King's Court to push through plans for the Las Vegas Night and help set up another meeting between Sonny and Trafficante.

Lefty was irate because I was reporting things to Sonny before I told him. I had told Sonny that we lost $2,400 on the book. Any loss for us was a loss for Lefty too.

"You didn't call me this morning," he says over the phone. "You were supposed to call me last night. You can't pick up a phone?"

"I missed you, then I called the club. Didn't he tell you I called?"

"The man never told me nothing. He's playing games with me. He knows I'm feuding with him because I don't like what's going on. I'm hurting, I'll tell you. I'm feuding and fighting with everybody because I can't get along with these people. I can't pay my bills."

"I called Boots's joint and asked for you, and you weren't there so he put Sonny on."

"How come he didn't tell me a goddamn thing? Let me tell you something. You're losing a lot of prestige because I'll tell you why. I've been scheming all day about there's something wrong. I hope you bail out next week, because we're not gonna owe a dime because whatever we owe next week, everybody is chipping in. This year is a different ball game or I'll send my own men down there."

"Why you getting mad at me? What's going on up there?"

"That don't concern you, Donnie. You're nobody as far as what we're talking about, him and I. You're on the outside. At least I give you the satisfaction of me telling you I'm arguing with him. You don't make no phone calls, what I gotta put a stop with you. I think it's gonna come to a head, and we're gonna break up with him and youse all belong to me."

"That's all right, I don't care."

"I gotta know where I'm at, that's all I'm telling

you. Lot of people invest a lot of money out there. I ain't like him. Throw a broad at him and he's happy."

Lefty never really went out chasing women. Sonny did a little more chasing, a fact that gnawed at Lefty.

"You know me when I go out of town with you," Lefty says. "I don't bother nobody, and I act the part of a man. Broads don't bother me. How the fuck could you invite your own sweetheart that you live with, then next day want to bring a cunt in? Boobie says, 'You bringing your wife down?' I says, 'Hey, Boobie, don't ever classify my wife with Sonny Black's girls. My wife's got too much class. I bring my wife when *you* bring your wives. Judy would understand, she's a good kid. But a *tramp*? The guy's sick, he's definitely sick."

While he was talking, the recording system on my phone was malfunctioning. I was afraid he would pick it up, so I brought it up first. "You hear this static?"

"Forget about the static."

"It's hard for me to hear."

"We're not talking about static! Let me explain something to you. When you had the problems with Mr. Mirra, he gave you up and he threw it in my lap. You know what hurted me, a slap in the face? I was there New Year's, wished Sonny and everybody luck. Mirra calls him up. And he takes the phone call. But listen, I'm not a phony. As long as I'm around, you're around. We don't accept no girls, shit like that."

"Why didn't he tell you I called?"

"He didn't tell me nothing because he thinks he's King Farouk. The whole world is disgusted with him."

"Hey, if we get stuck, he's gotta come up with the money."

"He has to come up with it. But that ain't the idea. He didn't tell me a goddamn thing. I says, 'You better stop bothering people.' That's all I told him, and I walked away from him. I said, 'Nobody understands you anymore.' I'll straighten this whole thing out. It's all bullshit. Let's stop this fucking nonsense. That's all I can tell you. Say hello to Tony."

*   *   *

I finally managed to get hold of Trafficante's man, Husick, and set the date for the Las Vegas Night: January 17.

Rossi, Shannon, and I met with Captain Donahue in the office at King's Court. Rossi told him that we had scheduled another Las Vegas Night and that important people would be there from both New York and Florida, so he wanted to make sure there wouldn't be any problems. Donahue assured us he would take care of everything.

Rossi handed him $200, "a little something for Christmas."

Lefty wasn't coming down for Las Vegas Night. He had been sick off and on for a month with flu or colds. "It's fucking eight degrees here," he says over the phone. "Fucking weather don't wanna break. That's why I'm scared to come out. I might get sick down there. Or drop dead on the fucking plane."

Also, Sonny had directed him to go to Miami instead, to consummate a deal for two keys of cocaine.

Two days before the event, Rossi, Shannon, and I picked up Sonny and Carmine at the airport. Sonny handed Rossi a brown paper bag. In it was $10,000 to be used as the "bank" for the Las Vegas Night. "Don't let this out of your sight," Sonny says.

Sonny had asked me to take $1,000 out of the shylock money for him. I handed him the ten $100 bills.

"Let's go to a mall," he says. "I want to find a card shop."

"Somebody's birthday or what?"

"I want to buy a card for Santo."

We drove to the Gulfview Square Mall in New Port Richey. He picked out a card that had a message about being such good "friends."

"This is cute," he says.

Made guys refer to each other as "friends," the same as saying "members." Sonny tucked the $1,000 inside the card.

On the day of the Las Vegas Night, Trafficante came to the Tahitian Motor Lodge and went to Sonny's room. We had the room bugged. Right away Trafficante said, "We can't talk in the room."

Afterward Sonny told us that everything was in order, and the money split for the night would be a third to us, a third to Trafficante, and a third for the guys that they brought up from Miami to work the games.

"He loved the card," Sonny says.

Everything was set up in the club. I had an antique slot machine in my apartment, and we decided to put it in the club for the night. There wasn't any money in it. It was just for fun. Captain Donahue had been paid, and he said he would make sure that the cars were all patrolling on the other side of the county.

We had a crew of six to work the games, plus our regular bartender and hostesses. We had a guy on the door. To get in the front door, customers buzzed from outside. The person at the door looked out the peephole to see who it was, make sure it was members or friends. Rossi and Shannon were going to sell chips and handle all the money out of the back storage room. I was going to work the front, collect the chips from the tables, and bring them back.

Rossi wrapped up Sonny's $10,000 in a box with Christmas paper and hid it in the furnace room, which adjoined the storage room. In there he also hid $2,000 of FBI money in the bottom of a brown paper bag under Christmas tree lights. He had a .22 Derringer Magnum pistol in a wallet holster. He hid that by taping it to the back side of the furnace. He kept his Walther .32 in a briefcase next to him.

The Las Vegas Night started at seven P.M. Sonny and Carmine were there representing New York. Husick and other cohorts were there representing Trafficante. By midnight the action was strong, the room was crowded with maybe a hundred gamblers. They were lining up in the storage room to buy chips. We already had a profit of several thousand dollars, and it was growing.

At one-fifteen A.M., I was in the storage room with the line of people buying chips. The warning buzzer sounded. Immediately I herded the customers out and locked the door behind me, leaving Rossi and Shannon locked in with the money and receipts.

I went to the front door. Nick, the guard, had hit the alarm buzzer. "Donnie, there's two uniformed cops outside."

I saw them through the peephole. They were Pasco County Sheriff's officers; one was a sergeant. "Don't open the door yet." I figured there was nothing to worry about since we had paid for protection, but I walked around the room to make sure there was no money on the tables, no cash anywhere, just chips.

Sonny was at our round table with Husick and others. I whispered to him, "There's two sheriff's guys outside. I'm going to talk to them, see what's going on."

I opened the front door. "Hi, Officers, what's the problem?"

"We had a complaint that there was a disturbance at the club," the sergeant says.

"No disturbance, no problems at all."

"Mind if we come in?"

I ushered them in. "Have something to eat? Drink?"

"I got an anonymous telephone call," the sergeant says, "and the caller stated that he had been gambling here and had lost a lot of money playing blackjack."

"There's no gambling here. We're running a charity event. Everything is chips. Nobody lost any money here."

He wanted to see the office. I walked him through the lounge.

"You got some pretty big people here," he says. "Some of the best clientele in Tarpon Springs."

"Well, people like to contribute to charity and have a good time."

The other cop came into the office. "I just won money on your slot machine. That's gambling."

"What are you talking about?"

He said that he had put a quarter in the machine and won a quarter back. He said that before they came in, he could see through a crack in the doorway that people were playing the slot machine and gambling at the tables.

"Come on, you couldn't see in here." The way the club was laid out, you couldn't see anything from the doorway. "And anybody can see that that's an antique slot machine."

"What are you, some fucking smart guy?"

"No. People are having fun and we're not bothering anybody." I couldn't let them push me around in front of Sonny. I couldn't let it get out of hand, either. "Why are you bothering us? Why don't you leave us alone?"

"Who's the owner of this place?" the sergeant says.

"I don't know."

"Who are you?"

"I'm just a customer, here to contribute to charity."

"Why you doing so much talking? You the spokesman around here?"

"Because I answered the door and let you in and you're asking me questions. Somebody's gotta answer your questions."

"What's your name?"

"Donnie Brasco."

"A fucking New York guinea, aren't you?"

"Well, I am from New York and I am Italian."

"You guys like to come down here and take over. Let me see some identification."

"I don't carry any."

"What's your Social Security number?"

"I don't have one. I don't work, and if you don't work, you don't need a Social Security number."

"You are maintaining a gambling place here. I'm gonna close the place down. I'm gonna call for a search warrant."

"I can't give you permission to use the phone."

He picked up the phone and dialed.

I hurried out to tell Sonny what was going on.

"Okay," he says, "get all the people out the back way."

I and the hostesses got everybody out of the club through the French doors while the two cops were in the office.

Sonny sat by himself at the round table, scowling. "That fucking Rossi. I thought he had the guy paid."

"He did, Sonny. I was right there when he talked to the guy. I saw him pay him off, and the guy said everything was taken care of."

"Tell him to get the fuck out here."

I knocked on the storage-room door and called Tony and Eddie out.

Rossi went over and sat down with Sonny and started to apologize.

"Don't say a fucking word," Sonny says. "You fucking embarrassed me in front of everybody. The old man's people here. People from Miami. You're just like all the others who say they're gonna do the right thing, and then they fucking embarrass me. I could fucking choke you, slit your throat."

Rossi turned angry.

I stopped him. "Tony, you better not say anything. Just let him cool down and I'll talk to him." I turned to Sonny. "It's really not his fault."

Sonny gave me a hard look. "Donnie, don't you say a fucking word to defend this fucking guy. It was Tony's responsibility. If we find out that cop fucked us, we'll chop him up. I'm going back to Brooklyn. I don't know what I'm gonna do about the future with this thing. Tony, you better come up with that fucking ten grand I gave you."

The sergeant came out. "Where'd everybody go?"

"I don't know," I say. "I guess they figured it was time to go home."

"Either of you other guys got I.D.'s? How come none of you guineas carry I.D.'s?"

The other cop stopped Shannon at the front door. Reinforcements arrived, more cops. It was now a full-fledged raid.

"All right," the sergeant says, "you three are going to jail."

"What are you talking about?" Rossi says.

"Failure to show identification."

"This is private property."

"Another New York smart guy. Handcuff them," he says to another cop.

"Maybe our I.D.'s are over in my apartment," I

say, "because all three of us were there this afternoon, and maybe we left them there."

They led Rossi, Shannon, and me out in handcuffs and drove us over to the apartments and walked us upstairs to my place. We were stalling and breaking balls. We were supposed to be badguys, so we were playing it like we were badguys. Plus, these cops deserved it. Rossi and Shannon sat on the couch while I went into my bedroom and looked around. "Well, mine isn't here, and I don't see theirs, either."

"You guys are really fucking wiseguys," the sergeant says. "That's all right. You're going to jail."

Now it was about two-thirty in the morning. They took us back to King's Court.

Sonny was still sitting at the round table, smoldering like a volcano about to go.

"Him too," the cop says. "We take all you New York guineas in, you'll understand a little better how we do things down here."

They put the cuffs on Sonny.

I wanted to smack these cops for hassling us, insulting us, for being unprofessional. Rossi and Shannon were both ex-cops. We all knew what proper procedures were for cops.

There was nothing wrong with these cops uncovering an illegal operation, which was the gambling at King's Court. But our undercover operation was being jeopardized because a couple of them were taunting us unnecessarily. What if Sonny blew up? What if somebody got trigger-happy because of all the insults and bullshit?

They marched the four of us out in handcuffs—three FBI agents and a Mafia captain.

Sonny leaned toward me. "Where's your identification?"

"Trunk of my car."

"Show it. Otherwise we're all gonna be in jail. We need somebody out on the street to get us out of the can."

In the parking lot I say to the cops, "Hey, I just remembered where my ID is. It's in the trunk of my car. I put it there so it wouldn't get stolen."

Shannon says, "Mine's in my glove compartment, I just remembered."

The cop had to take my cuffs off so I could open my trunk. "This is the last chance you get," he says.

Shannon and I produced our driver's licenses and were released.

Sonny was in the back of a patrol car, his hands cuffed behind him. The window was down. "Donnie."

I went over. The cops were talking together on the other side of the car.

"I got a knife in my pocket. Take it or they'll hit me with a weapons charge too."

I reached in through the window and into his jacket pocket and pulled out the long folding knife and slipped it into my pocket.

"Hey!" a cop hollers.

I had a frozen moment: Maybe he thought he saw a gun, or that I was cutting Sonny loose.

"Get away from that car! You don't want to be rearrested, do you?"

"No, sir." I got in Rossi's car and followed the sheriff's cars to the Pasco County Sheriff's Office in New Port Richey.

In the small jail they booked Sonny for resisting arrest and Rossi for gambling. I asked the officer what the bail was. He said it was $1,000 for Sonny and $5,000 for Rossi.

At four A.M., it was too late to find a bail bondsman, which was the route we wanted to take to protect our identities. Eddie and I headed for the Tahitian, to find Carmine.

I told Carmine what had happened after I got everybody out of the club.

"Donnie, all I got on me is a thousand dollars," he says.

We went back to the jail. They were photographing and fingerprinting Sonny.

"Tony," I say, "I only got enough money to bail one out, and it ain't you."

Shannon started laughing, I started laughing. Tony didn't laugh. They finished up with Sonny, we paid the bail.

"See you tomorrow," I say to Tony.

When they searched Sonny at the jail, they had found his driver's license in his pocket. It had his real name on it, but the name didn't mean anything to them. As his occupation he had given, "route sales-man, self-employed."

On our way to the hotel, Sonny was ripping mad. I couldn't get him to cool down about Rossi.

"Yesterday the Old Man gave us the Pasco County territory to do whatever we wanted," he says. "Now look how fucking embarrassed this leaves me. I'll fuck-ing strangle Tony."

"We had a lock on it, Sonny. Somebody must have snitched."

"Find out. Whoever gives us the snitch, we'll pay. Then we'll whack out the snitch."

"We'll try to find out."

Sonny and Carmine took the next flight out to New York. We got hold of a bail bondsman and bailed Rossi out.

We went to the club. The sheriff's boys had wrecked the joint. The money from the night was gone—Sonny's $10,000, the FBI's $2,000, about $8,000 in profits. They had taken both of Rossi's guns. They had emp-tied the desk and dumped everything all over. They had even torn apart boxes of Christmas ornaments and scattered them around. They had taken the slot machine.

Rossi was not in a good mood, anyway, after a night in that rattrap jail, and now this. "I'm gonna grab that fucking sergeant and smack him in the mouth. I want to go down there and tear that fucking station apart."

We were all steamed. We ourselves had conducted a lot of legal searches. You just search for what your warrant says, you don't wreck a place. We were out $20,000, half of which was Bonanno family money. We had embarrassed Sonny, and now there was the threat to kill the snitch. And we had to worry about whether the cops might stumble onto our real opera-tion and blow our cover. We had to worry about what really had happened to cause the raid.

The anonymous phone tip was a ruse because nobody lost much money and there were no hassles. But somebody had turned us in. We narrowed it down. Rossi had some beefs with another club owner who complained that we stole his business. Rossi was pretty sure that was the guy. But so what? We couldn't do anything. We couldn't tell Sonny. We had to keep Sonny from finding out.

The next day I called Sonny with a progress report: It was possible the charges would be lowered or dropped because of an illegal search, but the prosecutor wouldn't know for two or three days.

"You make sure Tony gets me that ten grand back," he says. "I don't care how he gets it." He wanted the bail money to repay Carmine, and he wanted his driver's license back. "What happened that they came to begin with?"

"Sonny, it was a fluke." I told him that Captain Donahue had been on the street until midnight and everything was okay. Then somebody lost a few bucks at the blackjack table, got pissed off, went outside, and called the cops. I figured it was safest just using the story the cops gave us.

"Listen, Donnie, there's a big gift in it if he can give us the guy who called."

"That's what we're working on now. In fact, Tony was on the phone with the captain for a couple hours yesterday."

"What's he doing on the fucking phone? It could be *that* guy we're talking about, and he could be wired. That's Tony's voice, that's better than fingers. Tell Tony to meet the guy in person. Let's start getting smarter instead of stupider."

"Okay."

"There's a tap on the phone, you hear it? There's an echo."

My recorder again. "It's this phone here, Sonny. They were supposed to come and change the wire, but they didn't come yet."

Sonny wouldn't talk to Rossi for about three weeks. I had to hear from Lefty every day about how I fucked up because I didn't keep a better control of Rossi to make sure *he* didn't fuck up.

"Get the fucking money from Tony," he tells me. "Remind fucking Tony that he's nothing without us. And listen, Donnie, forget about how it's not Tony's fault. You should be looking out for me, not Tony."

Finally Sonny said he had to have the money and told me to take it out of the shylock money and both of us bring it to New York.

Rossi and I each carried half the money. Sonny and Boobie met us at JFK, and we handed them the $10,000.

"Okay," Sonny says. "Now, I want you guys to start making connections for coke and heroin—especially the H, because I got the outlets up here. Also, I bought a machine to make Quaaludes, so find some connections for the powder to make them with."

Eventually the charges against Sonny were dropped. Rossi, however, was supposed to go to trial. We got it put off and put off until the entire operation was over.

One of the regular King's Court members brought in a doctor friend from Tarpon Springs. The doctor talked to Rossi about having friends in the Mafia. Talk got around to drugs. The doctor said he'd done a lot of dealing and had even been busted for drugs. In fact, he had access right now to $1 million worth of heroin— sixteen kilos—in Wichita, Kansas. He had just come back from Wichita. He said it was confiscated heroin in the possession of an ex-FBI agent. He said he could put together a deal for us. If he had known we were interested, he said, he would have brought a sample back with him.

I told Lefty and Sonny about the approach, and they wanted us to push it, get a sample.

The doctor said he would have a sample brought to Florida. A date was set for delivery.

I joined Lefty in Miami. The plan was that Rossi would get the sample from the doctor and bring it to us in Miami where Lefty had a guy on hand to test it for quality. Sonny was standing by in New York with a potential buyer. Lefty and I took a room in the Deauville to wait for Rossi.

I kept calling Rossi to see if the doctor had shown up. Lefty kept calling Sonny to say the doctor hadn't shown up yet. We didn't dare leave the hotel room together for fear that we'd miss the call from Rossi, saying he was on his way. It was like waiting for a sitdown. We ordered up room service, or one of us went across the street to get sandwiches at a deli.

Every couple of hours we made our phone calls. Rossi kept saying he hadn't heard from the doctor. After three days we gave up. I went back to Holiday, Lefty went back to New York.

We pursued the deal for weeks. The doctor said there was one delay after another in getting the sample to Florida.

"I'm embarrassed with this thing," Lefty says. "Everybody's disappointed up here. I'd like to shake him down for just the expense money. It hurted me. You gotta put your foot down. Grab him by the throat. I didn't say smack him around. Just grab him by the throat."

The three of us sat down to look at the situation—Rossi, Shannon, and me. Together we represented a lot of years of street experience. Rossi got it first. He says, "This guy's setting us up. Somebody's trying to do a number on us with this heroin. This guy ain't got access to any more heroin than the man in the moon. This is a setup by somebody."

We agreed. Rossi had it right on the nose. This doctor had been busted for drugs before. Somebody had him in a squeeze and was using him to trap us.

It could have been state or federal cops, or the DEA—the Drug Enforcement Administration. It could have been badguys, maybe amateurs who didn't know how to finish off the deal. We couldn't figure out exactly what it was. But somebody had this doctor in their clutches, and it looked like he was scared to go through with it.

Rossi decided to carry it out, lean on the doctor to bring us the sample. Nobody would ever see us touch it.

Rossi called the doctor and said he had twenty-four hours to produce the sample. That night the doctor showed up.

He came into the club at nine P.M. He was very

nervous. He took Rossi aside and told him he had tossed the sample into the shrubbery just outside the door.

The doctor had a drink at the bar. After a while Shannon ambled outside. It was pitch dark, which was great, because nobody could see anything. He felt around and found the little bag. He brought it into the office.

The next day we had it tested. It was talcum powder. The doctor swore, in a panic, that he didn't know, he had just accepted the sample. We believed him. Because if we had been legitimate badguys, for sticking us like this we might have killed him. At least we would have given him a bad beating.

Since we were agents, though, we couldn't really do anything. "Next time you want to play around with somebody," Rossi told him, "don't play around with the big boys."

We never found out who set him up to set us up. We had enough of a reputation that we were aware of the chances we could be set up. We could be set up by a law-enforcement agency to take a fall, which would have jeopardized the operation. Or we could be set up by badguys jealous of our success or their turf.

An undercover agent going by the name of Charlie Sacco—we called him "Charlie Chains" because he wore so much gold—was uncovering corruption and gambling involving the sheriff of a town near Charleston, South Carolina, and he set up a gambling hall. He brought Rossi into it because some of his clientele were Greeks that Rossi knew from the Greek community of Tarpon Springs and were frequent visitors to King's Court. Rossi, Shannon, and I made a few trips to the Charleston area to play our roles on behalf of Charlie Chains.

Rossi met a Greek named Flamos, who claimed he was from Harlem and could get us any kind of drugs in any volume we wanted.

"Don't bullshit me if you can't produce," Rossi says, "because the people I deal with in New York City won't stand for it."

The guy insisted he had great connections.

I came in as Rossi's New York man. Charlie had rented a condominium right on the beach at the Beach and Racquet Club in Isle of Palms, where we stayed. He made an appointment for Flamos to come and see me.

Rossi and I are lying on the beach. Flamos comes walking across the sand in street clothes. Rossi introduces me as his friend Donnie from New York. "Tell Donnie what you can get for us."

Flamos says he can get anything.

"Heroin," I say.

"I got a direct contact in Katmandu," he says. "But I need some front money to go to Katmandu, fifteen grand."

"Do I look like a fucking goofball or what? Katmandu?"

Flamos gets indignant. "I don't know you. How do I know you're straight? I'm from New York too. I got some friends up there that are righteous people."

"If you got the right friends up there, ask them to check out Donnie from Mulberry St. who's a friend of Lefty's. If your friends can't check out Donnie and Lefty from Mulberry Street, then your friends ain't worth shit."

Flamos turns to Rossi. "I don't want to get involved. Your friend's coming on too strong."

"Hey," I say, "you're coming on that you can come up with anything under the sun, so don't bullshit me."

"I'll come back in two days," he says.

The next day, Flamos comes back and comes right up to me. "Look, Donnie, I'm sorry if I offended you. I checked with my friends in Harlem, and when I mentioned Donnie and Lefty from Mulberry Street, these guys had nothing but the highest respect for Lefty, and they had heard of you being with him. Geez, Donnie, I didn't realize you're with the Bonannos."

"Hey, let's not have names here. We don't mention families. The bottom line is, can you get us the dope?"

"I can get the heroin, Donnie, but I got to go to Katmandu. Forget the fifteen, but I need five grand for traveling expenses."

"Forget the five and forget Katmandu. What could you bring here tomorrow?"

"Tomorrow? I got hashish in my stash. What I got is worth seventy-five grand on the street. I got to get twenty-five for it."

"All right, bring it over."

"Wait a minute, we gotta set up a correct deal, you know."

Rossi says, "What you do is, you deliver it to this warehouse we got, and when it's in there, you let us know, we'll have somebody check it. You come back, we'll give you the money."

"That's your correct deal," I say.

When he left, Rossi says to me, "We ain't giving this guy twenty-five grand. Once that shit's in the warehouse, it's ours. We'll give him five grand, and let him holler."

Flamos makes the delivery to the warehouse. Charlie Chains goes over and checks it and calls us to say that it's all there, good stuff. Rossi hands Flamos the money.

Flamos counts. "Ho, wait a minute, there's only five grand here."

"That's what you get," I say. "You don't want it, give it back and you're out everything. Because the hash stays with us."

"Oh, man, this ain't gonna go down with my people."

"Go to your people in Harlem if you want to, go see whoever the fuck you gotta see. They're gonna contact Lefty. Lefty's gonna say we gave you twenty-five and you must have glommed the other twenty. Who they gonna believe?"

So we got $75,000 worth of hash off the street at a cost to the government of only $5,000, while actually enhancing our credibility as legitimate badguys.

Lefty called me to Miami because he wanted us to look at a lounge together. He said that the lounge at the Sahara Hotel, next to the Thunderbird, might be available for $15,000, and Sonny gave us the green light to go after it.

"All the wiseguys from New York hang out at the

Thunderbird," he says. "We can get all the overflow. Because all the guys will come, New Yorkers and ex–New Yorkers like Joe Puma, and people will follow them. Get a good piano player."

We hung out at the bar in the lounge and looked the place over. We agreed that it looked good.

I was aware of the tension within the Bonanno family, because the infighting was causing tension with Lefty and Sonny. I couldn't ask a lot of direct questions about it, but I strained to pick up what I could. Partly that was for intelligence. Partly it was to make sure I stayed alive.

Now, at the hotel, Lefty gave me some news.

"The Commission met in New York. They named Sally Farrugia acting boss for how long Rusty is in jail."

Salvatore "Sally Fruits" Farrugia had been a captain.

"When Rusty gets out, Sally will step down," Lefty says. "And Sonny is now the main captain. Every family has a main captain. When Rusty gets out, Sonny wants to become consiglieri."

"Oh, yeah? I didn't know that."

"The consiglieri has to be voted by the whole family, you know, not appointed like the captains. Another thing, the Commission ordered the two sides in the family to keep the peace while Rusty's in the can."

"Is there gonna be peace or what?"

Lefty chuckles. "Let me tell you something. Sonny's strength is that he's close to Rusty."

The ABSCAM scandal broke, arrests were made, the story was all over the news. I didn't pay too much attention to it. I was too busy trying to dope out the power struggle within the Bonanno family.

I was in Miami with Lefty and a bunch of the guys. At three or four in the morning, after a night of bouncing around, one of the guys suggested that we go to Nathan's for something to eat.

I started to sit down with them. Lefty grabs my arm. "Sit over here at this other table. I want to talk to you."

We sat at a table over in the corner. "Donnie, what do you know about that boat we went out on?"

I started to answer when it hit me what he was driving at, and at the same time he whipped out a folded page from *Time* magazine, opened it up, and slapped it down in front of me.

"*That's* the boat, Donnie."

I was stunned. There, as part of a story about ABSCAM, was a picture of the *Left Hand,* the boat we had partied on, and a description of how the FBI had used it in the sting. My life was on the line right here, with how I handled this.

"Gee, I don't think that's the boat we were on, Left."

"Don't give me bullshit, Donnie. One thing I know is boats. We went out on a fucking federal boat!"

"I'll tell you this, Left, if that's the boat, we were in good company, and we were better than they were."

"Huh?"

"That fucking guy with the boat, he scammed congressmen and senators, and he tried to scam us. If he can scam those people, I ain't no Phi Beta Kappa that he can't scam me. But he didn't get a fucking thing on us, right? We had a great party and we walked away from it."

"You sure?"

"Hey, did they get us? We're sitting here, Left. We beat those FBI guys!"

"I don't know, Donnie," he says. He keeps shaking his head and looking at the picture. "I hope you know who the fuck you're messing around with. A fucking federal boat."

Lefty called me at my apartment. Tony Mirra was causing trouble. He had gone to the boss and put in another claim on me. Mirra said that I had worked for him at Cecil's disco when I first came around, and that entitled him to claim me.

"There's gonna be a sitdown on this, at Prince Street. Sonny and I have to go to the table and straighten this whole thing out. That's this afternoon. Last week Mirra won a decision that he gets $5,000 a week from Marco's."

Steve Cannone's social club was at 20 Prince Street. Marco's was a midtown restaurant that used to be Galante's place.

"Left, no way I'm gonna be with Mirra."

"You ain't got nothing to say about it."

17

THE SITDOWNS

Around the middle of March, informants were telling the FBI of unusual activity on Prince Street in Little Italy. An apparent series of sitdowns was taking place at 20 Prince Street, the social club owned by Bonanno consiglieri Steve Cannone.

"I gotta control my temper," Lefty says over the phone. "You have no idea what we went through. This went on for fucking eight days with this motherfucker, for you. I mean, heavyweights had to sit down. Saturday was the meeting in New York. I had a four-and-a-half-hour meeting about you again today."

"For what?"

"Don't say, 'For what.' "

"How come you never tell me? I don't even know what you're talking about."

"Who else is involved but Mirra?"

"Well, what's this guy want now?"

"I'll tell you what, you son of a bitch, fucking asshole that you are. You got me aggravated about this Rocky."

Mirra was always trouble. And now Rocky. The undercover cop's name was coming up too often. In addition to taking Rocky out on the ABSCAM boat, I had brought him up to the New York area and set him

up in the car-leasing business, the cover for his undercover operation. He had gotten involved with Mirra.
That there were sitdowns over me, involving Mirra
and Rocky, was not good news. "What about Rocky?"

"Rocky admitted that you made two hundred and
fifty grand in excess amount of money. I'm not burning my phone up, and you know what I'm talking
about. That you took a hundred and twenty-five off
him!"

"From where?"

"Anthony Mirra says that you shook Rocky down
and youse made it in fucking *junk money*!" Lefty's
voice was barely controlled. "I'm fed up with this
bullshit over here!"

"What are you talking about, junk money? I never
cut any junk money with him. Who did Rocky tell that
I cut two hundred and fifty grand?"

"Anthony Mirra and his men—don't you understand, you fucking jerk-off? I just got off the table."

Out of the blue, I was being accused of secretly
splitting up a $250,000 drug deal with Rocky. Next to
being a snitch, the worst thing you do is not split a big
score with your bosses. I didn't know what Rocky was
involved in. I didn't know what, if anything, he was
really telling Mirra. I couldn't risk trying to contact
Rocky because I couldn't trust his phone, and I wasn't
sure I could even trust him—I didn't know what kind
of situation he was in. There was no way I could find
out anything right now except from Lefty, and I had to
handle this conversation very carefully. I couldn't afford to say the wrong thing or give a wrong answer
that would further jeopardize either me or Rocky. But
without knowing the circumstances I couldn't be sure
what were the right things to say. All I knew immediately was that this kind of situation with sitdowns can
result in a decision that somebody has to go. I had to
react with badguy strength—I couldn't be pushed
around. "Rocky's lying, Left. I never cut any junk
money with him."

"I know he's lying."

"So what are you hollering at me for?"

"You're fucking laxed!"

"He's a liar. And Mirra's a liar."

"But your word don't count."

"Why does *his* word count?"

"Rocky already said it."

"Just because he said it first?"

"This son of a bitch passed a remark. You only get a denial. This thing has snowballed. It's a very, very dangerous thing. Now it's beyond Sonny. It's out of Sonny's hands now, your case. It's going all the way to the top. I got sent for today. Sonny didn't tell me what he wanted to talk about. Then when I was there, he says, 'Lefty, I want you to stay here.' Why? He says, 'Sally's coming down.' "

Sally Farrugia, the acting boss.

"All of a sudden Mirra walks in with two guys, give a kiss and all that. Sonny don't warn me what's going on. Another big sitdown. They had people from Canada down to represent this mother's claim over you, to represent this fucking scumbag because they heard big money, you understand? I warned I'm not giving you up. I die with you. If the Old Man was out, we'd have no fucking problem. Sally can't say nothing. He feels bad, but his hands are tied. He can only listen to people, and they're all making up stories. I went at Mirra today. I got up from the table, and I went at Mirra at the end of the bar. I called him all the cocksuckers in the world. I grabbed him. He says, 'I never said you got the money, but Donnie and this guy cut it up.' I says, 'Don't ever mention that fucking word *junk money*, you dirty cocksucker,' and that was it. Sonny says, 'Break it up.' I went at the fucking captains. His captain—visualize the guy that was in the papers where the old man went bye-bye—he put his hand on me. I says, 'Get your hand off me.' He says, 'You know who you're talking to?' I says, 'Get your fucking hand off me! I don't even know you.' The whole joint heard it. 'I'm no fucking mutt!' I says."

Mirra's captain was Caesar Bonventre, the zip who was one of Galante's bodyguards when he got hit, and one of those we figured was in on the hit.

"I'm in trouble. Then when I blow my top, Sonny says, 'You're supposed to listen.' 'I listen to my prick,'

I says. I had a big fight with Sonny. I stuck to my guns. I got witnesses. Consiglieri Stevie was there. Another main guy like Sonny"—Joey Massino, another powerful capo—"told me, 'Lefty, stick to your guns, I'll go back and tell that guy in the can.' "

"Was Rocky there today?"

"Are you kidding? Why would a scumbag like that be with us? Oh, I'll win you. But it'll go to the top."

"I thought this was settled. You told me two weeks ago."

"He wanted to be on our backs again. That's why I got mad at Sonny in front of him. In front of all the bosses I said, 'What are you, a piece of shit? This thing was settled with everybody, our family, our boss. This fuck does a thing like this again and gets away with it—why don't you open your mouth?' Then I went at the captains and got in trouble. I was chased off the table."

"What's with this guy?"

"Mirra is a low-life bastard," Lefty says. "He's a pimp, a fucking fag. With the bosses they called him a rat stool-pigeon bastard."

"You believe him or you believe me?"

"How many times you was in Cecil's?"

Cecil's was the disco that Mirra had a piece of, where I had hung out with him years before. I didn't know what this angle was, what answer was the safe one. I didn't know whether it was better for me to have been in Cecil's a little or a lot. I had to read between the lines and think quick. I hedged. "I was there like two, three times."

"He says you was there three, four times at the door."

"Left, I was at that door once." He was looking for evidence of whether I had worked for Mirra, which would give Mirra an edge in his claim of me. "I never got a dime. You know what I got? Free drink."

"While you were hanging in that joint, Cecil's, was Anthony Mirra a wiseguy then?"

"It was right around that time. I'm not sure."

"I said he wasn't a wiseguy when he got Cecil's because I wasn't married then. He's only straightened out three and a half years. I was six months after him. If Mirra wasn't a good fellow at the time you was there, his argument is no good. Sonny will check it out. Sonny's going to the Commission, you know, find out when he was straightened out, then they're going to revive it. I told him you met Anthony Mirra at my joint. I got you through the little guy"—underboss Nicky Marangello—"because I liked you very much. That's on record."

The question was whether Lefty or Mirra had introduced me into the crew. The fact was I had known Mirra first. Lefty was claiming he had introduced me to Mirra. In either event, way back then Lefty had gone to Marangello and put in an official claim on me—something Mirra had never done, as far as I knew.

"Caesar's on his side," Lefty goes on. "He says you were with him every night."

"I never saw Caesar there at Cecil's. He wouldn't know me."

"Donnie, you're fooling around with a dangerous man. I want this guy's head because he's looking for mine. He's telling his people, 'I live in Lefty's building. He lives on the eighth floor, I live on the sixth. If I got no coffee or butter or like that, some morning I'll stop and knock on Lefty's door.' In front of his men he says that. I says, 'I tell you what, Anthony Mirra, you stop at my door, I'll shoot you right in the head, because you're not my friend.' I want Rocky bad. I would hurt him only because he lied. I says to Mirra, 'You tell that motherfucker he belongs to me. I catch you in the fucking car with him, I shoot him in the fucking head. If you're in the fucking way, you die too.' The joint is bugged, Donnie. But I said what I had to say. I said I'm gonna put two bullets in his eyes, and I specify what caliber it's gonna be. Nobody in Brooklyn could control me today. You're not allowed to drink at a meeting. You know what four and a half hours is sitting down with politicians?"

"I know."

"No, you *don't* know. The fucking trouble with you."

"Well, you never explain to me."

"I *can't* explain to you. What I'm telling you now, you ain't supposed to know. See, you're treated like a *friend*, understand? Now, did you bring Rocky in town?"

This was the most delicate and dangerous subject of all. "Yeah, he came up there, why?"

"Now, Rocky come in through you. How I know Rocky is through you?"

"That's right. I met him down there. I met him in Lauderdale at the bar down there, I told you that, at Pier 66."

"The guy belong to you?"

"No."

"Donnie, we ain't saying different. But now you came in with him, you gave him the job. Remember what you say now. You put the guy there. Somebody put him in there. The guy that put him there was on the federal boat, the guy is a federal stool pigeon. Something's wrong with that joint."

This was Lefty at his most dangerous. He circled around, jumped here and there, but when he was on to something wrong, he wouldn't let go. Now he was circling around the truth, which was something that could get Rocky or me killed if it wasn't handled right.

"You put the guy there, Donnie. Now, who owns the joint?"

"I don't know who owns it now, Left."

"Donnie, who owned it before? Who's Rocky working for? You brought the guy down. The guy didn't know anybody in the fucking town. When I went there for a car, I had to check it out with Donnie. Donnie was the boss. The joint never left the hands. Now, Donnie, where do you take it from there? You can't answer that question. It's a serious thing. Where does this go, Donnie?"

"Left, I don't know."

"Think about it and don't go to sleep. Go sit down and have a cup of coffee and call me back."

I couldn't talk to Rocky. I couldn't talk to Sonny because I wasn't supposed to know any of this was going on. I needed to pump Lefty for information. If we had been face-to-face, at least I could have been gauging his expressions, sensing him better. I couldn't let any time go by. I called him back in a few minutes.

"Listen," Lefty says, "I'm asking you a question. The man admitted you made $250,000. Why would he rat you out?"

"That's because Mirra put the words in his mouth."

"Could you prove it?"

"How am I gonna prove it? Because he's probably scared of Mirra, that's the only reason. I'm sure the guy is okay. But I don't know why he would say, unless Mirra made him say it, that we cut up two hundred and fifty grand in junk money."

"He's a fucking stool-pigeon bastard. I won you and I'm gonna keep you. I says, 'I go all the way and die with the kid.' Ain't nobody having you. I don't like what Sonny did. He wants to compromise. He wants to give up Rocky for you. Sonny says, 'We own Donnie and we're giving up Rocky.' 'You give up my prick,' I says. Then, when I blew my top, he says to hold off. 'You don't want him,' he says. No, I don't want Rocky, but *he* can't have him. Mirra's a fucking swindling bastard. He's on the payroll out there, you know. He's out there every day from eight to three in the afternoon. Just tell me about Rocky and make me feel happy and go to bed with a clear head. You're not answering me, Donnie. Who put him there, Donnie?"

I hesitated, trying to think three questions ahead, how to slip out of this noose about my involvement with Rocky and the car business. "I just told you, he came up from Florida with me."

"Donnie, don't stutter to me. Ain't the question. You was the boss there. He admitted that. Everybody in the neighborhood knew it. You was the boss."

"So what's the big deal?"

"Whose business was it? Why'd you give it up?"

"Were we making any money out there?"

"Wasn't the question, that there. Who owns the company?"

"Left, I told you, it was a guy in California."

"A guy opens up a motherfucking Corvette joint with all new cars, you don't know his name."

"Left, there were three cars there. They closed that joint. All they're doing is running swag outa the back. Rocky told me—"

"Oh, come on. *Swag* to pay that kind of rent? What are you playing, games? Are you a fucking nitwit? The idea is, who put everybody there? Where'd it all stem from? Where'd youse meet? How come Rocky mentioned to Anthony Mirra about junk money and don't mention the boat, the stool-pigeon boat, the FBI boat? How come Rocky don't mention the federal boat? Take a guess who got him out of jail?"

"Who?"

"Go ahead, it's a guess you got coming."

"I don't know."

"Oh, you ain't gonna believe it. Rocky got him out."

"Rocky got Mirra out of jail? How?"

"I don't know, through paperwork. You figure it out. Rocky got him out, and he's paroled to them people out there. And he's on the payroll out there. So you figure it out."

I *couldn't* figure it out. It was news to me. "That's a good one."

"It ain't a good one. You got caught in the web. Donnie, you're my friend. I trust you an awful lot. Many times I had doubts about you. You don't understand the ins and outs of anything."

"So what do we do now? We just let this guy bullshit and lie to everybody?"

"Ain't the question. I didn't want to scare you from coming in."

"Hey, Left, I ain't afraid of anybody."

"You can't help me out. I have to handle it without you."

"I ain't afraid of Mirra, either."

Lefty gave a low chuckle. "Let me tell you something. Get off your fucking high horses and call me back later. You're fucking aggravating me."

"I'll listen to you, go ahead." Now I wanted to keep

him on the phone. I didn't want to risk losing contact, or letting him leave the house. I needed to know as much as possible, as soon as possible, about what was going on in the family and what I was facing.

"Donnie, what the fuck am I coming to Florida for? What am I, an impressionist? At least Jerry Chilli goes out there and has got fifty things going. He gets five grand a day. What have I got with you, Donnie? I got nothing but aggravation."

Jerry Chilli was a made guy under Alphonse "Sonny Red" Indelicato, a captain in the opposition faction. Chilli was a New Yorker who did a lot of business in Miami.

"The gimmick is, while you're laying lax, they got Rocky down with three witnesses, heavyweights. They scared him—you know, you put a gun to a guy's head, right? You're involved in a lot of heavyweights. I'm going right to the top with it. There's a lot of feuds going on. It has to go to the guy in Lewisburg, understand?"

The guy in the Lewisburg, Pennsylvania, federal penitentiary was Bonanno boss Rusty Rastelli. "Yeah."

"Rusty will hear about it for one reason, because I made Joey Massino a witness. I made Mirra take water. I'm in trouble with the zips today because I defied them. And I'm gonna pay for it. Because of my friend Donnie sitting on his ass out in Miami—and don't say different—about broads and shit like that, fine. Everybody likes to enjoy themselves. You're young, but you got a lax habit. Big fucking man. You're a big shit. You're busy getting the wrinkles out of your stomach. You don't even wanna work. Bookmaking ditto. You don't wanna do nothing, Donnie. You wanna be a playboy. This is what you wanted it to come to?"

"Of course not."

"You broke Tony in to that there. When I tell Tony I'm coming out, my plane ticket's supposed to be paid like they always was. When Tony got lax and you got lax, you thought Sonny was more important that I am."

"I never thought—"

"If you can't admit, just keep your mouth shut. You think I'm easy? How come you walk a chalk line with Sonny Black but you don't walk it with me? Get off your fucking ass. See, Donnie, I'm gonna say it once and ain't gonna say it no more. You come at me a couple times. You don't even realize when you come at me."

"No, I don't."

"You got one more strike with you. Not that I'm gonna hurt you. But I hold everything against. Like, 'Get your own bag' or something like that. When I walk in that town and I drop a suitcase, pick it up."

"Okay. How does Sonny stand tonight?"

"He's not giving you up, but he's not on your side. In other words, anything happens, I take the weight. Why ain't you blowing your top, why ain't you mad at Rocky?"

"I am." I was. I should never have brought Rocky in. I bent my rules to do a favor, because I didn't know Rocky. Now it was haunting me and I wanted to strangle him.

"One guy's gonna check both of youse out."

"Hey, Left, you know they got no problem checking me out."

"I don't give a fuck. If you did something wrong in life, it's for me to handle. Mirra cannot handle it. Sonny knows what he's doing. See what you did by being lax? There's no stopping here. The boss, the main guy in our family, had to sit down, and *he* can't straighten it out. Donnie, you told me you put Rocky there, and these things are gonna come out. You got anything fucking hidden?"

"I got nothing like that."

"Just promise me one thing. From here on in and to the longest day you live, you swear on yourself that you'll always abide my rules."

"I swear on anything, Left."

"Now. Will you face the guy?"

"That's right."

"I don't know if I can pull it off, because we're

fucking around with legitimate people now. If I can get Rocky down, you'll go along with the program?"

"That's right." I was making a risky move. "Legitimate people" were made guys. I wanted to attend a sitdown, which is restricted to made guys. I didn't want to face Rocky because I didn't know how jammed up he might be and what he might say, how much that might endanger us both. But I gambled that Mirra wouldn't produce Rocky at a sitdown. "Why should I be the fall guy?"

"Tell me now, because you're in Florida. If you got any fucking faults, go where the fuck you gotta go."

"I don't have any, Left."

"Who owns the company, Donnie? How come you backed away from the situation? Who put the fucking operation together? Donnie, you can't stutter there. You put him there. I can't lie to my people. If I gotta die over it, go down like a man. They gonna throw curves at you."

"Any curves they throw, Left, I'll be able to hit them. We get at the table and I'll prove to you that Rocky lied."

"Anthony Mirra says he knew him five years. I said, 'No, you're a fucking liar. We brought him from Miami.' Now you're on the table. Now I have to get off. They're gonna ask you these questions. I'm not gonna be there to defend you. First thing they're gonna ask: Who brought him into Miami? You did. Who brought him into this town up here? How did the operation start? Let me tell you something, Donnie. We got friends in that town. We can find everything out. That's what it'll come to, but I don't wanna prolong it. Why did Rocky give you up?"

"He's scared."

"Donnie. I know you like a book. I know every fucking move you make. I could tell you words from Milwaukee, word for word. See, everybody underestimates me. I know how lazy you are or how original you are. But now you're up in a different fucking category. You're into something that's beyond our reach. This fucking thing is exploding. And don't forget we're fooling around with zips. They'll keep on pecking. Greaseballs are motherfuckers. When a zip kisses, forget about it. They hate the American people. They hate the American wiseguys. I blew my fucking top, they hold it against me. You, they'll chew you up in a fucking minute. They got us in a barrel over Rocky and you. That's why Sonny Black wants me to give up Rocky. He feels it's shaky. He wants peace and he wants a compromise. This is why Sonny don't want you to come in, because you can't answer.

"If you get caught on the table, we're gonna lose. You ain't got the right answers. You ain't got the mentality. You got the brain, but you're gonna get hit with things. Once you stutter, they don't say nothing. They'll let you talk. Donnie, you got a headache. You can't answer these questions. You could tell it to Sonny, but when you get on the table and they throw curves at you, you're not gonna answer them."

"I'll hit the curves."

"You're not gonna hit no curves. You see, we got this Rocky on the table, right? Now, when he knows he's coming to see anybody, *he's* gonna bring everything out. So before he brings out about me being on a fucking boat, I have to tell everybody everything. I get sent for and they say it's a federal boat—what am I gonna say? I can't answer these questions without jeopardizing *you*, that you're a fucking sucker. They got me by the balls. They got you by the balls. You were on the fucking federal boat. But answer one fucking motherfucking question. How did you get this fucking jerk-off from the fucking boat to the fucking car shop?"

"Le-Le-Lefty, I told you—"

"Take your time. There's something wrong here."

"You ever think that Mirra's a rat? I'd say he's a stool pigeon, he made a deal with somebody."

"No, no, you can't say that, because if you call a guy like that a pigeon, you gotta back your words up or you're dead. He is nothing but a fucking rat. But could *you* call a wiseguy a rat? You can't answer that the way I want to. But I could, when I get through. So now I'm getting all the proof. I'm reaching out. Sonny don't even know what I'm doing. The guy I got, half the FBI can't hide nothing from him. I'll get all the bill of particulars. Because somebody's sticking Rocky up. They're taking his wallet. That's going to my friends. You I know about, your numbers on your American Express and everything. Tony in Milwaukee, I got his through Mike Sabella. I hope to God everything comes aboveboard. I'm gonna use my head while he's partying up all night tonight. They lied on the table today. The man that lies on the table has to die. But that's beside the point. I'm talking about something serious. I met the guy on the boat. Where'd the boat come from? I have to show them the fucking picture. What are they gonna do? That's what it's gonna come to."

"I still don't see how you say that's the federal boat."

"Donnie, I got pictures of it. What are you, crazy or what? I took pictures all over the boat. I go further. I'll get everybody's picture on that fucking boat. You want me to go further than that there? I can get it in a fucking week. I'll give you the fucking name of the stool pigeon."

"Well, let's go after him. Go to the table and call them liars."

"You can't call them liars. Donnie, you're involved with fourteen heavyweights now, going on for two weeks."

"I go with that guy, I walk, Left. I tell you that now."

"Ain't the question you walk. Over here I ain't got the right answers. I ain't got the right satisfaction with you."

"Why don't we just kill Mirra, that's all. Get it outa the way."

"No, no, we don't do that to friends."

"That's what he's trying to do to us."

"That's all right. He's doing that legally. Now I'll leave it up to Sonny what he wants to do. I'll get back to you."

"All right."

"It won't be now. Maybe a week from now."

When I hung up, I felt isolated. I didn't know what Mirra was going to do. I didn't know what Rocky was going to do. I couldn't go to New York. I had to wait it out.

Lefty called an hour later. His voice was very subdued, resigned.

"I just want you to understand that I feel I'm doing the right thing, so I thought I'd give you a call back. Only wish you could give me the right answers."

"Left, the only answers I give you are the truth."

"Like I say, they'll eat us up on the table. You made some fucking boo-boo, pal. You got me sick over it. The trouble we're having amongst ourselves. I tell you, Donnie, you don't make too many mistakes, but when you do, you start a fucking World War III. I gotta let it come to a head for one reason: I want this motherfucker. I want him bad. I want both of them bad. Somebody gotta pay the consequences. I didn't call you to worry you. I only called you for one fucking reason: to think and help me win this fucking war. Get your fucking bearings together and think. Put your head to the grindstone. I'm writing everything down and racking my brains out. I want to understand what's going on."

"I wish I knew."

"Donnie, once we get that thing straightened out, we open a legitimate business. Jesus Christ ain't gonna touch you. The motherfucking cocksucker."

"That's right. That no-good bastard. Left, what I'd like to do is really make a score and jam it up his ass."

"I tell you one thing, Donnie, the most hated guy on Prince Street is Mirra. So we'll just see till Rusty comes home. But whether we can survive these fucking sixteen fucking months, which them bosses say no wars allowed, I don't know. First guy fucks with a pistol, they'll break up the whole crew."

"That right?"

"They'll break it all up, dissolve it. All right, go to sleep. Don't worry about it."

18

THE HITS

There was no quick resolution to the sitdowns. I just had to stay cool and wait, for days, weeks. Lefty came down to Holiday, and Rossi and I were driving him to Miami, where he needed to talk to some people.

"I wanna get rid of all the old men," he says. "They can't do us no good. They're eighty years old. They don't wanna be bothered. Sonny tells me to call them to come to fucking wakes. Leave these people alone. You can't retire them. It's no good. Because they lose their prestige. We're stuck with them."

Lefty had been made an acting captain by Sonny, and he was sizing things up in the family. I tried to pump him a little on personnel. "Jerry Chilli's on the side with Caesar and them, right?"

"Both brothers are on the other side," he says, meaning both Joe and Jerry Chilli.

"Who's his skipper, who's he with?"

"He's with Sonny Red's man, Trinny," he says, indicating rival captains Alphonse "Sonny Red" Indelicato and Dominick "Big Trin" Trinchera. "One's kicking back to Trinny a G-note a week. The other one is kicking back three grand. That's why they got power, them two guys. Those brothers are making a ton of money. We ain't making it because we gotta walk the chalk line. This is what we're told."

"Joey Massino still got the coffee trucks?"

"Yeah. Joe Massino's got good men. They all love me. We grew up together and hung out together. He knows where the strength is."

349

"Joey goes to visit Rusty, huh?"

"Oh, yeah, he's *gotta* go see him. He doesn't know what's going on with Mirra. He can't butt in. When Joe Massino goes up there in a couple of weeks, he'll tell him."

"Well, Sonny's gonna do the right thing. I don't think anybody's gonna fuck over Sonny."

He ranted for a while about Mirra.

I say, "Well, he's not gonna go against you one on one, you know that."

"Ain't a fucking man in New York City would go up against me one on one, because I would do it cowboy-style, right on South Street, one block walking at each other. How many pistols you want? Two? Let's walk up against each other. One of us got to fucking die, or both of us die. That's what I would do. I wouldn't give a fuck, and don't forget it. I'll stay with Sonny and show honor."

"Well, Rusty knows that."

"Hey, let me tell you something. We were fighting a war, the Bonnanos. Rusty's my chauffeur. Because you know what kind of a fucking man I was, and he was the fucking *underboss*. And he had to listen to me while he was driving the car: 'Rusty, cut over here . . . leave my fucking window open.' He was a good wheelman."

But Rusty was a tough boss, Lefty went on. During a war Rusty was in Canada, and he called Lefty and ordered him to come up. He didn't even tell Lefty where he was, just where to go.

"I had four small kids. 'Go pack a grip,' he says. So I go pack a grip. Get on the fucking plane. Two pistols. Go to Canada, order a room. He says, 'I'm gonna meet three guys on that corner. Don't take your eyes off them. If anything happens to me, go all the way. Cops on the corner, blow them away.'

"Six fucking weeks he's got me out there. You're not allowed to make a phone call to your family. Good thing I had an ex-wife then who understood, never asked questions what happened to me or anything like that. Six fucking weeks. Now, I taught my new wife, Louise; 'Look, anything happens, you don't see me come in, don't you yell for anybody—he just didn't come home, you don't know nothing.' I says, 'You wanna cry, it's your fucking business. Don't ask anybody on the corner where I'm at or question my sister. Just say, 'He didn't come home—this is what my husband told me to say and these are his orders, and that's it.' ''

"Rusty knows what we got down here, right?"

"Oh, yeah. He knows everything. That's the trouble. They all know it."

"Donnie, listen to me carefully," Lefty says. It was Saturday night, April 11, and I had placed my regular call. "The car. Your friend's car. Meet me in Fort Lauderdale tomorrow."

"Why, what's the matter?"

"Why don't you just listen? Because I can cancel you out right now. I want you to come in alone. I don't know what name I'm going under. I'm gonna come in with some people. Could you get that car?"

That was Rossi's four-door Lincoln. "I guess so, why?"

"Donnie, don't say, 'I guess so, why?' Just say yes and you meet me in Lauderdale."

"Of course I can get it."

"I could use Spaghetti. But my friend and I want you. I'm trying to get in touch with Nick, because we cannot go in cold. I gotta go into that hotel for one day, and then we'll take it from there. Okay?"

"All right." Nick was the manager at the Deauville Hotel, Lefty's friend.

"That's all, pal. I'll explain everything. My friend requested you. You're coming in with us. I got work to do. If you don't like the idea, if you back out, fine, no problem. You go on back home. But I want to put you in on this, serious. Because we spoke about something, you and I, right?"

"I know what you're talking about."

"I got plane tickets, ten o'clock. Delta flight 1051, first-class, from Kennedy. We'll be there twelve-thirty tomorrow afternoon. You start coming in six hours before time. Drive in from Tampa with your big car.

You pick us up at the airport. Don't get there two hours before time. I don't want you seen there. You time yourself, stay away from the airport until time, you follow me?"

"Yeah."

"We just get in the car and we're gone. Now, you satisfied? Because I tell you, if you wanna back away from it, no problem, you go back and there's nothing said. I told you, two guys requested you, him and I. I'm taking full responsibility. He asked me if I wanted you. Okay?"

"All right."

Years earlier, Lefty had promised that when the time was right, he'd take me along. Now I was being taken on a hit.

From various conversations over the last couple of weeks I had pieced together just how the feuding Bonanno family factions lined up, just how ominous the friction was between them. Aligned with Rusty Rastelli were Sally Farrugia, consiglieri Steve Cannone, captains Sonny Black and Joe Massino. Against Rusty were captains Caesar Bonventre, Philip "Philly Lucky" Giaccone, Dominick "Big Trin" Trinchera, and Alphonse "Sonny Red" Indelicato and his son, Anthony Bruno Indelicato.

Sonny, as usual, had been discreet about everything. And especially since the sitdowns about me were still going on, he wasn't telling me anything. As close as we were, he was putting the family first, going by the rules. I probably would have been told more if I had been in New York. But everybody was being careful on the telephone. Lefty had been hinting at how everything was coming to a head, and had let me know that Sonny was the key to all the power, especially now that he had an alliance with Santo Trafficante. The opposing captains feared Sonny's expanding power.

I faced two major problems. One was that as an agent, I couldn't actually participate in a hit—in fact, it was our duty to prevent the hit if possible—yet as a badguy I couldn't turn down the invitation without losing credibility.

The other problem was that I wasn't at my apartment in Holiday, Florida. I wasn't anywhere near Florida. I was home. I hadn't been home for over a month. Over the years I had missed most of my children's important days. On this weekend my youngest daughter was being confirmed. Everything was quiet on the job for the moment, so I snuck home for the weekend. This was Saturday night. The confirmation was tomorrow, Sunday. So was the hit in Florida.

First things first. I had to go on the hit. Technically, since I wasn't a made guy, I could refuse and it wouldn't be held against me. Realistically, though, it would undercut the credibility I had been working to establish since 1976. If I didn't go, they would carry out the hit, anyway. I didn't know who the target was. I figured it was one of the wiseguys in the opposition faction, probably one of the four captains, but I didn't know who, so there was nobody the FBI could warn. And I didn't know where or when. They might go right out on the hit, or they might hang around and case the situation, wait for a good opportunity. At least if I was along, maybe I could find out who the target was enough ahead of time so I could tip off our guys so they could snatch him off the street.

I called Case Agent Jim Kinne in Tampa. He agreed that the only thing we could do is put a surveillance team on me from the time I got to Miami. When I hook up with Lefty and his crew, if I can find out soon enough who they're going to hit, maybe I can get to a phone. Or if I can't find out right away, the surveillance team can tail us until the last possible minute, until I signal or something, and they can stop us on a traffic violation or some bullshit charge. They could say they recognize us as mob guys, ask us what we're all doing down there together—apply a routine hassling that happens to these guys all the time. That way they probably wouldn't suspect a tip-off, yet it might be enough of a disruption to cause them to call off the hit.

Kinne would hurry to set up the surveillance. I would catch the first flight to Miami. It was a very dicey situation. The surveillance team could get spotted or lose us. Everybody with Lefty would be given a

gun, and I could be designated the triggerman. What
if the surveillance team is out of it and we're headed
for the hit and I'm the hitter—what the hell will I do?
I didn't know of any precedents for this situation.

But long before, when I had imagined the possibility
of this kind of situation, I had made a personal decision to cover it: Whatever the rules, if the target is a
badguy and it's him or me, he goes.

I called Rossi and laid out the situation. I would fly
into Miami. He would drive the big car to Miami for
me, then he would fly back to Tampa.

Now I had to tell my family that I would miss my
daughter's confirmation. We were going to have a
houseful of relatives and friends. Relatives were flying
in from all over. Not even my wife knew how deeply I
was involved now in the turmoil within the Bonanno
family.

First I told my wife. I said I got a phone call and I
had to return to Florida immediately. I wasn't going to
give her details, because I didn't want her to worry
any more than she already did. But she had overheard
me talking to Agent Kinne, and so she knew that the
mob wanted me to kill somebody.

I told her that it was a very important thing I was
involved in and that I had to go because somebody's
life might be at stake, and we were required to prevent a killing if we could. A lot of people were depending on me for this operation—it was the old story.
Beyond that, all I could tell her was not to worry. I
was never very good at talking about a thing like that
at a time like that.

She was furious and scared. She yelled at me and
cried. She hated the Bureau. How could I be put in
this position? Who was going to be there to protect
me? Why did I have to go, why not somebody else?
Why not somebody who didn't have a wife and children? She was shaking.

This was the lowest point since her accident.

My youngest daughter was now fourteen. I sat down
with her and told her I couldn't be at her confirmation
because something had come up with my job and I
had an obligation to do it and there was nothing I

could do about it. She cried and said, "Daddy, I don't want you to go because this is a special day for me."

But then she said she was mad that I would leave her on a special day but that at least she had her grandfather there to stand in for her.

I had to leave for the airport right away. I really had no choice.

I flew to Miami and picked up the car from Rossi. I drove to the Fort Lauderdale Airport, arriving five minutes before the scheduled arrival of Lefty's flight. Lefty's flight came, people filed off. No Lefty, no nobody.

I called Sonny in Brooklyn. "What's going on, Sonny? Nobody's here."

"We called it off."

"What do you mean, called it off?"

"Look, call the other guy, he'll explain it to you."

"Where's he?"

"He's home, Donnie."

I drove back to my apartment in Holiday. I needed the six hours to burn off my rage. My daughter's confirmation had gone on without me, and the hit hadn't gone on at all.

Then I called Lefty. He told me that he had gone to the airport and called back to Sonny as he was supposed to, and Sonny said it was canceled. "It was too late to call you," he says, "because you were already on the way from Tampa."

The hit was going to be on Philly Lucky. They called it off because he was down there by himself, and they decided they wanted to get three captains together, that it wasn't smart to hit them one at a time.

"I'm sorry, pal," Lefty says.

"That's all right. What the hell, you couldn't get in touch with me. Things like that happen."

"I know. That's it."

"Well, if it would have went, it would have been good, right?"

"I can't talk about it."

"I'm just saying—"

"No, I can't talk about that. If they'd have left it up to me, you know . . ."

"Next time, Left, don't ask me or say, 'You don't have to do it.' We got something to do, I do it. Don't ever feel that I'm gonna back out of something."

"You had a choice, though."

"What choice? We do things together. I'm not worried about no choice."

Anthony "Mr. Fish" Rabito was a fat wiseguy, maybe 5'9", 250 pounds, with a fleshy face, who once ran seafood restaurants. He was a bachelor and had an apartment at 411 East Fifty-Third Street in Manhattan. His apartment was popular with other wiseguys, who often used it as a place to take their girlfriends for an hour or so. He was a friend of Sonny's. Sonny said that Rabito was a good guy to contact and stay with when you have to work the streets during, say, a war.

On April 13, two days after the aborted hit, Lefty called.

"Donnie, listen to me carefully and listen good. I'm leaving with some people. I can't make no phone calls. If everything comes all right, you'll be in pretty good shape in New York. Understand?"

"Yeah, all right."

"You don't know all right."

"I'm just saying all right that you—"

"Because it might take two weeks. It might take a while. Now, this is the last time you're gonna hear from me. I'm being picked up in a little while. And don't call the other guy."

"Okay. Don't call nobody."

The only person he wanted me to call was Louise. He wanted me to call her twice a day in case she had any problems; at six P.M. when she got home from work, and at eleven P.M., before she went to bed, and to send her $1,000 for bills.

"And do me a favor, try to stay as close as possible just in case when something does come off, that we know where to contact you. In other words, like, I'll use the club. You understand?"

"Yeah."

"Because I'm gonna work from the street."

I alerted Case Agent Jerry Loar in New York. A surveillance team saw Lefty and Louise leave their apartment, get in his car, and drive to Rabito's building. Lefty got out carrying a brown paper bag and went to Rabito's apartment. Louise drove away.

I didn't hear from Lefty until five days later, when I finally learned that I had survived the sitdowns.

"I just got back from Brooklyn," he says. "Everything went good. We'll be all right. We're on top."

"Hey, that's good."

"But these motherfuckers, they was all *partying*. They thought I was clipped, you know? When I was missing? They had me fucking dead, these motherfuckers. So everybody's celebrating."

"Are they crazy or what?"

"Even Mike Sabella. He doesn't know that I know. But he was saying, 'That's a shame, but I'm glad I took his wife's jewelry.' "

Lefty had put up his wife's jewelry as collateral on a loan.

I say, "What a surprise he's gonna have, huh?"

"Unbelievable, these motherfuckers. Wait'll I talk to Blackstein tomorrow. He knew they thought I was clipped, but he didn't know it got *that* far."

Blackstein was Sonny Black.

"Those cocksuckers," Lefty says, "they don't know the surprise they're gonna *get* in a couple months. I got news for you, pal. Nobody bothers you no more. When that man comes out, you'll be in good shape."

"Oh, yeah?"

"I stuck with you all the way. And it's very surprising, he stood by you too."

"Blackstein?"

"Yeah."

"Good."

"Because what I did this here week, you're a lot better off tonight."

"Than last week, huh?"

"Ain't no way of stopping the situation. I can't go

into details. When you walk around, you can smack anybody you want in the mouth, that's all I can tell you."

"Anybody?"

"Anybody. When I get out there, you point them out to me, you smack them in the fucking mouth. Donnie, you're gonna be very shocked. Blackstein is so fucking happy."

He wanted me to meet him in Miami, where he would fill me in more on the results of the sitdowns.

"Do me a favor," he says. "Tell Tony bring a tie and a shirt. Not dress like a fucking Hoosier from Pennsylvania. I'm bringing down sharp clothes."

He put Louise on the phone. "Hi, Donnie, what you gonna do tomorrow?"

"Same thing I do every Sunday."

"No special plans? What kind of dinner you going to eat?"

"I don't know."

"It's *Easter*."

"I know, but I don't have any special buddy to spend Easter with anymore, you know?"

"Oh, we gotta fix that."

I started thinking about close calls and what would happen if Lefty or Sonny started adding things up. There was the time in P. J. Clarke's when I was with Larry Keaton and Larry was recognized as an agent and Lefty was told. And when were they going to get the call from the Chicago mob tipping them off to the fact that Tony Conte was an agent? Going way back, what about the guy at Jilly's in Brooklyn that I had once arrested? Would he see me again on the street and remember who I was? And there was the ABSCAM boat, and there was Rocky.

In the mob it's your close friend that will kill you. Here I was staying with Lefty all the time in hotels, with him twenty-four hours a day where any little slip could be noticed. I was dodging a lot of bullets, so to speak.

*   *   *

Rossi and I picked up Lefty at the airport in Miami. Mirra and his side had lost the sitdowns; I was okay.

"The case is closed," Lefty says. "There's no more. They lost, and they lost nationwide. New York, Miami, Chicago—they lost nationwide. Listen, that's why it took me fucking five days to go out and do what I had to do."

"That's good. Sonny happy now?"

"Forget about it, lit up like Luna Park. Well, I'm glad youse are satisfied, because this is the whole thing in a nutshell."

"Hey, Left, that's what we were working for all this time, right?"

"We're hurting, in the sense we don't have big money. But we have the power today. I'd rather have the power than the money. Because these guys have all got the money, and they don't know what to do with it no more. Where they gonna go? They can't run to nobody. They still got their captains. But who the captains gonna go to?"

"Are they still gonna be under Rusty, those guys?"

"Everybody's under Rusty. The law of the land. Nationwide. There's only one fucking boss."

"And that's it?"

"And nobody can take his place."

We went into the piano bar at the Deauville. Lefty told us that he, Sonny, Joey Massino, and Nicky Santora had been engaged in an important job in New York "for the Commission." He said that they had "put it together" and that in return they had been assured by the Commission that Rastelli would remain boss.

I didn't know what Lefty had done during his five days "working from the street" or what they had done for the Commission, or whether it was all one and the same. The FBI had kept him under surveillance for two or three days and nothing happened, so they abandoned it—they don't have unlimited manpower to keep everybody under surveillance for long periods. I assumed it involved a hit, because everything was typical of that—the secrecy and the working from the street, the fact that afterward all the serious problems raised in the sitdowns and going all the way up to the boss were solved. And finally the whole thing had been ratified nationwide by the Mafia Commission representing all the families. I figured that the paper bag Lefty had taken to Rabito's contained guns—that was a common way of carrying a bunch of them.

I couldn't ask direct questions. Supposedly I was experienced enough now as a connected guy to figure out certain things on my own, take what I was told, and, as Lefty liked to say, "leave it alone."

Even though everything pointed to a hit, I couldn't think of anybody that was missing. No bodies turned up.

We were sitting there listening to Lefty spin out his tale of trouble between family factions, shit with Mirra, all the difficult and violent solutions within the mob.

"Lefty," Rossi says, "I understand how we all like to make money. But what is the actual advantage to being a wiseguy?"

"Are you kidding? What the . . . Donnie, don't you tell this guy nothing? Tony, as a wiseguy you can lie, you can cheat, you can steal, you can kill people—*legitimately*. You can do any goddamn thing you want, and nobody can say anything about it. Who wouldn't want to be a wiseguy?"

A few guys from the New York crew were down having a good time. Rossi wanted to use the pay phone and didn't have any change. He asked one of the guys—the retired New York detective—if he had change for a dollar.

"Use these," the ex-cop says, handing Rossi four copper-colored metal discs the size of quarters. "They work good." He said that a few of the guys in New York had access to large supplies of these slugs at five hundred for fifty bucks—ten cents apiece.

Rossi used one in the phone and later turned in the other three to the contact agent.

The next afternoon we were sitting by the pool at the Deauville. Lefty was moaning and groaning about us not hustling enough. He wanted a lounge on the beach, for status. "Let's do it now," he says, "because

I'm older and tired." He complained about everything. "Promised about the racetrack. We embarrassed ourselves, it died. Promised about the Vegas Night, it died. Promised about bingo, it died."

Rossi went inside. Lefty complained that Rossi wasn't pulling his weight and that I wasn't leaning on Rossi enough. He droned on for another hour. At about four o'clock he says, "I think I'll go up and take a nap so I'll be fresh for when we go out tonight."

A few minutes later Rossi came out. "You won't believe what I did. I turned the air-conditioning up full-blast and took the switch off."

"Holy shit," I say. "We're gonna hear him screaming all the way out here at the pool. I ain't going up there for a while because he's gonna be going bullshit."

Lefty hated air-conditioning. Summers in New York or Tampa, in cars, in hotel rooms, he would not allow me to turn it on. He couldn't stand the cold air blowing on him. We'd be riding around on the hottest days with the car windows open. We had fights. I'd turn the air-conditioning on, he'd turn it off. I'd be drenched in sweat, he didn't sweat at all. "How can you not sweat in this car?" I'd say. "Ah, just keep the windows open and you don't need air-conditioning," he'd answer.

We always stayed together in hotel rooms. He always had a cold. Sometimes, even in the summer, he would turn the heat on in the room. "It's too damp in here," he'd say. "Lefty, you're fucking nuts. This is crazy. I'm getting another room." He chain-smoked his English Ovals. If I was lucky, he had a room where you could open the windows.

This time we were staying in one of the penthouse suites, the three of us together. Finally Rossi and I went up to the room.

"Donnie, you cocksucker! You did this!" Lefty is stomping around the nice cool room.

"What are you talking about?"

"You turned this fucking air-conditioning up, and it can't turn down!"

"Left, I haven't been in the room since we left it this afternoon."

"You fucking snuck up here and did this just to

break my fucking balls! Call the maintenance, get this fucking air-conditioning fixed!"

"Why don't you just turn it down?"

"It ain't got no fucking switch!"

Rossi is laughing so hard, he can barely stand up, because Lefty is hollering at me and not him.

"I couldn't even take a nap," Lefty rants on. "I been up here two fucking hours freezing my ass off!"

"Why didn't *you* call maintenance?"

"Because *you* did this thing!"

"Okay, I did it."

"You ain't going to dinner with me tonight!"

"Okay, I'll eat by myself."

Meanwhile Rossi is on his hands and knees. "Here it is," he says, pulling the switch out from under the couch. He puts the switch back on and turns the air-conditioning off.

The room is filled with too much cigarette smoke and too much Lefty, and it's making me crazy. I walk out. Rossi comes after me. I stop in the hall. "Tony, I'm going back in there and stab that motherfucker."

"Hey, Don—"

"I can't take him anymore. I'm gonna stab him. We'll just go down to the pool, let them find him up here. Who's gonna give a fuck if they find another dead wiseguy?"

"Hey, Donnie, take it easy."

With everything else there was to worry about, I had to take this daily shit. Rossi thought I was serious. That's how fed up I was with Lefty.

I talked to Lefty in the morning on May 5. It was a routine phone call. Nothing in his voice suggested anything unusual. Normal chitchat, good-bye.

I placed my usual call in the evening. Louise said Lefty wasn't there, she didn't know where he was.

I called the next morning. Louise said Lefty hadn't come home, she still knew nothing.

I called Case Agent Jerry Loar in New York. I told him that Lefty was missing. He said they had received word from two informants that three Bonanno captains had gotten whacked the night before: Philly Lucky, Sonny Red, and Big Trin.

The three had apparently been summoned to Brooklyn to a "peace meeting," to patch up differences, at a catering establishment. Our information was that's where they were murdered. No bodies had been found.

The heart of the opposition to Rusty Rastelli and Sonny Black had been whacked out all at once. The other main rival, Caesar Bonventre, was in jail in Nassau County, New York, on a weapons charge. But the word was that he had decided to come over to Sonny's side, anyway, and bring the zips.

Three days later Lefty called me in the afternoon. "I just got in."

"Did you talk to Louise yet?"

"I called her this morning for two minutes, that's all. You know why I come in, because she sent me all my clothes last night, whole box. She leaves the fucking pants out. She started crying at first. 'What are you crying for?' I says. 'I got the clothes.' "

"I sent her a grand, you know, because I didn't know how long you'd be gone."

He had been holed up at Rabito's apartment. "It's gonna be a while yet, but let me throw a curve at you."

"I'm listening, go ahead."

"Everything is fine. We're winners. A couple of punks ran away, but they're coming back. They came back. We gave them sanctuary."

"Is that right?"

"What we gotta do with you is, we gotta work out one more situation. I'm with that guy day and night. Have a little patience."

"Yeah, well, I figured something was going on, so that's why I just kept calling Louise. You don't know how long you're gonna be gone?"

"No. It's just that I'm dead tired tonight, and I'll be home the rest of the night."

"You gonna stay in, then?"

"Ah, till I get a call. You know what I'm talking about."

"Yeah."

"Everybody is satisfied. Them two guys out at the beach—don't mention names."

"Yeah." That was Joe Puma and Steve Maruca.

"They belong to us now. Now, don't talk to me, Donnie. But visualize what took place."

"Yeah, all right." I visualized the hits.

"You understand?"

"I understand what you're talking about."

"Now they're ours. How's the weather down there?"

"It's nice. Everything gets cleared up, maybe you can come down."

"Well, we'll see what happens. Right now I can't, I'm stuck over here. What's happening?"

"I'm looking at something, you know, might be worth maybe about ten grand or something."

"Ah, that'd be perfect, buddy. We can use it. I wanna clear up all these goddamn bills."

"That's why I figured I'd send that grand."

"She appreciated it."

"I figured you might be gone another five, six days."

"Well, now it'll be longer than that. Being that tomorrow's Mother's Day, everybody went home, you know. Everybody's laid up. I gotta go see him tomorrow morning."

"You still got another situation."

"Yeah. All right, buddy, so long."

Six days after the hits, the wife of Philip "Philly Lucky" Giaccone filed a missing-person's report on her husband with the Suffolk County, New York, Police Department.

On Tuesday, May 12, Lefty called and said that Sonny wanted to see me right away. I told him I needed a couple of days to clear up some business, then I would be up. "It's very important," he says, "so let me know as soon as you make arrangements."

I didn't have any business to clear up in Florida. But even in this instance I didn't want to seem too anxious. I was being summoned by Sonny for one of two reasons. Either I was going to be whacked, or I was going to be told about the hits and maybe involved in the "other situation" that was still left to take care of.

Either mission was crucial enough for me to make one arrangement, which didn't take long.

I flew into La Guardia on the afternoon of May 14, got off the plane, and immediately saw the agent I was to look for, Billy Flynn. I followed him silently into the men's room. He slipped me a wallet containing a transmitter. I dropped it into my sports coat pocket and went out.

I rented a car and drove to Graham Avenue and Withers Street in Brooklyn, and parked up the street from the Motion Lounge, arriving at about three-thirty. I didn't park right in front because I wanted to walk and case the block.

In recent weeks I had been in regular telephone contact with Jules Bonavolonta at Headquarters. Jules and I had been street agents together in New York. Working undercover, it was important to have one guy on the inside that you could trust totally to understand you and your situation, somebody that you could talk to as a close friend yet who at the same time had the skills to maneuver within the bureaucracy. Jules had become that guy for me. He could handle internal politics, get me authorizations and support. I called Jules all the time with frustrations: "You ain't gonna believe this," I would say when I had run up against some starch.

To the Bureau's credit, they consistently came around to our way of thinking after things were explained.

Lately Jules had been testing my condition. "Are you getting tired? You getting home enough? You think you should come out soon?"

Now, with the hits, Headquarters was nervous. When they found out that I was going to a meeting with Sonny, a couple of people thought that maybe he was setting me up, that they were going to kill me. I said, "What would they kill me for? I'm with Sonny. He's the one that asked me to come up." Jules agreed with me that Sonny wasn't setting me up.

Still, there was a lot of nervousness. Sonny was now

a target for retaliation. I was close to him—that made me a target too.

They wanted not only a surveillance team on me, which was reasonable, but they wanted SWAT guys hidden on the roofs. "Are you crazy?" I said. "In that neighborhood, Sonny's neighborhood, you're going to put guys on rooftops with rifles? Just put a good crew on the street, I'll be all right."

Jim Kallstrom was the coordinator of technical services, which includes surveillance teams. I specifically requested that I get a crew headed by Pat Colgan as street supervisor.

A surveillance crew is not just a passive monitoring outfit. If there's trouble, they have to move in. Most of the agents didn't know me except from pictures. They didn't know my way of talking, Sonny's way of talking. That, along with the static and interference that made transmissions chancy, could lead to the crew misunderstanding the conversation, making a move too soon, busting in on us, and screwing up our whole operation.

A surveillance team that screwed up was more dangerous to me than no surveillance team at all. If they got made on the street in that neighborhood, where's the first place a guy's going to go to tip somebody off? He's going straight to the Motion Lounge to tell Sonny Black, who is the main man in that neighborhood.

As I was walking up the block toward the Motion Lounge, I knew the surveillance team was there somewhere. I was looking for them to make sure they were in place. I am trained and experienced to spot such things on the street. I looked carefully. I knew they were there. I never made them. I never saw them at all. That's how good they were.

Sonny was waiting at the bar. The scene looked placid. Boobie was playing the electronic pinball machine. Charlie was behind the bar. Jimmy Legs was there. And there was one other guy I hadn't seen before. His name was Ray. He was, I later learned, Ray Wean, an informant for the FBI who did jobs with Joey Massino and with Sonny. In fact, it was Wean who had shot himself in the hand during the abortive burglary at the townhouse of the Shah of Iran's sister in 1980. Neither of us knew who the other really was at the time.

I walked in, gave Sonny, Boobie, and Jimmy a kiss and a hug—normal greetings. "How you doing?" "How's Florida?" Everything was normal. Sonny asked me to come into the back room. We sat at a card table.

"You know we took care of those three guys," were his first words. "They're finished. You got any reliable people in Miami?"

"Yeah, why?"

"Because one guy got away, Bruno. You know Anthony Bruno?"

Anthony Bruno Indelicato was Sonny Red's son. "I may have seen him, I don't know."

"I think he went to Miami because he's got a $3,000-a-day coke habit and he's got connections with the Colombians down there. I want you to find him. When you find him, hit him. Be careful, because when he's coked up, he's crazy. He's not a tough guy with his hands, but if he has a gun, you know . . ."

"Yeah, okay."

"He might be down there with his uncle, J. B. If you come across them both, just kill them both and leave them there in the street. You want me to send Lefty down there with you?"

"You kidding? I'd rather be by myself. That makes it so much quicker."

"Those two guys on the beach, Puma and that guy Steve, do you know them?"

"Yeah, I know them." Joe Puma and Steve Maruca. *The beach* was a phrase they used to indicate the Miami area.

"What do you think of them?"

"Joe Puma, I met a few times. What can I say? He didn't strike me as a stand-up guy."

"Now they're down there, they got the fear of God in them. Well, that's too bad for them. Their time has been coming. I got to do a lot of work."

"Sonny, you know me, I don't ask questions, I don't know nothing. There's a couple places down there that these guys hang out. I'll contact a couple of guys that I know. Once I get everything set up, then we can lay up for a few days down there and see what's going on."

"All right, any way you want to do it. Now, when I come down there, you got guns down there? I can't be walking around with nothing. I need two. You got two?"

"Yeah, we got a couple. One thing, I gotta have a description of the kid."

"I know him, but I can't give you any good description. He's like 140, 150 pounds. Smaller than you. Thin-faced kid. Italian-looking, dark. Always complaining about his bald head. In his late twenties. Bantamweight, petite-looking. He's a dangerous little kid. He's a wild man when he's coked up."

"High roller, huh?"

"Likes his broads."

"Suppose I come upon him, right? Then I get a chance to take him out, I don't have to call you and ask if it's okay?"

"No, no—go ahead, of course. You take him, leave him right in the street."

"All right, don't get excited. I'll do it right."

"I'm gonna come down maybe next week or so. Then I was gonna talk to the Old Man. Have you got a place to lay up over there now?"

"We can go to a lot of places down there. There's the Deauville. Broads. A stockpile of broads."

"All right. Now, we're leaving it to you to get down there."

"Joe and Steve are with you now, aren't they?"

"Yeah, because their guy is one of the guys that went." (Meaning Philly Lucky.) "It all comes in circles. We're gonna lock everything up over there. It's a tough situation. I got a lot of work to do. My game is a waiting game. Whatever happens, you get it when you can get it. It's coming to you one way or the other."

We went up on the roof to feed his pigeons. There was a guy up there hooking up a cable line for Sonny's TV. "Getting the Home Box up today," Sonny says.

He was tapping into the system illegally, like all the wiseguys do. He had ninety-five pigeons. "Out of ninety-five" he says, "we lose about four. Soon as I got the heater in there this winter, we never lost a bird from the cold."

He brought up the matter of Quaaludes. He wanted me to take some samples down to Florida and see if I could find a market. They were costing him eighty cents apiece, and he thought maybe we could get a dollar each for them.

We went downstairs. The guy named Ray had left. What none of us knew at the time was that he had left to call Pat Colgan, his contact at the FBI and coincidentally the guy who was running the surveillance team on me. He called Pat to tell him this guy named Donnie had just shown up from Florida, and he was apparently a good friend of Sonny Black's because they kissed and hugged, and apparently he was a pretty big drug dealer.

Sonny and I went across the street to the Caffe Capri for demitasse and cannoli. We sat at a table in the rear.

Sonny said he was making a lot of changes. "I'm forming a good crew, people you can go to bed with and trust."

I asked him about Mike Sabella.

"He thought I was gonna clip him," Sonny says, "but we had a good talk. He said he had stayed with the other side because they intimidated him, but I told him, 'You're my man now.' He was pleased. He'll be loyal."

He said that the day before the hits, Tony Mirra had said he was going with the opposition. On the day of the hits, Sonny called Mirra's uncle, Al Walker, and told him to come to the Motion Lounge. They sat him down, put a guy at either side of him, and made him sweat until word came that the hits had gone down. "When he heard that," Sonny says, "he turned ash-white. He thought we were gonna hit him too. But I just reamed him out about Tony, told him Tony was no good; and that he'd better recognize that and act right himself. He agreed, Donnie."

I asked him how Joe Puma and Steve Maruca would feel with me sitting them down and telling them the terms, since they were wiseguys and I wasn't.

"Don't worry about it. Long as you're my representative, they'll listen to you. I also want you to meet a guy I'm gonna send down with you, in case you need some help. You going to see Lefty later?"

"Yeah."

"Tell Lefty to call Sally Paintglass and have him meet me at the lounge at ten o'clock, and you be here too."

Sally "Paintglass" D'Ottavio was a made member of the crew who got his name because he owned a couple of auto body shops.

I left Brooklyn and headed for Manhattan. As I went across the bridge I saw that I had picked up a tail. It was an unmarked van with a white guy and a black guy. I was curious, but I didn't try to shake them. It didn't matter. I figured they were cops. I was going into Knickerbocker Village. They weren't going to do anything. I didn't see them again.

I didn't find out until two years later, when I was testifying, that these were N.Y.P.D. organized crime cops that had Sonny's club under surveillance since the hits. They had no idea who I was at the time. So they and the FBI were both surveilling the Motion Lounge at the same time, and neither knew the other was there.

Lefty was home, sick with a cold. We sat on the couch and I started to tell him about my conversation with Sonny.

"I already know what Sonny asked you to do," he says. "He's in control of the family now. Donnie, I'm really happy that he's having you clip Bruno, because it'll look good in the eyes of the bosses that you did some work. It's a good contract."

"Yeah, I'm glad, too, Left."

"The kid was supposed to be there. He didn't show because he was all coked up, too high."

He called Sally Paintglass and set up the meeting with Sonny. I said that before I went back to Brooklyn, I was going over to see my girl for a short while.

"All right," he says. "I would go with you to Brooklyn, but I'm dying here."

I did go to Jersey. I went across the George Washington Bridge to the Holiday Inn off Route 80, where I met with agents Jimmy Kosler, Jerry Loar, and Jim Kinne. I told them the whole story of the afternoon. Even though theoretically the conversation had been received from the transmitter and recorded, we couldn't count on that, so I wanted to relay the information as soon as possible. I gave them the transmitter because the batteries were shot, anyway.

I felt good. I wasn't a made guy, but I was given a contract to hit a made guy. And I was going to Miami to tell two other guys that they were now under Sonny. All the wiseguys could see how close I was to Sonny, who was becoming the main power in the family—aside from Rusty Rastelli, who was in the can.

The Motion Lounge was crowded at ten-fifteen. Sonny introduced me to Sally. "Donnie is with me, Sally. You can trust him as much as you trust me."

Sally Paintglass was about 5'9", sturdy, about five years older than me. He was a tough, greasy-looking guy with a weak chin. We agreed to meet three days later, on May 17, at Joe Puma's restaurant, Little Italy, in Hallandale.

Sonny says, "This is the first time in over ten years that the family has control over itself instead of being controlled by the Commission. Donnie, watch out for the kid. I got to get him before he gets me, because I can't rest at night and we can't go places until we get this kid. That's our only obstacle."

The next day I came into the Motion Lounge wearing the same brown-checked sport jacket I wore a lot in Florida.

"Donnie, you got to get rid of that fucking jacket."

"What's the matter with it?"

"You look like a fucking tourist. I don't even like it for Florida. Let's go get some fucking clothes that don't embarrass you."

He took me to a clothing manufacturer who was a friend of his, and I bought a couple of jackets and pairs of slacks. "I feel better now," Sonny says.

Boobie had told Nicky Santora that I needed some samples of Quaaludes to take back to Florida, and at the club Nicky said that he had to see a guy about it that afternoon. When I was about to leave to catch my plane, Boobie said the samples were over at Boot's place, the Capri Car Service across the street.

We walked over there. Boobie took a small brown paper bag out of the desk and gave it to me. I put it in my pocket and left for the airport.

On the Brooklyn-Queens Expressway, a car pulled alongside me. It was agent Pat Colgan, who was heading the surveillance team. He motioned for me to follow. We pulled off the road near the airport. I took the bag out of my pocket and opened it. The pills were in a plastic bag inside the paper bag. We counted twenty-five. We initialed and dated the bag, and Colgan took it with him to turn it in.

I went on to La Guardia and flew to Tampa.

19

THE CONTRACT

Rossi and I drove across Florida to Hallandale and went to Joe Puma's Little Italy restaurant. We walked in at seven P.M. Sally Paintglass was already there. We went over and sat down.

"Joe ain't here," Sally says. "I can't find him. The people here, his wife, they don't know where he is."

Puma, afraid we might be coming to whack him, had fled.

"I know. I just talked to Lefty. Sonny is ripping."

"His partner is supposed to be here at eight o'clock. I drove down from New York, drove straight through.

Then I found out this guy ain't here. I was fucking mad."

"The other guy know where he went?"

"I spoke to him on the phone. He went up north. So let Sonny put him on a fucking plane and let him come."

"That's what Lefty told Sonny: Tell these fuckers, Joe and Steve, to come up here. Sometimes Sonny's too easy."

"He figures the guys will be nervous if you call them up there," Sally says. "They're both a little scared. See, we're doing them a favor to come over here in their home grounds."

"Yeah, so they feel at ease."

"I brought my wife so the cocksuckers would feel comfortable. Because the other guy was dodging me all night. I said to him, 'Come to the hotel and have coffee. My wife's here, bring your wife.' "

It was a simple, if ominous, proposition. We were there to tell these guys that they belonged to Sonny. We wanted them to accept that and relax. We didn't want them to think they were still on the other side and be gunning for *us*.

Steve Maruca came in. He always looked like an intimidating old-time gangster. "Geez, it's hot in here," he says, sitting down with the three of us.

Compared to the last time, though, when I had seen him with Lefty, he looked nervous and whipped. His voice was a little shaky. "Ain't it hot here?"

Sally turned to me privately. "I don't want to be rude or nothing, but I don't know Tony. Could you tell him to go sit at another table while we discuss?"

Tony went to a table by himself.

Maruca fidgeted. "You say you got those three, uh . . ."

We explained to him that the three captains were gone, there was new leadership, everybody was now under Sonny Black.

"Does everything look good?" Maruca asks. ."Everything's settled?"

"Everything is finished," Sally says. "Just with that one guy. If you hear anything, right away call."

"I seen him, only met him once, at the wedding when Mike's son got married. I talked to him for a minute."

"It's a must," Sally says. "Anybody who sees him, it's a must."

I say, "He sniffs, you know. Three thousand dollars a day, he sniffs coke. That's why he's gotta come out of the woodwork, to get that shit."

"Wow," Maruca says. "How do you keep a habit like that?"

"He's a no-good fucking kid," Sally says. "Wanted to live off his father's record. Sonny Red. Very nice guy."

"I only met Sonny Red about three times," Maruca says, distancing himself quickly. "I don't know him."

"He was a gentleman," Sally says, "but everybody makes mistakes."

"Things like this happen," Maruca says. "You can't question."

"No, there's no questions," Sally says. "One thing you gotta realize. Anything happens, it happens for a reason."

Maruca clears his throat. "And you can't bring it up and you can't give opinions."

"There's a reason for everything that's right," I say.

"I wasn't aware, you know. Mike called me and said, 'Listen, everything's fine, just stand pat, and there's no more talking about it.' "

"Right."

"This is why they sent me down here at a big expense," Sally says, "because youse guys would feel comfortable. I mean, they didn't want to send two guys you didn't know."

"If they sent somebody we didn't know," Maruca says, "we can't talk to him. Gotta send somebody we know."

"What good is strangers?" Sally says. "So now you'll feel comfortable?"

"Yeah, yeah. Because I didn't do nothing wrong. When you don't do nothing wrong, you ain't got nothing to worry about, right?"

"Right," we say.

"Now my crew's in power," Sally says. "But Sonny Red, Phil Lucky, I'm gonna sit down and argue with them? They were in power long enough. Under-the-table power."

"But they were there," I say.

"Calling the shots," Sally says.

"I didn't know what the fuck was going on," Maruca says. "He wasn't telling me nothing at all. He was telling me very little."

"Now we're working under an honor system," Sally says. "You gotta be honorable amongst our fellows, right?"

"That's the way it's supposed to be," Maruca says.

"Well, you're with the right guy," I say, "with Sonny."

"Yeah, he's gonna be a big shot now," Sally says. "Because if the doors open up there, he moves. We're all under Sonny Black. Everybody."

"In other words, you told them—Sonny Black."

"Any problem, you call me," Sally says.

"There ain't no problem," Maruca says. "What have I got to lose here?

"You did the right thing," I say.

"If I'd have done something wrong, I'd have been loony."

We got back on the subject of Anthony Bruno Indelicato, my target. "See, he's got to come out," I say. "That stuff, when you take it, you're only high like twenty minutes. Then you need more. It's not like heroin where you stay four or five hours. That's why they get crazy."

"*Marone*," Sally says, "this guy needs sacks full."

"That's why it costs so much," I say. "So he's gotta come out of the fucking woodwork. He had connections down here for that stuff."

"I never saw him before," Maruca says.

"I met him three or four times," Sally says. "And I remember his mouth."

"The only time he does anything is when the coke is up," I say. "Otherwise, forget about it."

"Our guy over there said that he's capable of anything," Sally says.

"He might come in and start fucking shooting," I say.

"He come into the O.K. Corral," Sally says, "he didn't care."

"You gonna be around here?" I say. "Because I'm gonna be down here for a few days looking for this kid, so if I need something, you know . . . Can I get you over here?"

"Use my home number," Maruca says. "I'll come running. You want me heavy, just say, 'Come heavy.' "

"Okay."

"Just tell him it's chilly out, get dressed," Sally says.

"Okay."

"You don't wanna say that," Maruca says. "Just say, 'I'm buying a car and I want you to check it out.' "

"Okay. Nobody down here knows me. I'll know him, but he doesn't know me at all, so I can go in a lot of these joints. I'm at the Holiday Inn down here at the beach."

"How long you gonna be down?"

"I don't know."

"He'd like to go home sooner if he could clean the dishes up," Sally says. "For once we're independent, completely. There's no fucking dictators."

"That's right," I say.

"Hope Lefty's in favor," Maruca says.

"Forget about it," I say.

After the meeting I called Sonny to report.

"You're gonna have to do a lot of traveling back and forth for me," Sonny says. "Say hello to that fucking clownzo with holy underwears."

I called Lefty. He knew that Puma wasn't in Florida—he was in New York.

"I met here yesterday with him," Lefty says. "Everything is straightened out with him."

I told everybody that I was hitting a lot of joints looking for the kid. I did show my face around. I wasn't worried about running into him—or having somebody run to me with a tip that he was around the corner—which would have put me in a bad situation. After all, the mob was looking for him. So was the

FBI, which hoped to snatch him off the street for his own protection, at which time I could tell Sonny that I had done the job. If the mob and the FBI couldn't find him, I didn't have much to worry about.

The only thing some of the people at the Bureau were concerned about was that as word got round that I had the contract on Anthony Bruno, he might start looking to whack me out.

Sally and I stayed in the Miami area for about a week. Then Sonny called me. "I don't think he's down there. I think we got him up here in New York. So you go on back to Tampa."

A couple of days later, during my routine daily call, Lefty says, "What's happening?"

"Nothing. Just out seeing if I could hustle anything up, make some bread."

"I hope so. I hope so."

"Nothing going on?"

"No," he says. "Just buy today's *Post*, that's all."

"I don't get it down here until tomorrow."

"Tomorrow you get it. Give me a call in the morning."

The article in the *New York Post* had the headline: *MOB SNUFFS OUT AMBITIOUS BOSS.*

The article said that the body of Alphonse "Sonny Red" Indelicato had been found in a shallow grave in a vacant lot in Ozone Park, Queens, and described the body as "bullet-riddled." A couple of kids had been playing, and they say a cowboy boot sticking out of the ground.

Two close associates of his were missing and presumed dead. I found out that the day before the article, the New York Police Department had notified the FBI that the body was positively identified as Sonny Red, and that he had died of gunshot wounds.

I called the next morning. "I saw that article."

"Yeah. Heh! There's a lot of warm heat over here. Forget about it."

"Over that?"

"Yeah. Over a lot of things."

"We're all right, though, huh?"

"Lotta heat. But I can't say nothing. Our phones over here are no good no more, you know?"

Now that there was open warfare, with key family members being murdered, Headquarters wanted to pull me out and close the operation. They wanted to close it right away, by June 1. More murders were expected. Jules Bonavolonta felt that since I was close to Sonny and had been given a contract, I myself was a target to get whacked. I could understand their concern, but I didn't agree with it.

I was so close to getting made and becoming a real wiseguy that I could taste it. Soon Rusty Rastelli would be out of prison. I was sure that Sonny planned to move fast on it. He gave me the contract so that I would have that credential when he put my name up. He needed as a close ally a soldier he could trust and who could face other wiseguys as an equal. Sonny had already said that I would be doing a lot of traveling for him. As a made guy, I would have enormous clout as his emissary. I would be able to sit down with anybody. As a wiseguy, I would be Sonny's partner. Sonny could have used me almost like an ambassador, an intermediary with other families.

The help I could give to other investigations, as a made guy, was limitless. When it ultimately became known that I had penetrated the mob and become a made guy, it would humiliate the Mafia and end forever the myth of the Mafia's invincibility. I wanted to stay under until at least August.

There were arguments against becoming a made guy. Some felt that if I became made, I would have less flexibility and independence. I would no longer be excused for "dumb mistakes," which were really things I had done, moves I had made or not made, for the benefit of the investigation. I would have to do what they told me to do. I could be ordered to commit crimes. Jules was one of those against my staying in and getting made.

Primarily the question boiled down to safety. Nobody thought I was safe enough any longer. They felt that we had already made a bundle of important cases, and it wasn't worth the risk of staying under just to make a couple more. I felt safe enough. As much as it hurt to face ending the operation after five years, I had to accept the decision.

We had a meeting outside Washington, D.C., at the Crystal City Marriott. Rossi, Shannon, Jules, me, various supervisors, and Headquarters people and case agents. There were several other operations involved in one way or another with ours, and that made it rather complex to end our operation cleanly. We needed to give these other operations time to bring their work up to a point where they could do without me in the picture. They went around the table. Everybody was asked to cut estimated time. If somebody needed a month, they were asked to wrap up in two weeks. After going around and around, we got a fix on the amount of time needed by everybody concerned.

We set a date to end the operation: July 26.

Shortly after that, we had another meeting to finalize the ABC's of closing up. That was in New Jersey, at the Howard Johnson's near the George Washington Bridge. The two big items on the agenda were to determine what telephones we wanted to put wiretaps on, and which Bonanno guy we should approach first to tell of my true identity.

The two matters were related. Nothing about our operation would be made public until we had indictments, months down the line. In the meantime, when the operation ended on July 26, agents were going to reveal my role to the Bonannos so that they didn't go after me as an informant. Historically the mob did not seek vengeance against cops and judges, because that brings down too much heat on the mob. The second reason was that we wanted to stimulate a lot of telephone conversations that would contribute to the evidence of mob business, locations, conspiracy, who was who.

To pick up these conversations we needed wiretaps. For wiretaps we needed court orders. For court orders we needed to provide as much up-to-date supporting information as possible. We needed to be specific. You can't just walk into a court and get a hundred wiretaps. We needed to finalize these decisions now, so we could get the court orders and install the taps by the time I came out.

We pinpointed the most important phones to tap, those used most by the most important people, where the most business was transacted.

Then we turned to who to tell first. Almost everybody at the meeting said it should be Lefty. He was the most involved with me on a daily basis. He would get on the phones and scream to everybody and let slip all kinds of information.

I insisted that it had to be Sonny. Sonny was the top Bonanno guy on the street now. He was calm and cool and rational. Lefty would get on the phones and scream to everybody about everything under the sun. But Sonny would make more important calls and would be more specific. Sonny's orders would be more serious and would be taken more seriously. There was no question about it, it had to be Sonny.

They agreed on Sonny. Then the question was: Who should tell him? Some thought I should tell him. There was no way I would be the guy to tell him. That would be the worst kind of slap in the face. It would be rubbing salt into raw wounds. It would be unfair and unnecessary. It should be other FBI agents, including somebody Sonny has met before so that he will believe what he is told.

Everything was set. I went back to work.

Now the job no longer was to penetrate deeper into the family. I was simply to work for as much information as possible in the six weeks before I had to come out. Actually that wasn't so simple. I still had to play my role. I still had to maintain my personality and character—I couldn't start looking especially eager to learn things all of a sudden. For the mob it was business as usual, and it had to seem like that with me, too; which included navigating through the family warfare.

Some people at Headquarters wanted us to branch out all of a sudden and start asking questions of other people about other people, for some last-minute intelligence. But we resisted those requests. If we made a mistake of pushing too hard, suddenly we wouldn't even have six weeks anymore. We might have to pull out in a day.

Boobie's daughter was going to get married, and we were all invited to the wedding on June 20. I went up to New York on June 15 to be with Sonny and the crew. They were still looking for the kid, Anthony Bruno.

On my way into the Motion Lounge I ran into Nicky Santora. I said, "The kids's not in Miami, Nicky. We scoured the fucking place."

"We got a few feelers out now. We'll know this week. He might have crawled into a hole and stayed for a while. But when he comes out, we'll get him."

I went over to Manhattan to the Holiday Bar to see Lefty. We went out for a walk on Madison Street. He was aggravated with everybody, and a walk on the street was the only place he could really let his hair down. He wasn't getting a proper split of profits, he was being ignored or unappreciated or mistreated. His longtime loyalty wasn't counting for anything. Boobie was a phony; Joey Massino had all the men and money in the world and didn't know how to do anything; Sonny was greedy.

"They got all the connections and I'm a jerk-off. Who's gonna pay me? Sonny's trying to hold me back. Push me for like two hundred a week here, two hundred a week there, to pacify me. Meanwhile he's making like thirty thousand a week. Sooner or later he wants to get rid of me by making me a captain, but I gotta do it in Miami. He gives me a couple thousand, then I'm gonna go to Miami. Meanwhile they're knocking it down. Boobie's got fifteen hundred a week in salary. And they got all the junk. They took it all."

"How come you're not in on that?"

"Why? Because he's a greedy cocksucker," he says, meaning Sonny.

"You did all the work for him."

He grunts. "Donnie, they gave me the contract now

on the kid. Once I do that, the guy can go fuck himself."

"They found that one body, huh?"

"Yeah. That was a mistake. Joey Massino, he's the one fucked it up. Sonny's really hot about it."

Sonny Red's body, like the others, was supposed to have been chopped up and gotten rid of properly, not buried quickly and whole.

"You have no idea," Lefty says. "The guy choked." He put a hand to his throat in the gesture used about athletes who don't come through in the clutch.

"How'd you manage Big Trin?" I ask, "huge as he is?"

"I couldn't move him. Boobie could. Trin was all cut open and bleeding. There was little pieces around from the shotgun. Boobie got blood all over him trying to pick him up. I couldn't believe how strong Boobie is. He don't look it. But I was amazed. Boobie could move him. Then they cut him up and put him in green plastic garbage bags."

He said that the guys in on the hits were himself, Jimmy Legs, Nicky Santora, and a guy named Bobby Capazzio. When they came out of the building, Jerry Chilli told them that the kid was right around the corner.

"I said, 'Bobby, let's go over there.' He says, 'No, no, no, Lefty. Sonny Black told you to go to Brooklyn.' The kid was around the corner, Donnie. We could have boxed the corner."

So they went back to the Motion Lounge before going to Rabito's to hole up.

Having done that "work," Lefty was all the more disturbed with not getting a fair share of everything in the family.

"In fact, before the war started," Lefty says, "he says, 'Lefty, you come in on salary. We're going to be millionaires in three months.' I got shut out again. Who am I to speak up? And you wonder why I get aggravated. He knows I'd come at him. Because I'm gonna come at him. And what's he gonna do, sit down with the bosses? He can't sit down with the bosses, this man. He fucked up good. Now I got the contract for the kid. Uh-huh. Who the fuck you kidding? Only four guys can go. Me, Jimmy Legs, Nicky, and Bobby. What are you trying to do? I went there already. It's a suicide thing."

"To the house?" They had information that the kid was holed up in a house on a cul-de-sac in Riverhead, far out on Long Island.

"It's a bad corner. You come on the fucking block, the kid spots us, we're dead. Sonny wants us to hit pay dirt. Pay dirt? Sonny, who the fuck you kidding? There's your fucking answer. He wants to be a rich man before Rusty comes out."

He brought up the wedding. "Today he turns around in front of all the wiseguys and says, 'How many tables we got?' Four tables. 'Well, how you gonna situate them, because everybody wants to sit with me.' I says, 'Not me. Oh, no, I'll sit with my wife, with my friends. I wanna enjoy myself. I don't wanna stand at attention.' "

"Where they having the reception?" None of us was going to the wedding itself.

"At Shalimar's. Staten Island. Everybody's gotta carry a pistol. Even you gotta carry a pistol. You got one? I'll get you one. I know the right people. Two weeks ago he calls me. 'Lefty, you gotta meet me Saturday night. Stay with me, you and Nicky.' Boobie was there. So I went with them. I sit there with two pistols on me. They drank. I drank club soda. 'Lefty,' he says, 'you're beautiful, helluva guy,' he says. 'We're gonna go far.' He sits there playing with fucking birds. But when he's in trouble, he opens his gut. I don't stay with him no more. I used to spend day and night with him. This is my contract? Good. Now, sooner or later, if we whack this guy out, the bosses know I did it. I'll go capture this kid. I'll keep my mouth shut. I'll tell you one thing, it fucking hurts inside. It really eats your guts."

"Sure, you do everything you're supposed to do."

"How the fuck can he do this to me?"

"I don't know. You're fucking loyal."

"If Rusty comes home, it's all done. He's dead. Rusty'll kill him."

I went back to the Motion Lounge, and that night I stayed with Sonny at his apartment.

I had a transmitter in the pocket of my slacks. When we went to bed, I hung up my slacks and other clothes in the closet. We were close enough now so that either of us would have felt comfortable going into the other's pockets if we needed a couple bucks to go to the bakery or something. There was always that chance. But you don't sleep with your pants on. So I just hung them up and went to sleep on the pull-out couch.

At six forty-five, Sonny woke me up with coffee and rolls. We sat in the dining room in our shorts. It was his birthday. I gave him $200 as a present. I gave him his driver's license that I had retrieved from the Las Vegas Night bust, and the $1,000 bail money.

He gave me a pistol. He wanted everybody packing now because retaliation from the other side was a good possibility. The pistol was a blue-black German-made .25 automatic with the serial number scraped off the side of the barrel. It had a full clip of bullets.

"Carry this at all times, especially the wedding."

We talked about King's Court. He was anxious to get back together with Santo Trafficante.

"When you coming to Florida?" I ask.

"Maybe next week. There's gonna be a big meeting of the bosses next week, and I can't leave until after that." He started writing in a small blue notebook, where he kept the tab on his loan-sharking business. "I'm finally starting to make some money. I got thirty grand a week coming in. I got over seventy thousand on the street. If only I didn't have to dish out and support so many people."

We went upstairs to feed the pigeons. Sonny was in a quiet mood.

"You got any line on where Bruno is?" I ask.

"We have a line on him. We're gonna give J.B. a pass, though."

They weren't going to kill the kid's uncle. "How come?"

"You gotta give up something to lure the cat to you." We were quiet for a while as he moved around the coops.

"Donnie, I'm gonna put you up for membership when the Old Man gets out." He leaned over the railing. "I love you like a brother. I can't trust anybody else in this crew. I know they're telling stories. You I got faith in. I want you to make sure that if I get whacked or anything, my kids and my wife get what's coming to them from my partners. You understand? I gotta trust you to take care of my kids. They're supposed to get a G-note a week."

"You can trust me, bro."

"You know, these fucking pigeons, they can't just go out and fly fifty miles fast. You got to train them, get them in shape. They go ten miles in ten minutes now."

In the Motion Lounge, Lefty was talking with Jimmy Legs and Nicky Santora.

"Four guys got the contract," Lefty says. "What? Are you kidding? Everyone else is fucking earning!"

"Who's gotta go?" Nicky says.

"Me, you, Jimmy Legs, and Bobby—that's it. Nobody else is supposed to. Are you kidding me? Because that's the way he's doing things. In other words, Boobie's out. The other guys are making more money, out. Massino's crew is out. What do you do? You run into fucking death. That kid's sharp. He catches us coming in. Once you leave that parking lot, you're gonna be open. Sonny wants to go at nighttime. How you gonna see in the dark at nighttime?"

"Let's start Monday on it," Jimmy Legs says.

"You figure this'll be done in a week?" Nicky says. He was anxious to come down and hang out at King's Court. He had never seen the place, and now Sonny had given him permission.

"Well, we gotta put time in. We get lucky. Where's the credit card?"

They had some stolen credit cards they were using for various things.

"Why do you want a credit card?" Nicky asks.

"We can get a car from that."

"How we gonna bring the car back?"

"Leave the fucking car in the street."

"What about your guy with the cars? Can't we get a couple of cars over there? I mean, where Mirra's working."

"Mirra? Don't mention that fucking name in public. I can't go near him, Sonny says, right now."

"Why can't you go near him?"

"I don't know. When are you gonna get that car?"

"I ain't getting nothing," Nicky says. "You wanna do it properly, get two cars."

"Hey, as tight as you are with Sonny Black, tell him what you want to do. You start running around in a fugazy car—hey, we're going on a hit. If it's not a hit, it's a different story. You know what Philly Lucky sold only two weeks before he got hit—seven million cash? He had four trucking outfits over there. Young guy, fifty years old. He left seventy-five million. Handsome guy."

Lefty and Boobie met at the Holiday Bar on Madison Street. Some former cop in the New York Police Department was offering a copy of an up-to-date police report detailing the investigation of the Bonanno family, including surveillance reports and names of people who were going to be subpoenaed to appear before a grand jury. The guy wanted $5,000 for the report.

Lefty was urging its purchase. "The fucking thing is like a book. It goes back to May 4, the day before it happened on a Monday night, right? There was a meeting. They were observed. Just go to the family and let it come outa the kitty."

I drove Lefty to Brooklyn.

"Sonny and Joey are feuding," he says, "because Sonny's got more power. So Joey got an unlisted telephone number now. He ain't talking to anybody because of this feud with Sonny."

Lefty and Boobie talked to Sonny about the offered police report. Lefty came out of the Motion Lounge, disappointed. "He doesn't want it. He didn't want to pay the five thousand."

* * *

Lefty wanted to look at a new Cadillac he might buy. Nicky drove us to Queens to the dealer's to look at it. It was burgundy. Rock-bottom price was $15,300. Lefty decided to buy it.

They talked about looking for the kid, casing the house.

"Should I take the shotgun?" Nicky asks.

Lefty laughs. "Yeah, like last time, you shot the guy that ain't supposed to be shot."

They all laughed. One of their own guys, Santo Giordano, had been shot accidently in the hip and left paralyzed. That was their best joke of the day.

In the beginning of my undercover role as Donnie Brasco, I had occasional fears about the dangers of being an agent. Now I also had fears about the dangers of being a badguy. As things had now developed into family warfare, I could get whacked for being either an agent *or* a badguy.

Some mornings when I stayed at Sonny's I would get up and go into the bathroom and look in the mirror, and I would find myself thinking, Is today the day that I'm going to get whacked?

Lefty and I were having a lunchtime cappuccino at Caffe Capri.

"Tap Jerry Chilli's phones," he says. "He knows where the kid is. Tap Jerry Chilli's phones and we'll get the kid. I'll put a bug in Jerry's house. We'll visit him. He'll invite us, you know. Boobie goes there with a bullshit story. Puts a bug in there. And a bug outside, on a tree or something. Jerry was very close to the kid's father. Sonny Red's wife gave Jerry Chilli Sonny Red's car to sell for her. So we put a bug in Chilli's house on Staten Island."

"I hope so," I say.

"Now, you're gonna get straightened out, Donnie. But please, let me tell you. First of all, you and I are gonna do a little talking while we're away, where you come from and all that, because this is gonna come back on me."

Sonny came in and joined us. He said that Sally

Farrugia wanted to make some of the zips captains.
"But that would be crazy," Sonny says, "because those
guys are looking to take over everything. That's why
those three guys were killed—they went against the
zips, and the zips came over to our side. We were the
ones slated to get hit, but because Sonny Red screwed
the zips, they swung over to us. There's no way we can
make them captains. We'd lose all our strength."

He said he urged Sally to take a firmer hand as
acting boss until Rusty got out of jail.

"You're gonna be in shit's creek, Sonny," Lefty
says.

"Good. I been in shit's creek eighteen years."

"I advise you to be a little strong, because them
fucking zips ain't gonna back up to nobody. You give
them the fucking power, if you don't get hurt now,
you get hurt three years from now. They'll bury you.
You cannot give them the power. They don't give a
fuck. They don't care who's boss. They got no respect.
There's no family."

"Sally don't want no problems with us," Sonny says.

"Sure, I don't blame him. Look at the position he
got himself in."

"I mean, what if the guy stays in another ten years?
You think they're gonna let him out, especially with
this RICO law? So what we gonna do now, stand on a
corner? I'm starting from day one again."

"Yeah, but don't weaken," Lefty says. "You weaken,
you got a headache. You won't get a headache now.
You'll get it three years from now. They'll bury you.
I'm telling you, they'll bury you. Well, Sonny, you do
what you gotta do. Your word counts with me."

"I just can't go along with it. Because there are
some things I can't do for certain people, and some
things I did already."

"You do what you gotta do. You gotta put fear in
these guys."

"I don't put fear in there," Sonny says. "I put
friendship, you know? I almost didn't win the battle."

A bunch of us were sitting around the Motion Lounge
with guns in our belts, swapping stories—Sonny, Lefty,

Nicky, Jimmy Legs, and others. Sonny had ordered us to be armed at all times.

Jimmy Legs was packing a .45. Nobody used holsters. You carried your pistol in your sport-coat pocket or your belt. Jimmy Legs had a big belly, but the rest of him was skinny. He had no hips or butt. So when he'd walk around, the .45 kept falling down through his pants legs. He had this bright idea that he would sew a pocket on the inside of his pants at the small of his back and carry the gun in that pocket. So this evening he had just installed the pocket and was using it for the first time.

We were bullshitting about the world situation and how the United States should be tougher on other countries and not be pushed around. About how the liberals running our spy business should learn something from the methods of the KGB, which could do anything it wanted to in order to be effective.

Somebody brought up the different ways you could kill people in the spy business.

I told them a story about one of the methods. A KGB agent had an umbrella with a sharpened tip, and they put poison on it, and he'd walk by somebody and just prick him in the leg or arm with this umbrella.

They thought that was the greatest thing in the world. The CIA should be able to do that stuff and not be so answerable to Congress anymore, like it had been since Watergate.

We got to laughing at some of the stories, and Jimmy Legs suddenly took off for the john.

A few moments later we heard a commotion. Jimmy Legs came out of john dangling his .45 from his thumb and forefinger. "I had to shit so bad that I forgot about my gun pocket, and when I took down my pants and began, the gun fell in the bowl so I had to fish it out. Hey, if we had to go to war and I had to kill somebody, I'd just leave a little shit on it that'd get on the bullet, and all I'd have to do is nick somebody and I'd kill them with that poison just like the fucking KGB!"

* * *

The wedding reception for Boobie's daughter was scheduled for seven P.M. at Shalimar Caterers, 2380 Hylan Boulevard, on Staten Island. We started gathering at the Motion Lounge at about five P.M.—Lefty, Nicky Santora, Boots Tomasulo, Bobby Capazzio, Sonny, Charlie the bartender, and others.

The rules were that we would all stay around Sonny at all times, not leave his side, because this would be a good time for retaliation against him. Other families were going to be represented at the wedding, too, so we didn't know who might do what.

Some guys brought their wives or girlfriends. We were going to travel in a caravan, so we discussed how to get there and who was going with who.

We had to make sure everybody was packing. Nicky had a .45 that was too big for his waistband, so he gave that to Boots, and Nicky carried a little .32. I, of course, had my .25 automatic.

I drove with Boots and Nicky. Everybody was at the reception. Lefty and Louise, Jimmy Legs, Jerry Chilli, Mr. Fish Rabito, Dennis the cop, Nicky Marangello, Mike Sabella.

One notable absence was Joey Massino, which really ticked off Sonny and Lefty.

"That jerk-off is afraid to get caught out in the open," Lefty says, "that's all."

I sat at Sonny's table with Nicky, Charlie, and Boots. Everybody had a girlfriend except Boots and me.

It was a big, fancy reception with an open bar, a band, a prime-rib sitdown dinner. All kinds of wiseguys were there from different families, including Jerry Lang, the acting boss of the Colombo family. Boobie was proud, but quiet and controlled as always. We sat around Sonny and kept our eyes open.

There were photographers cruising around the room, but Sonny's rule was no photographs at any tables where his crew sat.

At about eleven P.M., we all went back to the Motion Lounge to relax for a while.

Sonny gave me $4,000 to put on the street in Florida as shylock money.

I flew back to Tampa the following day. I couldn't

carry the gun Sonny had given me on the plane, so I took the handle apart, scratched my initials and the date on the metal underneath, put it back together, and handed it to another agent at the airport for him to take to Florida.

On July 12, Nicky Santora called. "You know that kid from up here? We got word he's down there."

"Oh, yeah?"

"So we just wondered, maybe you could get a line on him or something. I think Miami. We're not positive, you know. It's more logical that he would be down there."

"I'll make a couple phone calls. Some good people down there."

"But, Donnie, you know, be careful, watch yourself."

On July 23, Lefty called. "That guy's coming out tomorrow. He's got something in the back of his head. I don't know what the fuck's happening."

Lefty had been feuding with Sonny for the way the crew was being handled.

"Have I ever told you what the fuck he did? He took half of my guys away. Who do you think he gave them to?"

"Who?"

"You'll never guess, Donnie. Who's our enemy?"

"Don't tell me he gave them to Al Walker."

"Thank you. The whole neighborhood is blowing their tops. He gave him Mike. He gave him Joe Puma. They're all disgusted. They're all gonna quit."

"You gotta be kidding me."

"And the trouble he's causing. He wants to know what they're doing for a living. They're all gonna rebel. So I went to see him. I said, 'Are you blowing your fucking top?' I start arguing with him. He said, 'I know what I'm doing.' "

"He's making those guys stronger," I say. "He's giving Al Walker, who's an enemy, other guys that are his enemies."

"Thank you. Jimmy Legs don't even want to come

around, and he belongs to me. I've got Steve in Florida."

"Instead of keeping them under control," I say, goading him, "he's giving them away."

"Thank you. I'm glad you understand all these things. That's what's gonna make us much stronger when the shit hits the fan. Listen, Donnie, I want to be under the, uh, the guy that's coming home. I'm allowed that request."

"Is that right?"

"Now, if I got it, I don't answer to nobody but him."

"That means I can go with you over to him, huh, Left?"

"That's it. You stay with me and we don't answer to nobody. Follow me?"

"Well, what do you want me to do now with this guy when he comes down here?"

"Go along with him. Just play it cool."

"All right."

"He's making all kinds of efforts. And so you know what the zips said? 'We don't like this guy, we don't trust him.' "

"Is that right?"

"They don't want him. He went over their heads. There's a feud going on. I don't care, Donnie. My guys are happy. I don't bother them, you know?"

"What's Joey M. doing?"

"Now they don't bother each other. He's buried himself. Joe Puma's in the hospital, and he makes the guy check in every day from the hospital. Ever hear anything like this? 'And don't go back to Florida until you check out with me,' Sonny tells him. Does not make sense. Well, that's good in our favor."

"Yeah."

"We don't bother our people."

"That's right."

"But this guy, I don't know what he's doing to himself. I'll tell you, Donnie, Sonny Black is in a fucking fog."

So Lefty was going to put me with him directly under the boss, Rusty Rastelli, when he got out of prison in a few weeks. I could never relate as closely to Lefty as to Sonny. But one thing about Lefty I could rely on: Everything he ever told me about the Mafia turned out to be true.

I prepared for my final weekend in the Mafia, my last days as Donnie Brasco, as the host of Sonny Black.

20

COMING OUT

Sonny was anxious to get back in Santo Trafficante's good graces, make sure everything was straightened out so we could move ahead and make all the money we could make through our hookup with Trafficante. He felt that a large part of his future was going to be in Florida.

Sonny and Nicky Santora came down on Friday, July 24, and had Rossi call Benny Husick to see if they couldn't set up a meeting for Saturday—not in Tampa, because Sonny felt there was too much heat on the both of them there, but in Holiday. Rossi reached Husick at the Bayshore Country Club in Miami. Husick said they would try to be in Holiday by five P.M. Saturday.

This weekend we had planned to pump Sonny and Nicky for everything we could get. For the last several weeks there had been a million little things to do to tie up loose ends, and we still played our normal roles so we didn't tip our hand. Now we were really coming to the end, and we could go for it, like a pitcher airing it out in the last couple of innings. We knew it would be the last time we would see them. We wanted them to talk about the murders, of course, but we would push conversations into any mob area we could bring up and grab anything that we could. It didn't matter if we went too far, because everything was history after this weekend.

We wanted to loosen them up right away. Friday night we went to Pappas Restaurant to eat, then bounced around to a few places. We went to Clearwater Beach to a hotel where there was a comedian performing. We went back to the club and finished up at about six A.M. Saturday morning. They were having a good time. They didn't talk business.

Trafficante and Husick arrived at the Tahitian Motor Lodge on the dot at five P.M. Saturday and went straight to Sonny's room. A few minutes later the three of them left the room and went to the coffee shop. They talked there for about forty minutes, then Trafficante and Husick got up, shook hands with Sonny, and left in Trafficante's Cadillac.

Sonny called Rossi and me into the coffee shop. He was ecstatic. The meeting had been terrific. He said that he had given Trafficante $2,000 and Husick $1,000 to split with the people who had worked that Las Vegas Night. Trafficante had said that the bust was "just one of those things."

"So we're back in his good graces," Sonny says. "Now you guys got to get your asses moving and start producing because I got us back in with this guy."

Bingo, gambling, numbers, dog tracks, drugs—everything was going to go big now, teaming up with Santo Trafficante. Florida was going to be ours.

They were in such a great mood that all they wanted to do was party. They wanted to celebrate and anticipate. It turned into a constant "go" weekend—they wanted to keep partying, we wanted to keep them up and talking as late as possible.

We partied all night at the club—Nicky Santora, Sonny Black, Eddie Shannon, Tony Rossi, and me. We had managed to get a little sleep Friday night. Saturday night, we didn't go to bed at all. Neither Nicky nor Sonny was interested in talking business, no matter how we tried to maneuver conversations. In addition to our own cocktail waitresses and bartender, waitresses from other local joints and regular customers came in and joined the party. In the early-morning hours Sonny took one of the girls back to the hotel.

The sun was up on Sunday morning. These were the last hours for the club and the operation. I took Nicky on ahead to Denny's for breakfast. Rossi and Shannon had to stay behind for a little while to check out the cash register and help the staff clean up.

When Nicky and I had left, Rossi told the help that they were getting a surprise two-week vacation with pay because we were going to close the club for renovations.

I was alone with Nicky at Denny's. There wasn't much time. I decided to take a shot at learning something about the murders of the three captains. I came in from an angle, asked about a couple of Colombo guys who had disappeared.

"They got clipped," Nicky said. "They were skimming drug money. They were mixed up in that with Sonny Red."

"That must have been something," I said, "that thing with him and Philly Lucky and Big Trin."

"I never saw anything like it in my life, Donnie. Big Trin was so huge. When that shotgun blast hit him, about fifty pounds of his stomach just went flying."

"What was it like with the other guys?"

"We'll talk about it later, Donnie."

Shannon and Rossi had walked in. I couldn't signal for them to leave. Nicky had not met Shannon before this weekend. He clammed up.

We had breakfast and went back to the Tahitian. Nicky and Sonny packed up, and Rossi and I took them to the airport. On the way Sonny kept drilling into us how we had to keep things going now that he was back on the right track with Trafficante, how we had to hustle for drug connections and build up the shylocking and gambling, and get going on the bingo and the dog track. Everything was really going to roll now.

Nicky realized he had forgotten something. "Donnie, I left my blue suede jacket in the motel room. It's got some important address books in it that I need.

Do me a favor and pick it up right away and send it to me?"

"Sure thing, Nicky."

We dropped them off at the airport. I felt relief and discomfort at the same time. I figured that I probably wouldn't see Sonny again, not even in court. I believed he was history. I couldn't make any big deal out of the good-bye.

"I'll talk to you tomorrow," I said.

I went back to the Tahitian and got Nicky's jacket out of his room, along with two address books and a pocket-size folder with personal papers and cards. I turned the stuff in to agent Mike Lunsford.

We cleaned out our apartments. The furniture was rented, so it was just a matter of gathering up personal stuff.

King's Court was locked up. The case agent would deal with it.

Later in the day Rossi flew to Washington, D.C., for his debriefing. I had to fly directly to Milwaukee to testify before the grand jury on the Balistrieri case. That case, like many others, had been held in abeyance until we wrapped up the whole operation. Eddie Shannon flew with me, just for double protection. After that I would go to Washington, D.C., for debriefing. For a couple of weeks I didn't have a chance to go home. After I went home for a few days I went to New York to start working with the U.S. Attorneys on the indictments.

I am not inclined toward soul-searching, and during this period I didn't have time to brood, anyway. I had some uncomfortable feelings because I felt close to Sonny Black. I felt a kind of kinship with him. But I didn't feel any guilt of betrayal, because I'd always maintained in my own mind and heart the separation of our worlds. In a sense we were both just doing our jobs. If he had found out who I was, he'd have whacked me out. He would have done it in the traditional way. He wouldn't have talked to me about it. He'd have set me up. Who kills you in that business is somebody you know. Maybe he would have had Lefty do it. Maybe he would have done it himself. It would have been cold-blooded.

Sonny was good at what he did. He wasn't a phony. He didn't throw his weight around. He was a stand-up guy. For reasons that are hard to explain, I liked him a lot. But I didn't dwell on the fact that I was going to put him in the can, or that he was going to get killed because of me. That's the business.

I knew that both Lefty and Sonny loved me in their own ways. Either would have killed me in a minute. It didn't have to be because I was an agent. They could have thought I was an informant. I could have lost a decision to Mirra, and they could have been ordered to kill me. They would simply have done it.

The difference between our worlds was that I wouldn't kill them. I would just put them in the can. I had a gut feeling that Sonny was going to be killed by his own people over this situation. I didn't like being responsible for anybody getting killed. But it wasn't my rules; it was their rules that would kill him. I didn't write those rules. Those rules were written by their society, not mine.

So I felt bad, but I didn't dwell on it. Nothing I did in my job was affected by any feelings I had for Sonny or anybody else. That was my discipline. Some guys have trouble dealing with that aspect. When one of my friends who had been working undercover was preparing to go to court, he said he couldn't look the defendants in the eye because he felt guilty for having deceived them. You just did your job, I told him.

You can't have those personal feelings in this business. I was not there to be buddy-buddy with these guys. I would not allow myself to become that emotionally attached. In my situation, my life was on the line every day.

On the first day after Sonny and Nicky went back to New York, Lefty tried to reach me in Holiday. On the second day, the agents visited Sonny Black.

Doug Fencl, Jim Kinne, and Jerry Loar went to the Motion Lounge.

Sonny knew Agent Fencl, and that was important.

Agents working "straight up" will on occasion drop in on mob guys like Sonny just to let them know they are around watching them, available to them if they ever get jammed up and want to share information. Some months before, Sonny and Lefty and I had been talking about ways of insulating ourselves against the law, and it was their opinion that the ones you really had to worry about were the FBI agents. Sonny said that a couple of agents stopped in the Motion Lounge once in a while, and he mentioned Fencl. "He's a nice guy, a gentleman. He doesn't bullshit. He just tells me exactly what's on his mind."

So Fencl was one that Sonny would be likely to trust and believe. The agents showed Sonny a photograph taken especially for this occasion. It showed me together with these three agents. They asked Sonny: "Do you know this guy? He's an FBI agent. We just wanted to tell you." They didn't offer him a deal, because a deal is always implicit, and a direct offer to a guy like Sonny would have been insulting to him.

Sonny gave away nothing by his expression or tone of voice. "I don't know him, but if I meet him, I'll know he's an FBI agent."

We tracked what happened after that through wiretaps and informants.

Just as anticipated, Sonny's first move after the visit was to call together the main men of his crew. Lefty, Boobie, and Nicky came to the Motion Lounge to meet with Sonny. Sonny told them there was no way I was an agent, that if the FBI had me, they must have kidnapped me and were maybe even brainwashing me.

For more than a week they kept the story to themselves while they looked for me. They reached out to the King's Court area, even called some of our waitresses. Lefty went to Miami, and he and Maruca scoured the area, checked all the hotels and haunts. They sent two guys from New York to Chicago, Milwaukee, and California to see if they could come up with anything.

After ten days Sonny called Santo Trafficante and told him about the agents' visit and what they had said. He didn't offer interpretations or explanations.

He sent word to Rusty Rastelli in prison. And then he called Paul Castellano, boss of the Gambino family, the boss of bosses.

The mob held several meetings in New York over this, making a damage assessment. They distributed pictures of me, snapshots taken over the years with Lefty or Sonny or others, all over the country, and all the mob families were put on alert to watch for me.

The bosses considered what to do. They decided to put an open-ended—open to anyone—$500,000 contract on me. There was a suggestion that they hit everybody in the mob that had anything to do with me. Obviously certain people were going to fall, but there was nothing we could do about it. You can't get a warrant to snatch anybody off the street, even for their own protection, without definite information that the person is going to get killed. Nobody's name came to us as a definite target.

Except mine. The FBI dispatched teams of agents to visit all the top Mafia bosses they could find and tell them face-to-face, Hands off this agent, he beat you, it's finished. If they hurt me, all the resources of the Justice Department would be focused on going after them—I and the FBI were not going to be intimidated.

On August 14, seventeen days after the agents had told Sonny about me, the bosses called a meeting in New Jersey. Sonny went to the meeting. I was not surprised. His options were either to turn informant, or to run, or to go to the meeting. He went to the meeting and disappeared.

Once we found out that Sonny was missing, I told Jerry Loar, "When you see them start taking his pigeon coops down, you can close your case on Sonny Black, because then he's history." About a week later a couple guys were on that roof taking the pigeon coops down.

A month later Sonny's girlfriend, Judy, called the New York office of the FBI, wanting to talk to me. When I got in touch with her, she said she was scared for Sonny and for herself, and she wanted very much to get together and talk to me about things. I said okay, and that agents would be in touch with her to arrange it.

We had to be careful, even with Judy, because of a possible setup. We needed a controlled situation. So we decided to have the meeting in Washington, D.C. Two agents picked her up, flew down with her, and brought her to the Marriott right by National Airport.

We went to the dining room to have dinner. The other agents sat at a table across the room.

She said she was frightened and worried, and she missed Sonny.

I said, "Judy, the chances are that Sonny is not coming back. My recommendation is that you not associate with any of those people anymore. They're not really your friends. Get on with your life."

"I know that now," she said. "But I had a good time with Sonny. I really liked him."

"So did I."

She was very sad, and she cried a little. "Donnie, I always knew that you weren't cut out for that world because you carried yourself different, you had an air of intelligence, you know? I knew that you were much more than just a thief. You were a good friend to Sonny and me. Sonny didn't have any ill feelings toward you."

"I'm glad to hear that."

She said he had told her about the agents coming to talk to him, and he didn't believe what they told him—there was no way I could be an agent, because of the things we had done together, the conversations we'd had, the feelings we'd had. "You know what he said? He told me, 'I really loved that kid.' He was really broken up when he found out that you were an agent, but he said that wouldn't change the way he felt because of the type of guy you were. You did your job and you did it right."

"I always liked Sonny," I said. "That hasn't changed with me, either."

"He told me he had this meeting in New Jersey. But that was all. Later I found out that just before he left for the meeting, he gave Charlie, the bartender, all his jewelry and the keys to his apartment and everything. The only thing he took with him were his car keys."

"He knew he wasn't coming back," I said.

"Yeah. Am I going to have any problems, you think?"

"No, I'm sure you won't. Don't worry about anything. Nobody's going to bother you. Just get on with your life and stay away from those people."

At the end, she said she felt better, was resigned to the fact that Sonny wasn't coming back, was glad for our talk.

"Call me anytime," I said.

We figured Sonny, Lefty, and Tony Mirra were the most obvious targets for mob hits because of me. Mirra, because he was the first guy to bring me into Little Italy, the first Bonanno guy I hung around with, and also because they thought he was a snitch. Our information was that they thought that his fight for me at the sitdowns was all a ploy, that he and I were actually working together for the FBI to advance my infiltration into the mob. Lefty and Sonny were obvious targets because of my association with them.

But the only definite contract we got word on was on Lefty. He was the only one we could protect from his own people. On August 30, a Sunday, agents snatched up Lefty just as he came out of his apartment building.

Mirra didn't get hit until March 1982. His body was found in a car in a parking lot at the corner of North Moore and West Streets, outside the building where Bonanno consiglieri Steve Cannone lived. Somebody had shot him four times in the head. He had $6,700 in his pocket.

On August 2, 1982, I started testifying in Room 318 of the Southern District Federal Courthouse in the racketeering trial of U.S. vs. Dominick Napolitano, et al.

On August 12, 1982, a badly decomposed body was found in a hospital body bag in a creek near South Avenue in the Mariner's Harbor section of Staten

Island. The body had been buried. Recent heavy rains had uncovered it and washed it up. The person had been shot. The hands had been chopped off—an indication of a Mafia hit and a special signal that the victim had violated mob security.

On November 10, five days before Lefty, Nicky Santora, Mr. Fish Rabito, Boots Tomasulo and others were sentenced, the body was identified through dental records as being that of Sonny Black.

I was sorry it was Sonny. I was glad it wasn't me.

EPILOGUE

When I emerged from undercover in 1981, there was no celebration, no homecoming, no resumption of normal life with my family. In fact, because of the death threats and the contract out on me, there was more fear in my family when I came out than when I was under. I began work immediately on preparation for the many trials, and I have testified in those trials all these six years.

Though I continue to testify when called upon, I resigned from the FBI in 1986, after seventeen years of service, to write this book. I am not in the federal Witness Protection Program. I and my family have moved our home once again to another part of the country. Except in matters relating to FBI activities or this book, I do not use the name Pistone. When I am with my family, I use the name they use. When I am traveling or engaged in anything other than testimony or family activities, I use any of several other names.

At forty-eight, I will begin a new life under a new name. Except for close friends and some government officials, no one will know that I am the man who lived this life as Joe Pistone and Donnie Brasco.

Looking back, would I do it again? Professionally, yes, there's no doubt in my mind that I would do it. Personally, it's a different matter. I missed ten years of a life with my family. I don't know whether that loss is worth it. But I do know that if I was going to do the job, I had to do it the way I did it.

Here follows a partial list of what happened to the major figures in this book:

Baldassare "Baldo" Amato: Convicted, "Pizza Connection" Case, New York, awaiting sentence.

Frank Balistrieri: Convicted, Milwaukee, 13 years; convicted, Kansas City, 10 years.

John Balistrieri: Convicted, Milwaukee, 8 years.

Joseph Balistrieri: Convicted, Milwaukee, 8 years.

Caesar Bonventre: Murdered, 1984.

Stefano "Stevie Beef" Cannone: Died, 1985.

James "Fort Lee Jimmy" Capasso: Not charged in our cases.

Bobby Capazzio: Missing, reports from informants that he was murdered.

Paul "Big Paul" Castellano: Indicted, "Commission" Case, murdered, New York, 1985.

Salvatore Catalano: Convicted, "Pizza Connection" Case, New York, 45 years.

John "Boobie" Cerasani: Acquitted in New York, pled guilty in Tampa, 5 years.

Jerry Chilli: Convicted, New York, fraudulent check charges, released 1987.

Joe Chilli: Not charged in our cases.

Anthony "Tony Ducks" Corallo: Convicted, "Commission" Case, New York, 100 years.

Joey D'Amico: Pled guilty, perjury, New York, 1987.

Aniello Dellacroce: Died, 1985.

Armond Dellacroce: Convicted, New York, failed to appear for sentencing, a fugitive.

Steve DiSalvo: Convicted, Milwaukee, 8 years.

Joseph Donahue: Indicted, Florida, committed suicide, 1983.

Sally "Paintglass" D'Ottavio: Indicted, New York, 1987.

Al "Al Walker" Embarrato: Not charged in our cases.

James "Jimmy Legs" Episcopia: Convicted, New York, 1983, 5 years.

Carmine Galante: Murdered, New York, 1979.

Salvatore "Sally Fruits" Farrugia: Not charged in our cases.

Philip "Philly Lucky" Giaccone: Murdered, New York, 1981.

Jilly Greca: Murdered, Brooklyn, 1980.

Benny Husick: Pled guilty, Tampa, 3 years.

Alphonse "Sonny Red" Indelicato: Murdered, New York, 1981.

Anthony Bruno Indelicato: Convicted, "Commission" Case, New York, 45 years.

Gennaro "Jerry Lang" Langella: Convicted, "Commission" Case, New York, 100 years.

Joseph Massino: Convicted, New York, 10 years.

Nicholas Marangello: Convicted, New York, 10 years.

Steve Maruca: Served several jail terms, not charged in our cases.

Anthony Mirra: Murdered, New York, 1982.

Dominick "Sonny Black" Napolitano: Murdered, New York, 1981.

Charles "Charlie Moose" Panarella: Sentenced to various jail terms in last ten years, on parole.

Alphonse "Allie Boy" Persico: Convicted, New York, 12 years.

Carmine "The Snake" Persico: Convicted, "Commission" Case, New York, 100 years.

Joe Puma: Died, 1985.

Anthony "Mr. Fish" Rabito: Convicted, New York, 8 years.

Philip "Rusty" Rastelli: Convicted, New York, 12 years.

Benjamin "Lefty Guns" Ruggiero: Convicted Milwaukee, Tampa, New York, 20 years.

Michael Sabella: Acquitted, Milwaukee.

Anthony "Fat Tony" Salerno: Convicted, "Commission" Case, New York, 100 years.

Nicholas Santora: Convicted, New York, 20 years.

Tommy Spano: murdered, 1984.

Antonio "Boots" Tomasulo: Convicted, New York, conviction overturned on appeal.

Santo Trafficante: Indicted, Florida, died 1987.

Dominick "Big Trin" Trinchera: Murdered, New York, 1981.

Mickey Zaffarano: Died, 1980.

UPDATE

July 1988

by Joseph D. Pistone

Since my book came out in hardcover, Peggy and I have been interviewed by *Time, People, 20/20,* and *Good Morning America.* I appeared on shows hosted by Larry King, Geraldo Rivera, and others.

More than anything else, those journalists, studio audiences, and people who phoned in, wanted to know more about how my investigation affected the Mafia, how those years undercover affected the Pistone family, and whether I would do it all again.

As a result of my investigation, the Mafia has changed some of its rules for membership. The mob has since reinstituted an old rule, that a proposed member must "make his bones" or kill someone, before he can become a made guy. They have done so because no agent would commit murder while posing as a bad guy.

Plus, two Mafiosi have to vouch for a proposed member. So now two wiseguys have to take the responsibility instead of just one. They have to say they have known the proposed member if not since childhood, then at least for fifteen to twenty years.

Meanwhile, increased pressure from enforcement, particularly from the FBI, has led many top-echelon mob members to become informants, more than at any other time in the history of the Mafia.

Of course, those defections and the more than 100 federal convictions we obtained have caused a leadership problem for the Mafia. With so many top guys out of action, there is a prevailing sense of mistrust and wariness in each family and in relations across family lines. I'm happy to say that the leadership problem is here to stay.

The Mafia's values are shifting. I helped speed up that process.

The oldtimers—who brought the values of the old country with them, who believed that whatever you did, you did it for the *crew* and, all the way up the line, ultimately for the organization—are dying off or are stuck in jail.

There, they are lamenting the fact that La Cosa Nostra—"Our Thing"—is becoming "My Thing" in the hands of the younger generation.

The new Mafia is made up mostly of guys born in this country, who are into easy living. They do not possess the same strong attachment to kinship and "family" honor that the old wiseguys did. This Americanization of the Mafia—coupled with law enforcement's concerted onslaught of indictments and investigations—is eroding the mob's power.

But there is another thing that is weakening the Mafia: as in the larger society, the Mafia subculture is facing the problem of drug abuse.

The Mafia has trafficked in narcotics for decades. It's true that only certain people in certain families get involved in large-scale importation and distribution, but everyone tries to traffic because of the profits to be made. However, very few of the older guys were users.

Now, despite the longstanding, unwritten Mafia rule

against using drugs, many of the younger members are addicted to drugs, particularly to cocaine.

Picture this: if you use cocaine, chances are you will never see more than a gram or two at any one time in your life; if you do become addicted, chances are you'll become a crook to support your habit, although probably not a very good one. Now imagine being an importer and distributor. You take control over kilos of the stuff. And you already make your livelihood as a crook. Chances are, as a Mafia coke addict, you'll eventuallly try to screw somebody in a deal and get whacked. If you live long enough, you'll make yourself crazy.

That's how it is. Members of the "Me Generation" Mafia are like kids in a coke candyshop.

When I appeared on talk shows, it seemed 99 percent of the audience was very pro about what the FBI did, and some people even said I was an American hero. For me, it is hard to think of myself as a hero—it was just a job, and I did it.

People wanted to know whether I felt I was on a mission to clean out the Mafia because I'm an Italian-American.

I didn't carry out the investigation on behalf of upstanding Italian-Americans. I wasn't an ethnic policeman. Truly, it didn't matter to me that it was the Mafia. I would have accepted any undercover assignment against any group the FBI targeted.

I am proud about how it turned out, however.

Italian-Americans have told me they are proud that I had the courage to do it and that I showed the nation that not all Italians side with the Mafia.

Some people even said they never realized the Mafia was not invincible. A lot of people thought the Mafia was an organization law enforcement couldn't do anything with. They were glad that our government got involved. It makes people feel good to know the myth of the Mafia has been broken.

Now we know the Mafia is not invincible.

It's also clear that the Mafia preys on Italians as well as other people.

At the very least, I think I helped destroy some fantasies. Unlike the images we got in movies like *The Godfather*, the Mafia in real life is repetitious. Conversations are mind-numbing. "What are we gonna steal today? How are we gonna steal it?"

On the other hand, some people asked, "How could you have done it to other Italians?"

I don't feel that way. I busted a group of people involved in illegal activities.

Not viewing the probe from an ethnic point of view was important for keeping a proper perspective. Another reason the investigation was successful was that I knew, no matter what I did, that I was not going to reform anybody in or around the Mafia, that the people I was getting close to were going to lie, steal, cheat, and murder whether I was there or not. My goal was to gather evidence for later prosecutions. I was not a social worker.

Some people also questioned the FBI's decision to give money to Lefty during the operation. Lefty was given about $40,000 by undercover agents Conti and Rossi because they were supposed to be "marks." They were paying him for his services as a "wiseguy" to insure they had the protection of the Bonanno family in the event another family tried to interfere with their business.

It was a good investment for a number of reasons. By giving him money, Conti and Rossi led Lefty to believe they were willing to become involved with him, and he trusted them as bad guys.

It helped the Bureau obtain valuable intelligence on all the mob families; we even became "partners" with three families in New York, Milwaukee, and Tampa. That information became evidence in court.

By giving Lefty money now and then, we saved many hours, perhaps years, of normal investigative work—work that wouldn't have necessarily led to evidence for indictments.

Six years in the Mafia didn't change my values, and if you ask my family, that's one reason the investigation was an unqualified success.

The time undercover barely changed me on the surface, either. I haven't had any problem dropping any of the habits or mannerisms I adopted during the course of the investigation.

I have retained some of the wiseguy attitude, however.

Wiseguys don't make reservations. They just waltz into a restaurant and give a name. Invariably, the maître d' says,"I'm sorry, we don't have a reservation in that name." And the wiseguy says, menacingly, "Whaddya mean, you don't have one?" And he gets a table right away.

I've done that a couple of time as a "citizen." Out of the corner of my eye I'll see Peggy shaking her head . . . but it works.

Most people back down from a confrontation in public, but in the wiseguy world, you don't back down. Not from waiters or salesmen or anybody. Instead of saying "forget about it" to yourself, you take the offensive right away. It's not bullying, at least in a physical sense.

But my brother will see me act this way, and he'll say, "Joe, you're not out with the wiseguys." My answer is,"Why should you be intimidated by somebody when you know you're right?"

Of all the mobsters I worked against, I've been asked the most questions about Lefty Guns Ruggiero.

Do I expect Lefty to try to kill me when he gets out of prison? He's eligible for parole in 1992.

I expect it. I also know the Mafia will try to kill him, since he took me in as an associate.

Here's a guy who is definitely of the old school. Lefty knows what he did was wrong, he knows a Mafia contract was put out on him, yet he has not turned stoolie. He has more resilience than most of the younger guys. Honor is so ingrained in him that it's more important than the strong possibility that he might get killed by his own peers. Lefty had steadfastly refused to cooperate with the government and join the federal witness protection program to reduce his sentence.

It's ironic, of course, that the Bureau arrested Lefty

in the first place to protect him, and that they have continued that protection during his trials and imprisonment, yet he has sworn to kill me—and that I am not eligible for federal protection. But that's the way it is. I have to depend on myself.

If Lefty survives long enough after his release to come after me . . . I can't worry about it. Whether he does it out of revenge, or if some other mobster tries to kill me to collect the $500,000 contract on my life, I'll be prepared. I carry a .38-caliber pistol at all times, and may the best man win.

I'm better than anyone I've ever met in or around the Mafia. I've got to feel that way. I'm one of the good guys—I didn't do anything wrong. I just did my job.

I take the normal precautions and live each day and try not to think about that contract.

I said try. I think about it sometimes. But I don't have nightmares about it.

The Mafia is not the first organization in the world to believe there's no such thing as bad publicity. Word on the street is that most of the wiseguys read this book when it came out in hardcover. Informants told FBI agents that, with the exception of Lefty, the wiseguys liked it. However, they added that I should not have written it. Their reactions didn't go any deeper than that; wiseguys are not proficient book reviewers.

While we don't know any more about their feelings about the book, those bare-bones comments tell a lot about the Mafia society. The remarks remind me of something Lefty said when he took it upon himself to educate me in the ways of being a wiseguy: what was so great about being a wiseguy, Lefty said, was that you can lie, steal, cheat, kill and it's all legitimate.

The people I met in the mob all regarded themselves as legitimate. Wiseguys do not think of themselves as being criminals or gangsters. They come from a subculture where crime is acceptable, normal, even "honorable." So the wiseguys are apparently happy that I portrayed them true-to-life.

The second reaction, that I shouldn't have written

the story, may be a sign that they still think of "Donnie Brasco" as having been "one of them" and that, in their minds, I betrayed them. That would figure. Mob guys believe cooperating with the government is morally reprehensible, that it is "criminal." When a wiseguy turns from the Mafia value system, he disgraces himself and his crime family, and the family loses respect in the neighborhood and with business associates.

Lefty's reaction to my book would be different, of course. It's a public reminder of the mob contract on his head.

I have been out of the FBI since September 1986, and as of this writing, I am still testifying for the government in cases against the Mafia. I am looking forward to the day when my testimony is no longer needed and I can put the past to rest and get on with the future.

I plan to write another book and to produce a movie about my career. Maybe I could hit the bestseller list again, or even win an Academy Award, but no one in my family will ever brag about it.

I'm referring not only to my immediate family, but also to my parents and my brother and sister, to Peggy's parents and brother and sister, and to other relatives.

My years undercover altered my relationships will all of them. I could never tell them what I was doing.

They knew I was undercover, but they worried about me because they didn't know when or if I was being secretive because I had to be, or if because somehow my personality was changing. That has happened to some undercover agents. I could never put their minds at ease during those years.

During the Mafia Commission and Pizza Connection trials, life got worse for our families instead of better. When I became a witness and my name and identity became public, I was guarded twenty-four hours a day. Peggy and the girls were safe, living far away under a different name. But the members of my family, and Peggy's, were frightened. My father-in-law was scared to start his car in the morning. No one would mention my name on the phone, fearing the lines might be bugged. Before long, it seemed danger existed everywhere. A few years ago, my sister-in-law and her husband owned a restaurant in New York. As it turned out, a man who ate there had ties with the mob. After my story broke in the newspapers, he told one of the Mafia chiefs he knew a way to get to me.

As for Peggy, the girls, and myself, my whole experience with the Mafia has changed our lives forever.

My oldest daughter still has not read this book. She says she does not want to relive the memories of my years undercover.

Today, Peggy, the girls, and I use different names when we travel, sometimes taking roundabout routes and separate flights.

When we meet people we have to invent stories about our past. We can't even say I was an FBI agent, something Peggy and I are proud of.

But those six years . . . Peggy says if it were to happen again, she would find a way out, that six years without a husband is too much.

I don't dispute it.

Including the six years during which I gave testimony as a key witness in the major trials, my family has now been involved with the Mafia for more than twelve years.

In fact, I have spent as much time with the lawyers representing the government's case as I spent with the mobsters.

As of this writing, we've moved six times in those twelve years, and the future holds more of the same.

Would I do it again? As I've said before, professionally, I would. Personally . . .

Put it this way. If Lefty and I meet again, I know we're not going to talk. And I know he isn't smart enough to be ironic. But I can imagine one last conversation:

"I'm proud of what I did, Lefty. If I had to do it all over again, yeah, I would," I'd tell him. "I exposed the Mafia. We got over a hundred convictions—"

"Yeah," Lefty would say. "That's real nice, good for you. You exposed us.

"But if you did so good exposing us, Donnie, whyzit you and your family gotta live a coverup for the rest of your lives?

ACKNOWLEDGMENTS

Special thanks are due the following friends and colleagues:

Richard Woodley who made my story readable.

Michaela Hamilton, my editor, with the fastest blue pencil in the East.

Carmen La Via and Peter Sawyer, my own special agents (literary) from the Fifi Oscard Agency.

Last but certainly not least the man who made it all possible
Mr. Louis Di Giaimo

ABOUT THE AUTHORS

JOSEPH D. PISTONE was an FBI Agent for seventeen years. He now lives under secret identity in an undisclosed location.

RICHARD WOODLEY has written numerous books, including DEALER: PORTRAIT OF A COCAINE MERCHANT and ROOKIE (with Dwight Gooden).